Lecture Notes of the Institute for Computer Sciences, Social Informatics and Telecommunications Engineering   208

Tegawendé F. Bissyande · Oumarou Sie (Eds.)

e-Infrastructure and e-Services for Developing Countries

8th International Conference, AFRICOMM 2016
Ouagadougou, Burkina Faso, December 6–7, 2016
Proceedings

 Springer

Editors
Tegawendé F. Bissyande
University of Luxembourg
Luxembourg
Luxembourg

Oumarou Sie
University of Ouagadougou
Ouagadougou
Burkina Faso

ISSN 1867-8211   ISSN 1867-822X (electronic)
Lecture Notes of the Institute for Computer Sciences, Social Informatics
and Telecommunications Engineering
ISBN 978-3-319-66741-6   ISBN 978-3-319-66742-3 (eBook)
https://doi.org/10.1007/978-3-319-66742-3

Library of Congress Control Number: 2017955569

Printed on acid-free paper

This Springer imprint is published by Springer Nature
The registered company is Springer International Publishing AG
The registered company address is: Gewerbestrasse 11, 6330 Cham, Switzerland

Preface

AFRICOMM 2016, the eighth in the series of the EAI Conferences on e-Infrastructure and e-Services for Developing Countries, held during December 6–7, 2016 in Ouagadougou, Burkina Faso, proved to be a unique and fantastic opportunity for African-rooted ICT4D. Scientists, practitioners, students, and professionals met to discuss research and development of efficient and effective infrastructures and solutions in situations of limited resources. This work is of utmost importance as it constitutes a key-enabler for the diffusion of ICT in developing countries.

In a concerted effort, following past experiences in Central and South African regions, participants interacted to discuss issues and trends, recent research, innovational advances, and in-the-field experiences related to e-Governance, e-Infrastructure, and e-Business with a focus on developing countries.

This volume of papers testifies of the exemplary efforts and sacrifices made by participants and the Organizing Committee. The excellent work supported an exciting program, and provides a unique insight in appropriate technology and practice. We thank the peer-reviewers and all involved for a job well done. Thanks to our colleagues from Burkina Faso, notably Prof. Oumarou Sie and Dr. Mesmin Dandjinou for excellent arrangements.

The papers, the commitment to participate, and the representation of research, practice, and interaction, made AFRICOMM 2016 a milestone event, not only for the ICT research community in Burkina Faso, but also for the West African region, notably the Côte d'Ivoire and Senegal, neighboring countries who sent the largest contingents for research.

Let these conference proceedings of AFRICOMM 2016 be a milestone of agency and empowerment for culturally aligned practices in e-Infrastructure and e-Services in developing countries.

Tegawendé F. Bissyande
Joseph Ki-zerbo

Conference Organization

Steering Committee

Imrich Chlamtac	CREATE-NET, Italy
Roch Glitho	Concordia University, Canada; IMSP, University of Abomey Calavi, Benin
Karl Jonas	Bonn-Rhein-Sieg University of Applied Science, Germany
David Johnson Meraka	CSIR and University of Cape Town, South Africa
Yacine Ghamri-Doudane	Université de la Rochelle, France
Bjorn Pehrson	KTH, Sweden

Organizing Committee

General Chair

Oumarou Sie — University of Ouagadougou, Burkina Faso

General Co-chair

Gertjan van Stam — SIRDC, Zimbabwe

TPC Chair

Tegawendé F. Bissyandé — University of Luxembourg, Luxembourg; University of Ouagadougou, Burkina Faso

Local Chair

Mesmin Dandjinou — Université Polytechnique de Bobo Dioulasso, Burkina Faso

Workshops Chair

Jonathan Ouoba — VTT Research Center, Finland

Publicity and Social Media Chair

Frederic Ouédraogo — University of Koudougou, Burkina Faso

Web Chair

Tiguiane Yelemou — Université Polytechnique de Bobo Dioulasso, Burkina Faso

Sponsorships and Exhibits Chair

Boureima Zerbo   University of Ouagadougou, Burkina Faso

Conference Manager

Barbara Fertalova   EAI (European Alliance for Innovation)

Technical Program Committee

Ernesto Damiani	Etisalat British Telecom Innovation Center; Khalifa University, UAE
Paolo Ceravolo	University of Milan, Italy
Pasteur Poda	Université Polytechnique de Bobo-Dioulasso, Burkina Faso
Tiguiane Yélémou	Université Polytechnique de Bobo-Dioulasso, Burkina Faso
Malo Sadouanouan	Université Polytechnique de Bobo-Dioulasso, Burkina Faso
Laurence Capus	Université Laval, Canada
Hatem Ben Sta	Laboratoire SOIE, Institut Supérieur de Gestion de Tunis, University of Tunis, Tunisia
Max Agueh	LACSC-ECE Paris, France
Roch Glitho	Concordia University, Canada
Patrick Chikumba	Malawi Polytechnic,University of Malawi, Malawi
Nizar Bouguila	Concordia University, Montreal, Canada
Eugene C. Ezin	University of Abomey Calavi, Republic of Benin
William Dedzoe	Inria, France
Christian Attiogbe	University of Nantes, France
Adam Ouorou	Orange Labs, France
Gertjan van Stam	SIRDC, Zimbabwe
Aurel Randolph	Ecole Polytechnique, Montreal, Canada
Fabien Houeto	Schlumberger, USA
Paul Kogeda	Tshwane University of Technology, South Africa
Karl Jonas	Germany
Thomas Djotio Ndié	LIRIMA, University of Yaoundé, Cameroon; Ecole Nationale Supérieure Polytechnique, Cameroon
Fréderic T. Ouédraogo	Université de Koudougou, Burkina Faso
Jonathan Ouob	VTT Technical Center, Finland
Tegawendé F. Bissyandé	Université du Luxembourg, Luxembourg

Visual Cryptography in Action: The Pay-with-a-Selfie Demo (Invited Paper)

Stelvio Cimato[1], Ernesto Damiani[2], Dina J.M. Shehadai[2],
Rasool Asali[2], Fulvio Frati[1], Chan Yeob Yeun[2], Joël T. Hounsou[3],
and Jacques P. Houngbo[3]

[1] Department of Computer Science, Università degli studi di Milano,
Crema, Italy
[2] Etisalat British Telecom Innovation Center/Khalifa University,
Abu Dhabi, UAE
[3] Institute of Mathematics and Physics, Benin

Keywords: Mobile payments • Visual cryptography

1 Application Scenario and Implementation

In developing countries, mobile technology is improving life conditions and providing new opportunities for economic development [3]. *Pay-with-a-Selfie* is a project funded by the Bill & Melinda Gates Foundation which provides a micro-payment framework for small business transactions at virtually zero per-transaction overhead and requiring no technological abilities beyond the one needed for taking a selfie [2]. Trust is enhanced by relying on Visual Cryptography (VC) schemes that make it possible the creation of shares [1, 4]. "Pay-with-a-Selfie" is not intended to replace the existing payment infrastructures, but to extend their reach to areas where connectivity is patchy, or to situations when the phones SIMs are absent or locked. The system's architecture includes two basic components: an app running on the supplier's and customer's smart-phone[1] and a desktop tool installed at the point of service. The current version of the app(s) has been developed using Android Studio, and enables the production of the shares and their exchange between the two parties. The desktop tool has been developed in Java and is used to reconstruct the images after both shares provided by the parties have arrived.

The actions that the parties and their apps are called to execute, and are shown in the "Pay-with-a-Selfie" demo, are listed below:

---

[1] The customer version, called the Purchaser app, includes some functionalities only and is distributed using a public app store. The Supplier app requires detailed registration at download and contains some additional checks for code integrity. We will provide the details of "Pay-with-a-Selfie" code integrity protection in a future paper.

1. (Purchaser/Purchaser App): Display the name of product/service to be exchanged and its price on the purchaser's phone using the captcha generator built in the customer's app
2. (Supplier): Take a selfie with the supplier's smart-phone showing the supplier, the purchaser and the customer's phone showing the captcha
3. (Supplier App): Convert the image it to black and white (performing dithering when necessary) and generate two shares;
4. (Supplier App) Send one of the shares and the original image to the purchaser's phone using a local Bluetooth connection.

The gray-scale image of a sample selfie showing two parties concluding the transaction, together with the price is shown in Fig. 1, as well as the black and white image generated internally by the Supplier App as input for shares' computation. From the implementation point of view is important to remark that computing the shares on the black-and-white dithered version of the selfie has enabled us to meet very stringent constraints in terms of execution and battery time on Android, even when our apps are executed on a cheap, low-memory smartphone. Also, besides being easily recognised by humans, people in our black-and white selfies have been consistently correctly tagged by the run-of-the-mill utilities available on board the phones and on the desktop computer. Once the purchaser's and supplier's phones get connected to the network, the two apps send the shares and the original image to a trusted remote service point, the *bank*, who reconstructs the image and (possibly interacting with a traditional payment infrastructure, or with a virtual currency system) ensures that the supplier gets the cash, and that the buyer gets the goods. It is important to remark that the "Pay-with-a-Selfie" desktop tool - the one used by the financial service point - supports grouping transactions involving a given supplier/purchaser until the total amount reaches a threshold where transaction costs are acceptable to both parties.

Fig.1. The selfie showing the parties and the price of the transaction. (a) the image in grayscale, (b) the same image in black and white

References

1. Cimato, S., Yang, C.-N.: Visual Cryptography and Secret Image Sharing. CRC Press (2011)
2. Cimato, S., Damiani, E., Frati, F., Hounsou, J.T., Tandjiékpon, J.: Paying with a selfie: a hybrid micro-payment framework based on visual cryptography. In: AFRICOMM 2015, pp. 136–141
3. Kochi, E.: How the future of mobile lies in the developing world (2012)
4. Naor, M., Shamir, A.: Visual cryptography. In: Proceedings of Eurocrypt 1994, pp. 1–12 (1994)

Contents

Mobile and Social Networks

A Mobile System for Managing Personal Finances Synchronously   3
Jabulani S. Dlamini and Okuthe P. Kogeda

Africa's Non-inclusion in Defining Fifth Generation Mobile Networks   14
Gertjan van Stam

Redesigning Mobile Phone Contact List to Integrate African
Social Practices   26
Pasteur Poda, A. Joëlle Compaoré, and Borlli Michel Jonas Somé

Analysis of the 2015 Presidential Campaign of Burkina Faso Expressed
on Facebook   33
*Frédéric T. Ouédraogo, Abdoulaye Séré, Evariste Rouamba,
and Soré Safiatou*

Towards Inclusive Social Networks for the Developing World   42
*Christian Akpona, Rose Gohoue, Herve Ahouantchede,
Fatna Belqasmi, Roch Glitho, and Jules Degila*

Multi-diffusion Degree Centrality Measure to Maximize the Influence
Spread in the Multilayer Social Networks   53
*Ibrahima Gaye, Gervais Mendy, Samuel Ouya, Idy Diop,
and Diaraf Seck*

Cloud, VPN and Overlays

Cloud Computing: Potential Risks and Security Approaches   69
Hassen Ben Rebah and Hatem Ben Sta

G-Cloud: Opportunities and Security Challenges for Burkina Faso   79
Didier Bassole, Frédéric T. Ouedraogo, and Oumarou Sie

Mobile VPN Schemes: Technical Analysis and Experiments   88
Daouda Ahmat, Mahamat Barka, and Damien Magoni

Proposals of Architecture for Adapting Cloud Computing Services
to User's Context   98
Kanga Koffi, Babri Michel, Goore Bi Tra, and Brou Konan Marcelin

SEMOS: A Middleware for Providing Secure and Mobility-Aware
Sessions over a P2P Overlay Network   111
  Daouda Ahmat, Mahamat Barka, and Damien Magoni

Xj-ASD: Towards a j-ASD DSL eXtension for Application Deployment
in Cloud-Based Environment   122
  Kanga Koffi, Babri Michel, Brou Konan Marcelin, and Goore Bi Tra

IoT, Water, Land, Agriculture

WAZIUP: A Low-Cost Infrastructure for Deploying IoT
in Developing Countries   135
  Congduc Pham, Abdur Rahim, and Philippe Cousin

Design and Implementation of an Internet of Things Communications
System for Legacy Device Control and Management.   145
  *Martin Saint, Aminata A. Garba, Audace Byishimo,
  and Rodrigue Gasore*

Classification of Water Pipeline Failure Consequence Index
in High-Risk Zones: A Study of South African Dolomitic Land   155
  Achieng G. Ogutu, Okuthe P. Kogeda, and Manoj Lall

Exploring Crowdfunding Performance of Agricultural Ventures:
Evidence from FlyingV in Taiwan   165
  Wen-I Chang

An Integrated RoIP Communication Network for Effective
Collaboration During Emergency and Disaster Management   174
  Quist-Aphetsi Kester

Head to Head Battle of TV White Space and WiFi for Connecting
Developing Regions   186
  *David Johnson, Natasha Zlobinsky, Albert Lysko, Magdeline Lamola,
  Senka Hadzic, Richard Maliwatu, and Melissa Densmore*

Networks, TVWS

Comparison of Different Antenna Arrays with Various Height   199
  *Chien-Hung Chen, Chi-Jie Hung, Chien-Ching Chiu,
  and Shu-Han Liao*

A Priority-Based Service Discovery Model Using Swarm Intelligence
in Wireless Mesh Networks   206
  Lungisani Ndlovu, Manoj Lall, and Okuthe P. Kogeda

Innovating Based on R tree and Artificial Neural Network for Hierarchical
Clustering in Order to Make QoS Routes in MANET   217
   Nguyen Thanh Long, Nguyen Duc Thuy, and Pham Huy Hoang

DNS Lame Delegations: A Case-Study of Public Reverse DNS Records
in the African Region   232
   Amreesh Phokeer, Alain Aina, and David Johnson

A Correlation Between RSSI and Height in UHF Band and Comparison
of Geolocation Spectrum Database View of TVWS with Ground Truth   243
   Richard Maliwatu, Albert Lysko, David Johnson, and Senka Hadzic

Learning

Usage of Online Business Advisory by Micro-entrepreneurs:
Case of Cloth Tailoring Enterprises in Uganda   253
   Fatuma Namisango, Gorretti Byomire, Maria Miiro Kafuko,
   and Asianzu Elizabeth

GIS Initiatives in Health Management in Malawi: Opportunities
to Share Knowledge   263
   Patrick Albert Chikumba and Patrick Naphini

Eliminate the Delay Backlog in the Conduct of Pedagogical Activities
by Distance Learning.   273
   Tiguiane Yélémou, Benjamin Sia, Théodore Njingang Mbadjoin,
   and Alain Jaillet

Crypto and Services

Spatial Cryptographic and Watermarking Technique for Authentication and
Security of Medical Images in a Cloud Based Health Information Systems. . .   281
   Quist-Aphetsi Kester

A Hybrid Lossy Compression Using 2-D Discrete Cosine Transform
and Visual Cryptographic Technique for Security of Multimedia
Image Data Communications in Internet of Things   292
   Quist-Aphetsi Kester

Modelization of Recipe in African Traditional Medicine with Visual
Ontology Approach, Iconic Sketch   304
   Kouamé Appoh, Lamy Jean Baptiste, Brou Konan Marcellin,
   and Lo Moussa

Technological Initiatives to Promote Science Growth in Mozambique   313
  Marangaze Munhepe Mulhanga, Venâncio Massingue,
  and Solange Rito Lima

The Shortcomings of Globalised Internet Technology in Southern Africa   325
  David L. Johnson and Gertjan van Stam

Author Index   339

Mobile and Social Networks

A Mobile System for Managing Personal Finances Synchronously

Jabulani S. Dlamini and Okuthe P. Kogeda[✉]

Department of Computer Science, Faculty of Information Communication
Technology, Tshwane University of Technology, Private Bag X680,
Pretoria 001, South Africa
Jabulani.1985@hotmail.com, KogedaPO@tut.ac.za

Abstract. Many SMMEs fail within their first year of operation in South Africa
mainly because of the lack of proper financial management skills. A number of
attempts have been made by way of software applications; however, these
attempts fail. This paper intends to design and implement a system that addresses
some of the financial management challenges faced by SMMEs. To achieve this,
features of similar systems were studies intensively through related work then
incorporated into our system design and then implemented. The main objectives
of the new system, was to make it possible for SMME owners to have access to
their financial information anywhere, have access to real time data, reduce the
amount of time needed to enter data in the system and a system that is easy to use.
Usability testing was done and the result was a system that was 20% better in
keeping records compared to the user's manual accounting system.

Keywords: Financial management · SMMEs · SMEs · Accounting system

1 Introduction

In the last five years, about 440000 SMME businesses closed down in South Africa [1].
Some of the contributing factors to the failures of most of the SMMEs were poor
business and financial management competencies [10]. To address the problem of lack
of proper business record keeping, much software has been availed over the years to
help business owners with their financial management but very few cater for the needs
of the SMME owners.

The problem with many of the accounting systems out there could be viewed as
complexity, whereby the accounting systems are not different to the manual accounting
practiced by any accountant who still writes on a piece of paper. This has led to most of
these software's to be only usable to people who have a strong accounting background
which most business owners do not have or require the users to have some form of
training before using them.

This paper seeks to develop an accounting system that will help SMME business owners with their financial management challenges regardless of their accounting background, by making it possible for them to have access to real time data, reduce the time needed to enter data, easy to use the system and make it accessible anywhere. This system was implemented Using PHP and MySQL database. To achieve the objectives mentioned above we automated some of the accounting processes, designed a user interface that is user friendly, did not use accounting jargon in the system instead used simple English for error recovery messages and information. This paper is organized as follows: In Sect. 2, we present related work. In Sect. 3, we present the system design and architecture. In Sect. 4, we present implementation. In Sect. 5, we present testing and results. We conclude the paper in Sect. 6.

2 Related Work

There has been a number of researches and projects done in the field similar to our research, some of these works are discussed in this section. A research was conducted to find out how the new web accounting system could work for SMEs and how these new systems could influence the adoption of International Financial Regularly Standards (IFRS) by SMEs and the factors that might influence the usage of web accounting by SMEs [8].

The product of this research was a system that made it easy for the users to gain access to it everywhere at any time because it was web based. The users did not need to have vast amounts of accounting knowledge just only basic computer skills. The reports design made it possible for the user to edit them in HTML, Excel, XML and some PDF applications. The application was accessible simultaneously by the operator and accountant or management. It was accessible using any computer with IE, Mozilla, and Opera.

This research is similar to our work because the researcher developed a web based accounting application specifically for SMEs with the aim of finding out if these systems could be adopted by the SMEs. The developed system accomplished similar objectives that we wanted to accomplish with our proposed system by making it easy for the users to access to the system everywhere at any time. Its design was in such a way that users did not need to have a vast amount of accounting knowledge just only basic computer skills. However this researcher's work is more of a direct translation of the manual or handwritten accounting, the gap in his work is the introduction of automation in the double entry system and report generation. This allows the user to enter transactions once and the rest happens in the background of the system.

Easy Books [5] developed accounting software that is free to use, but in order to use more of its features users had to pay $30 more to get access to its features. The software's design was to make it easy to use, as it did not require through knowledge of accounting. Reports were auto-generated in a functional layout and could be emailed or printed from the application. A built in calculator provided, as well as online backups. It provided 29 different types of accounts with accounting jargon names, such as "Accrual". MSEs in the developing world would unlikely use some of these feature. This software was similar to the proposed system because it incorporated some automation in its report generation, but differed when it came to its usage as it contained accounting jargon which we eliminated in our system with simple English to make it user friendly to those that do not have any accounting background.

IXpenselt [3] developed accounting software that enabled the user to keep track of his/her income and expenses; it also had the ability to generate graphical reports in PDF format. This software had some drawbacks which users were not very fond of, they found that entering data into the system was time consuming and the interface was too complex. As with Easy Books, it also offers online backups and monthly overviews of the different accounts. In addition, it included the ability to take a photo of the receipt to capture a transaction. This software is not similar to our proposed system because; its design was not so user friendly to the people who did not know much about accounting. The menu bars changing functions with every screen click and too many items on displayed on every screen made it to be not so user friendly. Users were complaining of the amount of time it took them to enter data into the system, while our system solved that problem by automating some of the processes. However it had some characteristic that we included in our system the printing of reports in pdf format.

Frogtek noticed that many of the SMEs did not track their sales or expenses because they do not have funds to procure the needed equipment to do that in their stores, these included things such as a point-of-sale system or a cash register, and those that were tracking them were doing it via note book [2]. Therefore, they then developed an accounting system that would help them in tracking their business dealing. They developed a point-of-sale application for the SMEs that enabled the users to be able to record all their operating expenses and revenues on their mobile phones or tablets. An external bar code connected to the phone via a wireless connection made it possible to record transactions in the system. All these application were compatible with Android smart phones or tablets that had a touch screen and synchronize with their web servers with this innovation from frogtek the users had access to financial reporting, personalize recommendation and improved services. This then enabled the SME owner to realize or be able to calculate their breakeven point and make personalized recommendations to customers.

This system is similar to the researcher study because it allowed the owners to keep track of their business records specifically sales and expenses. The system developed by frogtek still lacked other components needed for business accounting, these are bank transactions, capital investments financiers it only focuses on cash based accounting only. An addition of other components to this system is needed to make it more comprehensive and appropriate for business accounting.

SMEasy developed specifically to help South African small businesses owners who have no knowledge of accounting [9]. They developed an accounting system that allowed the users to enter their transactions only once and the system could do the double entry system the back end for the user. The accounting system had a simple screen, no complex menus and no accounting language used in it, which made it quite simple for the entrepreneurs and SMEs to understand. Being web-based made it possible for users to access it anytime and anywhere. The system enabled the users to be able to keep track of their business and personal money used in the business. It also allowed the use of company logos when creating quotations invoices, pays lips, and so builds the brand of your business.

It also had features that allowed a third parties such as an accountant to have access to the users' records by exporting the data.

This system is similar to our system, because it is for the South African SMME owners, who have little or no knowledge of accounting, and being hosted in the cloud, helped in making it accessible everywhere and the non-usage of accounting terminology helps in making it user friendly. The systems design meets most of the criteria related to researchers study, but still lacked or needs a better interface and navigation design.

The current model is not easy to navigate through the pages. A standard interface that would allow the switching between windows would make it easy to use, it also needs proper structuring to be more effect by grouping things in a chronological manner and make it easy to switch between windows by making it possible to have multiple windows open at the same time and switching between them.

3   System Design and Architecture

Before embarking on designing the user interface, we first had to design the database of the system. An entity relationship diagram is a graphical representation of an entity-relationship model [7]. The entity diagram shown in Fig. 1 shows the table used to store information in the database.

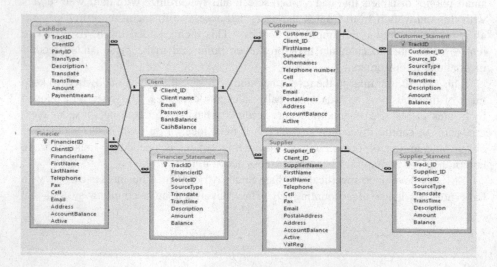

Fig. 1. Entity relationship diagram

The user interface was developed using PHP. The system was designed to have only one user working with the system having automation functions running in the background. Using the Use case diagram shown in Fig. 2, we describe how the user interacts with the system.

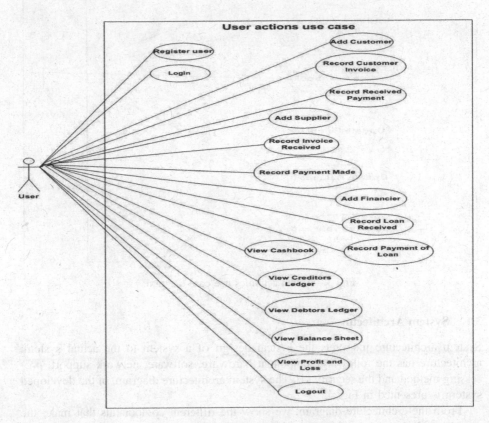

Fig. 2. User activities use case diagram

The interaction of the system with information that has been entered by the user is done through automation; the different automation processes of information are shown using the systems use case diagram presented in Fig. 3.

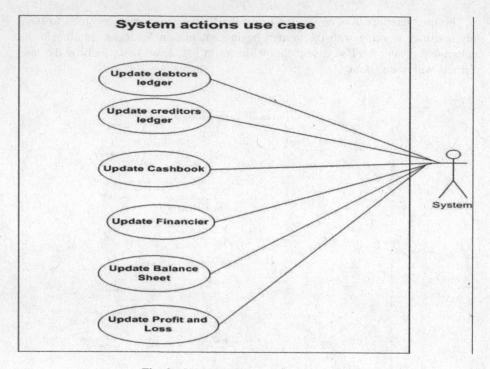

Fig. 3. System activities use case diagram

3.1 System Architecture

System architecture interprets the logical design of a system to the actual system; architecture has the following component hardware, software, network support, processing method and the security [4]. The system architecture diagram, of the developed system is presented in Fig. 4.

From the architecture diagram, we show the different components that make the system work these are; software services running in the server to make it possible for the users to interact with the application and the database. The database server is where the storage and processing of the users information occurs. Since the application is web based, users have to be connected the internet first before they can be able to use the application using the different browsers available that is Chrome, internet explorer, Firefox, etc.

A client may be a computer such as a desktops, laptops, note books which requires additional hardware or WiFi connection in order to connect to the internet. A mobile device is a device that can be carried by the user and is always connect to some network and does not require additional hardware to connect to the internet; these include smart phones and tables.

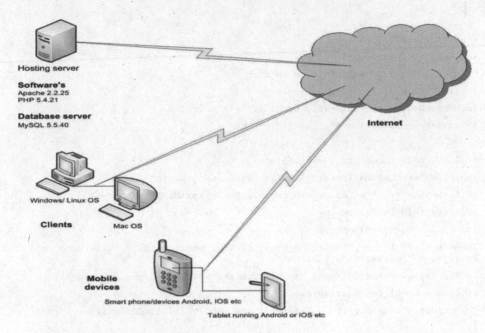

Fig. 4. System architecture

4 Implementation

The online mobile accounting management system was implemented using PHP scripting language. This system was connected to a database designed using MySQL to enable the users to save and retrieve data from the user interface.

The implementation of the system was separated into two parts these are as follows:

- Database- we used MySQL database found in XAMMP which is a free and open source cross platform web server solution stack package consisting mainly of the Apache HTTP Server.
- Interface- we used PHP to develop the interface because there are no costs of using PHP, and there are no licenses restrictions, it is 100% for free to use by anyone.

4.1 Database

To retrieve or save information in the "moneyb" database a connection string was created on the user interface this is shown in the database connection code.

```
session_start();
include("database.php");
//Get the date and adjust it by an hour
$systemDate = date("Y-m-d H:i:s");
$newTransDate = strtotime($systemDate." + 2 hours");
$transDate = date("Y-m-d", $newTransDate);


if($_REQUEST['SubmitBtn'] == "Login")
login.php?userT=$email&passT=$password&SubmitBtn=Login");
if($userName != "" && $password != "")//&& $clientName != "")
//verify info is filled in
{$dblink = openBase('moneyb');
$result = mysql_query("Select * from `client` where Email = '$userName' and
Password = '$password'", $dblink)
or die (mysql_error()."<p><a href='index.php'>Back to Logon Page</a>");
if($row = mysql_fetch_array($result))
{//include :"home.php");      //fopen("home.php");//$loggedOn = true;//$task
= "mess";

        $_SESSION['names'] = $row['ClientName'];

        $_SESSION['enter'] = $password;

        $_SESSION['clientId'] = $row['ClientID'];

        $_SESSION['clientTrackID'] = $row['TrackId'];

        $_SESSION['func'] = " ".$row['Functions'];

        $_SESSION['isLoggedOn'] = true;

        //echo "<tr>
 //<td>".$_SESSION['clientId']."
".$_SESSION['names'].""."".$_SESSION['clientId']."
".$_SESSION['names']."</d></tr>";

//update the last logon time
mysql_query("update `customer` set LoginDate = '".date('Y-m-d',
$newTransDate)."', LoginTime = '".date('H:i:s', $newTransDate)."' where
ClientId = '$userName'", $dblink);

mysql_close($dblink);

header("Location: home.php");

exit;
```

4.2   Interface

The use of PHP to develop the interface of the system has many advantages some of these are because, it is not platform specific it can run on any OS that is Linux, Mac OS, Windows and UNIX. Applications built on PHP are easy to scale up, which makes scalability easy when working with PHP. Hosting applications developed in

PHP is very easy since a lot of hosts do support PHP. Applications that are developed with PHP do not have any problems in terms of losing their speeds. Since it is a language that has been around for years it is a stable language that can be trusted.

4.3 Reports

To reduce the amount of work needed to enter data into the system, we automated some of the processes and these included posting to the cashbook, balance sheet, summary sales report, summary purchases report and the Profit and loss.

5 Testing and Results

After the successful implementation of the system, we set upon conducting a system and usability testing. In these tests, we did functional and non-functional testing on the system.

For the functional testing 40 individuals tested the system by performing certain tasks in it system then answered two questionnaires these are pre-test and post-test questionnaires. We wanted to get the following information from the tests:

1. If it was easy to learn and use
2. If it met the users financial information needs
3. If the users made many errors while using the system and if they would recommend it to others to try it out or not.

In one of the questions, we wanted them to compare the system with their manual bookkeeping method. Using Fig. 5, we present a diagram showing how the system rated against the user's manual system on a scale of 1–10.

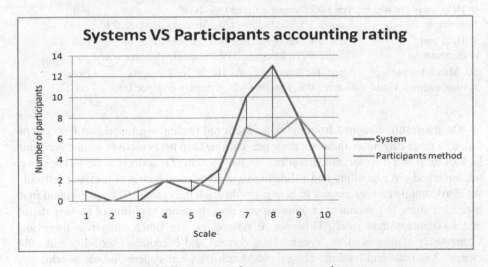

Fig. 5. Effectiveness of system vs. manual system

Unlike the functional testing whereby there was no specific selection criteria used to select or approach the testers, with this kind of testing, we needed people that have a programming background since we needed to test the system not just for its functionality but also to see if it met certain standards.

There are ten rules of system interaction, which are called heuristics because they are not specific to usability guideline [6]. When conducting the system testing we used Nielsen's 10 usability heuristics to develop the testing questions that were to be used for testing the system. The testers were given a case to complete in the system, and then answer questions paused to them on the questionnaire. The results of the tests that were carried on the system are shown in the Table 1.

Table 1. Usability testing results

Heuristic	Responses from questionnaires	Result
1. Visibility of system status	Agree 67%, Strongly agree 0%, Neither Agree or Disagree 0%, Disagree 33%, Strongly disagree 0%	Improvement
2. Consistency standards of the system	Agree 17%, Strongly agree 83%, Neither Agree or Disagree 0%, Disagree 0%, Strongly disagree 0%	Pass
3. Error prevention	Agree 0%, strongly agree 0%, Neither Agree or Disagree 83%, Strongly disagree 0%, Disagree 17%	Fail
4. User control and Freedom	Agree 0%, Strongly Agree 100%, Neither Agree or Disagree 0%, Disagree 0%, Strongly disagree 0%	Pass
5. Flexibility and efficiency	Strongly Agree 67%, Agree 33%, Neither Agree or Disagree 0%, Disagree 0%, Strongly disagree 0%	Pass
6. Recognition rather than recall	Agree 0%, Strongly Agree 67%, Neither Agree or Disagree 0%, Disagree 33%, Strongly disagree 0%	Improvement
7. Aesthetic and minimal design	Agree 0%, Strongly agree 0%, Neither Agree or Disagree 0%, Strongly disagree 67%, Disagree 33%	Pass
8. Help users recover from errors	Agree 0%, Strongly agree 0%, Neither agree or disagree 100%, Disagree 0%, Strongly disagree 0%	Fail
9. Help and documentation	Agree 0%, Strongly agree 0%, Neither agree or disagree 67%, Disagree 33%, Strongly disagree 0%	Fail
10. Match between system and real world	Agree 0%, Strongly agree 100%, Neither agree or disagree 0%, Disagree 0%, Strongly disagree 0%	Pass

On the results obtained from the non-functional testing, we found that the system failed in three categories these are error prevention, help users recover from errors and lack of help and documentation features on the system. To address these failures, we implemented error handling and validation in the system which was previous left out, we also compiled a user manual to help users through the system. They also found that it needed some improvement in other aspects and these are visibility of system status and recognition than recall. However, it passed in five other categories these are Consistency standards of the system, User control and Freedom, Flexibility and efficiency, Aesthetic and minimal design and Match between system and real world.

Based on the results obtained in the functional testing we concluded that the system is more effective in keeping records when compared to the participants' manual systems. 93% or 37 of the participants found the system to be more efficient as they rated it to be on 5 and above on a scale of 1–10 and that is a 20% improvement from the participants' manual accounting system.

6   Conclusion

In this paper, we first introduced the study by describing the challenges faced by SMMEs and the attempts that have been made to try and address the problems faced by SMMEs, we then discussed why they were not successful with their attempts. We then presented our system design to address some of the financial challenges face by SMMEs. Once the design was complete we started implementing the solution, here we used PHP and MySQL. To test the effectiveness of the solution we used questionnaires. These questionnaires were used to evaluate the system to see if it met its intended objectives through Functional and Non-Functional testing.

The final result of this testing proved that automating some of the system processes and hosting the system on the cloud helped the SMME owners in their financial management by reducing the amount of work needed for re-entering data, making data available in real time and making it simple to use even for those with little or no accounting skills this can be attested for by the results obtained from the tests. The results showed that the system was 20% better in keeping records when compared to the user's manual accounting system.

References

1. Fatoki, O.: The causes of the failure of new small and medium enterprises in South Africa. Mediterr. J. Soc. Sci. **5**(20), 922 (2014)
2. Products. http://frogtek.org/products
3. iXpenselt. http://www.fyimobileware.com/ixpenseit.html
4. Shelly, G.B., Cashman, T.J., Rosenblatt, H.J.: Systems Analysis and Design. Thomson course Technology, Boston (2006)
5. Easy Books. http://easybooksapp.com
6. Nielsen, J.: 10 Usability heuristics for user interface design (1995). https://www.nngroup.com/articles/ten-usability-heuristics/
7. Hoffer, J.A., Prescott, M.B., Macfadden, F.R.: Modern Database Management. Prentice Hall, New Jersey (2007)
8. Florien, M., Groza, C., Aldescu (Iacob), E.-O.: Using web technology to improve the accounting of small and medium enterprises: an academic approach to implementation of IFRS. Annales Universitatis Apulensis Series Oeconomica **13**(2), 280–289 (2011)
9. Product profile. www.tdh.co.za/pdf/SMEasy%20Product%20Profile.pdf
10. Naqvi, S.W.H.: Critical success and failure factors of entrepreneurial organizations: study of SMEs in Bahawalp. Eur. J. Bus. Manage. **3**(4), 98 (2011)

Africa's Non-inclusion in Defining Fifth Generation Mobile Networks

Gertjan van Stam(✉)

Scientific and Industrial Research and Development Centre, Harare, Zimbabwe
gvanstam@sirdc.ac.zw

Abstract. This paper identifies and unpacks a troubling phenomenon whereby Africans have historically been and currently are de-facto excluded from processes that set mobile network standards such as 3G, 4G, and (now) 5G. It combines technical and procedural observations and colonial discourses of computing, concluding that enshrined systems and processes that steer the changes in mobile technology disempower African inputs and represent a continuation of the single use of situated techniques, skills, methods and processes in the production of core mobile technologies, all conceptualised outside Africa.

Keywords: Mobile networks · e-infrastructure · Africa · Colonial discourse

1 Introduction

The conceptualisation, design and production of Information and Communications Technologies (ICT) are activities dominated by business and academia located in Europe, North America, and, since the last decennials, Asia.

Mobile network systems are defined in architectures that set the workings and interactions of core technology components, their access interfaces, and operations and management. The system standards and their specifications are mostly set by the 3rd Generation Partnership Project (3GPP) and the International Telecommunications Union (ITU), a body of the United Nations. The architectures define the system performances and set the device and operational requirements. The specifications aim to cater for anticipated user experiences, potential business cases, and requirements for deployment, operations and management for operators. In the running-up of the setting of definitions and standards of 5G—the fifth-generation mobile network—one recognises a re-iteration of enshrined practices mediated by the control of seemingly conditioned engineers embedded in centers of product development. The associated processes and collaborations invariably involve discussions and activities outside Africa. Africa is deemed silent while the particulars of 5G are being set in irrevocable decisions and related conceptual and textual artefacts.

This paper endeavours to focus on 5G development and Africa. It derives its findings from a reflexive science and use of an extended case method [1].

© ICST Institute for Computer Sciences, Social Informatics and Telecommunications Engineering 2018
T.F. Bissyande and O. Sie (Eds.): AFRICOMM 2016, LNICST 208, pp. 14–25, 2018.
https://doi.org/10.1007/978-3-319-66742-3_2

My studies are in the nexus of society and technology from an epistemological position and perspective in Southern Africa [2–4]. Reflective insights are gained from my engagement with practitioners and engineers active in the field of mobile networks in the time and space continuum of a participating researcher in the lived realm. The period of engagement spans from 1995, when I was strategist at the incumbent mobile operator in the Netherlands, up to the present, where I am research fellow in the government technology centre in Zimbabwe. It covers interactions in the West (Europe and North America), and in Sub-Saharan Africa.

I am a senior member of the Institute of Electrical and Electronics Engineers (IEEE) and encountered and interacted with experts in engineering facilitated by my professional affiliations and relationships. In particular, on the latest technologies, the work is informed by extended discussions and ethnographic interactions on the subject with experts in mobile technologies and the monitoring of literature, in the period 2010–2016. The ethnographic interactions took place in person, during travels in Africa, Europe, and North America. They were followed up with unstructured communications in the form of e-mails and interviews by means of voice calls from Africa. Thus, this study offers a fresh dimension of ethnography, different from traditional ethnography where the researcher is obliged to stay in the field in a given local for prolonged periods.

2   A Development Pattern of Mobile Networks, Void of African Involvement

There appears to be an eight years innovation cycle in the practice of mobile technology development. The first generation of digital mobile networks emerged in the early 1990's; the third generation of mobile networks (3G) were standardised in 2005, while the fourth generation (4G) mobile networks were standardised in 2013. The fifth generation is likely to be market-ready in the year 2020, with its development and standardisation being 'work in progress' till 2019 [5]. This sequence slots in well with the scheduling of the Olympic Games sporting events.

5G (Fifth Generation) means different things to different people. At its heart, it is heralded as a fundamental change in the way of thinking about mobile networks and wireless systems [6,7]. Among its priorities, the work on 5G is focusing on increases in the mobile data volume per geographical area, the number of connected devices in a given density, the user data rate, the speed of service deployment time, and a decrease in radio link latency [6]. However, these priorities are foreign to the peripheral areas in Sub-Saharan Africa where the majority of Africans live with low population densities, with limited transport infrastructure, and affected by the shortcomings of the globalised internet technology [8]. The omission of African inputs in the priority settings for 5G, especially catering for realities in non-urban centres, is a result of the practice that contributions to 5G architecture come from a core of network operators and technology players orienting on realities in cities and areas outside of Africa. The operators in this core are Vodaphone, Telefonica, NTT Docomo, China Mobile, ATT, and

Orange. They contrive with a conglomerate of four main technology players: Huawei, Alcatel-Lucent, Ericson, and Nokia Solutions and Networks. All these companies headquarter in either North America, Asia or Europe. From such positionality, their management is shielded and relatively unaware of the African realities.

As often in the field of technology, the development of 5G ICTs is sustained by a vendor driven, conservative, apolitical narrative of technocratic service delivery. This myopic and complacent practice thrives on a capitalitistic and neoliberal preponderance and a development paradigm based upon technology determination. Current systems of technical development involve a diverse and multi-layered arrangement of research and development, standardisation and intellectual property. This arrangement prioritises knowledge and knowledge practices generated outside of Africa and, therefore, represents a systemic obstruction and mires epistemic violence to inputs from Africa [4]. The dominating conglomerate of operators and manufacturers wields powers sustained by their influence in academia, finance, and politics, including politics of technology knowledge production and dissemination.

The process of 5G technology development involves white papers (e.g. [6,7]) and technical inputs (e.g. from a North American prespective [9]). These contributions align with a positioning of corporate industries for market dominance and the use of intellectual properties from their patent portfolios. At certain moments in time, these inputs solidify in decisions. For example, Radio Access Networks were defined, and linked with participants from North America, Asia and Europe only, during a 3GPP 5G-workshop, September 2015 in Phoenix, USA [10]. Such standardisation is framed as a zero-sum power game, disallowing the involvement of those not physically present. The standardisation meetings are open and contribution driven, however, the practicalities of enshrined practices safeguards a continued deployment and advocacy of intellectual and technical portfolios and capacities, without involving Africa. The outcomes are portrayed as *fait accompli* and often contain surprises to those unable to participate in the process. Africa remains implicitly and disapprovingly (mis-)represented.

Driven by Asian inputs, 5G focuses on vastly increased data transmission rates. European contributions target the opening up of vast sensor deployments across the world. Demands for efficient spectrum use and considerably reduced-latency-demands pushes technologies to use super high frequencies. Capability aspirations include the harvesting of the promises of the Internet-of-Things by the bolstering of network reliability that targets a 99.999% availability and lowering round-trip delay in the range of 1 ms. Through such performance, it is suggested, more applications in new fields can be allowed and 'security abilities' improve. Examples given are disaster avoidance through vehicle-to-vehicle communications. The Western-biased body of knowledge is supplemented by incidental contributions from researchers and companies, again from Europe, North America and Asia. An example is a much-cited contribution defining a *tactile internet* that can sustain holography, from a Technical University in

Germany [11]. The question that remains lingering and boggling critical minds is: where is Africa in this whole discourse?

As a matter of fact, there have been no significant African contributions for 5G. There exists neither a research agenda nor funding of African academic investigation and development within the current framing of 5G development, from an African point of view. There seems insufficient research and academic rewards in such positionality [12]. African research might be regarded idiosyncratic, and involvement with such research can have a negative effect on career development due the general omission of citations from researchers from Africa [13]. There is a sustained lack of funding for African research in Africa. In practice, all resources that flow out of the sanctified mobile technology processes—being understanding of process, intellectual and technical knowledge, quality information, theory, and secrets—flow to those involved in the process. When not part of the core team, it is hard to attain a proper comprehension of what is going on. The Western-centric processes of technology development represent a normative power system that Nicola Bidwell recognised as "complicit with systems that contribute to widening gaps between rich and poor, and urban and rural people" [14]. Bidwell's observation aligns with Paul Dourish and Scott Mainwaring who show that the discourse on ubiquitous computing—the prime source of ardent claims of the promises of 5G—sustains a colonial intellectual tradition [15]. Events and decisions made by non-Africans in distant meeting rooms have critical impacts on the use and benefits of technologies in Africa.

3 Technology Hegemony and a Discourse Set by Techno-Powers

The smooth and orderly flow and exchange of technologies are of critical importance for the domestic stability of a country. Dependency and domination can arise out of lopsided trade relations and, therefore, technology hegemony has the power to interrupt or disrupt commercial or financial flows or relations between countries. Technologies are a determinant of a community's (in)ability to guard its state, sovereignity and destiny. In a maritime analogy, Zaaiman [16] quotes Bryan McGrath, a naval expert at the Hudson Institute. McGrath explains the central proposition of the US Naval Strategy:

> that there is a global system in place that works to the benefit of the people of the United States and all other nations who participate in it. The system consists of tightly interconnected networks of trade, finance, information, law, people and governance, and the strategy posits that US. maritime forces will be deployed to protect and sustain the system [17, online].

McGrath's proposition is a modern rendering of *the invisible hand* mentioned in Adam Smith's writing in 1776. In his study of capitalist economy, Smith argued that participants in its processes

... generally, indeed, neither intends to promote the public interest, nor knows how much he is promoting it. By preferring the support of domestic to that of foreign industry, he intends only his own security; and by directing that industry in such a manner as its produce may be of the greatest value, he intends only his own gain, and he is in this, as in many other cases, led by an invisible hand to promote an end which was no part of his intention [18, p. 246].

Therefore, even unconciously, participants in 5G processes will orient towards maximising benefits for themselves to the detriment of Africa. In this light, it comes as no surprise that the current 5G development processes sustain the 'techno-powers' of established, non-African players. This syndicate is backed up by a development philosophy and master-narrative derived from a conceptualisation of capitalism, liberalism, and implicit orientalism, from the position and interests of the non-African center [19]. Subsequently, the barriers for participation in the development of 5G (or most ICTs, for that matter [20]) from Africa results in an opportunistic invasion and diminuting agency, leaving Africans no real opportunity to participate in a meaningful way. The Nigerian scholar Ekwuru [21] argues that globalisation links directly to cultural atrophy—the death of cultures, particularly those in Africa. The exercise of techno-power in 5G is a vivid example of such a globalisation.

The implicit claim of 'universal truth' like the one that '5G will be transformational' is imperialistic and false [12]. Due to the exclusion of the African voice, 5G development can only be partially fitting and context-biased. Light and Akama [22] draw on the work of Greenbaum and Halskov [23], to argue that it is an ethical and democratic imperative for everybody, including people that have historically been marginalised, to influence the decision-making processes that affect their communities and life. The design of computing e-infrastructures and architectures, such as in mobile networks equipment and services, does hard-code the conditions and possibilities of mobile networks in communities in Africa. The non-inclusion of potential contributions from Africa, whether from communities, governments, industry or academia, and an ignorance of the value of African world-views and economic realities and practices, leads to technologies and services unaligned with the daily experience, practice and needs in communities in large parts of Africa. Only if the fundamental interests of African people, especially the poorest and most marginalised, are incorporated into the design parameters of 5G, could 5G fulfil its claim to be truly transformational. Such an understanding of an agency of Africa and a related optimism is at odds with the widely held belief that Africa is steeped in poverty and under-development.

For Africa, the persistent master-narrative of under-development is a significant obstacle to meaningful participation. This master-narrative is advantageous to leaders of industry located outside the African continent but considerably hampers African participation in freely and fairly contributing to setting the agenda for 5G. A failure to participate feeds into the story of non-development. A circular and negative narrative relegates Africa to the subaltern and, in turn, pre-empts the development of African proposals and subsequently reduces the opportunity for Africans to influence the flows of resources that will result from a 5G roll-out. History repeats itself, and Africa will be forced to consume foreign 5G products, instead of creating African technologies to amplify its African, human intentions and realisation.

The bar set by the powers-that-be for an inclusion of African contributions to 5G are, in practice, excluding. Of course, this all feeds into a continuation of the master-narrative that the West must bring 'development', be it in the form of culture, commerce or technology [24]. Sometimes, a profession breaks through the glass ceiling and power-bar. For example, although much constrained by foreign influences also, there is ample evidence that medical research in rural areas in Africa has provided for African solutions that are of real value in African contexts. African research influences priorities and improves the fight against infectious and non-communicable diseases that affect millions of people. In technology, such research has not yet broken the thick glass ceiling created by hegemonic forces that prevent inclusion and equality, and sustain the continuation of a single narrative 'about Africa' of poverty, incapability and distance.

As an example of the dominant narrative-of-failure stands UNESCO Science Report *Towards 2030* [25]. In the report, the authors note that "unfortunately, many countries in Africa and Asia mainly are producing fewer inventions today than they did in the early 1990s, despite healthy rates of economic growth. An analysis of patents signed between 1990 and 2010 shows that 2 billion people live in regions that are falling behind in innovation. This decline is overshadowed by the extraordinary development in India and China: almost one-third of the 2.6 million patents filed worldwide in 2013 came from China alone" [25, p. 4]. In the linking of innovation with a growth-scenario, the UNESCO authors cover their eyes and align with a hegemonic master-narrative that economy and innovation go hand in hand. Sheneberger and van Stam [26] argue that such a narrative does not describe the economic reality in many African communities. In many parts of Africa, survival is at stake and generically everyone is an entrepreneur, utilising methods of improvisation [27]. As the African voice has been pushed into a subaltern state, there is a general lack of formal interaction. Most entrepreneurship takes place in the 'informal economy', where practice can be more robust than in the formal ones. Such economy is estimated to constitute more than half, sometimes up to 90%, of the economy in many African countries.

So, where are the African contributions for 5G, one might ask? It depends on the framing of one's outlook whether one can recognise them [28]. In current practice, 5G discussions are set in processes in which *individual* entities provide inputs, where engineers develop working groups, where engineers assess relative merits of technologies, and where engineers constitute the methodical power basis to integrate contributions into outcomes. Such processes do not align with African practices that focus on communal, dialogical, reciprocal, continuous, contextual behaviour [4,12]. Africa and its engineers cannot be readily understood through the lenses provided by international capital, (neoliberal) geopolitics, and mass culture [27].

Due to being invisible in the bigger world because of exclusion, Africans have forged a particular way of working. With regards to African engineering practice [27]—a practice which is salient in a locale over a substantial amount of time— African engineers do work in cooperation and communion. They align with a social, communal identity (Ubuntu, see [29]), continuously converse about that reality (Orality, see [30]) with the understanding that the success of others is the success of everyone (Relatio, see [26,31]). Activities happen in an environment where people know there is a need for forgiving to be able to live today and where people must convene to be able to live tomorrow (Dominatio). African engineers understand 'the living' are just an instance in time, part of a long line of ancestors. African engineers invest in social harmony, for those that will be after them (Animatio) [32]. This reading of African creative practices aligns with Ingold and Hallam [33], who contend that such forwards reading of creativity— in contrast with a backwards reading of innovation—shows its improvisational, temporal, relational, and performative agency.

An aside emerging from this reality is the absence of African references in mainstream academic literature. As the African scholars are relegated to sub-altern status, and with various forms of hegemony in publishing, and due to asymmetries in research relationships, citations to African publications hardly exist. Of course, any knowledge needs contextualisation and an appropriation by the interlocutors and the communities from which they operate; "If the end product of foreign academic research is a take-away text written in academic English, then the foreign academic appropriates local culture for private and foreign profit, leaving the local community objectified and exploited" [34, p. 4].

As with all humanities, people in Africa improvise [27]. Africans mediate the natural world in line with its practices, in context and positionality [4]. In that sense, African works adhere to framings, processes, and responds to needs and forms of appreciation understood in Africa. These requirements and satisfactions are at variance with those that govern the current 5G technology developments. It appears that for the current systems of 5G development, no input has been solicited to contribute to the framings, processes, needs assessments, and forms of appreciation instrumental in Africa. Governing processes seem set in stone. It appears that, as Mandani [35] already indicated, Africa can only solicit for the crumbs as 'hunters and gatherers' of raw data and as 'native informants' who collect and provide empirical data for processing in, and empowerment of, non-African industries (for a 5G example from Nigeria, see [36]).

The development of 5G is well under way, and the reality check as presented here shows little room for African contributions. The established teams of operators and equipment suppliers are well versed in their play. Although one must continue to contest the rules of this game and provide for alternatives, at present, there is little chance for Africa to assemble a team and play in the current 5G league. The contemporary processes do dominate, silence, objectify and normalise Africans and their communities. Therefore, for Africa, 5G will remain a hollow story of 'more of everything': more speed, more bandwidth, and faster response, unaligned with the African lived environment. Many people in Africa already struggle with the limited performance of 3G and 4G services, low investments per user, service shortcomings due to high latencies to distant service platforms, and an influx of services that leech African information to Western-controlled cloud-services. The result is a continued labelling of Africa being 'inmature', and an expanding digital exclusion [37]; the technological gap between the North and the South remains a tantalising reality. However, 5G, whatever it is going to be and when available, will be used by the destitute and powerful alike. Therefore, current academic exploits of 5G and Africa could focus on 'damage control' and how to mediate the inequality growing from 5G technologies that are forced upon Africa.

4   Potential African Contributions for Mobile Networks

To provide for future inclusion of Africa, processes, agendas, and content of global mobile network developments need contributions and participation from Africans. Such a standpoint aligns with discussions on innovating the economic order, for instance, by Varoufakis [38,39] or, anecdotally, Brand [40]. Understanding from Africa can lead to the furthering of circular, participative, and collaborative engagements. If the eight-year sequence holds, the next agenda is prone to be set around 2020. Due to its long lead times, Africa should position its conceptualisations as soon as possible.

Are there indications of the possible nature of African contributions to mobile networks? Deducing from reflexive, critical, longitudinal ethnographic work in Southern Africa, I suggest that the African realities can inform in the development of mobile networks, indeed. For an indication of such contribution, I exhibit two examples, (a) an embedding of human inclusiveness and frame bridging, and (b) a moral engineering within a paradigm of resource abundance.

Aligning Engineering with Human Cultural Behaviour
In practice, the worldwide growth of inequalities resulting from the roll-out of ICTs can be witnessed in their most heart-wrenching forms in the African urban/rural divide. In the so-called urban-jungle, survival is the mantra of the day. Here, by design, resources are scarce. Every conceivable use and utilisation is exercised in any manner. Besides, everything goes as, due to a combination of poverty, unfamiliarity and general lack of culture, people's behaviour and conduct are largely regulated by impulse.

Human suffering continues due to a design of zero-gaming of resource provisioning. To overcome an unequal resource distribution, future mobile networks could bridge frames to provide for the creation of networking commons. In an experimental design, Ouoba and Bissyandé [41] showed how with sensitivity to cultural practices and human behaviour in West Africa, new and contextually adapt e-services can be developed that make sense in context, utilising timely gatherings (cf. [42]).

Incorporating Communal Methods Within Resource Abundance
Africa is rich in the frequency spectrum. This richness blends with an enormous wealth of people, culture and environment. Africa is home to 15% of the world's

population and boasts of many and diverse cultures as well as a stunning amount of natural resources [43]. Sustainability involves the balancing of the community and individuals, embedding activities to interact with finite resources in an orientation of conviviality, inclusiveness and involvement of all people and stakeholders [44]. From such an outset, an African take on the essentials of mobile technologies is not only economically enriching but morally relevant.

With relatively low people densities in the majority of Africa's landmass, the second biggest continent in the world, spectrum is mostly not crowded. However, spectrum allocations are guided by old, rigid principles that guard the interests of the powerful, mainly living in urban areas. The realisation of this fix and the recognition of a 'spectrum dividend' has led some African scientists to explore the potential of (TV) White Space technologies [45,46]. Their reasoning involves embracing of the community, abundance, sharing, and the practice of authoritative communal (effectively a commons-based) governance. Potential outcomes are proposals for devising dynamic and fair access to dominated but unused spectrum, use of cognitive technologies, innovation of spectrum utilisation and monitoring in challenging environments, and the development of national and regional spectrum databases. These experiences can be generalised in mobile network technologies.

5   Conclusion

This extended case study of 5G and Africa shows enshrined systems and processes that steer change in core technologies, void of African inputs and participation. Africa is not consulted in defining the listing of needs from society, and Africa is not included in the development of techniques, skills, methods and processes used in the production of core mobile technologies.

The current methods of 5G technology development involve a relatively small group of operators and manufacturers that—in practice—dictate mostly the kind of technologies that are being developed. This dominating practice represents an instance of what I call super-colonialism. This extended form of colonialism includes international corporate business as a colonising party, complementary to countries that are known to have continued their meddling in African affairs in what is known as neo-colonialism. Super-colonialism incorporates the use of techno-powers, digital means of communications, ever increasing air-transport networks, technologies, global finance networks and aid, international treaties, and other frameworks, to exercise devious powers and vexations over distant peoples. By considering inputs from Europe, North America and Asia only, engineering systems are Western-centric, support functionalities that facilitate particular (Western) behaviour and circumstances, and neglect the needs of Africans. The current 5G processes and their implications are a continuation of imperialistic practice—albeit one with hardly a bridgehead in Africa—and is, in practice, a colonial meddling that mediates action in the African society in a manner that is foreign to its cultures and contexts.

Under a disguise of technocratic arguments, a limited group of operators and manufacturers—the establishment and elite—design technologies and implement irreversible choices on issues that not only affect themselves but everyone else in the world. Therefore, it is highly questionable if 5G will effectively support the social behaviours and contexts in Africa. In practice, 5G development will continue colonial practices whereby Africans are excluded from processes that frame standards and acceptable behaviour affecting the African societies.

To assure peace, equity, and justice, one must aspire to a mutual symmetric world. Thus there is a moral imperative to address the asymmetric power dynamics that exist in the development of mobile technologies. This questioning of contemporary practices necessitates the questioning of the methodologies, ethics and non-inclusive systems of technology development. Resulting artefacts and functionalities influence us all, as can be witnessed by all-and-sundry in the case of mobile technologies that a large part of the world population uses on a daily or weekly basis. The colonising effects of existing frameworks must be addressed. Its fall out is explained for Africa, but the effects could be well the same for other non-included people groups who are peripheral to the technical processes and dominant parties. In this respect, one can think of those living in rural and disenfranchised areas, anywhere in the world.

The agency of Africa, the second largest continent in size and with a fast-growing population, must be strengthened and incorporated in global technology developments. It is important that dedicated African research and development prioritises African challenges, situated within African and a global agendas. Such African research needs empowerment and sustenance. Globalisation will only be truly beneficial for all when it encompasses diversity. Contributions from the African experience must augment future mobile network technologies and their design in an collaborative effort to create a more just world. Local communities can flourish with and through technology, only, when inclusively developed. Technology contributions emerging from a crystallisation of African philosophy, notably Ubuntu (the belief in a universal bond of sharing) can contribute towards integration of the values of inclusiveness and reciprocity that need to underlie global networks. Africans should be heard in the mainstream of mobile network development, so that new technologies will not serve to marginalise the continent and colonise its people, but will rather enable Africans to play their rightful role in the global digital community.

References

1. Burawoy, M.: The Extended Case Method. University of California Press, Berkeley and Los Angeles (2009)
2. van Stam, G.: Is technology the solution to the world's major social challenges? In: IEEE Global Humanitarian Technology Conference (GHTC 2012), Seattle, WA, USA, 21–24 October 2012. IEEE (2012)
3. van Stam, G.: Experience in research and development in rural Zambia and Zimbabwe. In: RAE Workshop-4 'Enriching Engineering Education', Harare, Zimbabwe, 6–7 November 2014

4. Mawere, M., van Stam, G.: African engineering and the quest for sustainable development: levelling the ground for all players. In: Mawere, M., Nhemachena, A. (eds.) Theory, Knowledge, Development and Politics: What Role for the Academy in the Sustainability of Africa? Chap. 8, pp. 189–206. Langaa RPCIG, Bamenda (2016)
5. International Telecommunications Union: ITU towards "IMT for 2020 and beyond" (2016)
6. 5G PPP (Infrastructure Association). 5G Vision. Technical report (2015)
7. NGMN Alliance: NGMN 5G White Paper. Next Generation Mobile Networks Alliance (2015)
8. Johnson, D.L., van Stam, G.: The shortcomings of globalised internet technology in Southern Africa. In: Africomm 2016, Ouagadougou, Burkina Faso, 6–8 December 2016
9. ATIS. 5G Reimagined: A North American Perspective. Alliance for Telecommunications Industry Solutions, Washington, DC (2015)
10. 3GPP. The Mobile Broadband Standard RAN 5G Workshop - The Start of Something (2015)
11. Fettweis, G.P.: The tactile internet - applications and challenges. IEEE Veh. Technol. Mag. **9**(1), 64–70 (2014)
12. Mawere, M., van Stam, G.: Paradigm clash, imperial methodological epistemologies and development in Africa: observations from rural Zimbabwe and Zambia. In: Mawere, M., Mwanaka, T. (eds.) Development, Governance, and Democracy: A Search for Sustainable Democracy and Development in Africa, Chap. 6, pp. 193–211. Langaa RPCIG, Bamenda (2015)
13. van Stam, G.: Orientalism embedded in foreign narratives of technology for development. In: International Conference Chinoyi University, Chinoyi, Zimbabwe, 2–5 August 2016
14. Bidwell, N.J.: Moving the centre to design social media in rural Africa. J. Knowl. Cult. Commun. **31**(1), 51–77 (2016). AI & SOCIETY
15. Dourish, P., Mainwaring, S.D.: Ubicomp's colonial impulse. In: UbiComp 2012, Pittsburgh, PA, USA, 5–8 September 2012
16. Zaaiman, A.: National security: navigating the coming rough sees between USA and China. In: Women's Leadership in Peace-Building: Conflict, Community and Care, pp. 197–209. Africa World Press, Trenton (2015)
17. McGrath, B.: A New Look at an Old Maritime Strategy (2014)
18. Adam, S.: An Inquiry into the Nature and Causes of the Wealth of Nations. William Strahan, Thomas Cadell, London (1776)
19. Galtung, J.: A structural theory of imperialism. J. Peace Res. **8**(2), 81–117 (1971)
20. van Greunen, D., van Stam, G.: Review of an African rural internet network and related academic interventions. J. Commun. Inform. **10**(2) (2014)
21. Ekwuru, E.G.: The Pangs of an African Culture in Travail. Totan Publishers, Owerri (1999)
22. Light, A., Akama, Y.: Relations, structuring future social: the politics of care in participatory practice. Proceedings of the 13th Participatory Design Conference (PDC 2014): Research Papers, vol. 1, no. 1, pp. 151–160 (2014)
23. Greenbaum, J., Halskov, K.: PD a personal statement. Commun. ACM **36**(6), 47 (1993)
24. van Stam, G.: African engineering and colonialistic conditioning. In: Fifth International Conference on e-Infrastructure and e-Services for Developing Countries, Africomm 2013, Blantyre, Malawi, 25–27 November 2013
25. Schneegans, S., Eroöcal, D.: Unesco Science Report: Towards 2030. UNESCO Publishing, Paris (2015)

26. Sheneberger, K., van Stam, G.: Relatio: an examination of the relational dimension of resource allocation. Econ. Fin. Rev. **1**(4), 26–33 (2011)
27. van Stam, G.: African engineers and the quest for sustainable development: levelling the ground for all players. In: IEEE PES Power Africa, Livingstone, Zambia, 28 June–2 July 2016
28. van Stam, G.: Framing ICT access in rural Africa. In: 11th Prato CIRN Conference, Prato, Italy, 13–15 October 2014
29. Mawere, M., van Stam, G.: Ubuntu/Unhu as communal love: critical reflections on the sociology of Ubuntu and communal life in sub-Saharan Africa. In: Mawere, M., Marongwe, N. (eds.) Politics, Violence and Conflict Management in Africa: Envisioning Transformation, Peace and Unity in the Twenty-First Century, Chap. 9. Langaa RPCIG, Bamenda (2016)
30. van Stam, G.: Information and knowledge transfer in the rural community of Macha, Zambia. J. Commun. Inform. **9**(1) (2013)
31. Weijland, W.P.: Mathematical Foundations for the Economy of Giving (2014)
32. van Stam, G.: Thoughts on African content and implementation strategies involved in ICT access in (rural) Africa. In: HSRC, Seminar Series, Pretoria, South Africa, 25 March 2014. Human Sciences Research Council of South Africa (2014)
33. Ingold, T., Hallam, E.: Creativity and cultural improvisation: an introduction. In: Hallam, E., Ingold, T. (eds.) Creativity and Cultural Improvisation, Chap. 1. Berg, Oxford (2007)
34. van Stam, G.: Participatory Networks: Observations from Macha works. In: Participatory Networks Workshop at PDC 2014, Windhoek, Namibia (2014)
35. Mamdani, M.: The importance of research in a university (2011)
36. Wireless World: Gwandu seeks Africa's representation in 5G development (2015)
37. Unwin, T.: Ensuring that we create an internet for all. In: Stockholm Internet Forum 2013, Stockholm, Sweden, 23–23 May 2003
38. Varoufakis, Y.: The Global Minotaur. Zed Books, London (2015)
39. Varoufakis, Y.: And the Weak Suffer What They Must? Europe, Austerity and the Threat to Global Stability. The Bodley Head, London (2016)
40. Brand, R.: Revolution. Century, London (2014)
41. Ouoba, J., Bissyandé, T.F.: Leveraging the cultural model for opportunistic networking in sub-Saharan Africa. In: Fourth International IEEE EAI Conference on e-Infrastructure and e-Services for Developing Countries, Africomm 2012 (2012)
42. Bidwell, N.J., Reitmaier, T., Rey-Moreno, C., Roro, Z., Siya, M.J., Dlutu-Siya, B.: Timely relations in rural Africa. In: Proceedings of the 12th International Conference of the IFIP 9.4 Working Group on Social Implications of Computers in Development Countries, Ocho Rios, Jamaica, 19–22 May 2013
43. Unwin, T.: On the richness of Africa (2008)
44. Nyamnjoh, F.B.: Incompleteness: Frontier Africa and the currency of conviviality. J. Asian Afr. Stud. **50**(2), 1–18 (2015)
45. Johnson, D.L.: The white space opportunities in Africa. In: Fifth International Conference on e-Infrastructure and e-Services for Developing Countries, Africomm 2013, Blantyre, Malawi, 25–27 November 2013
46. Gweme, F., van Stam, G.: The potential for use of TV white spaces for the internet in Zimbabwe. In: Chinoyi International Conference, Chinoyi, Zimbabwe, 2–5 August 2016

Redesigning Mobile Phone Contact List to Integrate African Social Practices

Pasteur Poda[✉], A. Joëlle Compaoré, and Borlli Michel Jonas Somé

École supérieure d'Informatique, Université polytechnique de Bobo-Dioulasso,
01 BP 1091, Bobo-dioulasso, Burkina Faso
{pasteur.poda,joelle.compaore}@univ-bobo.bf, sborlli@gmail.com

Abstract. During the last decade, the design of social software involving the mobile phone contact list has been an active field of research. Systems, mostly those based on awareness, addressed many issues of social interest such as group communication or social ties building and strengthening. Yet, the mobile devices contact lists, as they are designed until now, do not efficiently take into account the social connections. Besides, the social connections are the principal provider of contact entries. Moreover, the current contact lists do not allow to efficiently retrieve/remember a contact who is forgotten or concerned by homonymy. Focusing on African social practices and behaviors, this paper proposed to redesign the contact list by integrating social relations that link people. This redesigning is accompanied with novel functionalities that will facilitate contacts retrieval, homonymy resolving and contacts remembering.

Keywords: Contact list · Contact information · Mobile phonebook · Mobile recommendation · Social relation · Social software

1 Introduction

One of the basic features offered on a mobile phone is the contact list. The contact list basically stores phone numbers, names and surnames of people who are the contacts of the mobile phone owner. The contact list primarily enables people to call their contacts without having to remember and dial the contacts phone number. Today, smartphones offer contact lists with elaborated features comprising a diversity of input fields that serve to identify and remember a contact entry. Some of the common input fields are for providing detailed information such as multiple phone numbers, names, surnames, email addresses, physical addresses, organization, notes about the contact, etc.

The social practices of African people make their contact lists to grow rapidly and significantly. A mobile phone can easily contain one hundred or more contacts entries. For example, a frequently observed social practice in African societies is that when a problem has to be solved, people use to resort to an acquaintance who, will in turn resort to his own acquaintance and so on until the right

© ICST Institute for Computer Sciences, Social Informatics and Telecommunications Engineering 2018
T.F. Bissyande and O. Sie (Eds.): AFRICOMM 2016, LNICST 208, pp. 26–32, 2018.
https://doi.org/10.1007/978-3-319-66742-3_3

one who can actually help solving the problem. In this endeavor to solve the problem, several types of social relations (mainly family and friendly) are mobilized and can spontaneously give rise to the creation of new entries in the contact lists. To formally argue this reality, the researches of Fiske [1,2] that explain how people construct social relations can be cited. Fiske stated that people in all cultures use the same relational models to generate most kinds of social interactions. However, based on his fieldwork among the Moose[1] of Burkina Faso, he noted that the Moose implement the models differently, in different domains, and in different relative degrees, than Americans. The "crowding" in contact lists causes the number of the rarely called contacts to be important. It also gives rise to more homonyms occurrences. These two realities, i.e. rarely called contacts and homonyms, together make the contact lists, even on smartphones, not always helpful when we need to remember a particular contact. Integrating African social practices in the design of the contact list software can contribute facing such a problem and can moreover provide additional smartness and usefulness to mobile phones. This paper stands for that and looks for providing African people with a mobile phone which is in phase with their social practices and behaviors.

In the remainder of this paper, we deal in Sect. 2 with related works, present in Sect. 3 the new design of the contact list, describe in Sect. 4 novel functionalities and conclude the paper with Sect. 5.

2   Works and Inventions Involving Mobile Contact List

An example of study addressing the cultural model of African countries has been to build, based on the cultural values of peasants, opportunistic networks for facilitating and automating the collection and synthesis of agricultural information [3]. In this paper, we are about to take into account African social practices and behaviors in the design of the mobile phone contact list. Several works and inventions related to mobile phone contact list were made. They covered systems built around the concept of awareness and besides many other issues were addressed. Some mobile systems, based on situation-awareness [4–6], are found under the vocabulary of recommendation systems. The principle of recommendation systems is to make the contact list smarter. Intelligent interactions with the mobile phone are introduced. Provide mobile phones with applications based on awareness together with efficient initiation of group communications has led to authors proposing a community-aware mechanism [7] that allows to efficiently select contacts in order to address them as a group. Mobile phones are thereby provided with a contact recommendation engine that help an initiator of a group efficiently constitute a group from his contact list. Hendrey et al. [8] invented a system for location-aware connections of telecommunication units involving group communications. They provide a way for automatically and/or selectively initiating communications among mobile users in a communication system that has the ability to determine a geographic location of mobile users.

---

[1] The Moose (or Mossis) are the ethnic majority of Burkina Faso.

Another aspect of social software that rely on mobile contact list is to make smartphones able to support mobile awareness and collaboration [9,10]. Systems that are able to disclose information about their users' presence motivated some authors [8] to redesign the smartphone contact list to provide cues of the current situations of others for the design of a mobile awareness application. The software interactions were designed based on social psychological findings. Many other works addressed contact information update and exchange. A method for updating automatically mobile phone contact list entries was disclosed [11]. Analyzing systems that provide phonebook and bookmarked links to web sites for mobile users, some inventors [12] found that the way in which they store, process, maintain and present or display this phonebook and browser information to their users is limited and imperfect. So, their invention disclosed updatable dynamic phonebook capabilities that provide a user with both contact information and dynamic network web content that can be updated by communications between a mobile device and a server. A system that proceeds with synchronization and updates through communications between the mobile phone and a data service provider was also proposed [13]. It enables the mobile phone to initiate an appropriate form of communication with one of the contacts given the circumstances. Regarding contact information exchange, a method [14] of sending contact list data from one mobile phone to another mobile phone allows to eliminate the need to re-key individual contact data. Short Message Service (SMS) or Multimedia Messaging Service (MMS) is used to exchange contact data between mobile phones within a group. A system for exchanging contact information was built based on an information server [15]. The location of the mobile device is used to gather contact information. To the end, the output of the system is a list of proximate users that is transmitted to the mobile device. This review of the literature lets us note that the idea of redesigning the mobile contact list to integrate African social practices is not yet addressed.

3   The New Vision of the Mobile Contact List

Traditionally, a mobile contact list is a contact database stored in a mobile equipment memory. It can be viewed as an object subjected to diverse transactions such as its use in social software. The proposed new mobile contact list is a set of linked entities $(C_j)_{1 \le j \le n}$ as the graph of acquaintances in Fig. 1 shows. Each entity C_j represents a contact and defines a node in the graph. A contact is generally a physical person who can be modeled using attributes and treatments as in object-oriented programming. The attributes serve to characterize a contact in such a way it is easy to identify him. Classically, the attributes include names, physical and email addresses, private and professional addresses, phone numbers and can provide an item for notes in order to add discretionary information about the contact, etc. The treatments to which a contact list may be subjected to are mainly operations for the contacts management: insertion, deletion, selection, update and displaying. A contact list is so defined as a set

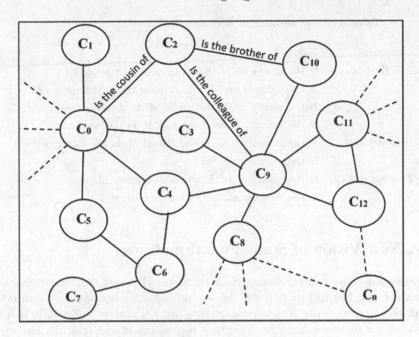

Fig. 1. Contact list as a graph of acquaintances

of n entities $(C_j)_{1 \leq j \leq n}$, each with specific values of the attributes and commonly shared treatments. Beyond this view, a contact list can be seen as a set of entities which are linked by social relations. In the graph of acquaintances of Fig. 1, the relations between the contact entities are the edges that link the different nodes. These ties between the contacts are the major foundation of the contact list redesigning we deal with. Any type of social relation can be considered. However, we focus on meaningful social relations that are of current and cultural considerations in daily life of African societies. Table 1 presents three categories of these relations without claiming exhaustivity. In the table, a tie is named according to the format "*Is_the_X_of*" where X denotes the type of relation. An edge in the graph that links two nodes C_k and C_l by the relation "*Is_the_X_of*" will carry the information that "C_k is the X of C_l". E.g.: let C_k and C_l be the contacts named respectively Ali and Alex and tied by the relation "*Is_the_brother_of*", we'll read that "*Ali is the brother of Alex*" (i.e., "*Ali is Alex's brother*" in good English).

In this new vision, the existing uses of the mobile phone contact lists are not affected. In particular, social software based on mobile contact list need not be modified. However, additional smartness is brought to some treatments regarding the contact lists.

Table 1. Some meaningful African social ties for contact list

Category	Name
Family ties	Is_the_father_of, Is_the_mother_of, Is_the_son_of,
	Is_the_daughter_of, Is_the_brother_of, Is_the_sister_of,
	Is_the_cousin_of, Is_the_uncle_of, Is_the_sister-in-law_of,
	Is_the_wife_of, Is_the_husband_of, Is_the_aunt_of, ...
Friendly ties	Is_the_classmate_of, Is_the_friend_of, Is_the_buddy_of,
	Is_the_comrade_of, ...
Professional ties	Is_the_colleague_of, Is_the_collaborator_of,
	Is_the_director_of, Is_the_hairdresser_of, ...

4   A New Vision of Some Functionalities

The proposed contact list will engender some novel smart treatments regarding contact list. For instance, it will be an interesting instrument of reminder. Indeed, the attributes of classical contact lists are not always sufficiently helpful when we want to remember who a contact represents in the real life. However, cultural practices that rely on social ties between people can be more helpful for remembering the contacts. Let us consider a contact list with a rarely contacted contact C_j. The simple visualization of the contact C_j information is not sufficient to remember who C_j is in the real life. Thanks to the new design of the contact list, social relations between C_j and other contacts can be displayed to help remember who C_j is (see *Algorithm 1*), and then initiate any form of communication with him. Another situation is the need to remember and select a contact C_j when there are L homonyms (see *Algorithm 2*). In this case, before initiating a communication with the desired contact, we need to select the right one. So, for each homonym of the list, its social ties with other contacts are displayed and analyzed until the right contact is identified. A third situation (see *Algorithm 3*) is the search for a contact C_j. We assume that we don't remember the contact information (including its names) and we just remember one of its social tie (e.g.: C_j is the cousin of C_k). The first thing to do is to execute a search operation on C_k, then filter out to display only the contacts which are linked to C_k by the right social tie. The contact C_j which is searched for is among these latter contacts (Table 2).

In addition to the three novel functionalities described above, the new contact list may provide new cues for the design of mobile awareness applications. The new cues may be based on the social relations that link the contacts. Moreover, as group communication is often performed with members of a community existing in the real life [7], social ties could facilitate the broadcast of social events (e.g.: weddings, funerals, family meetings, etc.) within a close group of contacts. Recommendation systems can work based on the social ties of a mobile device owner and suggest him the contacts with whom the information about a given social event must be shared.

Table 2. Algorithms of some novel functionalities

Algorithm 1	Algorithm 3
begin	begin
read C_j;	read C_k;
print C_j social ties;	print C_k social ties;
check social ties;	filter out social ties;
if C_j	check social ties;
then select C_j;	if C_j
endif	then select C_j;
end	endif
	end

Algorithm 2
begin
  read C_j;
  for $i = 1$ to L
    print C_i social ties;
    check C_i social ties;
    if C_i is the right C_j
      then select C_i; break;
    endif
  endfor
end

5 Conclusion

A new vision of the design of mobile devices contact lists was proposed and described in this paper. Social relations in the particular context of African social practices are the key of the new vision. The new contact list is a set of contacts linked to one another by social ties such as family or friendly ties. Three novel functionalities engendered by the new contact list make it a practical instrument of contacts reminder and homonymy resolver. We also noticed that the new contact list could provide new cues to some existing social software in the mobile domain. This paper acted as the birth stage of the new contact list as it was limited to the development of the idea rather than its implementation. However, our future work will focus on deepening the idea as well from its implementation aspect as to its potential appropriation by the targeted beneficiaries.

References

1. Fiske, A.P.: Structures of Social Life: The Four Elementary Forms of Human Relations. Free Press, New York (1991)
2. Fiske, A.P.: The four elementary forms of sociality: framework for a unified theory of social relations. Psychol. Rev. **99**(4), 689–723 (1992)

3. Ouoba, J., Bissyandé, T.F.: Leveraging the cultural model for opportunistic networking in Sub-Saharan Africa. In: Jonas, K., Rai, I.A., Tchuente, M. (eds.) AFRICOMM 2012. LNICSSITE, vol. 119, pp. 163–173. Springer, Heidelberg (2013). doi:10.1007/978-3-642-41178-6_17
4. Weißenberg, N., Gartmann, R., Voisard, A.: An ontology-based approach to personalized situation-aware mobile service supply. GeoInformatica 10(1), 55–90 (2006)
5. Min, J.K., Kim, H.T., Cho, S.B.: Social and personal context modeling for contact list recommendation on mobile device. In: Proceedings of the IEEE/WIC/ACM International Conference on Web Intelligence and Intelligent Agent Technology, vol. 3, pp. 381–384 (2008)
6. Plessas, A., Georgiadou, O., Stefanis, V., Komninos, A., Garofalakis, J.: Assessing physical location as a potential contextual cue for adaptive mobile contact lists. In: IEEE International Conference on Computer and Information Technology; Ubiquitous Computing and Communications; Dependable, Autonomic and Secure Computing; Pervasive Intelligence and Computing (CIT/IUCC/DASC/PICOM), pp. 1316–1324. (2015)
7. Grob, R., Kuhn, M., Wattenhofer, R., Wirz, M.: Mobile social networking for enhanced group communication. In: ACM International Conference on Supporting Group Work, pp. 81–90 (2009)
8. Hendrey, G.R., Tanaka, H.A., Koopman Jr., P.J.: Method and system for selectively connecting mobile users based on physical proximity. U.S. Patent No. 6,542,750. U.S. Patent and Trademark Office, Washington, DC (2003)
9. Oulasvirta, A., Raento, M., Tiitta, S.: ContextContacts: re-designing SmartPhone's contact book to support mobile awareness and collaboration. In: Proceedings of the 7th International Conference on Human Computer Interaction with Mobile Devices & Services, ACM, pp. 167–174 (2005)
10. Tang, J.C., Yankelovich, N., Begole, J., Van Kleek, M., Li, F., Bhalodia, J.: ConNexus to awarenex: extending awareness to mobile users. In: ACM SIGCHI Conference on Human Factors in Computing Systems, pp. 221–228 (2001)
11. Henri, F.M., Stephanie, L.W., Tong, Y., Yingxin, X.: Method of and system for updating mobile telephone contact lists entries. U.S. Patent Application No. 11/867, 287 (2009)
12. Guedalia, I., Guedalia, J.: System and method for dynamic phone book and network content links in a mobile device. U.S. Patent Application No. 11/638,272 (2006)
13. Apfel, D.A.: Unified contact list. U.S. Patent No. 7,139,555. U.S. Patent and Trademark Office, Washington, DC (2006)
14. Northcutt, J.W.: System and method of sharing a contact list among mobile phones. U.S. Patent No. 7,613,472. U.S. Patent and Trademark Office, Washington, DC (2009)
15. Chesnais, P., Wheeler, S., Pomeroy, S.: Methods and apparatus for organizing and presenting contact information in a mobile communication system. U.S. Patent No. 7,620,404. U.S. Patent and Trademark Office, Washington, DC (2009)

Analysis of the 2015 Presidential Campaign of Burkina Faso Expressed on Facebook

Frédéric T. Ouédraogo[1(✉)], Abdoulaye Séré[2], Evariste Rouamba[3],
and Soré Safiatou[1]

[1] Université de Koudougou, BP 376, Av. M. Yameogo, Koudougou, Burkina Faso
ouedraogo.tounwendyam@yahoo.fr, sore_safiatou@yahoo.fr
[2] Université Polytechnique de Bobo-Dioulasso, BP 1091,
Bobo-Dioulasso, Burkina Faso
abdoulayesere@gmail.com
[3] Université de Ouagadougou, BP 7021, Av. C.D.Gaulle, Ouagadougou, Burkina Faso
eva.rouamba@gmail.com

Abstract. Since the Arab spring, the social media have become more popular among young people in Africa. Their uses have been illustrated during political and social events that occurred recently in the continent. Not long ago, Burkina Faso has been a field of important political events, the insurrection followed by the presidential election. In this work, we study how Facebook has been used during the 2015 presidential campaign. We use a language model to analyze many Facebook pages of political parties and media. We find that the campaign debates have been focused on campaign slogans and on the candidates rather than their political programs. Our findings show that the Facebook pages content reflect the election result. The most quoted candidate has been the winner.

1 Introduction

The recent years have been characterized by the emergence of the social networking services in the Web, also called the Web 2.0. More and more people particularly young, are user of the social media like Facebook, Twitter, LinkedIn, Instagram and so forth, to build their social environment [2,4,5,9,13,14].

In the hardware side, the mobile phone is become a "hand computer" allowing more applications that concern the daily life and making the Web more reachable. The cell phone has become more and more accessible and the number of users is increasing in developing countries, particularly in Africa [1].

These social media opened a new way to the population, allowing them to participate in the social and political events that occur in their cities or anywhere in the world. The election of the American president Obama in 2008 who made use of the social media for the campaign, has shown that henceforth these new media should be taken in count in the political events [8,10]. After the revolutionary wave of protests in North Africa called Arab spring, the West African has

© ICST Institute for Computer Sciences, Social Informatics and Telecommunications Engineering 2018
T.F. Bissyande and O. Sie (Eds.): AFRICOMM 2016, LNICST 208, pp. 33–41, 2018.
https://doi.org/10.1007/978-3-319-66742-3_4

also known the experiment of social media during social and political protests. For instance, the civil society organizations in Senegal and Burkina Faso are particularly active and use the social networking services as their main media to spread information. Their succeeded experience is now referred as a model in other countries.

In this work, we investigate the 2015 presidential election campaigns expressed on Facebook. We consider the official period of the presidential campaign and we analyze the activities of the different members of political parties on the Facebook pages. We utilize the Netvizz application to retrieve the posts and comments made by the users on the Facebook pages of political parties and media.

Most parties or their candidates have at least a Facebook page or group but only few of them are used. The majority has less than ten posts and comments. This leads us to keep only the most important pages in our study. We use an 1-gram language model to analyze both the content and the structure of the pages. Our findings show that the debates of the electors were more oriented toward campaign slogans than the political programs of their candidates. The content of the Facebook pages reflects the election result. The most quoted candidate in the pages is the one who has been elected.

The rest of the paper is organized as follow; the Sect. 2 describes the data used; Sect. 3 presents our approach to analyze the page data; Sect. 4 presents the results and the Sect. 5 presents the relation work and discussion.

2   Data

This section describes the data used and the retrieving tool. Netvizz is an application designed to extract data of Facebook pages and groups, usually for research purposes. The personal information of users are hidden, therefore Netvizz provides freely anonymous data[1].

We retrieved the data of the Facebook pages of the main political parties of Burkina Faso during the first presidential campaign after the insurrection, that lasted from 8 to 27 of November 2015. We have discarded the pages which have less than 10 posts and comments during the campaign, constraining us to keep only two pages of the two important parties, MPP which stands for *Mouvement du Peuple pour le Progrès* and UPC which stands for *Union pour le Changement et le Progrès*.

The Facebook page of the UPC party has 121 posts and 3481 users have made comments on these posts. The Facebook page of MPP party has 283 posts and 3413 users have made comments. We also considered the presidential campaign activities on the media pages. Radio Omega, Lefaso and Burkina24 are the most important media which have the most frequented Facebook pages during the campaign. There are 2201 posts on the page of Radio Omega and 36018 comments have been made on these posts. Burkina24 has made 681 posts

---

[1] https://apps.facebook.com/netvizz/.

that received 15390 comments and Lefaso has 919 posts that received 18523 comments of users.

3   Approach

Our approach consists to act in two directions. First, We aim to study the content of the posts and the comments made by users. Afterwards, we want to analyze the structure of the pages. Indeed, the posts and comments can be view as a bipartite graph where an edge between two nodes represents an user that commented a post.

We base our content analysis on the language model [3] We use the *Bags of words* which is an unigram language model. The Bag of words provides corpus made of the terms of the text document. The text document is represented by a set of terms, where each term t is associated with the number of times $n(t)$ it appears in the document d. The term frequency *tf*, that gives the weight of terms in the document, is the normalized Bag of words.

We consider the Facebook page as a text document. The corpus is denoted by $C = \bigcup_i d_i$, where d_i is a text document of Facebook page. For different purposes, we define several corpuses depending on the text document considered.

4   Results

This section of the paper aims to present the main results of our contribution. We analyzed the content and the structure of the Facebook pages of parties, then we compare the quotes of the political parties and other topics expressed on the Facebook pages of the media.

4.1   Structure Analysis

We used the graph properties to represent and analyze the interactions of users on the posts of the pages. We consider the graph G whose the nodes are the posts and users that made comments on the Facebook page. An edge between two nodes of the graph means that an user represented by one node commented a post represented by the other node.

Netvizz provides each edge with a weight that represents the number of times an user commented a post and obviously the edges are always oriented toward the posts. We do not consider the weight and the orientation of the edges, accordingly the graph G that we obtain is unoriented and bipartite.

The page of the UPC party has 3 602 nodes and 18 750 links and the page of the MPP party has 3 696 nodes and 18 868 links between them. The two pages have approximately the same number of nodes and edges and this gives them the same density[2].

---

[2] We utilize the density definition of $\frac{2|Edges|}{|Nodes|^2 - |Nodes|}$.

We found that the density of the pages is roughly the same to similar study [7] done in U.S 2010 election. The comparison of the densities shows a satisfying use of the Facebook pages in the first post-insurrectional presidential. However there is an important contrast with the pages of other parties where most of them have less than 10 posts and comments.

The union of the two pages gives a graph G which has 7 089 nodes and 37 618 links. There are users that have commented both the UPC page and the MPP page. The common users are 209 and represent around 5 of the users of the party page. These users are probably not the MPP and UPC members but are members of other parties or internet surfers that spend time on Facebook (Fig. 1).

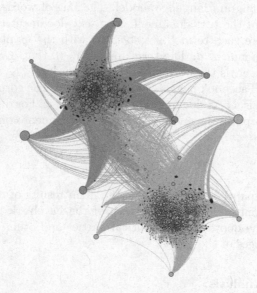

Fig. 1. Graph of posts and comments made on MPP and UPC Facebook pages during the presidential campaign of November 2015

The average path length of the graph G is 4 and its diameter is 8. The average path length is the average distance in number of edges between two nodes of the graph G. As the graph G is bipartite (posts and users), if the average path length is 2, then this means that averagely, any couple of users has commented the same post.

The average path length 4 of the graph G means that on average, between two users, there exists a third user that has commented a post with each of them. In the same ways, the diameter 8 of the graph signifies that for any couple of users there is at most two persons between them. The user comments are not spread but relative close, and this means some proximity of their interests in the pages.

4.2   Content Analysis

We utilize the bag of words model and we obtain for each Party Facebook page the probability distribution over its sequence of words which is the *tf* of the page.

Table 1 shows a comparison of the most important words in the posts and user comments made in the Facebook pages of UPC and MPP during the campaign. We have an overview of the main topics that have been debated during the campaign on the Facebook pages of parties.

We supposed that the words like employment, job, health, youth and poverty, usually quoted in the political agendas, should have the highest *tf* in the campaign debates. But, we observe that these words did not appear in the top ten of the Facebook pages of the two most important parties.

This shows that the main topics of the debate between the party members during the campaign were not focused on their political programs. We found that the words related to political programs have low *tf*, for instance the *tf* of *santé* quoted six times is 0.000781 and éducation quoted twice is 0.00026 for the MPP page. The same words are quoted once in the page of UPC. Surprisingly, the word textitpauvreté do not appear in the two pages. The debates on the Facebook pages of MPP and UPC are dominated by campaign slogans and centered on the presidential candidates, as shown in Table 1.

Table 1. Top ten of words based on the *tf* of the Facebook pages of the political parties UPC and MPP.

	UPC		MPP	
	Word	TF	Word	TF
1	Changement	0.1496	Bukina	0.1747
2	UPC	0.1414	Peuple	0.1123
3	Zephirin	0.1200	MPP	0.1044
4	Diabre	0.0954	Roch	0.1037
5	Progress	0.0769	President	0.0850
6	President	0.0527	Kabore	0.0779
7	Victoire	0.0302	Roch2015	0.0705
8	Burkina	0.0266	Progress	0.0520
9	Peuple	0.0145	Programme	0.0412
10	Insurrection	0.0133	Victoire	0.0291

Figure 2 shows a daily repartition of the number of posts and comments made by users on the Facebook pages of the parties UPC and MPP during the presidential campaign.

There is roughly the same amount of comments and posts in these two pages but the daily repartition gives interesting information. At the beginning of the campaign the UPC page received more comments than the MPP page. But some days in the middle of the campaign, there is practically no activity in the UPC page. This is not the case with the MPP page.

If the presidential campaign took end two days before the election day, we note that the parties did not observe this instruction. The political parties have posted campaign messages on their official pages after the 27 November, date of the end of the campaign. For instance, the MPP party has made 9 posts that received many comments on November 29.

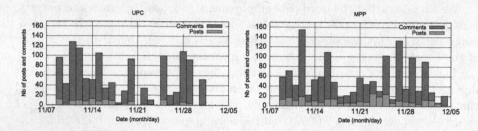

Fig. 2. Daily volume of posts and comments on political party pages

4.3   Campaign on Media Pages

Some media pages are popular among the youth of Burkina both within and at the diaspora. During the presidential campaign, these pages have been a field of debates between the different political members. Most of the internet surfers are accustomed to comment and to debate on the media pages long time before the 2015 elections.

We consider three media that are *Radio Omega, Lefaso.net* and *Burkina24*. Their Facebook pages are the most important regarding to the number of posts and comments made by the users during the presidential campaign. We found that these pages have received more posts and comments than those of political parties, see Table 2. The party pages have been created for the campaign purpose so they are not popular among internet surfers. In addition, their users are only among their party members. This may explain the pages of the political parties are less used than media pages by the internet surfers during the campaign.

Table 2. Basic statistics of the graphs of the media pages.

	Nodes	Edges	Avg. path length	Avg. degree	Diameter
Lefaso	19 442	64 160	3.85	6.6	10
Omega radio	38 219	191 398	3.85	10	11
Burkina24	16 071	45 852	3.87	5.7	8
Union of 3 pages	56 739	301 410	5, 6	10.6	12

The good coverage of the insurrectional protests of October 2014 by Radio Omega has made it rise among the most important radios in the city Ouagadougou. Since, Radio Omega has become more en more popular among the listeners. Table 2 shows that the Radio Omega has the most important Facebook page and even gets ahead of the online media like Omega and Burkina24.

In order to analyze the content of the media pages, we define classes of words for the main topics. This aims at quantifying the importance of topics on the media pages during the presidential campaign. Each class consists of words relative to the concerned topic. We compute the frequency of each word which is the number of times that this word appears in the pages.

Table 3 shows the different classes and their words. Obviously, each class may have tens of words that can represents it in the pages but we just kept those among the most important and relevant. For instance,

Table 3. Classes of words

Class	Words
UPC party	upc, diabre, zephirin, zeph
MPP party	mpp, kabore, roch, christian, marc
Political program	jeunesse, development, sante, travail, politique, ecoles, changement, energie, agriculture, programme, emploi, femme, enfant, justice
Transition government	kafando, zida, transition, martyrs, insurrection, isaac, michel

We compute the distribution of the frequencies of the classes. Figure 3 It shows that the MPP party has more references than the others in the comments and posts made during the campaign. The top word is the first name of the MPP candidate. The UPC party comes secondly. The reference to this party is fairly less than the MPP. The top word is also first name the party candidate.

However, we found that the political agendas of the parties did not interest the members during the campaign. The words like youth, job, education and the health are weakly mentioned in their Facebook pages.

The majority of the electors did not consider mainly the political programs of the candidates but their choice is lying on other considerations. Indeed, most electors are poorly or not literate and few of them know the democracy rules, so that they do not understand or even decline the advantages given by this political system.

We also found a significant number of quotes related to the government of transition on the posts and comments during the campaign. The transition, established after the insurrection, has done some acts before and during the campaign that has been perceived as favors to the MPP party. For instance, the weekly Council of Ministers has been moved to a city where the MPP party held a campaign meeting. This probably explains the relative high *tf* of the transition.

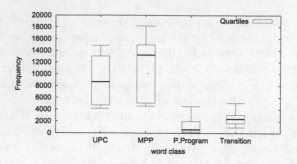

Fig. 3. Distribution of the frequencies of classes of words

5   Related Work

Since the emergence of social media and their integration in the political arena, many researchers are interested in their usage in the political campaign [2,6,7,10,14]. Most of earlier contributions concern the U.S. elections. The authors of this contribution [15] studied the influence of Facebook on the vote share in the U.S. 2008 Presidential primaries. This study shows that Facebook as a support, is an important indicator of candidate electoral success, in addition of the traditional measures. But Facebook had no impact on vote share for candidates who had not cultivated a social network presence during their campaign.

Another study has been made on twitter for the 2010 midterm election in the U.S. [7,11,12]. Smith has pointed out the level use of the Internet in 2010 campaign in U.S. and has shown that more than half of all American adults has used the Internet for political purpose [12]. Among them, 22% has made use of Twitter or other social media in 2010 campaign [11].

The authors of this work [7] have studied deeply the 2010 election campaign expressed on Twitter. They used thousands tweets of more than six hundred candidates of the three most important parties (Democrats, Republicans and Tea party) and analyzed the difference between them. Their main finding is the differences in the usage pattern of Twitter by the candidates. The Republicans and Tea party candidates have used Twitter more effectively than democrats. The authors have designed a model trying to predict candidate victory.

Our work belongs to the same stream of studies but we do not aim to predict victory of a candidate or party. We analyze the data of Burkina Faso 2015 election campaign on Facebook, mainly to find usage patterns and the main topics that dominated the elector debates.

6   Conclusion

In this paper we presented an analysis the campaign of the first post-insurrectional presidential election, expressed on Facebook. We utilized the

Netvizz application designed to retrieve the data of the Facebook pages and groups. Most of pages of political parties have few posts and comments leading us to consider only the pages of the most important political parties and media.

The analysis of the content has shown that the political programs of the candidates have not been debated by their members on the Facebook pages. We ranked the parties by the *tf* of words assumed to be their quotes in the posts and comments. We also found on the media pages similar results to those of the election.

Predict the results of the election is out of scope of this paper but our preliminary results show that it is possible to know, by the Facebook pages, the trends of opinions on social and political issues.

References

1. Porter, G., Hampshire, K., Abane, A., et al.: Youth, mobility and mobile phones in Africa: findings from a three-country study. Inf. Technol. Dev. **18**(2), 145–162 (2012)
2. Bruns, A., Highfield, T.: Political networks on twitter: tweeting the Queensland state election. Inf. Commun. Soc. **16**(5), 667–691 (2013)
3. Metzler, D., Lavrenko, V., Croft, W.B.: Formal multiple-Bernouill models for language modeling. In: SIGIR 2004, pp. 540–541 (2004)
4. Duggan, M., Smith, A.: The political environment on social media. Report of the Pew Internet Research Center, October 2016
5. Ellison, N.B., et al.: Social network sites: definition, history, and scholarship. J. Comput. Mediat. Commun. **13**(1), 210–230 (2007)
6. Larsson, A.O., Moe, H.: Studying political microblogging: twitter users in the 2010 Swedish election campaign. New Media Soc. **14**, 729–747 (2012)
7. Livne, A., Simmons, M.P., Adar, E., Adamic, L.A.: The party is over here: structure and content in the 2010 election. In: ICWSM (2011)
8. Miller, C.C.: How Obama's internet campaign changed politics. The New York Times, 49, November 2008
9. Perrin, A.: Social media usage: 2005–2015 (2015)
10. Smith, A.: The internet's role in campaign 2008. Pew Internet & American Life Project, 15 (2009)
11. Smith, A.: 22% of online Americans used social networking or twitter for politics in 2010 campaign. Report of the Pew Internet Research Center (2011)
12. Smith, A.: The internet and campaign 2010. Pew Internet & American Life Project, 15 (2011)
13. Stieglitz, S., Dang-Xuan, L.: Emotions and information diffusion in social media— sentiment of microblogs and sharing behavior. J. Manag. Inf. Syst. **29**(4), 217–248 (2013)
14. Stieglitz, S., Dang-Xuan, L., Bruns, A., Neuberger, C.: Social media analytics. Wirtschaftsinformatik **56**(2), 101–109 (2014)
15. Williams, C.B., Jeff Gulati, G.: What is a social network worth? Facebook and vote share in the 2008 presidential primaries. In: Annual Meeting of the American Political Science Association, pp. 1–17 (2009)

Towards Inclusive Social Networks
for the Developing World

Christian Akpona[1], Rose Gohoue[1], Herve Ahouantchede[1],
Fatna Belqasmi[2(✉)], Roch Glitho[1,3], and Jules Degila[1]

[1] IMSP, Porto Novo, University of Abomey-Calavi, Cotonou, Republic of Benin
[2] Zayed University, Abu Dhabi, United Arab Emirates
fatna.belqasmi@zu.ac.ae
[3] Concordia University, Montreal, Canada

Abstract. Social networks (e.g. Facebook) are becoming ubiquitous, especially in the developed world. However, they rely on two fundamental assumptions (i.e., reliable Internet connectivity, literacy) that exclude scores of potential end-users, especially in the developing world. Including these potential end-users will require lifting those two assumptions. This paper is a first step towards inclusive social networks in the developing world. It proposes and validates a two-layer system architecture. The proposed architecture allows end-users to access the social network with low-end cellular phones, using voice and Short Message Service (SMS), in addition to traditional access via a computer or smart phone, using keyboards. We have built a proof of concept prototype in which poorly literate end-users are included in two simplified dedicated social networks (a small farmers' social network and a motorcycle taxis' social network).

Keywords: Social networks · Developing economies · Inclusive social networks · SMS · Low-end cellular phones · Text-to-speech

1 Introduction

Social networks are becoming ubiquitous, especially in the developed world. Facebook, for instance, announced during the release of its third quarter 2016 results that it had more than a billion daily active end-users. There is still no consensus on the fundamental definition of a social network, especially as most social networks embed a plethora of heteroclite applications. In this paper we use the definition provided by Ref. [1], i.e., that social network sites are web-based services that allow individuals to construct a public or semi-public profile within a bounded system, articulate a list of other users with whom they share a connection, view and traverse their list of connections and those made by other users within the system. In the definition, publishing a comment is part of the profile construction, and accessing publications by other individuals is part of viewing and traversing the list of one's connections.

Social networks remain quite exclusive despite their popularity, especially in the developing world. One of the primary reasons is that accessing a Web-based service requires an Internet connection. However, according to the ITU-T [2], only 31% of

© ICST Institute for Computer Sciences, Social Informatics and Telecommunications Engineering 2018
T.F. Bissyande and O. Sie (Eds.): AFRICOMM 2016, LNICST 208, pp. 42–52, 2018.
https://doi.org/10.1007/978-3-319-66742-3_5

people in the developing world accesses Internet, compared to 77% in the developed world. Another reason is that constructing profiles, articulating lists of users, viewing and traversing list of connections are usually done via computers/smart phones' keyboards. A certain level of literacy is indeed required. Nevertheless, according to UNESCO [3], while the average literacy rate is generally above 80% in the developed world, it is usually below 50% in the developing world.

There are several compelling scenarios for inclusive social networks, especially in the developing world. Dedicated social networks are the most convincing; small farmers' social networks and motorcycle taxis' social networks are illustrative examples. This paper is a first step towards inclusive social networks in the developing world. It proposes and validates a two-level system architecture for inclusive social networks. The following section provides a critical overview of the state of the art. The proposed system architecture is presented in the third section. This is followed by a description of the proof of concept prototype. We conclude in the last section.

2   A Critical Overview of the State of the Art

Motivating scenarios and requirements are presented first, followed by critical overviews of the work on social networks for areas with poor Internet connectivity and of the studies on the use of social networks by poorly literate end-users.

2.1   Motivating Scenarios and Requirements

One can envision several compelling scenarios of dedicated social networks in the developing world. Let us start with a small farmers' social network. Farming and its myriad issues are of vital importance in most of the developing world. Most small farmers are barely literate and live in rural areas with poor Internet coverage. Information on evolving farming techniques and marketing news are both vital to their survival. In several developing countries, there are government officials who act as advisors and pay visits to small farmers now and then. One could imagine an inclusive social network that allows government officials to spread timely information to small farmers while allowing farmers to exchange information on the problems they face, as well as facilitate the exchange of best practices.

Let us move to a more urban/village setting and propose motorcycle taxis' social networks. Motorcycle taxis are common in several African countries (e.g. "zemi djan" in the Republic of Benin, "Boda boda" in Uganda). Some of the drivers are illiterate while others are university graduates. In some countries, they are renowned as being highly politicized, as in the Republic of Benin. One could well imagine a dedicated social network where they could exchange ideas on on-going political events. This very social network could easily act as a dispatching system since there is usually no centralized taxi dispatching system for these motorcycle taxis. A driver dropping a client near a given landmark (e.g. church, mosque, or other sort of landmark) could publish a comment to signal the number of clients waiting for taxis at that point. Another driver who retrieves the publication might decide to go to the landmark in order to pick up one of the clients. She/he would then respond to the comment to signal to the other drivers that she/he is going to that site.

A first requirement on the envisioned inclusive social network is obviously the ability to cope with poor Internet connectivity. The second one is to address the possibility of its use by poorly literate end-users. Beyond these two requirements, which are easily derived from the use cases, there are three additional requirements that need to be taken into account. The first is the possibility to access the social network with very low cost phones that support only voice and SMS. This reflects the fact that small farmers and the motorcyle taxi drivers are not at all likely to own high-end phones.

The second additional requirement is that the social network should offer the full set of social networking services to all end-users. The third additional requirement is re-use. The envisioned social network should re-use the infrastructure that has already been deployed whenever possible to reduce deployment cost. This deployed infrastructure includes the rich cellular network infrastructure as well as the exclusive social network infrastructure.

2.2   Social Networks for Areas with Poor Internet Coverage

Reference [4] proposes a social network that addresses the poor Internet connectivity issue. In the use case, Vijay, who has lost his goose, posts a comment on the community social network, in the hope that other members of the community will comment back on the whereabouts of the goose. The paper assumes that Vijay and the other members of the community are literate enough to understand highly intuitive graphical user interfaces. It is also assumed that they might eventually get help from trusted literate friends and family members for some of the social network operations.

The proposed architecture relies on the GSM infrastructure where it exists, and uses delay tolerant networking (DTN) to cater to areas where there is no GSM coverage [4]. DTN [5] is an overlay network that runs on top of transport layers and provides a store and forward mechanism to overcome intermittent Internet connections. In the architecture, this overlay is built on top of the very phones used by the members of the community. This means that the phones are expected to have short-range radio interfaces such as Bluetooth to take advantage of social encounters for communicating, acting as nodes of the DTN overlay. Low-cost phones with only voice and SMS support could not be used, and thus this system does not meet our requirements. The architecture does re-use the existing infrastructure as stipulated in our requirements. However, it does not re-use the existing infrastructure to the fullest extent since the social network infrastructure is not re-used at all.

We have previously proposed SNS4D, a social networking system for developing countries [6]. The system architecture proposed here actually builds on that system. SNS4D enables ubiquitous access by offsetting the poor Internet connectivity with the rich SMS access provided by cellular networks. It offers the same set of services to end users with SMS access and end-users with Web access. However, it assumes that all end-users are literate enough to use SMS, and this assumption does not hold in many parts of the developing world. As mentioned in the same paper [6], it is important to note that some existing social networks (e.g. Facebook) allow access by SMS. However, the set of services offered through this access is usually restricted. It is also important to note, as mentioned in the very same paper [6], that social networks accessible exclusively via SMS have also been deployed, especially in India (e.g. Gupshup). It is obvious that neither the existing social networks that provide SMS access for a sub-set of functionality nor SMS-based social networks meet all our requirements.

Daknet [7] tackles the general problem of Internet connectivity in the developing world. It provides mobile ad hoc connectivity by following a model similar to the traditional postal system. Data is transmitted over short point-to-point links between kiosks and portable storage devices. Kiosks store the original content the end-users wish to transmit via the Internet. The portable storage devices mounted in vehicles such as buses and motorcycles retrieve the content from the kiosks and transport it "physically" to hubs that are wireless Internet access points. Daknet is content-agnostic and social network services may be built on top of it. However, the poor literacy issue remains to be solved.

2.3 Use of Social Networks by Poorly Literate End-Users

Voice is certainly the most natural modality that even barely literate end-users could use to interact with social networks. Several voice-enabled social networks have been proposed in the literature, although they do not usually target poorly literate end-users. Voice is rather used for convenience by literate end-users. Vehicular social networks are the archetypes. RoadSpeak [8] is one example. It enables voice chats between drivers on popular roadways and relies on an underlying social network overlay. The motivations are entertainment, utility and emergency. These voice-enabled social networks assume Internet connectivity, and are generally not accessible with low cost phones.

Spoken Web [9] provides a general architecture for a Web where sites are created and browsed with voice via ordinary phone calls. It re-uses the telecommunication infrastructure, provides Web access to poorly literate end-users, and low cost phones can be used. Its key concepts are voice sites, voice numbers and voice links. Voice sites are interconnected with voice links and are accessed by calling the associated voice numbers. The calls are mapped onto the underlying telecommunication infrastructure. The sites can be created via phone calls using simple voice-driven interfaces. While this architecture includes poorly literate end-users in Web browsing and voice site creation, it does not give any insights into how to design Web complex-based services such as inclusive social networks.

Reference [10] describes an architecture that enables Internet access with voice (and SMS). It is known as SiteOnMobile. Low cost phones can be used, just as we envision in our architecture. The architecture re-uses the telecommunication infrastructure, as with the spoken Web architecture. It uses concepts such as TaskLet, which enables a Web of page to become a Web of tasks. A smart gateway is used to convert SMS patterns into TaskLet invocations. Text to speech conversions are performed on the web content accessed by the end-user. Just like SpokenWeb, SiteOnMobile includes poorly literate end-users in Web browsing, but does not give any insights into how to design complex Web-based services such as inclusive social networks.

3 Proposed System Architecture

Figure 1 shows the proposed system architecture. It is comprised of two layers: a front-end layer and a back-end layer. The front end layer is made up of an access sub-layer and a mediation sub-layer. The architectural assumptions and principles are presented first, followed by a description of the functional entities and the interfaces. The last sub-section discusses the procedures.

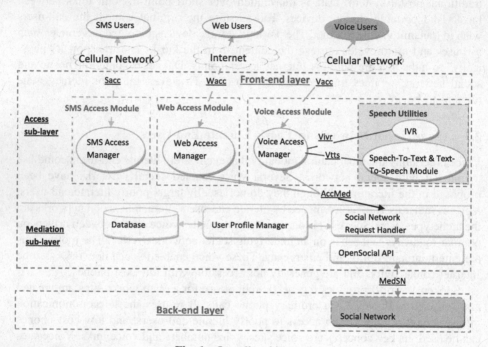

Fig. 1. Overall architecture

3.1 Architectural Assumptions and Principles

Our key assumption is that there is cellular network coverage wherever there is poor Internet connectivity. This is not farfetched at all, since according to an ITU-T report [2], cellular network coverage has now reached 89% in the developing world. Furthermore, this assumption helps us avoid more tenuous assumptions, such as the one made in Ref. [4] (i.e., the support of short-range radio connection by all phones for DTN connectivity) that are much less likely to hold in many parts of the developing world.

The first architectural principle is that we build on the deployed social network infrastructure in addition to the cellular network infrastructure. We use the OpenSocial standard [12] for that purpose. It is a set of programming interfaces that enable the development of social applications that are portable and inter-operable across the social networks that support the standard. The back-end layer of our proposed architecture could be any social network that supports OpenSocial (e.g. Google+ social network). The front end can be considered as a social application running on top of OpenSocial.

The second architectural principle is that text is used as the common denominator for requests (e.g. account creation, publication, and others). The key reason is that the existing social networks that could be used as a back-end layer via OpenSocial only support text as the interaction modality – voice is not supported. Requests made by voice users in our architecture are thus always translated into text, and textual comments retrieved from the back-end are translated into voice for voice users.

3.2   Functional Entities and Interfaces

The access sub-layer has four functional entities: SMS access manager, Web access manager, Voice access manager and speech utilities. The SMS access manager, the Web access manager and the voice access manager entities offer the Sacc, the Wacc and the Vacc interfaces, respectively, to enable access by SMS users, Web users and voice users, respectively. The Sacc and Vacc interfaces bridge cellular networks and our proposed inclusive social network, and their implementation could rely on cellular modems. Wacc is nothing more than the usual interface for accessing Web-based services, and it can be implemented as a simple Web page. The speech utilities include the Interactive Voice Response (IVR) system and the speech to text (STT) and text to speech (TTS) systems. They are accessible via the Vivr and Vtts interfaces, respectively.

Vivr and Vtts are modelled according to the Representational state transfer (REST) principles. REST is an architectural style for designing distributed client-server applications. In REST, each resource is identified by a unique Uniform Resource Identifier (URI) and is accessed via a subset of HTTP methods. The most common of these methods are GET, POST, PUT, and DELETE, which can be used to read, create, update and delete a resource, respectively. Reference [12] provides an overview. The list of resources defined by Vivr interface are shown in Table 1 for illustration purposes, along with the URI of each resource and the HTTP methods that are supported. The call-back resource is used by the IVR to send back a notification to the voice access manager about the termination of an ongoing communication session. The same applies to sending back the notification about the termination of a TTS or an STT request. The call back resources are used because the recording and the translation requests may take time and therefore the initiating requests may timeout before the processing has been completed.

The mediation sub-layer mediates between the access sub-layer and the back-end layer. For instance, when a comment is retrieved from the social network in the back-end layer, it ensures that the comment is dispatched to the correct access manager. It comprises a database, a user profile manager and a social network request handler. The database contains information such as the access manager to which end-users are connected at any given point in time. It is updated by the user profile manager. The social network request handler processes requests from the access sub-layer and interacts with either the user profile manager (e.g. updating the access manager used by an end-user) or the OpenSocial API (e.g. publication of a comment). Every end-user has two accounts: one in the social network of the back-end and the other in the inclusive social network. The first account is transparent to the end-user and is automatically created by our system. The access sub-layer and the mediation layer interact via the AccMed interface. AccMed is also modeled according to REST principles.

Table 1. VIVR rest interface

Resources	Operation	HTTP method: resource URI
List of sessions	Create: establish a new communication session between an end-user and the IVR	POST: http://www.ivrSNS.com/
A specific session	Read: get information about a specific communication session	GET: http://www.ivrSNS.com/{idCom}
	Delete: end a specific communication session	DELETE: http://www.ivrSNS.com/{idCom}
Recording	Create: record a specific session	POST: http://www.ivrSNS.com/{idCom}/record/
A specific recording	Delete: delete a specific recorded communication session	DELETE: http://www.ivrSNS.com/{idCom}/record/{idRecord}
Call-back	Create: send back a notification to the voice access manager	POST: http://www.voiceAccessManager.com/ivr

3.3 Procedures

New account creation and information publication procedures are described below for the purpose of illustration.

New Account Creation: To create a new account using voice commands, the following steps are followed:

- The end-user calls the phone number for the voice access manager, which transfers the call to the IVR.
- The end-user then chooses the option to create a new account via the IVR menu. He/she follows the voice steps offered by the IVR to enter the required information (e.g. the pseudo name, the first and last names, the password). The communication is saved in a voice file on the IVR side.
- At the end of the communication, the IVR informs the voice access manager and sends it the URI of the recorded voice file. The voice access manager then calls the appropriate API on the STT to translate the voice commands into the corresponding text request, and then sends the request to the social network request handler for processing.
- The social network request handler instructs the user profile manager to create a new user profile in the local database and then issues a new account creation request which it sends to the back-end social network. The local profile includes information such as the request-ID and the access manager from which the request was received. When an account creation confirmation is received from the back-end social network, the request handler transfers the response to the originating manager. If the end-user has asked for a confirmation, the voice access manager uses the TTS to create a speech file that corresponds to the received response (the output file will be stored on the TTS side), creates a voice call between the IVR and the end-user and instructs the IVR to play the output file to the user by giving the IVR the URI of the appropriate file.

To create a new account via SMS, the end-user sends an SMS message to the phone number associated to the SMS access manager, which transfers the request to the social network request handler. The process then proceeds in the same way as for the voice request, creating a new account on the back-end side. When the response is sent back to the SMS access manager, it creates the appropriate SMS response and sends it to the end-user, if the latter has asked for a confirmation. The same procedure is applied for account creation via the Web, except that the end-user communicates with the system via the Web.

Publication: The publication procedure is similar to that of account creation. We therefore summarize the main steps for voice publication and focus on the differences. To publish new information, the end-user calls the voice access manager and he/she is put in contact with the IVR. After choosing the appropriate option from the IVR menu, the end-user dictates the information to be published to the IVR, which stores it in a voice file. The access manager transcribes the posted information into text before issuing a publication request towards the back-end. It also retrieves the end-user contact list from the back-end and sends a notification to the SMS members that requested to be informed about new publications. The Web and voice end-users will be informed when they connect to the system and explicitly ask for new publications.

4 A Proof of Concept Prototype

Figure 2 depicts the overall prototype setup. We first introduce the implemented scenarios. This is followed by a short description of how the TTS/STT tools have been customized for Fon, a vernacular language of the Republic of Benin. We end with a description of the prototype itself including its setup.

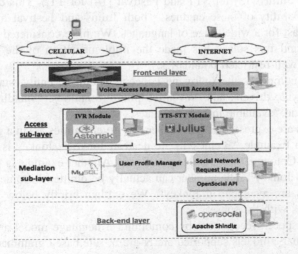

Fig. 2. Prototype setup

4.1   Implemented Scenarios

We have implemented two scenarios. The first relates to the small farmer social network. The second deals with the dispatching functionality of the motorcycle taxis'
social network we discussed earlier. In the first scenario, we consider a simplified
poultry epidemic situation in a given area. Sika (a farmer) notices the death of two
chickens on her farm. She is a voice user and publishes the information on the social
network. This triggers a series of publications by other farmers in her network. Dossou,
a voice user, indicates that five of his chickens have died, and Ablawa, who is an SMS
user, subsequently signals the death of six chickens on her farm.

Jean, the veterinarian who is also a member of the small farmer social network, is a
Web user. Upon receipt of this series of publications, he realizes that there is a poultry
epidemic. He then publishes a message through his Web interface to tell the farmers
that preventive pills are available (for sale) at a specific veterinarian pharmacy in the
area. We assume that there are several veterinarian pharmacists in the area and that Jean
knows the type of medicine each one sells.

In the second scenario, Bossou, a motorcycle taxi driver who is a voice user,
notices that there are two clients waiting for a taxi at a specific place. He publishes this
to the other drivers who are looking for clients. Pierre is one of these drivers and is an
SMS user. Upon receipt of the publication, he decides to go to that place to pick up one
of the clients. He notifies the other drivers via a publication. Kokou is another driver
and an SMS user. After receipt of the two publications, he realizes that there might still
be one client waiting. He decides to go to pick her/him up and notifies the group via a
publication.

4.2   Customization of the STT and TTS Engines

There is no STT/TTS engine readily usable for the Fon language. This has led us to the
customization of Julius [13] for STT and Festival [14] for TTS. This choice is motivated by the flexibility of these engines – both Julius and Festival have been customized in the past for a wide range of languages. We have considered a very limited
subset of Fon, and this subset has made the implementation of the two scenarios
possible, within well-restricted boundaries.

The sub-set comprises the following concepts: number, entity, state, and place.
Farmers, motorcycle drivers, and preventive pills are entities. "Standing in", "going
to", "dead in", and "available in" are the states.

All sentences are expressed as "A number of a given entities are in a given state in a
given place". For example, "3 chickens are dead in Jonkey". Jonkey is a well-known
neighborhood in Cotonou, the capital city of Benin. Another example is "A motorcycle
client is going to Jonkey". The number can actually be omitted in some cases such as
"Preventive pills are available in Jonkey". We explain briefly below how we have
customized Julius with the subset.

Julius offers speech recognition by combining a language model and an acoustic
model. The language models supported are N-gram, rule based grammar, and isolated
word recognition. The acoustic model can be monophone or triphone, or a combination. Reference [14] can be consulted for tutorial-level information. We have used

isolated word recognition and a very simple grammar, with two sentence structures. The first is when the number is not omitted and the second is when it is. A specificity of FON that was factored in is that "number" (when not omitted) comes after "entity". This leads to the following sentence structure "entity number state place". A combination of monophones and triphones were used. The numbers were limited to the digits from 1 to 10, the places to 5 well-known Cotonou neighborhoods.

4.3   Prototype

The prototype setup is shown in Fig. 2. The modules inside the same rectangle with solid borders are deployed on the same machine. The SMS and voice end-users communicate with the front-end layer via their cellular network operator. The users' SMSs and voice calls are routed to the number of a SIM card on a GSM modem (i.e. HUAWEI E153) connected to the machine running the front-end layer modules. The voice calls are automatically routed to the voice access manager. The SMS access manager uses a Java library (i.e. SMSLib API) to receive and send SMS messages via the GSM modem.

The IVR module is implemented using Asterisk, a free and open source software framework for building communications systems. Asterisk supports a number of VoIP signalling protocols. In our prototype, we use the session initiation protocol (SIP). We use an Oktell SIP-GSM gateway [15] to bridge between the GSM and SIP domains on both the signalling and the media planes.

The back-end social network is implemented using Apache Shindig, the reference implementation of OpenSocial API specifications. It is open source and it assists in the building and hosting of new OpenSocial applications.

5   Conclusion

Social networks currently exclude scores of potential end-users de facto, especially in the developing world. This is due to the two fundamental assumptions on which they rely on: Internet connectivity and literacy. This paper has made a first step towards inclusive social networks by proposing and validating a new system architecture. It is a first step; there are several research directions possible in this area. We have assumed good cellular network connectivity wherever there is no Internet connectivity. Although the assumption is not farfetched, it should be possible to omit it for some situations. However, omitting that assumption should not be replaced by a less realistic assumption (i.e. the support of short-range radio connection by all phones in order to enable opportunistic connections). More research is needed. We envision inclusive social networks as dedicated social networks or as closed groups of general purpose social networks. Ontologies need to be developed to formalize the vocabularies used in the dedicated areas. This is a key to the optimal customization of the TTS and STT tools. Social networks are certainly the most complex social media that exist today. However, there are other social media (e.g. blogs, podcasts) that have become as exclusive as social networks. Architectures are also needed to make them more inclusive.

References

1. Boyd, D.M., Ellison, N.B.: Social networks: definition, history and scholarship. J. Comput. Mediat. Commun. **13**, 210–230 (2008)
2. ITU-T, ICT facts and figures. www.itu.int/en/ITU-D/Statistics/Documents/.../ICTFactsFigures2013.pdf
3. UNESCO: The official source of literacy data. http://www.uis.unesco.org/literacy/Pages/default.aspx
4. Vallina-Rodriguez, N., Hui, P., Crowcroft, J.: Has anyone seen my goose? Social network services in developing regions. In: 2009 International Conference on Computational Science and Engineering (2009)
5. Fall, K.: A delay-tolerant network architecture for challenged internets. In: Proceedings of SIGCOMM (2003)
6. Ahouantchede, H., Belqasmi, F., Glitho, R.: SNS4D: an Online social network system for developing countries. In: Fourth International IEEE EAI Conference on e-Infrastructure and e-Services for Developing Countries, Africomm 2012, November 2012
7. Pentland, A., et al.: DakNet: rethinking connectivity in developing nations. IEEE Comput. **37**(1), 78–83 (2004)
8. Smaldone, S., et al.: RoadSpeak: enabling voice chat on roadways using vehicular social networks. In: SocialNets 2008, April 2008
9. Agarwal,. S.K., et al.: The Spoken web: a web for the underprivileged. In: ACM SIGWEB Newsletter, Summer 2010
10. Manjunath, G., et al.: Delivering mobile eGovernance on low end phones. In: 2012 IEEE International Conference on Mobile Data Management (2012)
11. Hasel, M.: Opensocial: an enabler for social applications on the web. Commun. ACM **54**(1), 139–144 (2011)
12. Belqasmi, F., Fu, C., Glitho, R.: RESTful web services for service provisioning in next generation networks: a survey. IEEE Commun. Mag. **49**(12), 66–73 (2011)
13. Lee, A., et al.: Recent development of open source speech recognition engine Julius. In: APISIPA ASC (2009)
14. Beutnagel, M., et al.: The AT&T next-gen TTS system, Joint Meeting of ASA (1999)
15. http://www.oktellpbx.com/gateways/, June 2001

Multi-diffusion Degree Centrality Measure to Maximize the Influence Spread in the Multilayer Social Networks

Ibrahima Gaye[1,2]($\boxtimes$), Gervais Mendy[1,2], Samuel Ouya[1,2], Idy Diop[1,4], and Diaraf Seck[1,3]

[1] Cheikh Anta Diop University, Dakar, Senegal
{gervais.mendy,diaraf.seck}@ucad.edu.sn, samuel.ouya@gmail.com
[2] École Supérieure Polytechnique, Laboratoire Informatique-Réseau-Télécom (LIRT), Dakar, Senegal
gaye.ibrahima@esp.sn
[3] Faculté Sciences Économiques et de Gestion, Laboratoire Mathématiques de la Décision et d'Analyse Numérique (LMDAN), Dakar, Senegal
[4] École Supérieure Polytechnique, Laboratoire Imagerie Médicale et Bio-Informatique (LIMBI), Dakar, Senegal
idy.diop@esp.sn
http://www.ucad.sn

Abstract. In this work, we study the influence maximization in multi-layer social networks. This problem is to find a set of k persons, called seeds, that maximizes the information spread in a multilayer social network. In our works, we focus in the determination of the seeds by proposing a centrality measure called *Multi-Diffusion Degree* (denoted by C_{dd}^{MLN}) based on *Independent Cascade* model. We consider the $top-K$ persons as the most influential. This centrality measure uses firstly, the diffusion probability for each person in each layer. Secondly, it uses the contribution of the first neighbors in the diffusion process. To show the performance of our approach, we compare it with the existing heuristics like *multi degree centrality*. With software R and *igraph package*, we show that *Multi-Diffusion Degree* is more performant than the benchmark heuristic.

Keywords: Centrality measure · Diffusion probability · Influence maximization · Mapping matrix · Multilayer social network

1 Introduction

Nowadays the social networks become more and more popular and varied. For example: *facebook*, *viadeo*, *linkedin*, *twitter*, $\cdots$. In these networks, often we find the same persons. A person may have an account in many social networks. With the unified authentication, the e-mail address, the similarity [1], $\cdots$, we can identify the same persons in different social networks. So, we can see these social networks as an aggregation of several networks Fig. 2. We call it *MultiLayer*

© ICST Institute for Computer Sciences, Social Informatics and Telecommunications Engineering 2018
T.F. Bissyande and O. Sie (Eds.): AFRICOMM 2016, LNICST 208, pp. 53–65, 2018.
https://doi.org/10.1007/978-3-319-66742-3_6

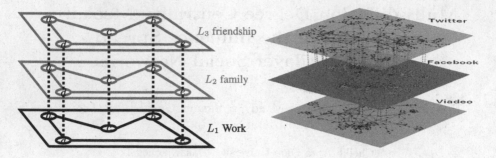

Fig. 1. $MLSN$ dialed of three layers

Fig. 2. Multilayer social network (3-layers)

Social Network [2,3] and we denote $MLSN$. These networks appear in different contexts: according to their natures (online, offline, hybrid), according to them semantic natures (contact, communication, time, context, etc.). Social network can dial several types of relationships. In the analysis of social networks, it is important to differentiate between these links. So, each nature of link can be seen as a layer and all as a $MLSN$. In the Fig. 1, we have an example of $MLSN$ dialed of three types of relationships: family, work and friendship. We can explore these networks in many fields: in the field of air transport [2], in the theory of online games [4]. A complete example of multiplex (or multilayer) network model can be found in [5]. Several of these works are mainly theoretical. A MSN uses a multidimensional set where each dimension is a relationship between two persons. Recently, the MultiLayer Networks were applied to the study of strength of social ties in multilayer interactions [6]. The social networks analysis (SNA) which attracts many attention thanks to its varied fields of application. For example in marketing, the use of the online social networks gives a big potential. It is more effective than traditional techniques of marketing. For a good visibility of a new product, organizations can use the publicity word of mouth in the social networks [7,8]. This approach is known under the expression of influence maximization problem in the social networks [9]. The problem consists to find a small set of $k - persons$ (i.e. the seeds) in the social network that maximizes the influence spread in a small delay. But The social networks increase in a considerable way. The same persons in several networks can be identified with its e-mail, the unified authentication technology. So, these networks can be an aggregation of one social network with several types of relations. Each types of relation is considered as a layer. The resultant social network is known under the name of MultiLayer Social Network denoted by $MLSN$. The influence maximization problem can be applied in these networks. The goal is to find the most influential persons in the $MLSN$. Mathematically, we can define this problem by the Eq. (1)

$$S_k^* = argmax_{S \subseteq V, \ |S|=k} \ \sigma(S) \tag{1}$$

where:

- V is the set of persons of the MutiLayer Social Network ($MLSN$)
- S is subset of V
- $\sigma(S)$ is an activation function that gives the influenced number of persons by the seeds S
- S_k^* the set of persons that maximises the diffusion in $MLSN$

As application examples, a politician, during the electoral campaigns, wants that his program will be known by many voters. He can search in $MLSN$ (like *twitter* ∪ *facebook* ∪ *viadeo*, A divided network according to the type of links, etc.) the most influential individuals and proposes them his program. These individuals will influence their neighbors. These latter, in turn, influence their neighbors, ⋯. In marketing field, if a company wants to sell product, it may find the most influential costumers in a $MLSN$ (like *twitter* ∪ *facebook* ∪ *viadeo*) and gives them the product freely. These costumers will influence their neighbors, so now.

This paper is organized as follows. First, we will develop an introduction, a related work and we will give our contribution. Secondly, we will model the $MLSN$ with the graphs. Thirdly, we will propose an heuristic to give the most influential persons by developing the benchmark spread models. Finally, before to conclude and to give some future works, some simulations will be made to show the performance of our approach.

2   Related Work and Contribution

Several works are effected in influence maximization in the single and multilayer social networks. Some works focus in the spread models [9,10,21] while others in the determination of seeds. [12,16,17,20,22]. In this same point of view, some studies have been done in the goal to treat the network before to determine the seeds [13]. In this latter, the authors purpose to prevent the information feedback toward the seed nodes. Kempe et al. [16] are the first to attack the influence maximization problem. It's very difficult to choose the $k - persons$ that maximise the $\sigma(S)$ function. They show that, if $\sigma(S)$ function is modular and monotone, with the Greedy hill climbing algorithm under the LT and IC model, an approximation of 63% is guaranteed. Some heuristics like *degree*, *closeness*, ⋯ centrality [3,14], *eigenvector* centrality [15], consider the $top - k$ persons as the most influential in the network. But most of these works are applicable in the single networks. Yet, the results in single networks can not be used in multilayer networks. It is important to observe that results for single networks do not always generalize to multilayer networks. As an example, in [17], the authors show that the $k - shell$ index [18] proposed to identify the influential persons in single networks loses its effectiveness in interconnected networks, so they introduce a new measure which considers both structural and spreading properties. So far the works in the process of influence maximization in the multilayer social networks do not focus on diffusion probability and contribution of first neighbors. In this paper, to consider these deficient, we propose an heuristic called centrality of *Multi-Diffusion Degree* and we denote it by C_{dd}^{MLN}. This centrality measure is based on the work of [12].

3 Multilayer Social Networks Modeling

In this part, we give a modeling of multilayer social networks. It's very important to model the system before to exploit it. The goal of this modeling is to give an heuristic which gives the most influenced persons that maximizes the influence for a small delay. A system that has several interaction can be modeling by a multilayer network.

Example, Let, an aggregation of the social networks *facebook*, *viadeo* that represent respectively the first and the second layer (see Fig. 3).

In this same problem, the age group is very important to maximize the influence. The social network will be parted according to there age group. Each group is considered as a layer.

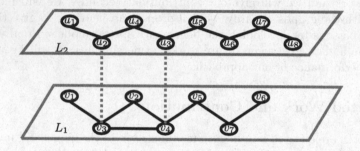

Fig. 3. Two layers social network

A person is modeling by a node and the link between two persons is modeling by an edge. The $k-th$ layer of a multilayer social network is represented by a graph denoted by $L_k(V_k, E_k)$.

- $V_k = (V_k^1, V_k^2, V_k^3, \cdots, V_k^{n_k})$ represents the set of persons of the layer k
- E_k represents the set of links of two persons of the layer k.

A multilayer social network is represented by a MultilLayer Network denoted by MLN. It is defined by $MLN=(L_1, L_2, L_3, \cdots, L_n, MM)$.

MM represents the union of mapping matrices between the layers. To build the mapping matrice between the layers $k-th$ and $k'-th$ denoted by $MM_{k'}^k$, we define an equivalence relation as follow:

$V_k^i \, \Re \, V_{k'}^j$ if:

1. $V_k^i \in L_k$, $V_{k'}^j \in L_{k'}$
2. $(V_k^i$ - $V_{k'}^j)$ a mapping edge (the same persons of the layer L_k and $L_{k'}$)

$\Re$ is an equivalence relation because it is reflexivity, The symmetry and transitivity. We consider the $MLSN$ of the Fig. 3, $L1$ represents $facebook$ and $L2$ $viadeo$. $v3$ and $u2$ represent the same person respectively in $facebook$ and $L2$ $viadeo$. We have also, $v4$ and $u3$ that represent the same person. $v7$ in $facebook$ hasn't a representative in the others layers. So, we have: $v3 \Re v3$ and $v3 \Re u2$. To build the mapping matrix $MM_{k'}^{k}$, we consider the equivalent relations between the persons of layers $k - th$ and $k' - th$. The mapping matrix $MM_{k'}^{k}$ of $k - th$ and $k' - th$ layers is defined below:

$$MM_{k'}^{k} = \begin{array}{c} \\ V_k^1 \\ V_k^2 \\ V_k^3 \\ \vdots \\ V_k^{n_k} \end{array} \begin{array}{cccccc} V_{k'}^1 & V_{k'}^2 & V_{k'}^3 & \cdots & V_{k'}^{n_{k'}} \\ \left(\begin{array}{ccccc} a_{1,1}^{k,k'} & a_{1,2}^{k,k'} & a_{1,3}^{k,k'} & \cdots & a_{1,n_{k'}}^{k,k'} \\ a_{2,1}^{k,k'} & a_{2,2}^{k,k'} & a_{2,3}^{k,k'} & \cdots & a_{2,n_{k'}}^{k,k'} \\ a_{3,1}^{k,k'} & a_{3,2}^{k,k'} & a_{3,3}^{k,k'} & \cdots & a_{3,n_{k'}}^{k,k'} \\ \vdots & \vdots & \vdots & \ddots & \vdots \\ a_{n_k,1}^{k,k'} & a_{n_k,2}^{k,k'} & a_{n_k,3}^{k,k'} & \cdots & a_{n_k,n_{k'}}^{k,k'} \end{array} \right) \end{array}$$

where $a_{i,j}^{k,k'} = 1$ if $V_k^i \Re V_{k'}^j$ else 0

After building MM, we define the equivalence class of each node v_k^i denoted by $class(v_k^i)$. For all mapping matrix $M_{k'}^k$ with k' a layer different to the layer k, if $MM_{k'}^k(v_k^i, v_{k'}^j) = 1$ then $v_{k'}^j$ belongs to $class(v_k^i)$. In Table 1, we have the mapping matrix of the $MLSN$ of the Fig. 3. As $\Re$ is an equivalence relation then it is réflexive and symmetric. In $MM = MM_1^1 \cup MM_2^1 \cup MM_1^2 \cup MM_2^2$.

MM_1^1 and MM_2^2 represent the unit matrix which do not have big importance on this model. MM_2^1 et MM_1^2 are transposed, they have the same information. So the mapping matrix is defined by the Eq. (2).

$$MM = \bigcup_{\substack{k,k' \in \{1 \cdots n\} \\ k \succ k'}} MM_{k'}^k \tag{2}$$

where n is the number of layers. The mapping matrices of the Fig. 3 is therefore reduced to the matrix MM_1^2.

Table 1. $MM = MM_1^2$

$$MM_1^2 = \begin{array}{c} \\ V1 \\ V2 \\ V3 \\ V4 \\ V5 \\ V6 \\ V7 \end{array} \begin{array}{cccccccc} u1 & u2 & u3 & u4 & u5 & u6 & u7 & u8 \\ \left(\begin{array}{cccccccc} 0 & 0 & 0 & 0 & 0 & 0 & 0 & 0 \\ 0 & 0 & 0 & 0 & 0 & 0 & 0 & 0 \\ 0 & 1 & 0 & 0 & 0 & 0 & 0 & 0 \\ 0 & 0 & 1 & 0 & 0 & 0 & 0 & 0 \\ 0 & 0 & 0 & 0 & 0 & 0 & 0 & 0 \\ 0 & 0 & 0 & 0 & 0 & 0 & 0 & 0 \\ 0 & 0 & 0 & 0 & 0 & 0 & 0 & 0 \end{array} \right) \end{array}$$

In MM, we have $class(u1) = \{u1\}$. it has not representative in the others layers. All elements of the column of $u1$ are 0. $class(v3) = \{v3, u2\}$ because $MM_2^1(v3, u2) = 1$.

4 *Multi-diffusion Degree* Centrality Measure

In this part, we propose metric to determine the persons that maximize the influence in the $MLSN$ based on the Independent Cascade Model (ICM) that is a spread model. First, we develop the two benchmark spread models. Then, we propose the heuristic that gives the seeds persons.

4.1 Spread Models

In the influence maximization problem, it's very important to have a spread model that is also a $NP\ hard$ problem. In these works, there are two benchmark heuristics that are the Linear Threshold Model (LTM) [16] and the Independent Cascade Model (ICM) [16,21]. These two spread models are defined in single social networks. In [10], the authors propose an adaptation of the ICM in multilayer networks. In [11], the authors propose also an adaptation of the LTM.

LTM: In this model, a node u, inactive at time t, can be activated by its neighbors v active. Let $p_{v,u}$ the diffusion probability of v on u, let θ_u the activation Threshold of v (Social resistance) chosen randomly between $[0,1]$. If the sum of the influence factor of all active neighbors of v is bigger than the threshold activation θ_u, so u becomes active and forever. The activated node participates it also in the activation of its inactive neighbors. A recent works [11] in multilayer social networks, a node participates in the activation of all its neighbors in all layers. They define for each node v, an activation threshold denoted $Th(v)$ (Eq. 3)

$$Th(v) = a(\theta^G + \theta_v^L) \tag{3}$$

where a is an activation factor to adjust the threshold, θ^G the global threshold and θ_v^L the local threshold in the layer of v.

Mathematically, they define the LTM by the Eq. (5). The Eq. (4) represents the condition of Th.

$$\sum_{v\ active\ and\ v\in N(u)} p_{(v,u)} \prec 1 \tag{4}$$

$$\sum_{v\ active\ and\ v\in N(u)} p_{(v,u)} \succ Th(u) \tag{5}$$

ICM: In this model, a node u can try to activate one time these inactive neighbors. Let $p_{u,v}$ probability that the node u speeds up the node v. At time t, if v is active, it can activate these inactive neighbors at time $t + 1$. In the $MLSN$, we have some works in the $MLSN$. The information spread in all layer via the node that are some representative [10]. A node can activate these neighbors in all layers.

4.2 *Multi-Diffusion Degree*

In this paper, we propose an heuristic for maximizing the influence in the $MLSN$ based on the works of [12] that use the neighborhoods of level ℓ in the single social networks. The proposed heuristic uses the neighborhoods of level 1. We call it *Multi-Diffusion Degree centrality* and denote it C_{dd}^{MLN}. We propose a mathematical model for this heuristic. Let the node v_k^i, the $i-th$ node of the layer k. To determine its centrality measure ($C_{dd}^{MLN}(v_k^i)$), we define $P_{v_k^i}$ that is the diffusion probability of v_k^i in the layer k. In the Eq. (6), we give the contribution of v_k^i in the layer k in the diffusion of information.

$$P_{v_k^i} * C_d^k(v_k^i) \tag{6}$$

where $C_d^k(v_k^i)$ is the degree centrality measure (number of neighbors) of v_k^i in the layer k. But the v_k^i can have some representatives in the others layers. we determine the contribution of each representative. For each node v_k^i, we consider the contribution of all members of $class(v_k^i)$ in the information diffusion. So, the contribution is the sum of contributions of each representative of $class(v_k^i)$ (the same person in all layers). We use the equivalence relation defined above to determine these representatives. The Eq. (6) will be applied to each member of $class(v_k^i)$. The importance of a person may be different from one layer to another. The diffusion probability is defined for each layer. And the number of neighbors in the same layer is used (the degree centrality measure in the single networks). The Eq. (7) gives the contribution of v_k^i in all layers in the diffusion process.

$$\sum_{v_{k'}^{i'} \in class(v_k^i)} P_{v_{k'}^{i'}} * C_d^{k'}(v_{k'}^{i'}) \tag{7}$$

After we determine the contribution of v_k^i in all layers of the multilayer social network, we determine the contribution of the neighbors of each representative of $class(v_k^i)$ in the same layer and in the other layers.

In the same layer, we have the contribution of each neighbor of $v_k^{i'}$ in the Eq. (6). This contribution of all neighbors of $v_k^{i'}$ in the same layer is the sum of the individual contributions. It is defined by the Eq. (8).

$$\sum_{v_k^{i'} \in N^k(v_k^i)} P_{v_k^{i'}} * C_d^k(v_k^{i'}) \tag{8}$$

where $N^k(v_k^i)$ represents the set of neighbors of v_k^i in the layer k.

But, neighbor nodes can be in many layers. So, them contribution doesn't limit in them layer. They participate in the spread process in all layers. For each neighbor, we determine its equivalence class and we determine its contribution in its layer itself. Then, we define a set $N(class(v_k^i))$ that is the set of neighbors of all representatives of v_k^i. We have in the Eq. (9) the contribution of all neighbors of all representatives of v_k^i in them layer.

$$\sum_{v_{k'}^j \in N(class(v_k^i))} P_{v_{k'}^{i'}} * C_d^{k'}(v_{k'}^{i'}) \tag{9}$$

$v_{k'}^j$ also can have some representatives in other layers. So, we consider its equivalence class. In Eq. (10), we have the contribution of $v_{k''}^j$, neighbor of a representative in all layers.

$$\sum_{v_{k''}^l \in class(v_{k'}^j)} P_{v_{k''}^l} * C_d^{k''}(v_{k''}^l) \tag{10}$$

In Eq. (9), we have the contribution of each neighbors of the representative but in the same layer where is the representative. Yet, a neighbor can have some representatives in the other layers. In Eq. (10), we have the contribution of a neighbor in all layers. The contribution of all the neighbors in all layers is defined in the Eq. (11).

$$\sum_{v_{k'}^j \in N(class(v_k^i))} \left(\sum_{v_{k''}^l \in class(v_{k'}^j)} P_{v_{k''}^l} * C_d^{k''}(v_{k''}^l) \right) \tag{11}$$

The Eq. (11) presents some redundancies. Many persons can be some neighbors of several networks. So, they are evaluated many times. For example, in the Fig. 4, we have $class(V3) = \{V3, U2\}$ and $class(V4) = \{V4, U4\}$. $V3$ and $V4$ are neighbors in the layer $L1$. $U2$ and $U4$ are neighbors in the layer $L2$. So, them contribution will be calculated two times. To prevent these redundancies, we build a set that is the union of all class of each neighbor. So, in a set, there isn't repetition, so each neighbor will be evaluated one time. In the Eq. (12), we have the contribution of all neighbors without the redundancies.

$$\sum_{\substack{v_{k''}^l \in \cup class(v_{k'}^j) \\ v_{k'}^j \in N(class(V_k^i))}} P_{v_{k''}^l} * C_d^{k''}(v_{k''}^l) \tag{12}$$

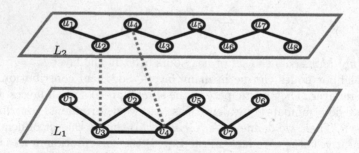

Fig. 4. Redundancy between two nodes

Now, the *Multi-Diffusion Degree* centrality of v_k^i denoted by $C_{dd}^{MLN}(v_k^i)$ is the sum of the contribution of v_k^i in all layers (Eq. 7) and the contribution of all neighbors i all layers (Eq. 4). We define this centrality measure in the Eq. (13). The $top - k$ will be considered the most influential persons in the $MLSN$.

$$C_{dd}^{MLN}(v_k^i) = \sum_{v_{k'}^{i'} \in class(v_k^i)} P_{v_{k'}^{i'}} * C_d^{k'}(v_{k'}^{i'}) + \sum_{\substack{v_{k''}^{l} \in \cup class(v_{k'}^{j}) \\ v_{k'}^{j} \in N(class(V_k^i))}} P_{v_{k''}^{l}} * C_d^{k''}(v_{k''}^{l}) \quad (13)$$

5 Experiments and Results

In many works, like [10, 11], some proofs show that the multilayer social networks are more effective than if we consider them as a single network. So, to show the performance of our approach, we compare our approach to some heuristics defined in the multilayer networks. In our simulations, we give the influenced number of persons by our approach and the *multi-degree centrality* defined in [20]. We select the $top - k$ given by our approach and the benchmark approach under the IC defined in [10] model. We determine the number of influenced nodes by the two set of seeds.

Table 2. The characteristics of the both multilayer networks

Networks	Aggregation	RT layer	RP layer	MT layer
Can. 2013	N = 348537	N = 340349	N = 85867	N = 233735
	M = 991855	M = 496982	M = 83535	M = 411338
NYC. 2014	N = 102439	N = 94574	N = 7928	N = 50054
	M = 353496	M = 213754	M = 8063	M = 131679

5.1 Data

In our simulation, we use the two multilayer social networks $Cannes2013$[1] and $NYCLIMATEMARCH2014$ (see Footnote 1) [19]. The characteristics of these two networks are detailed in the Table 2. These two networks are extracted in the $Twitter$ network. They include three layers denoted by $\{RT, RP, MT\}$.

A user can ReTweet (RT) another user's tweet. This means that the user is endorsing a piece of information shared by the other user, and is rebroadcasting it to her/his own followers.

A user can RePly (RP) to another user's tweet. This represents an exchange from a user to another as a reaction of the information contained in a user's tweet.

A user can MenTion (MT) another user in a tweet. This represents an explicit share of a piece of information with the mentioned user.

---

[1] http://deim.urv.cat/manlio.dedomenico/data.php.

Here, for each event, we build a multilayer network composed by L = 3 layers $\{RT, RP, MT\}$, corresponding to the three actions that users can perform in Twitter, and N nodes, being N the number of Twitter users interacting in the context of the given event. A directed edge between user i and user j on the RT layer is assigned if i retweeted j. Similarly, an edge exists on RP layer if user i replied to user j, and on MT layer if i mentioned j.

5.2   Parameters and Benchmarks

We use the *multi-degree* centrality heuristic adapted by M. Magnani et al. [20] as benchmark. In this heuristic, they search all neighbors of v and its representatives in all layers. It is given by the Eq. (14).

$$\delta(v) = |P_{eqIMi}(\bigcup_{i\in[1..n],(u,v)\in E_i} u)| \tag{14}$$

In this equation, we determine the equivalence class of the node v. For each representative, they use the degree centrality defined by Kempe et al. [16] for each representative in of each layer where is this equivalent node. To show the performance of our approach, we determine the seeds given by our heuristic by selecting the $top-k$ and the seeds given by the benchmark heuristic by selecting also the $top-k$. We measure the number of influenced nodes by these two heuristics by using the IC, defined in [10], as spread model. A spread probability is generated for each node randomly between 0 and 1. The iteration numbers is fixed at 3 for $NYClimateMarch2014$ network and 4 for $Cannes2013$ network.

5.3   Results

To show the performance of our model, we determine the $top-k$ (seed set) given by our heuristic and that defined in [20] (benchmark model). We determine the influenced number of nodes by each seed set under the IC model. In the Figs. 5 and 6, we use the multilayer social network $Cannes2013$. In the Figs. 7 and 8, we use the multilayer social network $NYClimateMarch2014$.

In the Figs. 5 and 7, we have determined the influenced number of nodes according to the number of seeds given by our heuristic and the benchmark heuristic. Here, we take various seeds S_k given by these two approaches. The values of k varies between 5 and 30. After the number of iterations fixed for each network, we determine the number of influenced nodes by these two seed sets. For the two experiment networks, in each set S_k, our heuristic spreads more information than the base model. In the theoretical part, we use of neighbors of level 2. The seed nodes are the nodes that are the most neighbors of levels one and two. This theoretical result is justified by the simulations of these two figures.

In the Figs. 6 and 8, we determine the number of influenced nodes according to the iteration numbers by using the S_{30} sets (given by our heuristic and the benchmark heuristic). The results show that for each iteration, our heuristic gives

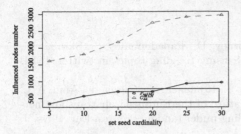

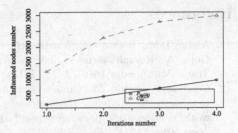

Fig. 5. Number of influenced nodes according to the seeds given by C_{dd}^{MLN} and P_{eqIMi} heuristics

Fig. 6. Number of influenced nodes according to the iteration numbers with 30 seeds given by C_{dd}^{MLN} and P_{eqIMi} heuristics

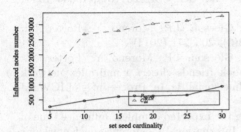

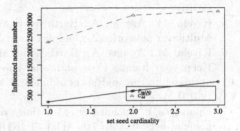

Fig. 7. Number of influenced nodes according to seeds given by C_{dd}^{MLN} and P_{eqIMi} heuristics

Fig. 8. Number of influenced nodes according to the iteration numbers with 30 seeds given by C_{dd}^{MLN} and P_{eqIMi} heuristics

better results than the benchmark heuristic. In the theoretical part, a probability that a node spreads the information was taken into account. We don't only look at the node that has more neighbors but the one that does more pressure on its neighbors. From the first iteration, our heuristic spreads more information than benchmark heuristic.

6 Conclusion

In this paper, we treat the influence maximization problem in multilayer social networks. First, we model this network by using the equivalence class and generated the mapping matrices between all layers. Then, we defined a new heuristic that uses neighbors of level 2 and a spread probability of each person in each layer. This heuristic is based on the propagation model IC. The software R and $igraph$ package are used to show the performance of our approach. In the future work, it is interested to adapt this centrality measure under LT model.

References

1. Aiello, L.M., Petkos, G., Martin, C., Corney, D., Papadopoulos, S., Skraba, R., Goke, A., Kompatsiaris, Y., Jaimes, A.: Sensing trending topics in twitter. IEEE Trans. Multimedia **15**(6), 1–15 (2013)
2. Cardillo, A., Zanin, M., Gomez-Gardenes, J., Romance, M., Garcia del Amo, A.J., Boccaletti, S.: Modeling the multilayer nature of the European air transport network: resilience and passengers re-scheduling under random failures. Eur. Phys. J. Spec. Top. **215**(1), 23–33 (2013)
3. Magnani, M., Micenkov, B., Rossi, L.: Combinatorial analysis of multiple networks (2013), arXiv preprint 1303.4986. http://dblp.uni-trier.de/db/journals/corr/corr1303.html
4. Szell, M., Lambiotte, R., Thurner, S.: Multirelational organization of large-scale social networks in an online world. Nat. Acad. Sci. USA **107**(31), 13636–13641 (2010)
5. Kivela, M., Arenas, A., Barthelemy, M., Gleeson, J.P., Moreno, Y., Porter, M.: Multilayer networks. J. Complex Netw. **2**(3), 203–271 (2014)
6. Kivela, M., Arenas, A., Barthelemy, M., Gleeson, J.P., Moreno, Y., Porter, M.: Keep your friends close and your Facebook friends closer: a multiplex network approach to the analysis of offline and online social tie. In: Proceedings of ICWSM (2014)
7. Domingos, P., Richardson, M.: Minimizing the expected complete influence time of a social network. In: 7th ACM SIGKDD International Conference on Knowledge Discovery and Data Mining (2001)
8. Tsiporkova, E., Boeva, V.: Multi-step ranking of alternatives in a multi-criteria and multi-expert decision making environment. In: 7th ACM SIGKDD International Conference on Knowledge Discovery and Data Mining, pp. 2673–2697 (2006)
9. Domingos, P., Richardson, M.: Mining the network value of customers. In: 7th ACM SIGKDD International Conference on Knowledge Discovery and Data Mining (2001)
10. Domingos, P., Richardson, M.: Spreading processes in Multilayer Networks, arXiv:1405.4329 v5 (2014)
11. Li, C., Zhao, Z., Huang, J.Z., Luo, J., Fan, J.: Multi-layer networks for influence Propagation over Microblog. Bull. Adv. Technol. Res. **6**(5), 60–72 (2012)
12. Gaye, I., Mendy, G., Ouya, S., Seck, D.: New centrality measure in social networks based on independent cascade (IC) model. In: 2015 3rd International Future Internet of Things and Cloud (FiCloud), pp. 24–26 (2015)
13. Gaye, I., Mendy, G., Ouya, S., Seck, D.: Spanning graph for maximizing the influence spread in Social Networks. In: Proceedings of the 2015 IEEE/ACM International Conference on Advances in Social Networks Analysis and Mining 2015, pp. 1389–1394. ACM (2015)
14. Solé-Ribalta, A., De Domenico, M., Gómez, S.: Centrality rankings in multiplex networks. In: ACM Conference on Web Science - WebSci, pp. 149–155. ACM Press, New York (2014). http://dl.acm.org/citation.cfm?id=2615569.2615687
15. Sol, L., Romance, M., Criado, R., Flores, J., Garcia del Amo, A., Boccaletti, S.: Multiplex PageRank. Chaos, Woodbury (2013)
16. Kempe, D., Kleinberg, J., Tardos, E.: Maximizing the spread of influence through a social network. In: Proceedings of the 9th ACM SIGKDD International Conference on Knowledge Discovery and Data Mining (2003)

17. Zhao, D., Li, L., Li, S., Huo, Y., Yang, Y.: Identifying influential spreaders in interconnected networks. Phys. Scr. **89**, 015203 (2014)
18. Kitsak, M., Gallos, L.K., Havlin, S., Liljeros, F., Muchnik, L., Stanley, H.E., Makse, H.A.: Identification of influential spreaders in complex networks. Nat. Phys. **6**, 888–893 (2014). doi:10.1038/nphys1746
19. Omodei, E., De Domenico, M., Arenas, A.: Characterizing interactions in online social networks during exceptional events. arXiv:1506.09115v1 [physics.soc-ph] (2015)
20. Magnani, M., Rossi, L.: The ML-model for multi-layer social networks. In: International Conference on Advances in Social Networks Analysis and Mining (ASONAM), pp. 5–12 (2011)
21. Pintado, L.: Diffusion in complex social networks. Games Econ. Behav. **62**(2), 573–590 (2008)
22. Zhou, J., Zhang, Y., Cheng, J.: Preference-based mining of top-K influential nodes in social networks. Fut. Gener. Comput. Syst. **31**, 40–47 (2014). Elsevier

Cloud, VPN and Overlays

Cloud Computing: Potential Risks and Security Approaches

Hassen Ben Rebah[1(✉)] and Hatem Ben Sta[2,3]

[1] Higher Institute of Technological Studies, Mahdia, Tunisia
ben_rebah_h@yahoo.fr
[2] SOIE Lab, LR11ES03, Higher Institute of Management,
University of Tunis, 2000 Tunis, Tunisia
hatem.bensta@gmail.com
[3] Higher Institute of Computer Science, University of Tunis El Manar,
2080 Tunis, Tunisia

Abstract. Cloud Computing is a new technology, widely used in different areas, allowing easy and on-demand access through the internet to a shared set of configurable computing resources. The adoption of this new technology within companies is restricted by security constraints. In this paper, we present the most significant risks that could affect organizations intending to deploy Cloud technology and security measures to be in place to reduce the impact of risks based on a literature review.

Keywords: Cloud computing · Potential risks · Counter-measure · Threat

1 Introduction

Cloud Computing is a new processing scheme in which computer processing is performed in the Internet "Cloud" [1]. This new technology based on virtualization has become essential in the progress and provision of IT services for organizations. It is considered by them as a method to raise automatically their abilities of storing, deploying web services, database management and sharing data without affording in new infrastructure, training new employer, or licensing new software. In spite of all this advantages, clients are still not enthusiastic to deploy their business in the cloud [2] since it presents new security issues which has not been well realized [3] and which needs to be carefully evaluated before any engagement in this area [4]. According to a survey conducted by Fujitsu Research Institute in 2010, 88% of potential cloud consumers are afraid of who has access to their data, and demanded more caution of what goes on in the backend physical server [5]. The main contribution presents the potential risks related to cloud computing environment and security measures to reduce the impacts of these risks based on literature review.

This paper is divided into two sections: the first section presents Cloud Computing technology: its models, its services and its characteristics. The second section presents the potential risks related to this technology and the safety measures to be in place to reduce the impacts of these risks. It contains also a literature review of previous research involving several evidence classifications of risks that affected the cloud environment. Finally, we will wrap up our paper with a conclusion.

© ICST Institute for Computer Sciences, Social Informatics and Telecommunications Engineering 2018
T.F. Bissyande and O. Sie (Eds.): AFRICOMM 2016, LNICST 208, pp. 69–78, 2018.
https://doi.org/10.1007/978-3-319-66742-3_7

2 Cloud Computing

According to the National Institute for Standards and Technology (NIST)[1], cloud computing is a model for enabling ubiquitous, convenient and on-demand network access to a shared pool of configurable computing resources (e.g., networks, servers, storage, applications, and services) that can be rapidly provisioned and released with a minimal management effort or service provider interaction [6].

2.1 Cloud Computing Architecture

Cloud computing is composed of two sections: the front end and the back end. These latters are connected with each other through a network infrastructure, normally the Internet. Front end is that the user can see, it includes the hardware and software equipments necessary to access the cloud (e.g. Web browsers like Internet Explorer or Firefox) and the back end is composed of cloud computing services such as servers, data storage and various computers. Traffic control operations, administration system and user request are managed by a central sever. It keeps some rules and uses particular software named middleware. This last permits networked computers to communicate with each other [7, 8]. End user is able to use the cloud computing services via the Internet network from any location (home, work, etc.) and through any device (phone, laptop, etc.). Generally, these services are governed by a service-level agreement (SLA) between customer and cloud service provider (CSP), it specifies requirement, quality of service, cost, etc.

2.2 Cloud Computing Characteristics

Cloud computing has five key characteristics as described by Melland Grance:

- On-demand self service: a consumer can one-sidedly provide computing capabilities when necessary automatically without contacting the hosting provider [6, 8].
- Broad network access: the hosted application is available over the network and accessed through standard mechanisms that promote use by heterogeneous thin or thick client platforms such as laptop, Smartphone, etc. [6, 8].
- Resource pooling: the provider's computing resources are shared to serve multiple consumers using a multi-tenant model, with different physical and virtual resources dynamically assigned and reassigned according to consumer demand [6, 8].
- Rapid elasticity: cloud service can be rapidly and elastically provisioned and released to quickly scale up or down commensurate with demand [6, 8].
- Measured service: cloud computing resource can be monitored, controlled, and reported providing transparency for both the provider and the consumer of the utilized service. Cloud computing services use a metering capability which allows to control and optimize resource use based on pay per use model [6, 8].

---

[1] http://www.nist.gov.

2.3   Cloud Computing Deployment Models

Cloud computing represents four deployment models:

- Private cloud: the cloud infrastructure is set up for exclusive use by a specific organization which incorporates many consumers such us business units [9, 10].
- Community cloud: the cloud infrastructure is shared by a specific community of consumers from organizations that have the same interests such as mission and policy [9, 10].
- Public cloud: The cloud infrastructure is made available to a big number of consumers and owned by a service provider [9, 10].
- Hybrid cloud: The cloud infrastructure is a composition of two or more different cloud (private, community, or public) that remain unique entities [9, 10].

2.4   Cloud Computing Service Models

Cloud computing offers three types of services:

- Software as a Service: the ability provided to the user is to use the provider's applications running on a cloud infrastructure. The applications are available to various clients through a thin client interface such as a web browser [6, 11].
- Platform as a Service: the capacity allowed to the user to deploy on the cloud infrastructure consumer-created or acquired applications created using programming languages, libraries, services, etc. [6, 11].
- Infrastructure as a Service: The ability available for the user to provide him with IT infrastructure (processing, storage networks, etc.) [6, 11].

3   Security Problems in Cloud Computing

The immaturity of cloud computing technology has posed many issues such as security [12, 13], virtualization [14], network [15] and fault tolerance problems [16]. But security issues are the most important ones for the consumer who is seeking a comfortable service in terms of integrity privacy, availability, etc. According to a research conducted in 2009 by Fujitsu on problems of cloud computing from the user viewpoint which revealed that security problems are the most important ones with 73% [1]. The security problems associated with cloud computing is being treated by different organizations and several studies done by many researchers. These latters have classified them in different dimensions. Cloud Security Alliance (CSA) is a non-profit American organization formed to advance the use of the best practices for providing security assurance within cloud computing and provide education on the uses of cloud computing to help secure all others forms of computing [17]. This organization defined in 2010 a guideline that describes necessary security considerations for performing critical tasks on a cloud computing divided into 13 domains (e.g. Governance and enterprise risk management, compliance and audit, application security, Identity and access management, virtualization, etc.) [1]. The European Network and Information Security Agency (ENISA) estimated in a report submitted en 2009 35 types of security risks in cloud computing [18]. Gartner 2008 fixed seven security issues that must be verified by the customer before choosing a cloud computing provider (e.g. privileged user access, regulatory compliance, data location, data segregation, recovery, investigative support and long-term viability) [19]. [11, 20] presented a categorization of security issues for cloud computing focused on its service models (SaaS, PaaS, and IaaS) who identified the main liabilities in this type of systems, the most important risks found in the literature and all available counter-measures for these threats and vulnerabilities. [17] gave the key security issues in cloud computing environment (e.g. data transmission, network security, data privacy, data integrity, etc.) and presented some recommendations to reduce the impacts of these risks. [21] provided two categorizations of security issues related to cloud computing (threats for cloud service users and threats for cloud service providers) based on analysis of its technical components. This classification was also justified by [22] through a systematic literature review.

3.1   Potential Risks Related to Cloud Computing

In the literature, there are many definitions of the term "risk". According to the ISO/CEI 13335-1:2004 risk means "The potential that a given threat will exploit vulnerabilities of an asset or group of assets and thereby cause harm to the organization. It is measured in terms of a combination of the probability of an event and its consequence". With threat means "a potential cause of an incident that may result in harm to a system or organization" and vulnerability means "a weakness of an asset or group of assets that can be exploited by one or more threats" [23].

In 2009, ENISA presented a report in which it suggested the most nine influential risks on organizations mentioned below:

Loss of governance: when using the cloud infrastructure, the cloud client gives supervision to the cloud provider on various issues [24]. This loss of governance relies on the cloud service models for example in case of IaaS, organization cedes hardware and network management to the provider, while SaaS also cedes OS, application, and service integration in order to give a turnkey service to the cloud service customer. This loss of control can result a lack of confidentiality, integrity and availability of data [21].

Lock-in: lock-in means incapability of the cloud user to move from one provider to another or migrate data and services back to an in-house IT environment. This introduces a reliance on a specific cloud provider for service provision, especially if data portability, as the most important feature, is not enabled [24]. According to [21], this risk can also affect a cloud provider (Supplier Lock-in) when several supplier-dependent modules or workflows are used for integration or functionality extension.

Isolation failure: multi-tenancy and shared resources are a two essential feature of cloud computing based on the virtualization technology. Although this technology is utilized by many providers to maximize the use of hardware [25] but it has many gaps because it is not designed to offer strong isolation properties for a multi-tenant architecture [26]. In fact, it leads hackers to a full access to the host and cross-VM side channel attacks to take out information from the specific VM on the same machine [22]. Also, data from multiple occupiers is saved in a shared database, the threat of data leakage among these occupiers is high [27].

Compliance risks: traditional service providers are subject to external audits and security certifications. If a cloud service provider does not adhere to these security audits, then it results an obvious decrease in client trust [28]. This risk arises because of lack of governance over audits and industry standard assessments [17]. Organizations which implement the audit and compliance to the internal and external processes search to get certification. These enterprises may be put at risk since cloud computing service providers may not be capable to show evidence of their own compliance with the necessary needs or may not permit an audit by cloud customer [29].

Data location: generally, when a customer uses the cloud, he does not know the exact location of his data and he also does not have any supervision over the physical access techniques to that data. The majority of cloud service provider possesses data centers in many places in the world. This situation can be considered as an issue in several cases [30]. On the one hand, the cloud provider should not only store and process data in specific jurisdictions but should also respect the privacy regulations of those jurisdictions in different countries all over the world [31]. On the other hand, it is hard to determine the appropriate security procedures are in place to protect customers' data [32].

Management interface compromise: the customer management interface that cloud providers give is accessible through the internet. These interfaces offer users the possibility to access to a large set of resources. This may pose a real menace if web browser vulnerabilities are there. This includes customer interfaces supervising many virtual machines and, more than that, cloud provider interfaces supervising the operation of the entire cloud system [18].

Data protection: cloud computing shows various data protection risks for both cloud customers and providers. In some cases, it may be difficult for the cloud user to effectively check the data handling practices of the cloud provider and, therefore, to be certain that the data is handled in a legal way. This issue is more complicated in cases of multiple transfers of data, e.g. between federated clouds. An organization cannot verify how a cloud provider handles its data and thus cannot establish either the practices employed are lawful or not. Data flowing from the Internet is full of malware and packets intended to lure users into unknowing participation in criminal activities. Although this defiance is more difficult, some cloud providers have obtained certified levels regarding to data handling [24].

Insecure or incomplete data deletion: in fact, the user who can erase data is in relation with the separation issue which is defined by multi-tenant usage mode [33]. In a public cloud, a user can ask the provider to delete completely some of his data. This request can be impossible or undesirable because the copies of data are on multiple disks belonging to many data centers located in several countries around the world and are shared with other customers [34]. In this case, data is supposed to be removed completely from the cloud but according to the physical characteristics of storage support, the data still exit and may be restored. This problem can be considered as a major risk to the users [35].

Malicious insider: this risk which is well-known to most organizations is a result of staff hired by cloud service providers. Those employees are offered a level of access that may enable them to get confidential data and complete control over the cloud services without any risk of detection. Cloud Service Providers show little or no transparency on how they hire employees, how they give them access to cloud resources or how they monitor them. Bad insiders can directly affect financial consequences and productivity of organizations [26, 36].

The table below represents the list of risks mentioned above classified in terms of their types and their impacts to the organizations. The impact is listed as "Medium" which is scored as1and "High" which is scored as 2 (Table 1).

Table 1. Classification of potential risks of cloud computing

Risk	Type	Impact 1: Medium - 2: High
Loss of governance	Organizational	2
Lock-in	Technical	1
Isolation failure	Technical	2
Compliance risks	Organizational	2
Management interface compromise	Technical	2
Data protection	Technical	1
Insecure or incomplete data deletion	Technical	2
Malicious insider	Technical	2
Data location	Technical	2

3.2   Counter-Measure of Potential Risks

The successful implementation of cloud computing technology requires the development and implementation of several security management policies and mechanisms. In the following table, we present some safety measures to reduce the impacts of potential risks of cloud computing mentioned above.

In Table 2, with reference to a literature review, we have listed the measures of security that must be applied by cloud service providers and the organizations to reduce the impacts of the potential risks of cloud computing.

Table 2. Risks and counter-measure

Risk	Counter-measure
Loss of governance	• Execute carefully Service Level Agreements (SLA) • Define clearly the role and responsibility between cloud service provider, cloud service user, data owner related to data ownership, access control, infrastructure maintenance • Secure and maintain properly all documents which should be available to the customer at all times • Define common frameworks for certification such as COBIT or ISO [4, 29, 36]

(*continued*)

Table 2. (*continued*)

Risk	Counter-measure
Lock-in	• Promote standardized technology and Application Programming Interface (API) • Use Free Libre Open Source Software (FLOSS) which accompanied increasingly standardization initiatives such as Apache CloudStack, OpenStack and Eucalyptus • Develop applications based on a generic functional base such as LibCloud or Deltacloud in the case of IaaS and SimpleCloud in the case of PaaS • Choose a specialist technical operator (Technical cloud brokers) that avoids lock-in and uses simultaneously several cloud services • Establish an exit strategy • Implement the hybrid cloud model which can solve the problem of compatibility issue [22, 29, 36–38]
Isolation failure	• Implement a better security practices for installation/configuration • Monitor environment for illegal changes/activity • Develop strong authentication and access control for administrative access and operations • Promote Service Level Agreements for patching and vulnerability remediation • Conduct vulnerability scanning and configuration audits • Use effective encryption methods to guarantee data isolation between clients [22, 26, 29, 36]
Compliance risks	• Conduct internal and external audits regularly on a basis to verify cloud service provider to match terms, standards and regulations • Ensure that cloud service provider should give evidence that data, saved only in geographic locations, allowed just by a formal contract (SLA) • Ensure that requirements meet the data location • Comply location with well-defined laws and regulations • Incorporate and document laws and regulations formally in governance policies [17, 29, 36, 39]
Management interface compromise	• Provide remote access with a secure protocol • Patch completely web browser vulnerabilities before providing remote access • Promote a strong authentication strategy (avoid only a simple authentication by password) • Plan periodic and efficient OS and hardware hardening procedures on the cloud system [26, 29]
Data protection	• Ensure that cloud service provider abides by all the regulations, including HIPPA and FISMA, within the same country, regarding cloud security • Make sure that cloud service provider has to meet the legal systems under different jurisdictions without so much visibility where the data resides and how it is set up through various legal jurisdictions [22]

(*continued*)

Table 2. (*continued*)

Risk	Counter-measure
Insecure or incomplete data deletion	• Ensure that the provider should define policies to set up procedures for the destruction of persistent media before getting rid of it • Ensure that providers should define very strong encryption strategies [22, 26]
Malicious insider	• Require transparency in all information security and management practices in addition to compliance reporting • Determine and report security breach notification processes • Promote strict supply chain management and conduct a comprehensive-supplier assessment • Make sure that human resource requirements are part of legal contracts [26, 29, 36]
Data location	• Offer information to consumers about where their data stored and processed • Ensure that cloud service provider should guarantee safe operation of the cloud data center to grant a secure physical location for customers' data • Verify that the cloud service provider should store and process data in specific jurisdictions and respect the privacy regulations of those jurisdictions [36, 40, 41]

4   Conclusion

Cloud computing is an economic and technological revolution in which computing resources are provided as a service over the Internet. However, adoption of this technology remains low due to of several safety problems related to virtualization technology, deployment models, service models and network architecture. In this paper, we have focused on the potential risks related to cloud computing and we suggested a number of controls that could be considered for the mitigation of these controversial issues. Several studies have demonstrated that the adoption of hybrid cloud computing can be an effective strategy for a wide variety of companies which are more concerned with security. What are the limitations of this model? And does it really meet the growing needs of security companies?

References

1. Okuhara, M., Shiozaki, S.T.: Security architectures for cloud computing. Fujitsu Sci. Tech. J. **46**, 397–402 (2010)
2. Kuyoro, S.O., Ibikunle, F., Awodele, O.: Cloud computing security issues and challenges. Int. J. Comput. Netw. **3**, 247–255 (2011)
3. Wang, Q., Wang, C., Li, J., Ren, K., Lou, W.: Enabling public verifiability and data dynamics for storage security in cloud computing. In: European Conference on Research in Computer Security, pp. 355–370 (2009)

4. Brender, N., Markov, I.: Risk perception and risk management in cloud computing: results from a case study of Swiss companies. Int. J. Inf. Manag. **33**, 726–733 (2013)
5. Fujitsu Research Institute, Personal data in the cloud: A global survey of consumer attitudes. http://www.fujitsu.com/downloads/SOL/fai/reports/fujitsu_personal-data-in-the-cloud.pdf
6. Mell, P., Grance, T.: The NIST definition of cloud computing (v15), National Institute of Standards and Technology (NIST) (2009). http://nvlpubs.nist.gov/nistpubs/Legacy/SP/nistspecialpublication800-145.pdf
7. Jadeja, Y., Modi, K.: Cloud computing - concepts, architecture and challenges. In: International Conference on Computing, Electronics and Electrical Technologies (2012)
8. Saggar, R., Saggar, S., Khurana, N.: Cloud computing: designing different system architecture depending on real-world examples. Int. J. Comput. Sci. Inf. Technol. **5**, 5025–5029 (2014)
9. Zissis, D., Lekkas, D.: Addressing cloud computing security issues. Future Gener. Comput. Syst. **28**, 583–592 (2012)
10. Al Morsy, M., Grundy, J., Müller, I.: An analysis of the cloud computing security problem. In: Proceedings of APSEC 2010 Cloud Workshop (2010)
11. Subashini, S., Kavitha, V.: A survey on security issues in service delivery models of cloud computing. J. Netw. Comput. Appl. **34**, 1–11 (2011)
12. Begum, F.: Cloud computing and its security concerns a survey. Int. J. Res. **3**, 1082–1088 (2014)
13. Raj, B.J.: Cloud computing security issues in infrastructure as a service. Int. J. Adv. Res. Trends Eng. Technol. **2**, 246–250 (2015)
14. Shwetha, S.: Survey on security issues and problems in cloud computing virtual machines. Int. J. Comput. Sci. Inf. Technol. **4**, 755–760 (2013)
15. Patidar, P., Bhardwaj, A.: Network security through SSL in cloud computing environment. Int. J. Comput. Sci. Inf. Technol. **2**, 2800–2803 (2011)
16. Bala, A., Chana, I.: Fault tolerance- challenges, techniques and implementation in cloud computing. Int. J. Comput. Sci. Issues **9**, 288–293 (2012)
17. Padhy, R.P., Patra, M.R., Satapathy, S.C.: Cloud computing: security issues and research challenges. Int. J. Comput. Sci. Inf. Technol. Secur. **1**, 136–146 (2011)
18. European Network and Information Security Agency (ENISA). https://www.enisa.europa.eu/publications/cloud-computing-risk-assessment
19. Gartner. http://www.infoworld.com/article/2652198/security/gartner–seven-cloud-computing-security-risks.html
20. Hashizume, K., Rosado, D.G., Fernández-Medina, E., Fernandez, E.B.: An analysis of security issues for cloud computing. J. Internet Serv. Appl. **4**, 1–13 (2013)
21. Lee, K.: Security threats in cloud computing environments. Int. J. Secur. Appl. **6**, 25–32 (2012)
22. Latif, R., Abbas, H., Assar, S., Ali, Q.: Cloud computing risk assessment: a systematic literature review. Future Inf. Technol. **276**, 285–295 (2013)
23. The Great Seal of the seal of approval. https://law.resource.org/pub/in/bis/S04/is.iso.iec.13335.1.2004.pdf
24. Kulkarni, G., Gambhir, J., Patil, T., Dongare, A.: A security aspects in cloud computing. In: IEEE 3rd International Conference on Computer Science and Automation Engineering, pp. 547–550 (2012)
25. Pearson, S., Benameur, A.: Privacy, security and trust issues arising from cloud computing. In: IEEE Second Conference on Cloud Computing Technology and Science (2010)
26. Shah, H., Anandane, S.S., Shrikanth, S.: Security issues on cloud computing. Int. J. Comput. Sci. Inf. Secur. **11**, 25–34 (2013)

27. Hashizume, K., Rosado, D.G., Medina, E.F., Fernandez, E.: An analysis of security issues for cloud computing. J. Internet Serv. Appl. **4**, 1–13 (2013)
28. Chou, Y., Oetting, J.: Risk assessment for cloud-based IT systems. Int. J. Grid High Perform. Comput. **3**, 1–13 (2011)
29. Tripathi, A., Mishra, A.: Cloud computing security considerations. In: IEEE International Conference on Signal Processing, Communications and Computing, pp. 1–5 (2011)
30. Kleber, V., Schulter, A., Westphall, C.B., Westphall, C.M.: Intrusion detection techniques for grid and cloud computing environment. IT Professional IEEE Comput. **12**, 38–43 (2010)
31. Julisch, K., Hall, M.: Security and control in the cloud. Inf. Secur. J. Global Perspect. **19**, 299–309 (2010)
32. Khajeh-Hosseini, A., Sommerville, I., Bogaerts, J., Teregowda, P.: Decision support tools for cloud migration in the enterprise. In: IEEE International Conference on Cloud Computing, pp. 541–548 (2011)
33. Adineh, M., Hariri, N.: Risks identification and ranking in information technology projects based on cloud computing. Kuwait Chapter Arab. J. Bus. Manag. Rev. **3**, 216–277 (2014)
34. Ayala, L.C., Vega, M., Vargas, L.M.: Emerging threats, risk and attacks in distributed systems: cloud computing. Innov. Adv. Comput. Inf. Syst. Sci. Eng. **152**, 37–51 (2013)
35. Rahul, S.S., Rai, J.K.: Security & privacy issues in cloud computing. Int. J. Eng. Res. Technol. **2**, 1–6 (2013)
36. Youssef, E.A., Alageel, M.: A framework for secure cloud computing. Int. J. Comput. Sci. Issues **9**, 487–500 (2012)
37. Viseur, R., Charlier, E., Van de borne, M.: Comment gérer le risque de lock-in technique en cas d'usage de services de cloud computing? 16ème colloque CREIS-TERMINAL (2014)
38. Hwang, K., Li, D.: Trusted cloud computing with secure resources and data coloring. IEEE Comput. Soc. **14**, 14–21 (2010)
39. Rittinghouse, J.W., Ransome, J.F.: Cloud Computing: Implementation, Management, and Security, pp. 301–308. CRC Press, Boca Raton (2010)
40. Julisch, K., Hall, M.: Security and control in the cloud. Inf. Secur. J. Glob. Perspect. **19**, 299–309 (2010)
41. Kumar, A.: World of cloud computing & security. Int. J. Cloud Comput. Serv. Sci. **1**, 53–58 (2012)

G-Cloud: Opportunities and Security Challenges for Burkina Faso

Didier Bassole[1(✉)], Frédéric T. Ouedraogo[2], and Oumarou Sie[1]

[1] Université Ouaga I Pr Joseph KI-ZERBO, Ouagadougou, Burkina Faso
dbassole@gmail.com, oumarou.sie@gmail.com
[2] Université de Koudougou, Koudougou, Burkina Faso
ouedraogo.tounwendyam@yahoo.fr

Abstract. In this paper, we try to clearly outline the opportunities of cloud computing in the context of developing countries, while helping stakeholders grasp the challenges ahead. In particular, we consider the case of the G-Cloud project engaged by the government of Burkina Faso to boost the ICT economy, improve administration-citizen relations, and strengthen the education system. Through this article, we try to show the actors, that the G-Cloud to be a vector of opportunities and sustainable development for Burkina Faso, pre-conditions and challenges are facing particularly in terms of security in the cloud environment and the challenge on the supply in sufficient quantity and quality of electric power.

Keywords: G-Cloud · Opportunities · Security chalenges · Developing countries

1 Introduction

Around the globe, we are witnessing the momentum of cloud computing technology, which allows providers to make both hardware and software infrastructure available on demand as services via the Internet. In an era where resources must be intelligently managed and expenses reduction has become a priority, cloud computing has been positioned as a powerful vector of the economy. Indeed it provides opportunities in various sectors of development, contributing in a rational management of economic, human and infrastructural resources. For developing countries such as Burkina Faso, with embryonic economies where citizens and governments face diverse overlapping priorities, cloud computing can be leveraged as a concrete opportunity for sustainable development based on an efficient exploitation of IT infrastructures. Nevertheless, given the context of developing countries where technological challenges are immense, cloud computing projects must check the capability of stakeholders to ensure the availability, reliability and security of the infrastructure of the hosted applications and of stored data.

This paper is an effort from the academic community to clearly outline the opportunities of cloud computing in the context of developing countries, while

© ICST Institute for Computer Sciences, Social Informatics and Telecommunications Engineering 2018
T.F. Bissyande and O. Sie (Eds.): AFRICOMM 2016, LNICST 208, pp. 79–87, 2018.
https://doi.org/10.1007/978-3-319-66742-3_8

helping stakeholders grasp the challenges ahead. In particular, we consider the case of the G-Cloud project engaged by the government of Burkina Faso to boost the ICT economy, improve administration-citizen relations, and strengthen the education system [2,3].

The remainder of this paper is structured as follows: Sect. 2 discusses related works. Section 3 enumerates the opportunities that the G-Cloud project will help realize if/when fully implemented. In Sect. 4, we will detail challenges, in particular security challenges, that arise in the design and implementation of the G-Cloud project in the context of a developing country. We provide discussions on the impacts of security issues as well as propositions on mechanisms to secure the cloud. We conclude this work in Sect. 5.

2   Related Works

The emergence of cloud computing as a technological advance of the 21st century, several studies highlighted the opportunities that such a model of service can offer to developing countries. In [5], Mathias and Baldreck highlight the benefits of cloud computing for small and medium-sized enterprises of developing countries. The authors discuss the potential of cloud computing in Africa and the challenges associated with the use of the services offered. In [6], Juster by analyzing the benefits of cloud computing for developing countries, shows that Cloud Computing can bridge the gap in development between the developed and developing.

Hong-Linh [7] focuses on the opportunities of cloud computing to the field of education and research in developing countries. Needs infrastructure and software for countries with weak economies related to cloud computing profits overshadow not however challenges in terms of security applications and data especially for less advanced nations economically, technically and where the legislation on the protection of personal data is not yet in the beautiful fixed. Because of its operation, Cloud computing has both of legal risk for the customer and technical and operational risks due to the loss of control of the client on its own data processing. It also introduces new risks, whether for the sharing of responsibilities, the location of the data or sharing.

3   G-Cloud: Opportunities for Burkina Faso

Cloud computing is a major technological shift from traditional computing. It leverages virtualization on remote servers and distributed pooling of storage resources to provide remote (i.e., users can be geographically distant from servers) data processing and application computing. This yields substantial savings in various resources (including energy, storage, human resources, etc.) and thus, an economy of scale particularly for countries under development. Based on a new economic model that is to provide services and applications available online through network (e.g., in a web service mode) based on an on-demand policy and billing to the use, cloud computing has now turned into an obvious opportunity for the information and communication technology sector and also for the sector of entrepreneurship in developing countries. The main services offered by Cloud Computing can be summarized as follows [15]:

- The infrastructure as a Service (IaaS): it provides the entire infrastructure stack that delivers the computer infrastructure and it leverages significant technology, services, and data center investments to deliver IT as a service to customers. It delivers hardware such as servers, Server virtualized and application, data center virtualized, memory, flexible storage and application, CPUs, disk space, network connectivity, flexible local area networks (LANs), firewalls, security services, etc.
- The platform as a Service (PaaS): it provides the development environment and delivers operating systems and associated services over the internet without the need to download or installs applications on end-user computers.
- The software as a Service (SaaS): Software-as-a-Service is a software distribution model in which applications are hosted by a vendor or service provider and made available to customers over a network, typically the internet. This may relate to business applications, customer relationship support (CRM), Finance (ERP), online payment, electronic marketplace (for the TPE/PME), etc. (Fig. 1).

  Apart from these main service delivery models a number of variations exists, namely [5]:
- The communication as a Service (CaaS): based on SaaS, it delivers audio/video communication, collaborative services, unified communications, e-mail, instant messaging sharing data (web conferencing).
- The network as a Service (NaaS): based on IaaS, it provides Internet managed (warranty of throughput, availability, etc.), virtualized networks, Virtual Private Network (VPN) combined with Cloud Computing, flexible bandwidth services and demand.

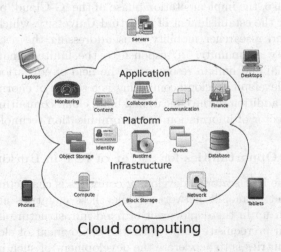

Cloud computing

Fig. 1. Cloud computing delivers services

In the light of the services offered by cloud computing, there emerge a number of opportunities for countries with weak economies and in all sectors of activity. We will focus on cloud computing opportunities in three areas of development for the developing countries: education and research sector, sector of the technologies of the information and communication, sector of entrepreneurship.

3.1   G-Cloud: Opportunities for Education and Research in Burkina Faso

Education and research in developing countries are generally characterized by several challenges related mainly to the access to resources (teaching and related work material), and to the lack of qualified teachers [7]. Given the inadequacy of budget allocations for addressing these challenges, cloud computing may be suitable for alleviating several difficulties.

Indeed, leveraging cloud computing services, education and research stakeholders can quickly implement e-Learning, e-science and e-research platforms while establishing strategic networking within the scientific and academic communities. Another advantage of cloud computing for education and research is that it will allow mobility and emulate ubiquity. As a result, work initiated in a given location can be continued in another in another location via the cloud, without any need to duplicate or synchronize the supporting documents.

To face the shortcomings in budget, savings can be made at certain levels including the purchase of terminals. Storage and computing capabilities are deported into remote servers, and thus personal computers require less CPU and hard drive capacity. Furthermore, cloud computing adoption can limit the installation of a slew of software on personal computers, a hazard for spreading viruses and pumping energy to supporting redundant task processing. One can finally compensate for the accidental loss of data on personal terminals by saving documents in the cloud.

In Burkina Faso, the implementation phase of the 'G-Cloud' platform can be a springboard for the establishment of a Virtual University, which will facilitate online courses and researcher mobility, thus addressing the needs of an ever-growing university community. In response to the limited financial resources (including material and human resources in the field of education and research of the countries developing), cloud computing is a source of enormous to exploit opportunities. In addition to the educational field, cloud computing offers opportunities for the sector of information and communication technologies.

3.2   G-Cloud: Opportunities for Sector of ICT in Burkina Faso

The context of the ICT sector in developing countries is characterized by a very rapid development of mobile networks, while these countries attempt to find solutions to catch up in the deployment of fixed infrastructure and broadband networks. A main prerequisite however for the deployment of cloud computing in developing countries is to accelerate the development of such infrastructures. Other prerequisites for deployment are the constant availability of sources of stable energy and water, in quantity and quality, for cooling of servers which must remain constantly active. Unfortunately, these conditions are not always met in these countries.

Cloud computing investments are therefore an opportunity for developing countries in the sense that efforts to satisfy the conditions necessary to its deployment will contribute to reduce the digital gap between developed and developing countries. The physical proximity of Cloud resources with the end user will have the immediate impact of the budget earmarked for the bandwidth savings and will guarantee some level of access speed to resources in the cloud.

Opportunities to gain immediate access to the latest innovations and for an organization to move from heavy investment in ICT infrastructure, in particular, in data centers, are a godsend for the reduction of the digital gap. As an illustration, in the context of implementation of the G-Cloud, the government of Burkina Faso undertook the creation of a national, 5740 km-long, backbone, and will have to improve connectivity and communications in a country that lacks basic digital infrastructure. Also, the realization of a technology park of 80 ha with a virtual point landing and an internet exchange point is considered in the South of Ouagadougou, the capital city [3,4].

The G-Cloud project participates in the reduction of the digital gap with the deployment of 513 km of optical fiber, and connecting more than 800 public buildings in the capitals of the thirteen regions of the country, as well as the establishment of an e-Government platform [1].

3.3   G-Cloud: Opportunities for Youth Entrepreneurship in Burkina Faso

In Burkina Faso, entrepreneurship and self-employment are essential vectors in the fight against unemployment of young people, and an engine for sustainable development. Unfortunately, entrepreneurship of youth in Burkina Faso faces several factors, mainly the lack of capital. The advent of cloud computing can contribute inexorably to boost entrepreneurship in countries with weak economy.

There is an increasing, and often unbalanced, competition between firms from developed countries and those of developing countries. To reduce operating costs, streamline investment, improve productivity and boost innovation, cloud computing can be leveraged by lower-economy companies to reduce investment costs in ICT infrastructure. With cloud computing, organizations, institutions and businesses will no longer have the need to invest heavily in computing resources, and requiring a heavy and costly internal management.

The availability of online services gives also the possibility to access more appropriate computer equipment in a pay-per-use model which is suitable in an economic environment where businesses seek to maximize investment and reduce operating costs while reaching competitiveness and performance for businesses.

Despite the benefits that come with cloud computing, its adoption and implementation in developing economies is confronted by a variety of challenges. One can find several arguments against cloud services in developing countries. However, the most critical one remains the security challenges. Indeed, an essential concern of cloud computing setups in countries where the technological challenges are immense, remains to guarantee the security of the cloud infrastructure, applications, and data.

4   G-Cloud: Security Challenges for Burkina Faso

Lose control of its data and entrusted to a third party in a cloud computing environment can create specific problems due to the geographical dispersion of data in multiple treatment centers.

This new context calls for lawyers to include provisions to better protect the interests of each and other. It should therefore be made in contracts in an environment Cloud Computing of the provisions strengthened in terms of security and data availability.

Indeed, in an outsourced computing environment, such as the Cloud, the end-user must obtain guarantees on levels of service for solutions to which he subscribes. The provider must be able to justify the levels of service on which he has committed, through a service contract, and provide clients with the means and tools to track these service levels over time.

In addition, at least the following aspects should be addressed [10,11,17]:

- The securisation of network connections: int the order to avoid attack methods such as phishing, fraud, and exploitation of software vulnerabilities. Avoid attackers to access critical areas of deployed cloud computing services, allowing them to compromise the confidentiality, integrity and availability of those services.
- The authentication of persons accessing the data: the security and availability of general cloud services is dependent upon the security of software interfaces or APIs that customers use to manage and interact with cloud services. These interfaces must be designed to protect against both accidental and malicious attempts to circumvent policy.
- The encryption of data: Data protection is the most important security issue in Cloud computing and encryption is a key technology for data security. In the service provider's data center, protecting data privacy and managing compliance are critical by using encrypting and managing encryption keys of data in transfer to the cloud.
- The data access controllability: the possibility to the data owner to perform the selective restriction of access to his data outsourced to cloud and denied the access to persons without permissions.
- The backup of data: the ability to retrieve data when an undesirable operations corrupt or delete them.
- Traceability of access and actions on data.
- The certification of organization and security procedures of the Cloud Computing provider.
- The duty of information reinforced the claimant on security incidents.
- The establishment of regular testing of procedures for the recovery of data and procedures in the event of discontinuance of the service.

- The level of quality of service: the customer must have a right to look at the quality of the services and the level of performance of the service, with a contractual commitment on the part of the contractor;
- The location of data: Cloud has no borders, one must have a commitment on the places of storage of data, and ensure that the regulations of the countries are in compliance with the regulations to which the client is subject or that it wishes to have.
- The conditions for termination of contracts including the reversibility of the service: in the event of breach of contract or change of supplier, the customer must ensure the recovery and destruction of its data on provider infrastructure after his migration.

4.1 The Legal Framework of the G-Cloud

A regulatory environment meets the international requirements in terms of protection of personal data and security of data exchange is the first pillar for a successful development of Cloud Computing.

Since geographic dispersion of data is an important factor associated with cost and performance of the cloud, an issue that deserves mention relates to regulatory arbitrage, which means that cloud vendors can take advantage of loopholes in regulatory systems of certain jurisdictions to reduce risks. Economies worldwide vary greatly in the legal systems. Experts expect that, at least for the short run, countries are likely to update their laws individually rather than acting in a multilateral fashion [9,10].

Due to the newness, jurisdictional arbitrage is higher for the cloud compared to the IT industry in general. In this regard critics are concerned that cloud providers may store sensitive information in jurisdictions that have weak laws related to privacy, protection and availability of data [12,16]. Given the cloud's significance to economic competitiveness and national security, policy makers need to look at developments in cloud-related institutions in other countries and take proactive measures to enact and enforce laws for developing the cloud industry.

In implementing data center according to the rules of the art offering the guarantees of continuity of service, rapid accessibility and secure backup of data according to international standards is another pillar of the G-Cloud.

4.2 The Energy Challenge for Security, Performance, and Availability

The security, performance, and availability are essential pillars in the cloud environment. Availability without fault and the guarantee of continuity of service require a constant availability of electricity to power data centers and a mechanism for cooling without fault. Landlocked climate Sudano-Sahelian, Burkina Faso knows country an energy deficit estimated in 2016 to 110 kwh/day [18] and water resource deficiency [19].

One of the challenges for Burkina Faso to ensure proper security for the G-Cloud is the challenge on the supply in sufficient quantity and quality of electric power in accordance with the need for power and stability required by the hardware. The distribution and consumption of electrical energy by computer equipment off a lot of heat and generally, the temperature quickly exceeds the thresholds recommended for the proper functioning of the equipment. A cooling device is therefore necessary. It is mainly based on the cooling of equipment, directed by forced cold air with forced convection or/and cooling water. Availability is an index that is measured by the ratio between the time during which the service is available and the total time required use either the sum 'uptime + downtime'.

Availability = uptime service/(time uptime + downtime of the service)

The energy efficiency index or PUE (Power Usage Effectiveness) is used to determine the energy actually available for computing resources. It allows to measure the efficiency of a data center and its ecological footprint.

With appropriate levels of security, trust and governance, service providers can provide a secure environment for company data and applications. For this, in the context of G-Cloud, it will ensure an adequate (quantity and quality) supply of electric power in accordance with the need for power and stability required by the hardware.

5   Conclusion

Cloud computing technology is increasingly used and it gives promising approaches for the government, public and private sectors of education and research, ICT, entrepreneurship, etc.

However, customers are also very concerned about the risks of Cloud Computing if not properly secured, and the loss of direct control over systems for which they are nonetheless accountable.

In developing countries, several arguments against cloud services can be discussed. The most critical one remains the security challenges. Cloud providers need to guarantee some aspects of security, performance, and availability for organizations to be more comfortable in service consumption.

References

1. Le Burkina Faso lance la construction d'une plateforme G-Cloud. http://www.jeuneafrique.com/264882/economie/burkina-faso-lance-construction-dune-plateforme-g-cloud/. Accessed 16 Sept 2015
2. G-CLOUD, la nouvelle trouvaille en informatique au Burina Faso. http://www.gouvernement.gov.bf/spip.php?article1574. Accessed 16 Nov 2015
3. G-cloud: l'avenir est dans le NUAGE - les avantages techniques - les avantages Economiques - les avantages Politiques et Sociaux. http://www.anptic.gov.bf/gcloud/
4. Mise en place d'un cloud gouvernemental: réduire les dépenses, gagner en rapidité et en flexibilité. http://news.aouaga.com/h/86603.html

5. Mathias, M., Baldreck, C.: Cloud computing concerns in developing economies. In: The Proceedings of the 9th Australian Information Security Management Conference (2011). http://ro.ecu.edu.au/ism/127

6. Juster, K.I.: Cloud computing can close the development gap. Salesforce.com. www.salesforce.com/assets/pdf/misc/IT-development-paper.pdf. Accessed 8 Nov 2011

7. Hong-Linh, T., Tran-Vu, P., Nam, T., Schahram, D.: Cloud computing for education and research in developing countries. doi:10.4018/978-1-4666-0957-0.ch005

8. Greengard, S.: Cloud computing and developing nations. Commun. ACM **53**(5), 18–20 (2010). http://cacm.acm.org/magazines/2010/5/87255-cloud-computing-and-developing-nations/fulltext. Accessed 8 Nov 2011

9. Parekh, D.H., Sridaran, R.: An analysis of security challenges in cloud computing. (IJACSA) Int. J. Adv. Comput. Sci. Appl. **4**(1), 38–46 (2013)

10. Kuyoro, S.O., Ibikunle, F., Awodele, O.: Cloud computing security issues and challenges. Int. J. Comput. Netw. (IJCN) **3**(5), 247–257 (2011)

11. Subashini, S., Kavitha, V.: A survey on security issues in service delivery models of cloud computing. J. Netw. Comput. Appl. **34**(1), 1–11 (2010)

12. Kaufman, L.M.: Data security in the world of cloud computing. IEEE Secur. Priv. **7**(4), 61–64 (2009). doi:10.1109/MSP.2009.87

13. Baikie, B., Hosman, L.: Green cloud computing in developing regions - moving data and processing closer to the end user. In: the 2011 Technical Symposium at ITU Telecom World Proceedings, Geneva, Switzerland, 24–27 October 2011, pp. 24–28

14. Nir, K.: Cloud computing in developing economies: drivers, effects, and policy measures. In: PTC 2010 Proceedings. University of North Carolina-Greensboro, pp. 1–22 (2010). Accessed 8 Nov 2011

15. Mell, P., Grance, T.: The NIST definition of cloud computing. National Institute of Standards and Technology Special Publication 800–145, September 2011

16. Edwards, J.: Cutting through the fog of cloud security. In: Computerworld, Framingham, 23 February 2009, vol. 43, no. 8, p. 26, 3 pages

17. Cloud Security Alliance: Security Guidance for Critical Areas of Focus in Cloud Computing V2.1. http://www.cloudsecurityalliance.org/csaguide.pdf

18. Délestage en 2016: De fort à modéré, prévoit la SONABEL. http://www.burkina24.com/2016/03/04/delestage-en-2016-de-fort-a-modere-prevoit-la-sonabel/. Accessed 4 Mar 2016. Par Abdou ZOURE

19. Pénurie d'eau à Ouagadougou: Un déficit de plus 27.000 m^3 en 2016. http://www.burkina24.com/2015/03/13/penurie-deau-a-ouagadougou-un-deficit-de-plus-27-000-m3-en-2016/. Accessed 13 Mar 2015. par Redaction B24

Mobile VPN Schemes: Technical Analysis and Experiments

Daouda Ahmat[1,2]($\boxtimes$), Mahamat Barka[2], and Damien Magoni[3]

[1] Virtual University of Chad, N'Djamena, Chad
daouda.ahmat@uvt.td
[2] University of N'Djamena, N'Djamena, Chad
mahamat.barka@gmail.com
[3] University of Bordeaux – LaBRI, Bordeaux, France
magoni@labri.fr

Abstract. A new class of Virtual Private Networks (VPN), which supports both security and mobility, has recently emerged. Called mobile VPN, these systems provide not only secure tunnels but also session continuity mechanisms despite location change or connection disruptions. These mechanisms enable secure sessions to survive in dynamic/mobile environments without requiring a renegotiation of security keys during the session resumption phase. In this paper, we compare four open-source mobile VPNs in terms of functionality and performance.

Keywords: Mobile VPN · Resilient session · Seamless resumption

1 Introduction

A Virtual Private Network (VPN) provides increased security between two remote entities that exchange data through untrusted networks such as the Internet [1]. VPN systems prevent against various attacks such eavesdropping or replay. However, traditional VPNs fail to support the mobility of users. Indeed, network failures automatically break-up secure tunnels and involve a subsequent renegotiation that is then necessary to reestablish broken tunnels. Such a negotiation involves expensive computational operations in order to restore tunnels as well as transport and application layers connections. This phase of negotiation causes not only significant latency but also presents risks of Man-In-The-Middle attacks. Traditional VPNs can not therefore effectively operate in dynamic and/or mobile environments.

Mobile devices and dynamic environments become pervasive in the Internet. However, for instance traditional VPN infrastructures do not support session continuity result from location change or network reconfiguration. After each connection disruption, key renegotiation process is needed to restore broken tunnel. In order to address network failures resulting from location changes or network reconfigurations, several solutions were proposed in the literature [2–7].

© ICST Institute for Computer Sciences, Social Informatics and Telecommunications Engineering 2018
T.F. Bissyande and O. Sie (Eds.): AFRICOMM 2016, LNICST 208, pp. 88–97, 2018.
https://doi.org/10.1007/978-3-319-66742-3_9

2   Mobile VPN Technologies

Up to now, several mobile VPN solutions have been proposed in various research papers. In this section, we describe some leading examples of mobile VPN systems and technical concepts in this area proposed in literature.

2.1   N2N

In opposition to most dynamic VPN systems, these systems have the advantage to be fairly scalable and to have ability to communicate across NAT and firewalls. Decentralized P2P VPN are flexible and self-organizing infrastructures that enable users to create their own secure networks upon an untrusted network. A layer 2 peer-to-peer VPN (see Fig. 1), called N2N [2], and ELA [8] topologies are very similar despite the fact that N2N is based on the OSI layer 2 whereas ELA is based on the OSI layer 3. However the use of super nodes in N2N limits its full scalability as these nodes have a more important role than the other nodes and thus they can weaken the overall strength of the N2N network and may even break its connectivity if they fail.

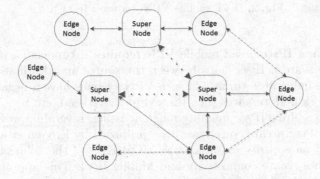

Fig. 1. Example of N2N topology.

Freelan [9] is a multi-platform and open-source peer-to-peer VPN that abstracts a LAN over the Internet. Based over the UDP protocol, the Free-LAN Secure Channel Protocol (FSCP) is designed to be secure and efficient, and it tries to reduce the network overhead. In addition, Freelan systems can be configured to act according to a client/server, peer-to-peer or hybrid model whichever suits best.

2.2   IPSec + Mobile IP

Mobile VPN systems based on both IPsec [10] and Mobile IP [11] have been proposed several times such as in [7,12–15], in order to attempt to overcome the inherent mobility drawbacks of traditional VPNs. Nevertheless, as explained in [16], many problems arise from the combination between IPsec and MobileIP. In order to overcome these problems, a model has been proposed which is based on the use of two HAs (Home Agents) - internal HA and external HA - and two FAs (Foreign Agents) - internal FA and external FA - by Vaarala et al. in [17]. However, this model imposes the use of three imbricated tunnels ({x-MIP{GW{i-MIP{original packet}}}}), as shown in Fig. 2.

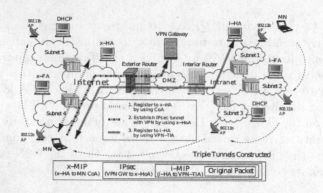

Fig. 2. IETF mobile VPN (source: IETF).

In addition, a IPsec-based mobile VPN requires n tunnels (n security layers) when there are n IPsec hops between the source and destination entities. Therefore, the imbricated tunnels in such VPN systems have a negative impact on their network performances (i.e., throughput, overhead, etc.).

In order to address IPsec mobility inherent issues, several improved schemes based on the IPsec architecture have been proposed by Eronen et al. in [4,18], or [19]. Based on security extensions to MOBIKE [4], the solution described in [19] combines secure connectivity and Mobile IPv4. This approach resolves considerably the issues notified in [16] such as overhead, NAT traversal or mobility problems due to the combination of IPsec and Mobile IPv4. These solutions are however not free of scalability issues and network overhead that they inherit from IPsec and Mobile IP.

Based upon the NEMO architecture [20], the mobile VPN scheme presented in [21] provides secure connectivity between vehicles for public transportation. In other words, this model provides secure vehicle to vehicle (V2V) communications as well as secured communications between passengers in the same (or in a different) vehicle. As the above mobile VPN solutions, this current model is designed to use the best properties of MOBIKE and Mobile IP.

The dynamic VPN approach proposed in [22] enables to use alternately IPsec in Full-Mesh mode or in Hub mode with a centralized IPsec Gateway. The first mode is only used when routing problems occur. This architecture extends MOBIKE in order to support dynamic tunnels. However, this model is not designed to support mobility.

Another proposal leveraging MOBIKE is presented by Migault in [23], where they propose an alternative End-to-End security (E2E) architecture based on their own MOBIKEX protocol, which extends the MOBIKE mobility and multihoming features to multiple interfaces and to the transport mode of IPsec. Based on a topology organized in communities, peer-to-peer (P2P) mobile VPN systems have also been proposed such as ELA [8] or N2N [24].

2.3 HIP-Based Mobile VPN

The Host Identity Protocol (HIP) [3,6] is an architecture that provides both mobility and multihoming services. HIP introduces a new name space that enables the separation between the host identity, called Host Identity Tag or HIT, and the host location, as shown in Fig. 3. Each HIP host is uniquely identified by the public key of its public/private key pair. When a mobile node changes its point of network attachment, its IP address is then changed and the new IP address will be communicated to its correspondent hosts. However, in addition to remaining at an experiment stage for some years, HIP introduces a new layer between the transport and the network layers in the OSI stack. This implies that the host's operating system must be modified in order to use HIP although a user-space implementation does exist.

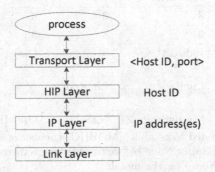

Fig. 3. HIP layer within the TCP/IP stack.

In order to provide both security and mobility, HIP has been extended in two subsequent proposals: Hi3 [25] and SPEAR [26]. Previously known as P2P SIP-over-HIP (p2pship), SPEAR was originally designed for SIP-based communication applications (i.e., SIP proxy), allowing users to make peer-to-peer voice/video calls, without the help of a centralized SIP infrastructure. It now supports various protocols and applications. HIP is used as data transport, making the connections secure and enabling features such as mobility and multihoming.

3   Evaluation

In this section, we present a functional analysis as well as the experiment environment and the results of the evaluation of our approach MUSeS [5] and three state-of-art solutions, namely: N2N, HIP and MOBIKE.

3.1   Functional Analysis

Table 1 describes the technical comparison between MOBIKE, N2N, HIP and MUSeS. Indeed, all these systems are based on UDP to exchange information in both handshake and re-handshake steps. The MUSeS middleware has the smallest number of exchanged packets for these two phases of communication. While both HIP and MUSeS proceed through direct connection, MOBIKE is based on indirect secure connection (through an IPSec gateway) and N2N is based on triangular negotiation in both handshake and re-handshake phases. For the two first systems, mobility is limited. This means that only *N2N Edge Node* and *MOBIKE client* can be really mobile.

Table 1. Comparison of the evaluated mobile VPN systems.

Mobile VPN system	MOBIKE	N2N	HIP	MUSeS
Handshake packets	8	3	3	2
Re-handshake packets	6	3	3	2
Secure connection mode	Indirect[1]	Triangular[2]	Direct	Direct
Mobility supported by systems	Limited[3]	Limited[3]	√	√
Implementations	StrongSwan [27]	N2N [2]	OpenHIP [28]	MUSeS [29]

[1] An IPsec Gateway is needed to establish MOBIKE connections.
[2] Both peers connect to a Super Node before establishing a direct connection.
[3] Only a client (or Edge Node) can be mobile.

Security Analysis: A Mobile VPN enables, in one hand, to secure communication and to keep open application sessions during location change. In other hand, mobile VPN is free to session key renegotiation in the resumption phase. These two technical properties are needed in secure mobile environments. Despite their interesting properties, the systems that operate in autonomous and mobile environments are constantly subject to some security challenges such as DoS and replay attacks.

To prevent replay attacks, MUSeS packets are built by adding sequence number to their headers. In other words, each packet is separately identified by its sequence number added to its header. Thus, when a packet is replayed, it will be automatically detected and subsequently it will be destroyed.

In the resumption phase, a Re-hello is generated and then sent in order to restore interrupted session without using session key renegotiation mechanism. However, Re-hello packet could be replayed because it does not contain a sequence number in order to detect replay attack. Thus, a malicious user that has infiltrated the network could then send a succession of Re-hello packets with the aim of perpetrating Denial-of-Service (DoS) attacks. In addition, the receiver peer cannot determine which packet is the last one received among other received packets, otherwise this problem could be solved easily. In concrete terms, on receiving Re-hello, the receiver peer processes it in order to resolve and, the challenge and before finishing, it receives another, again another, etc. Finally, the target peer will be saturated by a flooding of Re-hello requests. Furthermore, HIP could be vulnerable to DoS attacks in the resumption phase as shown in the paper analyzing HIP protocol security [30].

To address this security issue, MUSeS assigns a timestamp when sending to each Re-hello packet in order to recognize the freshest request among received requests. In this way, the MUSeS system tries to prevent DoS attacks that use an uninterrupted sequence of Re-hello packets. Due to their mobility, flexibility and autonomy, P2P-based VPN systems are unfortunately not totally invulnerable to intrusion of malicious users. Indeed, in fully decentralized P2P networks, each peer can join and leave the network at any time and usually without any authentication. In our system, authentication is guaranteed by using challenge messages.

Typically, to authenticate a peer over the network, a node encrypts a random challenge message and sends it to its corresponding peer. On receiving this message, the corresponding peer decrypts it and sends the same message to the initiator peer. Thus, the initiator peer ascertains the identity of the corresponding peer.

The HIP protocol is designed to be resistant to Denial of Service (DoS) and Man in the Middle (MitM) attacks, and when used with ESP enabled, it provides DoS and MitM protection to upper layer protocols, such as TCP and UDP.

In N2N and MOBIKE however, there can be no secure tunnels without a N2N-Super-Node or a MOBIKE-GW. In other words, when N2N-Super-Nodes and MOBIKE-GWs are unavailable, any secure communication is then impossible. The HIP protocol and MUSeS do not suffer from these impairments.

Although MUSeS offers a solid security mechanism in remote communication between two peers, there is, however, a security weak point in local applicative connections. Unlike communication between two MUSeS peers, local communication between MUSeS and applications is not secured. This means that an unauthorized user application launched by a malicious user should establish connection with a remote honest MUSeS or eavesdrop exchanged traffic between MUSeS and local applications. This untrusted communication should cause security issues.

On the one hand, to prevent external malicious processes to connect to MUSeS, only local applications are authorized to connect to MUSeS by loopback address. On the other hand, only the root user can catch, by using *tcpdump* or *wireshark*, local traffic passed through from local applications to the MUSeS middleware and conversely. Therefore, plain text data exchanged between local applications and MUSeS are protected.

Mobility Analysis: MOBIKE and N2N are both based upon permanent virtual addresses in order to identify separately mobile nodes. However, when N2N-Super-Node and MOBIKE-Gateway (MOBIKE-GW) change their network points of attachment, any mobility would be possible. Thus, these systems have limited mobility. Indeed, MOBIKE authorizes only the mobility for initiators. However, in addition to mobility, MOBIKE supports also multi-homing for initiators. This means that MOBIKE mobile nodes can have several network interfaces and use them in order to support network link breakdown. In opposition to MOBIKE, all two endpoints of a N2N tunnel keep up mobility.

HIP introduces an interesting scheme of mobility and multi-addressing over IPv4 and IPv6 networks and it is designed to work in a NAT-less environment. Indeed, the HIP hosts do not change identities during location changes; this implies network addresses changes. Each HIP host is identified by its public key that is self-certified, called *Host Identity* (HI). Thus, when a mobile node changes its IP address, it notifies its currently active peers by sending a control packet containing its new location. When correspondent peers change simultaneous their location, the previous notifying method fails and a deadlock will occur. However, HIP introduces a *rendezvous* mechanism in order to address this simultaneous mobility issue. Unlike previous mobility methods, MUSeS proposes a new mobility scheme based on identifiers provided by a DHT infrastructure [31].

Each MUSeS host is identified separately by a name and an address defined as coordinates taken from the hyperbolic plane.

An *Interruption Detection* mechanism is introduced by MUSeS to detect failures and to subsequently activate the SRM module. SRM is based on keepalive messages which are periodically sent. Thus, when network failures occur within lower layers, communication will be temporarily interrupted and failures will be confined within SRM and hidden to higher layers. Due to these properties, mobility is transparent to both user applications running over MUSeS middleware and all the other MUSeS modules, except the SRM component. Therefore, loopback connections established between MUSeS and local applications survive to networks failures despite network attachment point change events, for instance.

3.2 Performance Analysis

In order to assess those four VPN technologies in a mobility scenario, we have used a tool called Network Emulator For Mobile Universes (NEmu), developed by Vincent Autefage and presented in [32].

An experiment has been carried out with the above implementation in a dynamic environment composed of one mobile node. A mobile node inside this environment has the ability to leave one network (one virtual router) in order to join another one (another virtual router). This event causes a network failure during the move until a possible subsequent reconnection. This disruption is transparent for the application and it does not prevent the MUSeS system from continuing to run despite the fact that the mobile node is disconnected for a moment. Technically, in our experimentation, the node mobility consists in causing an artificial failure on a virtual network interface. We disconnect a virtual wire from a virtual switch and reconnect it on another virtual switch. The MUSeS system hides this network change not only to the user's application but also to the remote corresponding node.

Figures 4, 5, 6 and 7 show the evolution of the throughput between the two corresponding applications over time. For all systems, the network interruption happens at the 40th second after the start of the experiment and the throughput instantly drops to zero in the time intervals [40 s; 60 s]. This means that the disruption duration is 20 s. The connectivity is reestablished at the network and CLOAK level at the 60th second. However, due to latency, the throughput remains at zero after the 60th second until the effective recovery. This latency varies from one system to another. Indeed, whereas MUSeS middleware has a latency of 3 s (see Fig. 7), MOBIKE, N2N and HIP protocols have respectively latencies of 12 s (see Fig. 6), 51 s (see Fig. 4) and 13 s (see Fig. 5).

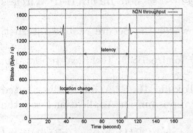

Fig. 4. N2N resumption latency.

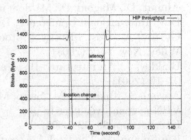

Fig. 5. HIP resumption latency.

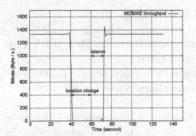

Fig. 6. MOBIKE resumption latency.

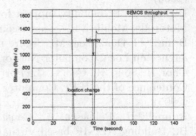

Fig. 7. MUSeS resumption latency.

4 Conclusion

Disrupted networks, due to both poor-quality devices and technical skills deficiency, are pervasive in developing countries, particularly in Africa. In theses areas, secured resilient sessions are needed to overcome both security and performance issues inherent to connection disruptions. In this paper, we have presented four open-source mobile VPN solutions, have provided a detailed technical analysis of those systems and have compared them in terms of functionality and performance. Results show that MUSeS is a competitive solution for providing secure and mobile communications.

References

1. Berger, T.: Analysis of current VPN technologies. In: The First International Conference on Availability, Reliability and Security, ARES 2006, 8 pp. (2006)
2. Deri, L., Andrews, R.: N2N. http://www.ntop.org/products/n2n/
3. Moskowitz, R., Nikander, P.: Host Identity Protocol (HIP) architecture. IETF RFC 4423 (2006)
4. Eronen, P.: IKEv2 mobility and multihoming protocol (MOBIKE). IETF RFC 4555 (2006)
5. Ahmat, D., Magoni, D.: MUSeS: mobile user secured session. In: 5th IFIP Wireless Days International Conference, Dublin, Irland
6. Gurtov, A.: Host Identity Protocol (HIP): Towards the Secure Mobile Internet. Wiley, New York (2008)
7. Binkley, J.: An integrated IPsec and mobile-IP for freeBSD. Technical report, pp. 01–10 (2001)
8. Aoyagi, S., Takizawa, M., Saito, M., Aida, H., Tokuda, H.: ELA: a fully distributed VPN system over peer-to-peer network. In: Symposium on Applications and the Internet, pp. 89–92 (2005)
9. Kauffmann, J.: The freeLAN secure channel protocol (2011). https://github.com/ereOn/libfscp/blob/1.0/fscp.txt
10. Kent, S., Seo, K.: Security architecture for the internet protocol. IETF RFC 4301 (2005)
11. Perkins, C.: IP mobility support for IPv4. IETF RFC 3344 (2002)
12. Motorolla: Mobile VPN, secure connectivity on the move. White paper (2008)
13. Braun, T., Danzeisen, M.: Secure mobile IP communication. In: 26th IEEE Conference on Local Computer Networks, pp. 586–593 (2001)
14. Choi, H., Song, H., Cao, G., La Porta, T.: Mobile multi-layered IPsec. In: 24th Joint Conference of the IEEE Computer and Communications Societies, pp. 1929–1939 (2005)
15. Ruppelt, R., Pelinescu, A., Constantin, C., Floroiu, J., Sisalem, D., Butscher, B.: Building ALL-IP based virtual private networks in mobile environment. In: International Work on Informatic and Mobile Communication over Wireless LAN, Research and Applications (2001)
16. Adrangi, F., Levkowetz, H., Statement, P.: Mobile IPv4 traversal of virtual private network gateways. IETF RFC 4093 (2005)
17. Vaarala, S., Klovning, E.: Mobile IPv4 traversal across IPsec-based VPN gateways. IETF RFC 5265 (2008)

18. Devarapalli, V., Eronen, P.: Secure connectivity and mobility using mobile IPv4 and IKEv2 mobility and multihoming (MOBIKE). IETF RFC 5266 (2008)
19. Karbasioun, M.M., Berenjkub, M., Taji, B.: Securing mobile IP communications using MOBIKE protocol. In: International Conference on Telecommunications (2008)
20. Devarapalli, V., Wakikawa, R., Petrescu, A., Thubert, P.: Network mobility (NEMO) basic support protocol. IETF RFC 3963 (2005)
21. Petrescu, A., Olivereau, A.: Mobile VPN and V2V NEMO for public transportation. In: 9th International Conference on Intelligent Transport Systems Telecommunications, pp. 63–68 (2009)
22. Ishimura, K., Tamura, T., Mizuno, S., Sato, H., Motono, T.: Dynamic IP-VPN architecture with secure IPsec tunnels. In: Symposium on Information and Telecommunication Technologies (2010)
23. Migault, D., Palomares, D., Herbert, E., You, W., Ganne, G., Arfaoui, G., Laurent, M.: E2E: an optimized IPsec architecture for secure and fast offload. In: International Conference on Availability, Reliability and Security, pp. 365–374 (2012)
24. Deri, L., Andrews, R.: N2N: a layer two peer-to-peer VPN. In: Interntional Conference on Autonomous Infrastructure, Management and Security, pp. 53–64 (2008)
25. Gurtov, A., Korzun, D., Lukyanenko, A., Nikander, P.: Hi3: an efficient and secure networking architecture for mobile hosts. Comput. Commun. **31**(10), 2457–2467 (2008)
26. Koskela, J.: A Secure Peer-to-Peer Application Framework (SPEAR - A Secure Peer-To-Peer Services Overlay Architecture) (2010). https://archive.li/ycvnN
27. Steffen, A.: StrongSwan. http://www.strongswan.org
28. Henderson, T.: OpenHIP. http://www.openhip.org
29. Ahmat, D.: SEcure MObile session. http://www.labri.fr/magoni/cape/
30. Aura, T., Nagarajan, A., Gurtov, A.: Analysis of the HIP base exchange protocol. In: Boyd, C., González Nieto, J.M. (eds.) ACISP 2005. LNCS, vol. 3574, pp. 481–493. Springer, Heidelberg (2005). doi:10.1007/11506157_40
31. Tiendrebeogo, T., Ahmat, D., Magoni, D., Sié, O.: Virtual connections in P2P overlays with DHT-based name to address resolution. Int. J. Adv. Internet Technol. **5**(1), 11–25 (2012)
32. Autefage, V., Magoni, D.: Network emulator: a network virtualization testbed for overlay experimentations. In: 17th IEEE International Workshop on Computer-Aided Modeling Analysis and Design of Communication Links and Networks, pp. 38–42 (2012)

Proposals of Architecture for Adapting Cloud Computing Services to User's Context

Kanga Koffi[1(✉)], Babri Michel[2], Goore Bi Tra[2],
and Brou Konan Marcelin[2]

[1] Ecole Doctorale Polytechnique de l'Institut Nationale Polytechnique Félix
Houphouët Boigny (EDP/INPHB), UMRI 78: Electronique et Electricité
Appliquée Laboratoire de Recherche en Informatique et Télécommunication,
Yamoussoukro, Ivory Coast
`koffi.kanga@larit.net`
[2] Institut National Polytechnique Félix Houphouët Boigny (INPHB),
UMRI 78: Electronique et Electricité Appliquée Laboratoire de Recherche
en Informatique et Télécommunication, Yamoussoukro, Ivory Coast
`{michel.babri,goore,kmbrou}@inphb.edu.ci`

Abstract. In cloud computing service providers offer services to be used by
customers. Given the increasing number of clients and also the variety of their
needs, some users adjust services to their context. Also context may differ from
those services. For this, we propose in this paper a set of tools (architecture and
algorithm) for achieving this adaptation taking into account the specificities
related to the context of the user. This set, knowing the services offered by
suppliers, enables the user to make an adjustment using methods to construct the
user context and the research service related to this context. The result obtained
after the different tests carried out shows that our tool could be a better simulation environment of research and selection service adaption like in other
environments.

Keywords: Cloud computing · CloudAdapt · Cloud architecture · Adaptation
of services · Context awareness · Cloud computing simulator

1 Introduction

Talking about service adaptation in cloud computing deserves explanations. In fact
cloud computing is a service delivery model which involves two types of actors which
are suppliers and customers. In this model, clients who are the users pay proportionally
to their consumption just like water, electricity gas, fuel and other services. In this
condition, cloud computing becomes the fifth supply model like the last mentioned.

Today, with the advent of internet of thing and also given the high mobility rate of
cloud computing services users in the process of service consumption, users would like
to adjust those services to their context. Context could refer to desired functional
characteristic that is to say the working material environment (CPU value, screen size,
Ram value etc. …) and the geographic location of users. This work aims at finding a tool
to carry out experiments work to adapt services to the context of the user. In other words

© ICST Institute for Computer Sciences, Social Informatics and Telecommunications Engineering 2018
T.F. Bissyande and O. Sie (Eds.): AFRICOMM 2016, LNICST 208, pp. 98–110, 2018.
https://doi.org/10.1007/978-3-319-66742-3_10

it aims to develop a set of tools for performing an adaptation of service. In other words it is meant to set up a simulator for performing an adaptation of services. In the literature, several simulation tools exist. However, those tools are used to carry out precise experimentations due to the diversity of their architecture (network, ecological environment, etc. .....). Thus, in Sect. 2 of this article, we shall present the simulation tool in cloud environment that are known to us. We shall end this section with a summary on those tools by highlighting the common points and also possible differences. In Sect. 3, the research problem will be presented in order to justify the completion of this current work. As for Sect. 4 it will give way to our simulation platform by presenting its architecture, its functioning and differents components necessary for its implementation and the underlying data model to achieve the adaptive function assigned to it. We shall conclude in Sect. 6 after discussion in Sect. 5 while generating possible future works.

2 State of the Art

In research, any theory must go through an experimentation or simulation phase before its validation. Thus, research works in cloud computing found their experimentation through a simulator. In the literature several simulators (tools) exist. Here we will present some of them we consider representative for the area in which these tool are used and their architecture without forgetting the various features.

2.1 Cloud Simulator Architecture

2.1.1 Cloudsim Architecture

The cloudsim architecture is shown on Fig. 1. This architecture has a layered structure. At the lower level is its simulation engine SimJava, which allows the implementation of required functions for a high level simulation. On the upper level (network) are the network management function between the different Data centers. As for the resources they are in this architecture from the previous allocation services (VM, CPU, MEMORY and bandwidth) in this architecture of cloudsim there is also the presence of "broker" and "cloudlet". In fact brokers manage the creation and the destruction of

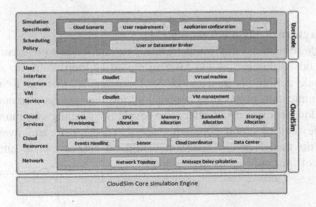

Fig. 1. Architecture of CloudSim [7]

VM. In its uppermost layer there is the user code outlining the characteristics of physical machine (number of machine and their technical specificity).

2.1.2   GreenCloud Architecture [11, 15, 20]

GreenCloud here is an extension of the simulator network NS-2. Basically speaking, it implements energy management in data centers environment. The objective of this simulator is to reduce energy consumption at the data center level while facilitating the consumption of cloud services by users. Also this simulator appears as the basis for the design, manufacture, use and disposal of IT resources with minimal environmental damage. Its includes a datacenter (containing physical machines), cloud computing users (who consume the services), or the switch nodes (for communication between different cloud spread infrastructure)

2.1.3   Architecture of CloudAnalyst [11]

CloudAnalyst is an extension of CloudSim [5]. Therefore, its architecture (Fig. 3) would be inspired and included that of Cloudsim. The difference between the two architectures lies in the integration of a graphical user interface (GUI) in that of Cloudanalyst. Mathematically speaking, the architecture of CloudAnalyst is the sum of that of cloudsim and graphical interface management functions of GUI (Fig. 4). (Fig. 2)

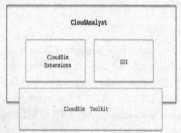

Fig. 2. Architecture of CloudAnalyst   **Fig. 3.** Perspective view of CloudAnalyst [13]

2.1.4   Architecture NetWorkcloudSim [11]

According to these authors, this simulator has been designed to overcome the short-comings of cloudsim, GreenSim and MDSim regarding their ability to allow deployment of network aplications in a cloud. So NetworkCloudSim is a simulator that supports communication between an application and the various elements of the network from a cloud computing. It offers two levels of planning communication tasks between the devices of cloud computing service consumers and available virtual machines. To do this, NetworkCloudSim would be appropriate to simulate a networking protocol for applications in the cloud.

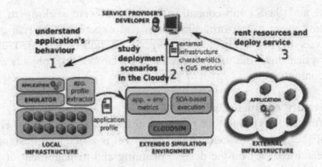

Fig. 4. Architecture EMUSIM

2.1.5 Architecture EMUSIM

This tool was developed to predict the behavior of the applications hosted on cloud computing platforms. Its implementation has required the use of two systems: AEF (Automated Emulation Framework) for emulation applications and CloudSim for the simulation of cloud computing. In its architecture (Fig. 4), we notice the presence of cloud service providers, users, local and external infrastructure to assess the behavior of applications.

2.1.6 Architecture DCSim (DataCenter Simulator)

This tool was developed to overcome the need for evaluation of datacenter management systems. It offers its members a virtual IaaS infrastructure. In its architecture there is the presence of datacenter containing each of the physical machines. Each physical machine hosting multiple virtual machines. On these machines are installed applications.

2.1.7 Architecture GroudSim (Grid and Cloud Simulator)

This simulator is an event-based tool (any changes that might occur in the grids or cloud computing) designed for grid computing applications. For event management it uses threads. According to its authors, given its reputation acquired in various areas of IaaS, it could be used in cloud computing management through IaaS and consideration

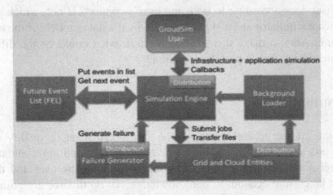

Fig. 5. Architecture of GroudSim

platforms PaaS and SaaS. Subsequently, the authors were seeking to integrate an Askalon to allow users to perform simulation and experiment in real environment. After an analysis of its architecture in Fig. 5, GroudSim included cloud events (withdrawal physical machine to VM), users (User GroudSim), objects and entity of grid or cloud computing.

2.1.8   Architecture of Open Cirrus

According to (the authors), this tool would be a testbed sponsored by HP, Intel and YAHOO in collaboration with some organizations. It is a free tool designed for cloud computing research focuses on the design, planning and management of resources at the Datacenter. The designers of this testbed have set the following objectives:

- boost research at the level of cloud computing system
- encourage research on new cloud computing applications
- to produce data collections in cloud computing
- make available to users of **source code** and **APIs** necessary to enable services (Application s) to interact with him.

2.1.9   Limitation of these Architectures

Given these architectures, one notices that their different authors have made huge contributions. However, some aspects of the services, users and their contexts and their profiles have not been taken into account.

3   Research Problem

In this literature review, it appears that excellent research works have been done. Those works have led to the development of cloud computing simulators of which we have presented the most representative in terms of their features and interesting architectures. However, these simulators still suffering limitation making it impossible to perform, some work including the adaptation or adjustment of services taking into account the specificities related to the user and his working environment, its physical characteristics and also the conditions under which a service could be consumed. The question that arises in this conditions is the following: is there a tool for achieving adaptation or adjustment of services according to taste and user's context? If not, which architecture could have such a simulator and also what would be the data model for the operation of this architecture. Also to make this simulator smart, what could be the different tools (algorithms) necessary for its perfect operation?

4   Contribution

The state of the art we presented reveals the significant level of quality of research conducted in order to establish a more complete cloud computing simulation framework. However some aspects, profile and context for both the user and the services have not been taken into account to our knowledge. To do this we are going present a

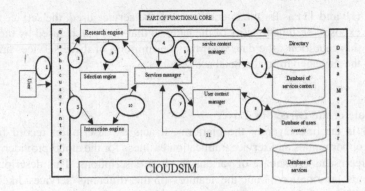

Fig. 6. Architecture of our proposal

tool with methods and algorithms to give intelligence to the architecture shown in Fig. 6, and data models to the research, the selection of services and interaction with the user.

4.1 Architecture of Our Proposal

Our architecture consists of two main parts:

- GUI: it allows dialogue or interaction between the user and the tool through the part of the user queries emissions and the simulator answers
- a functional kernel consists of a data manager and a functionality manager or application manager. In this second part, *the data Manager* consists of the sources of management of different contextual elements that are: service settings and user settings without forgetting services directories and data sent from the services. As for *functionality manager,* it abounds in research functions and service selection as well as interactions included during these phases.

4.2 Our Proposal Operation

The functioning of our architecture follows the steps explained below.

Step 1:   First, the user connects to the cloud platform based on information related to his profile (email, name, password, etc.).

Step 2:   After this step, the user can conduct the research services to consume (2); or interact with services (3).

Step 3:   If the user is looking for services, service manager of the platform receives from the service directory the list of services relevant to the user context (4).

Step 4:   In (5) the user comes into contact with the service context manager to request different services contexts actually stored in the context database service (6). Also the service manager contacts the context user manager (7) to request the context of the existing user in the context of database thereof (8). If the desired service is found, it can be consumed if befits the context thereof.

Step 5:   **(10 and 11)** as for the interaction with the service used, the service manager exposes the functionality of the latter so that they can be used by the user. In this conditions, the data from the consumption of these services are sent to the manager from the database services.

4.2.1   Role of the Directory Layer

This layer is the first layer of the platform. It acts as description record figure by providing opportunities and service publication easiness for the cloud provider. In other words, it represents a database of various services descriptions. This description contains various information about the features of the differents services likely to be consumed. These features are used to check if the services that the user wants to consume are compatible or adapted to its context. Therefore, the directory sends the list of services adapted to the context of the user via the service manager.

4.2.2   Role of the Service Manager

The service manager is the second layer of architecture. He is responsible for managing the process of adaptation and restitution of adaptation results (relevant services) to the user. Indeed, this layer is responsible for managing adaptation during the search for service to find a list of relevant services in the context of the user and also during interacting with the Cloud computing services to dynamically adapt the services after possible changes occurring in the context of the user (change of location, change the level of energy for moving objects, change of system operation, size of the ram, etc.)

4.2.3   Role of the Context Layer

In a context of restitution to the user of cloud services a service adapted to its context and the change of the same context, we take charge in our platform the service context so as to improve the quality of adaptation. To do this, we endow this layer with two (2) elements: the context of service and the user context. The context of service is responsible for managing the different contexts in which a cloud service can be consumed. Thereby, he receives from cloud providers the differents contexts in which each service can be used; it stores these settings in a database (DB service context) and then restores them through the service manager when services related are sought by users. As for the user's context manager, it captures the context of a user and the stock in a database (DB user context). In this context the database user is invoked using procedures, functions and components we have set up for this purpose.

4.3   Method of Construction of the User Context Profile

In the cloud, the consumption of a service is achieved through the user's connection to the provider's service platform. So in our architecture platform, this connection is made from a graphical interface in which the user declares preferences of services corresponding to his taste consumption. In our architecture; we classify preferences in the following categories:

- preferences related to service content (**Pc**)
- preferences related to the display of data, network characteristics, the cost of services, language, etc. (**Pa**)

Thus defined Pa and Pc, the entire global preferences is obtained by the union of the two previous categories. Let **P = U PaPa** with **Pc = {P1, P2... Pn}**. Preferences being defined, we define the context based information related to the user's environment, his working device, his network at his session and also his balance. This information is represented as follows:

C is set of user context and Cj is element of the user's context (with $j \in [1, k]$, where k is the maximum number of context item).

The needs of service consumer being in constant change and also given the large number of services offered to users by suppliers, possible conflicts between the preferences (Pa) and contextual information could occur. In that way we offer in our platform CloudAdapt an algorithm called **UserContexte(0 algorithm) is used** to overcome such problems. This algorithm has the role to check whether each **Pi** preference of the user corresponds or not to contextual information. Therefore, it helps determine preferences compatible with the contextual information of the user when - tries to connect with the cloud platform. In this connection, our platform recovers **(Capture (SC, EC))** session's information **(SC), environment context (EC),** its working device **(DC)** and network **(CN)** and stores **(Save ((SC, EC), UC)** in a database (user context). (Fig. 7)

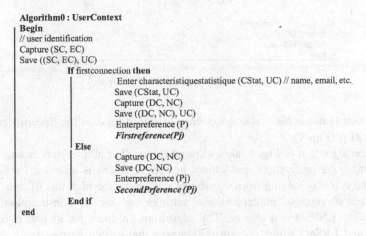

Fig. 7. Pseudo code of usercontext

Operation of the "UserContext" algorithm:

This algorithm in its operation goes through the following steps:

Step1:   **user identification**

In this step, the user entered his login, password and other information likely to help in his identification through the procedure **Capture (SC, EC)** and then stores the backup or through the **Save** procedure **((SC, EC) UC).**

Step2:   **checking connections**

At this stage our algorithm checks whether the user is logging in on our platform for the first time.

If this is the *case, step 1* is executed and then the user is invited to make known their preferences through **EntrerPreferences** procedure **(P).** In this case the procedure **FirstPreference (Pj) (Fig.** 8) in turn analyzes the preferences to determine which is compatible with the characteristics of the user environment to a successful adaptation of this preference. This algorithm takes as input the set of user preferences and produces at its output two (2) preference lists with their content in the overall set of user preferences. Indeed, the set of lists are: the list of preferences to satisfy **(LPSat)** and those that cannot be met **(LPNSat).**

Algorithm1. FirstPreference

Input : p = set of user preference
Output : LPSat = list of user preference for satisfaction
LPNSat = liste containing preferences which cannot be satisfied

Begin
J is integer = 0
n is integer // number of preference
            While j ≤ n
                        If can_satisfyPj,(Pj) **then**
                        Add (Pj, LPSat)
                        Else
                        Add (Pj, LPNSat)
                        Endif
            J ++
            End while
Ruturn (LPSat)
Return (LPNSat)
End

Fig. 8. Pseudo code of FirstPreference

If the user is not at his first connection, our algorithm uses the **SecondPreference** procedure **(Pj) (Fig.** 9).

Here the algorithm of **Fig.** 8 takes as input the set **P** of all preferences and **LNPSat** list containing the preferences that cannot be met. This list is included for user preferences and contexts ranging from significant way given the high rate of user mobility and different changes of implementation settings and service consumption, the list could undergo LNPSat real change. This algorithm produces for its part two (2) lists **(LNPSat** and **LPSat)** which contain preferences that cannot be met again and compatible preferences easy to meet. To produce these two lists, this algorithm **"Secondpreference"** research in **P** the preferences compatible with the characteristics of the user's environment and the latter does not exist in **LPNSat.** Depending on the case, this preference may or not be added to LPNSat. If **Pj** belongs to **LNPSat** with other values then it will be removed from and added to **LNPSatLPSat.**

If **LPSat**, have multiple values, our algorithm gives priority to the new value set by the user during the current session compared to values from **LPNSat.** However if after

---

Algorithm2. SecondPreference

Input : p = set of user preference
LPSat = list of user preference for satisfaction
LPNSat = liste containing preferences which cannot be satisfied
Output : LPSat = New list of user preference for satisfaction
LPNSat = New liste containing preferences which cannot be satisfied

---

Begin
J is integer = 0
n is integer // number of preference
VP(j) is array of string
    While j ≤ n
            If can_satisfy,(Pj) **then**
            If LPNSat⊃ V(Pj) Then
            delete (Pj, LPNSat)
            Else
                If can_satisfy(VPj) then
                delete (Pj, LPNSat)
                endif
              add (Pj, LPSat)
            End if
            //
            If LNPSat contain Pj whith other values **then**
                If LPNSat ⊃ V(Pj) **Then**
                delete (Pj, LPNSat)
                add (Pj, LPSat)
                Else
                add (Pj, LPNSat)
                End if
            End if
        J ++
        End while
Ruturn (LPSat)
Return (LPNSat)
End

Fig. 9. Algorithm SecondPreference

connecting to the platform the user does not specify preferences, the algorithm automatically takes into account the preferences stored in previous contexts.

4.4   Service Research Method

To return a list of relevant cloud computing services in the context of the user, we endowed our architecture with research functions to perform this task. In this way, this research function uses the components of the layer are the followings **"service manager"**, **"applicant"** and **"adaptive model"** component.

The component "applicant" is responsible for finding and sending a list of items representing the contexts of services found in the second component is the **"adaptive model"**.

4.4.1   Service Research Steps

In the process it performs the following steps:

Step 1:   It receives from the service directory a list of relevant services in relation to the request sent by the user.

Step 2:   It contacts in his turn the service context manager to request the services found in the list of services provided by the directory.

Step 3:   It receives from the service context manager, the different contexts in a given format.

Step 4:   He sends different documents (files) to the second component that is "adaptive model".
            At this stage, rest of the search of appropriate services is devoted to the second component that follow.

Step 5:   Reception of the document containing services contexts of **step 4.**

Step 6:   The component "adaptive model" ask the context layer and more specifically to the manager component of the context of the user, the current user context. He then receives from this manager the current context of the user in a precise format.

Step 7:   Set the correspondence between the context of the current user and for each service matching the user query. It is performed through a comparison between the content elements of both documents (containing both services and user contexts).

Based on this comparison, the algorithm returns to the user the appropriate services to its context, therefore likely to be consumed.

5 Discussion

In order to contribute to the ever growing success of cloud computing, research must develop tools for performing laboratory work experiments. Also given the increasing cost of simulation environments, it would be appropriate to devise and propose alternatives. In this paper, the recommended an alternative tool to make an adjustment services through a new architecture, data models and algorithms to give intelligence to this architecture. So what does a cloud provider get by adopting this tool? Also what do customers earn by consuming cloud services hosted on infrastructure using such architecture?

In fact, such an architecture could allow a cloud computing provider to detect and store the different contexts of use of a service and also to capture the contexts of users during the consumption of services. As for the customer, he can benefit from the consumption of services compatible with its context (may vary depending on the mobility of the client). As for the researcher, our architecture will enable him to analyze the effects (quality of service, energy consumption level) that could be produced by using our tool and its architecture.

6 Conclusion

The objective in this paper was to propose an architecture and algorithm allowing the provision of services to adapt operations as profiles and contexts related not only to users but also to the different cloud services. To do this first we had reviewed and presented in the different architectures and objects of database model for these architectures. Then we presented our architecture, structure, operation and algorithms for the construction of the context profile. This algorithm is part of a set of tools for the coordination and operation of our architecture. The analysis of this architecture shows that the appropriate services from the latter satisfy the needs of the user if their contexts of use are consistent with those of their consumers. Also taking into account aspects related to data storage could be used to adjust the size of services to be consumed and working tools of users.

References

1. Farh, M.: A low approach é e agents for the allocation of resources in the Cloud Computing, Doctoral dissertation, University é Mohamed Khider-Biskra (2015)
2. H umane, P., Varshapriya, J.N.: Simulation of cloud infrastructure using cloudsim simulator: a practical approach for researchers. In: 2015 International Conference on Smart Technologies and Management for Computing, Communications, Controls, Energy and Materials (ICSTM), pp. 207–211. IEEE, May 2015
3. Krzywda, J., Tärneberg, W., ÖStBerG, P.O., Kihl, M., Elmroth, E.: TelcoClouds: modelling and simulation. In: Closer (2015)
4. Kecskemeti, G.: Dissect-CF: a simulator to foster energy-aware scheduling in infrastructure clouds. Simul. Model. Pract. Theory **58**, 188–218 (2015)
5. Kaur, R., Ghumman, N.S.: A survey and comparison of various cloud simulators available for cloud environment. Int. J. Adv. Res. Comput. Commun. Eng. **4**(5), 605–608 (2015)
6. Malik, A., Bilal, K., Malik, S., Anwar, Z., Aziz, K., Kliazovich, D., Buyya, R.: CloudNetSim++: a GUI based framework for modeling and simulation of data centers in OMNeT ++, 29 October 2015
7. Tian, W., Xu, M., Chen, A., Li, G., Wang, X., Chen, Y.: Open-source simulators for Cloud computing: comparative study and challenging issues. Simul. Model. Pract. Theory **58**, 239–254 (2015)
8. Serrano, N., Gallardo, G., Hernantes, J.: Infrastructure as a service and cloud technologies. IEEE Softw. **2**, 30–36 (2015)
9. García-Galán, J., Trinidad, P., Rana, O.F., Ruiz-Cortés, A.: Automated configuration supporting infrastructure for migrating to the cloud. Fut. Gener. Comput. Syst. **55**, 200–212 (2015)
10. Sá, T.T., Calheiros, R.N., Gomes, D.G.: CloudReports: an extensible simulation tool for energy-aware cloud computing environments. In: Mahmood, Z. (ed.) cloud computing, pp. 127–142. Springer, Cham (2014)
11. Ahmed, A., Sabyasachi, A.S.: Cloud computing simulators: a detailed survey and future direction. In: 2014 IEEE International Advance Computing Conference (IACC), pp. 866–872. IEEE, February 2014
12. Liu, J., Zhou, Y., Zhang, D., Fang, Y., Han, W., Zhang, Y.: Muclouds: parallel simulator for large-scale cloud computing systems. In: Ubiquitous, December 2014
13. Malhotra, R., Jain, P.: Study and comparison of cloudsim simulators in the cloud computing. SIJ Trans. Comput. Sci. Eng. Appl. **3**(9), 347–350 (2013)
14. Ray, S., De Sarkar, A.: Execution analysis of load balancing algorithms in cloud computing environment. Int. J. Cloud Comput. Serv. Archit. (IJCCSA) **2**(5), 1–13 (2012)
15. Zhao, W., Peng, Y., Xie, F., Dai, Z.: Modeling and simulation of cloud computing: a review. In: 2012 IEEE Asia Pacific Cloud Computing Congress (APCloudCC), pp. 20–24. IEEE, November 2012

16. Rak, M., Cuomo, A., Villano, U.: Mjades: concurrent simulation in the cloud. In: 2012 Sixth International Conference on Complex, Intelligent and Software Intensive Systems (CISIS), pp. 853–860. IEEE, July 2012

17. Fittkau, F., Frey, S., Hasselbring, W.: CDOSim: simulating cloud deployment options for migration software support. In: 2012 6th IEEE International Workshop on the Maintenance and Evolution of Service-Oriented and Cloud-Based Systems (MESOCA), pp. 37–46. IEEE, September 2012

18. Wickremasinghe, B., Calheiros, R.N., Buyya, R.: Cloudanalyst: a cloudsim-based visual modeller for Analysing cloud computing environments and applications. In: 2010 24th IEEE International Conference on Advanced Information Networking and Applications (AINA), pp. 446–452. IEEE, April 2010

19. Papakos, P., Capra, L., Rosenblum, D.S.: Volare: context- aware adaptive cloud service discovery for mobile systems. In: Proceedings of the 9th International Workshop on Adaptive and Reflective Middleware, pp. 32–38. ACM, November 2010

20. Liu, L., Wang, H., Liu, X., Jin, X., He, W.B., Wang, Q.B., Chen, Y.: GreenCloud: a new architecture for green data center. In: Proceedings of the 6th International Conference on Autonomic Computing Industry Session and Communications Industry Session, pp. 29–38. ACM, June 2009

21. Wickremasinghe, B.: CloudAnalyst: A CloudSim-based tool for modeling and analysis of large scale cloud computing environments. MEDC Proj. Rep. **22**(6), 433–659 (2009)

SEMOS: A Middleware for Providing Secure and Mobility-Aware Sessions over a P2P Overlay Network

Daouda Ahmat[1,2(✉)], Mahamat Barka[2], and Damien Magoni[3]

[1] Virtual University of Chad, N'Djamena, Chad
daouda.ahmat@uvt.td
[2] University of N'Djamena, N'Djamena, Chad
mahamat.barka@gmail.com
[3] University of Bordeaux – LaBRI, Bordeaux, France
magoni@labri.fr

Abstract. Mobility and security are major features for both current and future network infrastructures. Nevertheless, the integration of mobility in traditional virtual private networks is difficult due to the costs of re-establishing broken secure tunnels and restarting broken connections. Besides session recovery costs, renegotiation steps also present inherent vulnerabilities. In order to address these issues, we propose a new distributed mobile VPN system called SEcured MObile Session (SEMOS). Based upon our CLOAK peer-to-peer overlay architecture, SEMOS provides security services to the application layer connections of mobile users. Secure and resilient sessions allow user connections to survive network failures as opposed to regular transport layer secured connections used by traditional VPN protocols.

Keywords: Connectivity · Mobility · Overlay · P2P · VPN · Security

1 Introduction

Mobile devices and wireless networks have progressively provided increased connectivity for users. However, such extended connectivity often comes at the expense of vulnerabilities to attacks such as eavesdropping. Malicious users can infiltrate public open networks and attack legitimate traffic. Virtual Private Networks (VPN) are offering high security to the network traffic [1]. Traditionally, these systems allow the user to securely and remotely communicate with its Intranet through insecure public networks such as the Internet. Security services provided by these infrastructures are robust against malicious users attacks. However, traditional VPNs fail to support users' mobility. Indeed, network failures automatically break-up secure tunnels and involve a subsequent renegotiation that is then necessary to re-establish broken tunnels. This renegotiation requires expensive computational operations in order to restore tunnels

© ICST Institute for Computer Sciences, Social Informatics and Telecommunications Engineering 2018
T.F. Bissyande and O. Sie (Eds.): AFRICOMM 2016, LNICST 208, pp. 111–121, 2018.
https://doi.org/10.1007/978-3-319-66742-3_11

as well as transport-layer and application-layer connections. This phase of negotiation causes not only significant latency but also presents risks of Man-In-The-Middle (MITM) attacks. Traditional VPNs can not therefore effectively operate in dynamic and mobile environments. In addition, lack of means, disrupted-environments and unsteady networks, due to both poor-quality devices and technical skills deficiency, are pervasive in developing countries, particularly in Africa. In these areas, secured resilient sessions are needed to overcome both security and performance issues inherent to connection disruptions.

In this paper, we propose a new mobile VPN-like system called SEcured MObile Session (SEMOS). This system is designed to support both the mobility and the security of SEMOS entities. We have implemented a prototype and have tested and evaluated it by running experiments upon an emulated mobile network. We have compared its features and performances to three other existing solutions namely HIP, N2N and MOBIKE that propose open source implementations. Results show that our solution provides more features and exhibits better connection resumption performances.

This paper is an extended version of our previous work presented at Wireless Days 2012 in Dublin [2]. This new version includes an exhaustive state of the art, a more detailed description of the SEMOS underlying P2P overlay network called CLOAK and a comparative evaluation of three existing similar and open source solutions (i.e., HIP, MOBIKE and N2N), with respect to features and latency performances. In addition, we have extended MUSeS properties by adding several useful design features. In order to avoid name conflicts, we have also changed the name of our solution from MUSeS in [2] to SEMOS in this paper.

2   Related Work

Up to now, several mobile VPN solutions have been proposed in various research papers. In this section, we study some interesting existing solutions that address the design of mobile VPNs. Mobile VPN systems based on both IPsec [3] and Mobile IP [4] have been proposed several times such as in [5–8], in order to attempt to overcome the inherent mobility drawbacks of traditional VPNs.

Nevertheless, as explained in [9], many problems arise from the combination between IPsec and MobileIP. In order to overcome these problems, a model has been proposed which is based on the use of two HAs (internal HA and external HA) and two FAs (internal FA and external FA) by Vaarala et al. in [10]. However, this model imposes the use of three imbricated tunnels ($\{$x-MIP$\{$GW$\{$i-MIP$\{$original packet$\}\}\}\}$).

In addition, an IPsec-based mobile VPN requires n tunnels (n security layers) when there are n IPsec hops between the source and destination entities. Therefore, the imbricated tunnels in such VPN systems have a negative impact on their network performances (i.e., throughput, overhead, etc.).

In order to address IPsec mobility inherent issues, several improved schemes based on the IPsec architecture have been proposed by Eronen et al. in [11,12], or [13]. Based on security extensions to MOBIKE [11], the solution described in [13] combines secure connectivity and Mobile IPv4. This approach resolves considerably the issues notified in [9] such as overhead, NAT traversal or mobility problems due to the combination of IPsec and Mobile IPv4. These solutions are however not free of scalability issues and network overhead that they inherit from IPsec and Mobile IP.

The dynamic VPN approach proposed in [14] enables to use alternately IPsec in Full-Mesh mode or in Hub mode with a centralized IPsec Gateway. The first mode is only used when routing problems occur. This architecture extends MOBIKE in order to support dynamic tunnels. However, this model is not designed to support mobility.

Another proposal leveraging MOBIKE is presented by Migault in [15], where they propose an alternative End-to-End security (E2E) architecture based on their own MOBIKEX protocol, which extends the MOBIKE mobility and multihoming features to multiple interfaces and to the transport mode of IPsec. Based on a topology organized in communities, peer-to-peer (P2P) mobile VPN systems have also been proposed such as ELA [16] or N2N [17].

In opposition to most dynamic VPN systems, these systems have the advantage to be fairly scalable and to have ability to communicate across NAT and firewalls. Decentralized P2P VPN are flexible and self-organizing infrastructures that enable users to create their own secure networks upon an untrusted network. N2N and ELA topologies are very similar despite the fact that N2N is based on the OSI layer two whereas ELA is based on the OSI layer three. However the use of super nodes in N2N limits its full scalability as these nodes have a more important role than the other nodes and thus they can weaken the overall strength of the N2N network and may even break its connectivity if they fail. Freelan [18] is a multi-platform and open-source peer-to-peer VPN that abstracts a LAN over the Internet.

The Host Identity Protocol (HIP) [19,20] is an architecture that provides both mobility and multihoming services. HIP introduces a new name space that enables the separation between the host identity, called Host Identity Tag or HIT, and the host location.

3   System Description

3.1   Design

As shown in Fig. 1, SEMOS is a communication layer directly used by the applications. SEMOS is using another communication layer called CLOAK which enables the creation and management of a P2P overlay network above any IP network [21]. This system is designed to provide traffic security and session continuity. Applications produce data and send it to the SEMOS middleware. Data is then sliced in packets that are encrypted and authenticated. Unlike IPsec or TLS which rely on IP addresses to define the identity of the communication entities, SEMOS relies on permanent device identifiers called *names* provided by CLOAK. SEMOS can keep a user session active despite a connection disruption and can resume an interrupted secure session.

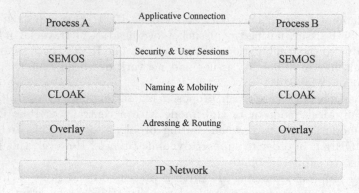

Fig. 1. Architecture overview.

3.2 Overlay

CLOAK is an architecture for building P2P overlay networks which are autonomous and dynamic. A new peer can join any peer already inside the overlay usually by setting up a transport layer connection such as TCP with this peer. The new peer is then offered an overlay address which is unique and dependent on its location in the overlay. These virtual addresses or coordinates are taken from hyperbolic plane and used by a greedy routing algorithm for forwarding the data inside the overlay.

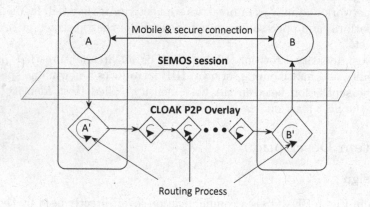

Fig. 2. Routing through the P2P overlay network.

CLOAK was originally defined in our paper [21], which presented the protocols and modules of the architecture with details and reported simulation results upon static and dynamic networks concerning routing success ratio, path length and stretch, as well as DHT performances. The DHT scheme defined by CLOAK is fully explained in our paper [22]. The Fig. 2 shows how a packet is routed over CLOAK.

3.3   Permanent Identifiers Details

The CLOAK system provides a lookup service based upon distributed tables that consist of pairs defined as $<ID_{CLOAK}, @_{overlay}>$.

Figure 3 describes the mobility mechanism provided by CLOAK. When a CLOAK node joins the network, it stores the pair $<ID_{CLOAK}, @_{overlay}>$ into the DHT, where ID_{CLOAK} is its permanent identifier and $@_{overlay}$ is its virtual temporary address. Thus, after moving within the network or leaving the network, when the node reconnects to the network, it will update the pair $<ID_{CLOAK}, @_{overlay}>$ by replacing its old address $@_{overlay}$ by its new address that determines its current location. Only ID_{CLOAK}, which is a permanent identifier, is used to identify the endpoints of a session in order to keep sessions active despite connection disruptions.

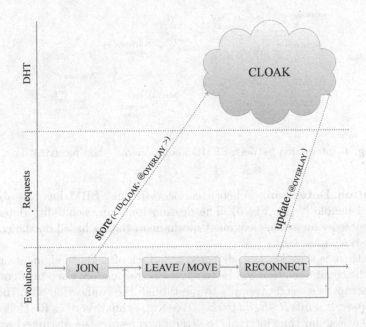

Fig. 3. Mobility scheme based upon the CLOAK DHT.

3.4   Architecture

As shown in Fig. 4, the SEMOS system is based on four main components:

- The Session Security Module (SSM) manages security services such as confidentiality, integrity and protection against replay attacks;
- The Session Reliability Module (SRM) is designed to provide fault-tolerant secure user sessions; In a nutshell, SRM offers user session continuity service that survives despite connection disruptions caused by lower layers failures;

- The Local Connection Manager (LCM) handles multiple local TCP connections in order to support several simultaneous user applications;
- The Port Forwarder (PF) enables to forward destination ports into local ports in order to intercept and process traffic and finally to send it.

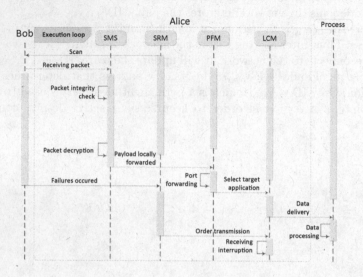

Fig. 4. Interaction between SEMOS components when receiving data.

Interruption Detection: When a connection fails, SRM has the ability to detect and handle it (see Fig. 5). The destination's unreachability detection is made possible by an acknowledgment mechanism that is based on the exchange of *request-reply* messages.

When there is a packet loss, detected by a lack of acknowledgment or a wait timeout, the communication will be temporarily suspended. Each peer concerned by an interrupted session attempts to reestablish the connection with the corresponding peer. It sends *Re-Hello* packets (see Fig. 7 that describes Re-Hello packet structure) at regular time intervals to attempt to restart the disrupted session.

Session Identifier: When a mobile SEMOS entity wishes to communicate with a remote corresponding node, these two peers compute together, in the *handshake* phase, a unique value in order to singly identify each session following the same principle as with a socket connection. When *Alice* sends a *Hello* message (see Fig. 6 that describes the Hello packet structure) to *Bob* to start the communication (*handshake phase*), *Alice* generates a partial session ID (*pSessID-a*) and sends it to *Bob*. After receiving *pSessID-a*, *Bob* also generates a partial session ID (*pSessID-b*) and sends it to *Alice*. Each corresponding user determines the final session ID (SessID) by concatenating the partial session IDs: SessID = pSessID − a ⊙ pSessID − b, where ⊙ represents a concatenation according to lexicographic order.

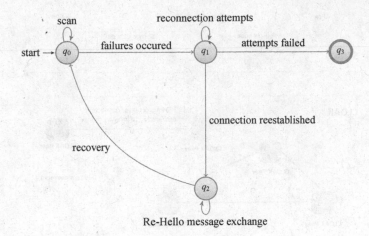

Fig. 5. Failure detection and recovery mechanism.

Hello Packet
   Header
      Routing Header
         Src ID = $ID_{CLOAK}Src$
         Dst ID = $ID_{CLOAK}Dst$
      Additional Header Fields
         Packet Type = flag 0
         RC P = Source port
         DST P = Destination port
         IsConnectionOK() = Yes / No
   Payload   % partial session ID
      PSess ID = uuid() $\odot$ SRC Port

Fig. 6. Hello packet structure.

Re-Hello Packet
   Header
      Routing Header
         Src ID = $ID_{CLOAK}Src$
         Dst ID = $ID_{CLOAK}Dst$
      Additional Header Fields
         Packet Type = flag 2
         IsResumptionOK()=T/F
   Payload
      Sess ID = SEMOS ID
      SEQ NBR = Last packet ID

Fig. 7. Re-Hello Packet Structure

The communication, identified by a SessID, can be therefore started between the two actors. Precisely, a partial session ID (pSessID) is essentially computed by a combination between a source port number (psN) and a peer ID (pID): pSessID = psN $\odot$ pID.

Secure Mobility: In our model, the concept of secure mobility is a way to allow mobile users to keep an established secure session active when the underlying system connection fails until a subsequent new connection is started. In other words, when a user changes its location as shown in Fig. 8 or when its connections are disrupted by network failures, the user session survives as long as necessary to resume the communication.

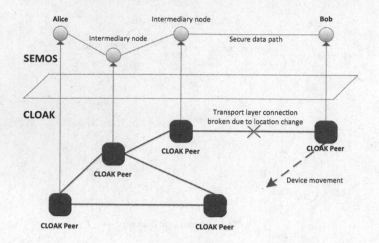

Fig. 8. User mobility with ongoing secure session.

4 Experiment

In order to assess those four VPN technologies in a mobility scenario, we have used a tool called Network Emulator For Mobile Universes (NEmu), developed by Vincent Autefage [23]. Furthermore, NEmu is an emulator that enables the creation of virtualized roaming or mobile devices which is needed in our scenario. The virtual machines run on top of QEMU using the Debian OS. QEMU virtual hosts are interconnected by virtual switches emulated by the Virtual Network Device (VND) software. In order to emulate roaming or mobile devices, NEmu uses the Network Mobilizer (*nemo*) software module.

Table 1. Experiment results.

System	Location change	Average latency	Maximum latency
HIP	20 s	16 s	21 s
MOBIKE	20 s	13 s	19 s
N2N	20 s	49 s	92 s
SEMOS	20 s	4 s	11 s

We have used a minimal FTP-like application based on the OpenBSD version of *nc* in order to experiment on the four different mobile VPN solutions presented. Table 1 provides the average results of ten experiments for each of the four systems. Location change duration showed in the second column is the same for all systems, it is defined as a parameter in NEmu. The third column shows the average latency for each system over ten rounds of experiments.

These results show that SEMOS has the smallest average and maximum values for the latency due to communication resumption. Besides, failures do not cause any packet loss despite the long duration of disruption.

5   Conclusion

In this paper, we have presented a new solution called SEMOS for the simultaneous security and mobility of end-to-end connections. SEMOS is based on our P2P overlay system called CLOAK which provides dynamic naming, addressing and routing services. SEMOS builds upon CLOAK to provide secure and resilient sessions to the applications run by mobile users. In other words, user sessions can be paused for any period of time and can be restarted without the cost of renegotiating security parameters. In addition, SEMOS makes disruptions at lower layers completely transparent to the user applications and to their remote corresponding peers. The secured mobility and roaming of SEMOS user communications is thus ensured. The SEMOS middleware is designed to support several user applications simultaneously.

We have implemented a prototype of SEMOS as a middleware inserted between user applications and our CLOAK P2P overlay middleware. Currently, applications using the SEMOS API to implement secure and mobile sessions, must be recompiled. Devices running these applications must also run the CLOAK middleware and belong to a CLOAK overlay. SEMOS is implemented in C and can be downloaded at [24].

We have compared its features to three existing similar solutions: HIP, MOBIKE and N2N. We have also evaluated the performances of SEMOS and the corresponding implementations of the other solutions in an emulated dynamic network environment by using NEmu. We have shown that HIP is the closest solution for providing all the functionalities offered by SEMOS. We have also observed that the latency resumption of SEMOS was the smallest of the four evaluated implementations, which places it as an interesting alternative to existing solutions.

Our future work will consist in completing and improving our current implementation as well as integrating a key management scheme suitable for dynamic networks to provide the users with a means to exchange or generate secret keys in-band. To this end, we have designed a key generation technique based on the Shamir's secret sharing method and using multiple disjoint paths in the overlay, for creating a secret key without requiring certificates such as in Diffie-Hellman [25]. We are currently evaluating this technique and we plan to insert it in the negotiation phase of a SEMOS connection.

References

1. Berger, T.: Analysis of current VPN technologies. In: The First International Conference on Availability, Reliability and Security, ARES 2006, 8 pp. (2006)
2. Ahmat, D., Magoni, D.: Muses: mobile user secured session. In: 5th IFIP Wireless Days International Conference, Dublin, Ireland

3. Kent, S., Seo, K.: Security Architecture for the Internet Protocol. IETF RFC 4301 (2005)
4. Perkins, C.: IP Mobility Support for IPv4. IETF RFC 3344 (2002)
5. Binkley, J.: An Integrated IPSEC and Mobile-IP for FreeBSD. Technical report, pp. 1–10 (2001)
6. Braun, T., Danzeisen, M.: Secure mobile IP communication. In: 26th IEEE Conference on Local Computer Networks, pp. 586–593 (2001)
7. Choi, H., Song, H., Cao, G., La Porta, T.: Mobile multi-layered IPsec. In: 24th Joint Conference of the IEEE Computer and Communications Societies, pp. 1929–1939 (2005)
8. Ruppelt, R., Pelinescu, A., Constantin, C., Floroiu, J., Sisalem, D., Butscher, B.: Building ALL-IP based virtual private networks in mobile environment. In: Research and applications, International Workshop on Informatic and Mobile Communication Over Wireless LAN (2001)
9. Adrangi, F., Levkowetz, H., Statement, P.: Mobile IPv4 Traversal of Virtual Private Network Gateways. IETF RFC 4093 (2005)
10. Vaarala, S., Klovning, E.: Mobile IPv4 Traversal across IPsec-Based VPN Gateways. IETF RFC 5265 (2008)
11. Eronen, P.: IKEv2 Mobility and Multihoming Protocol (MOBIKE). IETF RFC 4555 (2006)
12. Devarapalli, V., Eronen, P.: Secure Connectivity and Mobility Using Mobile IPv4 and IKEv2 Mobility and Multihoming (MOBIKE). IETF RFC 5266 (2008)
13. Karbasioun, M.M., Berenjkub, M., Taji, B.: Securing mobile IP communications using MOBIKE protocol. In: International Conference on Telecommunications (2008)
14. Ishimura, K., Tamura, T., Mizuno, S., Sato, H., Motono, T.: Dynamic IP-VPN architecture with secure IPsec tunnels. In: Symposium on Information and Telecommunication Technologies (2010)
15. Migault, D., Palomares, D., Herbert, E., You, W., Ganne, G., Arfaoui, G., Laurent, M.: E2E: An optimized IPsec architecture for secure and fast offload. In: International Conference on Availability, Reliability and Security, pp. 365–374 (2012)
16. Aoyagi, S., Takizawa, M., Saito, M., Aida, H., Tokuda, H.: ELA: a fully distributed VPN system over peer-to-peer network. In: Symposium on Applications and the Internet, pp. 89–92 (2005)
17. Deri, L., Andrews, R.: N2N: a layer two peer-to-peer VPN. In: International Conference on Autonomous Infrastructure, Management and Security, pp. 53–64 (2008)
18. Kauffmann, J.: The freelan secure channel protocol (2011). https://github.com/ereOn/libfscp/blob/1.0/fscp.txt
19. Moskowitz, R., Nikander, P.: Host Identity Protocol (HIP) Architecture. IETF RFC 4423 (2006)
20. Gurtov, A.: Host Identity Protocol (HIP): Towards the Secure Mobile Internet. Wiley, Hoboken (2008)
21. Tiendrebeogo, T., Ahmat, D., Magoni, D., Sié, O.: Virtual connections in P2P overlays with dht-based name to address resolution. Int. J. Adv. Internet Technol. 5(1), 11–25 (2012)
22. Tiendrebeogo, T., Ahmat, D., Magoni, D.: Reliable and scalable distributed hash tables harnessing hyperbolic coordinates. In: 5th IFIP International Conference on New Technologies, Mobility and Security (2012)

23. Autefage, V., Magoni, D.: Network emulator: a network virtualization testbed for overlay experimentations. In: 17th IEEE International Workshop on Computer-Aided Modeling Analysis and Design of Communication Links and Networks, pp. 38–42 (2012)
24. Ahmat, D.: SEcure MObile Session. http://www.labri.fr/~magoni/cape/
25. Ahmat, D., Magoni, D., Bissyandé, T.: End-to-End key exchange through disjoint paths in P2P networks. ICST Trans. Secur. Saf. **2–3**, 1–15 (2015)

Xj-ASD: Towards a j-ASD DSL eXtension for Application Deployment in Cloud-Based Environment

Kanga Koffi[1(✉)], Babri Michel[2], Brou Konan Marcelin[2],
and Goore Bi Tra[2]

[1] Ecole Doctorale Polytechnique de l'Institut Nationale Polytechnique Félix
Houphouët Boigny (EDP/INPHB), Côte D'ivoire UMRI 78: Electronique
et Electricité Appliquée Laboratoire de recherche en informatique
et télécommunication, Yamoussoukro, Côte d'Ivoire
koffi.kanga@larit.net
[2] Institut Nationale Polytechnique Félix Houphouët Boigny (INPHB),
Côte D'ivoire UMRI 78: Electronique et Electricité Appliquée,
Laboratoire de Recherche en Informatique et Télécommunication,
Yamoussoukro, Côte d'Ivoire
{michel.babri,kmbrou,goore}@inphb.edu.ci

Abstract. In this paper, we propose an extension of the grammar of an application deployment constraints description language from a cloud computing platform. To do this, we draw a meta data model proposed by [1] for an application deployment in a cloud. This meta model, we extend j-ASD for the consideration of compatibility constraints or conformity between the virtual image data file formats used by the components of the virtual machines and those target sites that are deploying Smartphones, PC, etc. ...

Indeed for a full deployment of applications from a cloud environment on high mobility rate (Smartphone, PC, etc. ...), it occurs to ensure compliance of the data formats of these environments to that of Cloud platform. This conformity proves a prerequisite for deployment on a device from a cloud. To address these compliance constraints, we formalize them in matrix form and propose the use of a constraint solver.

Keywords: Application deployment · Software component description language constraint · Cloud computing · Deployment plan

1 Introduction

Designing application requires an approach called life cycle. This approach, in whatever form (V, waterfall, spiral ...) includes a number of activities (design, implementation, validation, deployment, and administration) regardless of the approach [1]. These activities include the deployment is a complex process ranging from the production of the application and uninstall it [2].

© ICST Institute for Computer Sciences, Social Informatics and Telecommunications Engineering 2018
T.F. Bissyande and O. Sie (Eds.): AFRICOMM 2016, LNICST 208, pp. 122–132, 2018.
https://doi.org/10.1007/978-3-319-66742-3_12

Today, with the emergence of the Internet of Things monitoring the development of service models in the Cloud, mobile device users want to use their applications on their phone, tablet and other materials with high rates of mobility. In this context, the deployment of applications becomes an important activity with its constraints corollary, given the diversity of deployment sites and components that make up these applications.

Faced with this dilemma, the research tried to find solutions to the architecture and deployment platform [2], the definition of deployment constraints languages [3] to describe the application to deploy, and the constraints of facilities. In this paper we propose an extension of this language to the specificities of a Cloud to benefit users of the benefits in terms of computing power and the Cloud profitability. Also in order to cover all the deployment activities, we integrate other deployment constraints are not supported, namely the management of data formats, image management from various file virtualization to deploy. The rest of the paper is organized as follows. In Sect. 2, we are a state of the art in this field. Section 3 is devoted to our contribution. We end with a conclusion while generating few prospects for our future work.

2 State of the Art

Several research studies describing the tools and procedures around the deployment exist. But to our knowledge, these are almost always intended for fixed topologies machines and/or known at the time of deployment and therefore not relevant to our context. This section presents some research related to the application deployment.

Fractal Deployment Framework (FDF) [4], is a tool that provides a generic in deploying applications. It consists of a deployment description language, a set of components, and user interfaces.

The deployment unit is an archive that contains the binaries and software deployment descriptor. The main limitation of this tool is the static nature of the deployment although a static deployment plan qualifies in relatively stable environments such as grid computing, this type of tool cannot be used in environments characterized by a topology network dynamics as cloud environments. Another limitation of FDF is that it does not provide heuristic dynamic reconfiguration that allows the incorporation of machinery malfunction situations for example.

Software Dock [5], it provides a Framework for the configuration and deployment of software. It uses a system of events and mobile agents to control deployment activities such as installation and activation. Deployment life cycle includes the installation, activation, deactivation, updating, uninstalling and reconfiguring. The deployment system uses a client/server architecture associated with event management system. A server called "release dock" is installed at the manufacturer's website. A customer called "fi eld dock" is installed at each site software consumers, which acts as an interface for the release dock. However, Software Dock does not allow the description of the software architecture and deployment constraints. Software Dock also offers a centralized, static deployment process that does not meet the needs of dynamic reconfiguration and deployment of open environments.

R-OSGi [6] is a middleware that uses the standards of the OSGi specification to support the management of distributed modules. Upon deployment, R-OSGi can be used to execute a distributed application simply indicate the deployment locations of deferent modules. The developer of an R-OSGi application has full control over how the application is distributed. Manual control of the deployment process and its configuration in a large scale environment left is a very complex task and represents for us a very important human intervention in the deployment process. In addition, R-OSGi is only intended to create static software deployments that cannot be used in environments distributed large-scale open as ubiquitous systems and P2P.

Dearle et al. proposed in [7] middleware, MADME (Monitoring Automatic Deployment and Management Engine) for deploying and managing applications consist of one or more components called Cingal-bundle. Deployments constraints are specified with the Deladas language. The deployment administrator specifies an initial deployment target, then the deployment system tries to generate a configuration that describes the process of deploying the application components. After initial deployment, the deployment system verifies the satisfaction of the initial target and redeploys the application if necessary. This approach has similar motivations to ours. Indeed, one of the reasons is the reduction of human intervention in the deployment process by automatically generating the deployment plan. However, the proposed middleware is not usable in environments with an unpredictable topology. In addition the user of the tool must restart the entire deployment process. Upon the occurrence of a disconnection or failure for example.

A DSL-Based Approach to Software Development and Deployment on Cloud [8]: In this work, Krzysztof Sledziewski et al. present an approach incorporating a DSL for the development and deployment of applications in a Cloud. In this approach the authors propose that developers use a DSL for describing the model associated with the application. This model is then translated into a specific code and automatically deployed in a cloud. This approach is specific to a deployed in a Cloud and facilitates the work of the administrator to deploy. However, the proposed approach does not take into account the conditions or deployment constraint to satisfy.

A DSL for Multi-scale Deployment and Autonomic Software [9]: In this article, Raja BOUBEL and Al. present a progressive work that aims to define and test a DSL dedicated to autonomic application deployment in multi-scale environments. In these environments, the network topology may vary according to hardware failures.

In this work the authors design a DSL to support the expression of constraints and properties related to autonomic application deployment in multi-scale environments. However, they do not provide in their DSL prior restraint activation, deactivation, installation, application uninstall.

J-ASD [3]: A middleware for autonomic software deployment. It consists of a set of software that can best meet the deployment problem of a distributed application regardless of the execution context. In other words this middleware performs independently (with minimal human intervention as possible) a deployment that meets a set of constraints defined by the deployment administrator. It is able to self- adapt and automatically resolve some problems associated with the instability and the opening of the environment. It is based on:

- A specific language (DSL) for the description of deployment constraints called j- ASD DSL
- A network service to automatically detect deployment target sites
- A bootstrap middleware for the preparation of the execution environment
- A constraint solver for solving constraints and deployment plan generation
- A deployment support and an adaptable mobile agent system for the execution and supervision of deployment activities
- A deployment algorithm.

However j-ASD, in defining the conditions to be met for a deployment does not take into account the level of use of the battery devices, characteristics that are related to cloud virtual machines and images of virtualized applications, formats data images to deploy.

3   Contribution

In view of the existing work, more deployment-related issues seem to be resolved. In particular, the deployment constraints related problems (install/uninstall). Nevertheless, some aspects of the deployment as part of activation, deactivation and update components seem not yet to find solutions.

An analysis of existing studies shows that configure and deploy of application in a large scale environment such as the Cloud is not easy. This complexity is due to the multitude of components, the heterogeneity and the large number of target sites in an environment with high levels of mobility (and therefore variable topology) that make up an application. So our contribution is as follows:

- Taking into account the given file formats to deploy the devices from virtual machines in cloud platforms.
- Extension of the grammar description language deployment constraints J-ASD DSL initiated by [3] to take into account other constraints (i) pre-deployment, (ii) relating to the use of the battery deployment target sites from a cloud platform (iii) network latency which is based on the deployment plan and also the power of the processors.

3.1 Modeling the Inclusion of Data Formats (Fig. 1)

In Fig. 1, our model shows different class with roles based on their attributes.

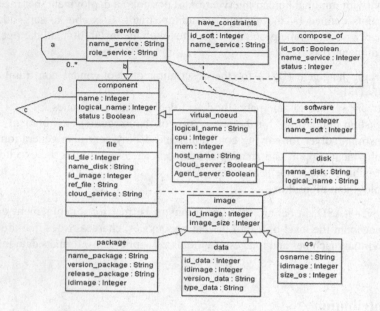

Fig. 1. Meta data model for deployment in the cloud [1]

In the following table, we present these different classes and their role in the process of deploying an application (Table 1).

Table 1. List of class in Fig. 1 and their respective roles

Class	Roles
Application	Is characterized by an application name, version, and an ID. It may consist of components (class has) and also its use requires the satisfaction of certain vis-à-vis stress-related services to its components (stress class)
Composant	A component appears as the component of an application. It is also characterized by a name, version and status (on/off)
Service	This class is characterized by name, a role and also may depend on the operating state of other services (reflexive link a)
Contrainte	Determines if a service is available for the proper functioning of an application. In which case an adaptation of the application to another service arose

(continued)

Table 1. (*continued*)

Class	Roles
Comporte	Materializes the creation of an application from components. For proper operation, the component needs the availability of several services (b) or as other components (reflexive link c)
Virtual_noeud	Represents a virtual machine. It is characterized by a name, CPU frequency, memory value, 2 Boolean attributes (cloudserver and agent_cloud) whether the node is a server or client
Disk	This class embodies the place of deployment of the virtual machine. It is characterized by a logical name (LOGICAL_NAME), size (size), an identifier (name_disk). It consists of a set of files (file).
File	Represents the element to be virtualized to form an image. It has the following features: a Id_image representing the corresponding image, the disk on which it is stored, its reference (path, a boolean flag to see if it is a file server to a virtual machine server
Image	Represents the file element (file) virtualized. it is characterized by the set of packages that make up the data and the OS with which it is compatible
Package	Each package of the image has a name (name_package), a version (version_package) and a release (release_package) that distinguish it from other packages
Data	Here this class characterizes the image because it determines the version (version_data) Image data type (or format) (type_data) data, and the data source (source_data)
OS	This class in turn determines the operating system on which an image can be deployed. It has a name (osname), size (size) for the space installation requires a distribution (os_distribution) and version (os_version)

3.2 Constraints Description Language Extension j-ASD DSL Based on the Model of Fig. 1

J-ASD DSL is a language with a simplified and intuitive grammar. This grammar is developed using Xtext[1] which is a specific languages Development Framework. As stipulated in the j-ASD DSL precursors, an application consists of one or more components. Each is defined by an identifier, a version, execution url or implementation but also by a set of software dependencies, hardware constraints and deployment constraints. So from the j-ASD DSL grammar presented in a we extend this grammar to battery usage constraints (PowerPref) potential deployment sites, internet network latency constraints (NetLatency) and also to the constraints CPU power (MIPSPref Million Instructions Per Second) and also to the constraints of the data format as shown in b in the same conditions given the high rate of mobility in Cloud environments.

---

[1] http://www.eclipse.org/Xtext.

a- J-ASD DSL language grammar Xtext

```
grammar eu.itsudparis.inf.JASDDsl with
org.eclipse.xtext.common.Terminals
generate jASDDsl
Model:
Software=Software
Components+=Component+(HostConstraints+=HostConstrain
t*)?
Deployment=Deployment;
Software:
"Software" "{"
"Name" "=" name=ID
"Version" "=" ver=INT
"Components" "=" components+=(ID)*
"}";
Component:
"Component" "{"
"Name" "=" name=ID
"Version" "=" ver=INT
"Url" "=" url=STRING
("Dependencies" "=" dependencies+=ID*)?
"}";
HostConstraint:
"HostConstraint" "{"
"Name" "=" name=ID
constraints+=(OsPref | CPUPref |
RAMPref | HDPref | NetSpeedPref)*
"}";
Deployment:
"Deployment" "{"
{Deployment} members+=MemberDecl*
```

```
"}";
MemberDecl:
component=ID "@" localisation=Localisation
("with" constraints+=(ID)*)?;
OsPref:
"OSNameContains" name=STRING;
CPUPref:
"CPULoad" InfSup val=INT "%";
terminal InfSup:
"<" | ">" | ">=" | "<=";
RAMPref:
"RAM" sym=InfSup val=INT "MB";
HDPref:
"HD" sym=InfSup val=INT "MB";
NetSpeedPref:
"NetSpeed" sym=InfSup val=INT "kb/s";
Localisation:
IPv4 | NetName | Val | Interval | All;
terminal IPv4:
INT '.' INT '.' INT '.' INT;
NetName:
STRING;
Val:
INT;
terminal Interval:
INT ".." INT;
terminal All:
"all";
```

b- Extension given to grammar j-ASD DSL language

```
'contribution to the extension of the grammar
'J-ASD DSL# puissance de la batterie
PowerPref :
"Power" sym=InfSup Val=INT "%";
# network latency
NetLatency :
"NetLat" sym=InfSup Val=INT "ms";
# puissance du processeur
MIPSPref :
"MIPSPval" sym=InfSup Val=INT "MIPS";
'Extension into account the meta data model
# Data format
Format :
"format" "=" name=STRING ;
DataConstraint:
"dataConstraint" "{"
"Name" "=" name=ID
"Version" "=" ver=INT
"type" "=" name=STRING
"source" "=" name=STRING
"}";
```

So as defines our extension grammar highlights a number of constraints to be satisfied to make a full deployment. In this work, as we make a deployment from a cloud, we propose the use XMPP protocol [11] for the management of network discovery sites belonging to the deployment plan. If network discovery services are defined and the constraints of compliance (yes compatibility) of defined data format property, our second contribution is working to formalize and solving these constraints as a constraint satisfaction problem (CSP) that can find solution using a constraint solver. As part of our prototype we chose the open source constraint solver Choco [11] to be consistent with [9].

3.3   Formalization and Resolution of Constraints

As part of j DSL-ADS, the constraint satisfaction problem is constructed from a set of integer variables (compliance matrix) and a set of constraints on these variables. Under these conditions we model the CSP program with the following:

- A set C software components forming the application to deploy
- Let $C = \{C1, C2, C3, \ldots, Cn\}$
- A set S deployment target sites detection network discovery service
- A given compliance matrix (Cfm) modeling the compliance or non-compliance of file images of the data formats supported by virtual machines from components that they have with those of deployment sites is such that:
  - Cfm (Ci, Sj) = 1, if the component Ci has the same data format as the site Sj
  - Cfm (Ci, Sj) = 0, if the component Ci has the same data format as the site Sj
- A Q set of constraints on the Si sites (e.g. Powerload, Netlatency ...)
- A set of constraints on the variables Cfm (Ci, Sj)

---

c-Example of J-ASD Program DSL written taking into account the constraints of data format compliance for deployment

---

```
Software {
Name=niveau_de_test
Version=1
Components=ramSize display
}
Component {Name=RamSize
Version=1
Url=http://x.fr/RAM-Size.jar }
Component {Name=display
Version=1
Url="http://x.fr/Display.jar"}
HostConstraint {Name=Display-Constraint
CPULoad > 80%
RAM >= 40 MB
OSNameContrains "Linux"}
Deployment {
RamSize @ all
display @ 2 with Display-Constraint
}
********************
extension taking into account our contribution to the constrained
********************
*** definition of the characteristics of the component niveau_batterie
Component {
Name=niveau_batterie
Version=1
Url="http://x.fr/niveau_batterie.jar"
}
*** definition of CONSTRAINT deployment contraint3
dataConstraint {
Name=contraint3
version = 2
Type = ".exe"
OSNameContains "Windows"
}
*** component deploying niveau_batterie
*** on all sites is considering the contrainte3
Deployment {
niveau_batterie @ all with Constraint3
}
```

In this j-ASD DSL program, we have a description of deploying an application called "niveau_de_test" consists of the following components: ramsize - Display - niveau_batterie characterized by their name (Name), their version, the URL of storage. The program also includes a set of constraints (Display-constrained constraint3), which are constraints on the size of the RAM memory, the processor occupancy and operating system.

The deployment constraints (activation) Niveau_batterie mean that the component must be deployed on all sites that respect Contrainte3 constraint. This constraint on the data format of the images of virtual machine files.

Formally this means:
Niveaubatterie $\forall \in C, \forall$ If $\in S$
If ((version = 2) and (type = ".exe") and (osname = "Windows")) then
Cfm (niveaubatterie, Si) = 1
else Cfm (niveaubatterie, Si) = 0
As for the second constraint, it means that the display component must be deployed (on) a set of two sites that satisfy the constraint "Display-Constraint", it is formally expressed by:
Display $\forall \in C, \exists$ S1, S2 $\in S$ such que:
If ((CPULoad> 80%) and (ramsize $\geq$ 40 MB) and (osname = "linux")) then
Cfm (display, S1) = Cfm (display, S2) = 1
else
Cfm (display, S1) = Cfm (display, S2) = 0

4 Conclusion

In this article we presented our contribution to the application deployment problem solving from a Cloud by providing an extension to the grammar of deployment constraints description language j-ASD DSL. These deployment constraints relate to the compatibility of data formats virtual images of the component files. This set of constraints is in solution using a constraint solver for calculating a deployment plan.

Our proposed extension can be used to manage the power consumption, latency network's management to ensure full deployment from a cloud-based environment. Also it helps enable deployment of equipment in a variable topology environment.

For now we continue our work with the deployment of OSGi Framework. However, the use of new deployment unit as SCA applications (Service Component Architecture) (Open Service Architecture Collaboration 2007) with Frascati platform [Seinturier 2009 Seinturier 2012] as deployment media is a natural extension of j-ASD DSL.

References

1. Etchevers, X.: Déploiement d'applications patrimoniales en environnements de type informatique dans le nuage. Other. Université de Grenoble, 2012. French. <NNT: 2012GRENM100>. <tel-00875568>
2. Dibo, M.: UDeploy: une infrastructure de déploiement pour les applications à base de composants logiciels distribués. Other. Université de Grenoble, 2011. French. <NNT: 2011GRENM001>. <tel-00685853>

3. Matougui, M.E.A., Leriche, S.: j-ASD: un middleware pour le déploiement logiciel autonomique. NOTERE/CFIP'12: Conférence Internationale Nouvelles Technologies de la Répartition/Colloque Francophone sur l'Ingénierie des Protocoles, Oct. 2012, Anglet, France. Cepadues. <hal-00757154>
4. Quinton, C., Duchien, L.: Vers un Outil de Configuration et de Déploiement pour les Nuages. JLdP - Journee Lignes de Produits, Nov 2012, Lille, France. pp. 83–94. <hal-00747319>
5. Flissi, A., Dubus, J., Dolet, N., Merle, P.: Deploying on the grid with deployware. In: CCGRID, pp. 177–184 (2008)
6. Eysholdt, M., Behrens, H.: Xtext: implement your language faster than the quick and dirty way. In: Cook, W.R., Clarke, S., Rinard, M.C. (eds.) Companion to the 25th Annual ACM SIGPLAN Conference on Object-Oriented Programming, Systems, Languages, and Applications, SPLASH/OOPSLA 2010, Reno/Tahoe, Nevada, USA. SPLASH/OOPSLA Companion, pp. 307–309. ACM, October 2010. doi:10.1145/1869542.1869625
7. Rellermeyer, Jan S., Alonso, G., Roscoe, T.: R-OSGi: distributed applications through software modularization. In: Cerqueira, R., Campbell, Roy H. (eds.) Middleware 2007. LNCS, vol. 4834, pp. 1–20. Springer, Heidelberg (2007). doi:10.1007/978-3-540-76778-7_1
8. Dearle, A., Kirby, G.N.C., McCarthy, A.: A framework for constraint- based deployment and autonomic management of distributed applications. CoRR, vol. abs/1006.4572 (2010)
9. Sledziewski, K., Bordbar, B., Anane, R.: A DSL-based approach to software development and deployment on cloud. In: 24th IEEE International Conference on Advanced Information Networking and Applications, AINA 2010, Perth, Australia. AINA, pp. 414–421. IEEE Computer Society, April 2010. doi:10.1109/AINA.2010.81
10. Boujbel, R., et al.: A DSL for multi-scale and autonomic software deployment. In: The Eighth International Conference on Software Engineering Advances, ICSEA 2013, pp. 291–296 (2013)
11. The Choco Team: Choco: an open source java constraint programming library. Ecole des Mines de Nantes, Research report (2010). http://www.emn.fr/z-info/choco-solver/pdf/choco-presentation.pdf
12. Saint-Andre, P., Smith, K., Tronçon, R.: XMPP: The Definitive Guide: Building Real-Time Applications with Jabber Technologies. O'Reilly Media, Inc. (2009)

IoT, Water, Land, Agriculture

WAZIUP: A Low-Cost Infrastructure for Deploying IoT in Developing Countries

Congduc Pham[1(✉)], Abdur Rahim[2], and Philippe Cousin[3]

[1] University of Pau, Pau, France
`congduc.pham@univ-pau.fr`
[2] CREATE-NET, Trento, Italy
`abdur.rahim@create-net.org`
[3] Easy Global Market, Sophia Antipolis, France
`philippe.cousin@eglobalmark.com`

Abstract. Long-range radio are promising technologies to deploy low-cost Low Power WAN for a large variety of IoT applications. There are however many issues that must be considered before deploying IoT solutions for low-income developing countries. This article will present these issues and show how they can be addressed in the context of African rural applications. We then describe the WAZIUP low-cost and long-range IoT framework. The framework takes cost of hardware and services as the main challenge to be addressed as well as offering quick appropriation and customization possibilities by third-parties.

Keywords: LPWAN · Low-power IoT · Low-cost IoT · Rural applications

1 Introduction

There are many opportunities for IoT applications in Africa and Fig. 1 shows some typical applications where remote monitoring facilities could greatly increase quality and productivity in a large variety of rural applications.

However, Africa's countries are facing many difficulties – lack of infrastructure, high cost of hardware, complexity in deployment, lack of technological eco-system and background, etc. – when it comes to real deployment of IoT solutions [1], especially in remote and rural areas which are typical of the Sub-Saharan Africa region. In this context, IoT deployment must address four major issues: (a) Longer range for rural access, (b) Cost of hardware and services, (c) Limit dependency to proprietary infrastructures and (d) Provide local interaction models. The WAZIUP project targeting deployment of low-cost IoT in sub-saharan Africa addresses these issues that are presented below.

Longer Range for Rural Access. Traditional mobile communication infrastructure (e.g., GSM/GPRS, 3G/4G) are still very expensive to deploy IoT devices. Moreover, they are definitely not energy efficient for autonomous devices

© ICST Institute for Computer Sciences, Social Informatics and Telecommunications Engineering 2018
T.F. Bissyande and O. Sie (Eds.): AFRICOMM 2016, LNICST 208, pp. 135–144, 2018.
https://doi.org/10.1007/978-3-319-66742-3_13

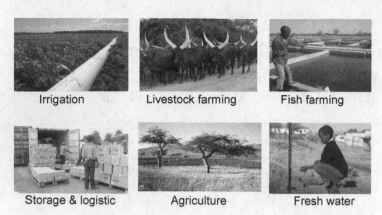

Fig. 1. Some ICT fields of IoT opportunities in rural environments

that must run on battery for months. Short-range technologies such as IEEE 802.15.4 can eventually be used by implementing multi-hop routing to overcome the limited transmission range but this can only be envisaged with high node density and easy access to power scenarios such as smart-cities environments. They can hardly be considered in isolated or rural environments.

Recent Low-Power Wide Area Networks (LPWAN) – Sigfox^{TM} or Semtech's LoRa^{TM} technology – provide a much more adapted connectivity answer for IoT in remote areas as a star topology with a central gateway or base station can be deployed. Most of long-range technologies can achieve 20 km or higher range in LOS condition and about 2 km in urban NLOS [2]. LoRa technology that can be privately deployed in a given area without any operator has a clear advantage in the context of developing countries over Sigfox which coverage is entirely operator-managed.

Cost of Hardware and Services. Commercial IoT devices are definitely too expensive for very low-income countries. In addition, these highly integrated devices are difficult to repair with their parts being hardly locally replaced. The availability of low-cost, open-source hardware platforms such as Arduino definitely pushes for a Do-It-Yourself (DIY) and "off-the-shelves" design approach: the Arduino Pro Mini based on an ATmega328 microcontroller has a high performance/price tradeoff and can be used to build a low-cost generic sensing IoT platform with LoRa long-range transmission capability for less than 10 euro. In addition, these boards also benefits from the support of a world-wide and active community of developers and a large variety of software libraries are available.

Commercial LPWAN gateways use advanced concentrator radio chips to listen on several channels and radio parameters simultaneously. The cost of such concentrator alone is more than a hundred euro. In the context of smaller scale rural applications, simpler "single-connection" gateways can be built using the same radio components than those for end-devices. Again, with "off-the-shelves" embedded Linux platforms such as the Raspberry PI the cost of an LPWAN gateway can be less than 45 euro.

Limit Dependency to Proprietary Infrastructures. Along with the world-wide IoT uptake a large variety of IoT clouds platforms offers an unprecedented level of diversity which contributes to limit dependency to proprietary infrastructures. Most of these dedicated IoT platforms have free account offers that, despite some limiting features, can largely satisfy the needs of most agriculture/micro and small farm/village business models. In order to take advantage of all these infrastructures, the design of an IoT versatile gateway should highly decouple the low-level gateway functionalities from the high-level data post-processing features to maximize the customization of the data management part. Furthermore, by privileging high-level scripting languages such as Python, the customization process can be done in a few minutes, using standard REST API interfaces to IoT clouds. Therefore, rather than focusing on large-scale deployment scenarios, easy integration of low-cost "off-the-shelves" components with simple, open programming libraries should be the main focus of IoT platforms in developing countries. WAZIUP provides code and example templates for quick appropriation and customization by third-parties.

Provide Local Interaction Models. With unstable and expensive accesses to the Internet, data received on the gateway should be locally stored. In addition, a versatile gateway is also an interesting feature where it should be possible to turn the gateway into an end computer by just attaching a keyboard and a display, and using visualizing data locally. With standard wireless technologies such as Wifi or Bluetooth, it is also interesting to provide local interaction with the end-user' smartphone/tablet to display captured data and notify users of important events without the need of Internet access. Figure 2 summarizes the various interaction models.

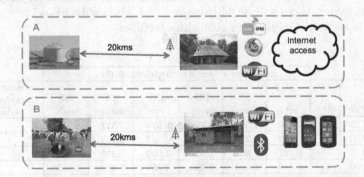

Fig. 2. Deployment scenarios in developing countries

Case A depicts an Internet access based on traditional technologies such as 3G/4G or DSL+WiFi. This Internet connection can be either privately owned or can rely on some community-based access. Case B depicts a fully autonomous gateway scenario: data from remote devices are collected and stored by the gateway and smartphones/tablets using standardized technologies such as WiFi or Bluetooth can provide user-friendly access – through a web server – to the data on the gateway.

The rest of the article is organized as follows. Section 2 gives some details on the long-range Semtech's LoRa technology used in WAZIUP project. In Sect. 3, we present the WAZIUP IoT platform that has been designed specifically to address the needs and constraints of low-income developing countries, illustrating how the project addresses the 4 issues previously identified. We conclude in Sect. 4.

2   Review of Long-Range Transmission and Low-Power WAN

2.1   Semtech's LoRa Technology

Semtech's LoRa (LOng-RAnge) technology [3,4] uses a well-known spread spectrum approaches. The high receiver's sensitivity is achieved by largely "spreading" data bits in both frequencies and time, thus reducing drastically the throughput. But then, the sensitivity at the receiver can be as low as -148 dBm in the 433 MHz band (-137 dBm in 868 MHz band). Range and throughput mainly depend on 2 parameters: BW and SF. BW is the physical bandwidth for RF modulation (e.g., 125 kHz). With larger bandwidth, higher effective data rate can be achieved, but reduced sensitivity is the cost to pay. SF is the spreading factor and the lower the SF, the higher the transmission rate with a decrease of the immunity to interference. In LoRa, each bit of payload information is represented by multiple chips of information and the ratio between the nominal symbol rate and chip rate is the spreading factor. For instance, with $SF = 6$ (minimum value), there will be 64 chips/symbol while with $SF = 12$ (maximum value), this ratio will increase to 4096 chips/symbol.

LoRa mode	BW	SF	time on air in second for payload size of						max thoughput (255B packet) in bps
			5 bytes	55 bytes	105 bytes	155 Bytes	205 Bytes	255 Bytes	
1	125	12	0.958	2.597	4.235	5.874	7.512	9.150	223
2	250	12	0.479	1.217	1.872	2.527	3.265	3.920	520
3	125	10	0.281	0.690	1.100	1.509	1.919	2.329	876
4	500	12	0.240	0.608	0.936	1.264	1.632	1.960	1041
5	250	10	0.140	0.345	0.550	0.755	0.959	1.164	1752
6	500	11	0.120	0.304	0.509	0.693	0.878	1.062	1921
7	250	9	0.070	0.183	0.295	0.408	0.521	0.633	3221
8	500	9	0.035	0.091	0.148	0.204	0.260	0.317	6442
9	500	8	0.018	0.051	0.082	0.115	0.146	0.179	11408
10	500	7	0.009	0.028	0.046	0.064	0.083	0.101	20212

Fig. 3. Time on air for various LoRa modes as payload size is varied

Figure 3 shows for various combinations of BW and SF the time-on-air of a LoRa packet as a function of the payload size in bytes. The maximum throughput is shown in the last column with a 255B-payload packet. Modes 4 to 6 can provide quite interesting trade-offs for longer range, higher data rate and immunity to interferences.

Currently, LoRa uses unlicensed spectrum bands that are usually somehow regulated in many countries. In Europe, LoRa transmissions fall into the Short Range Devices (SRD) category where the ETSI EN300-220-1 document [5] applies: transmitters are constrained to 1% duty-cycle (i.e., 36 s/h) and a maximum transmission power of 14 dBm in the general case. The global duty cycle enforcement usually limits the node's total transmission time, regardless of the frequency channel. The 36 s duty-cycle is however, in most cases, quite sufficient to most of deployed IoT applications. Advanced mechanisms that implement radio activity time sharing approach can provide an elegant solution to the duty-cycle limitation as well as providing QoS levels that is definitely lacking in most of long-range technologies. In sub-saharan Africa, the regulation may differ from one country to another and our low-cost LoRa IoT platform can be adapted to follow these regulations. For instance, when deploying in Senegal, we use the 863–865MHz band with a maximum transmission power of 10 dBm.

2.2 LoRa LPWAN Network Deployment and Architecture

The deployment of a LoRa LPWAN can rely on an operator but its most interesting feature is to allow completely ad-hoc deployment scenarios. Although P2P communications between devices are possible (mesh topology), the large majority of sensing applications have mainly uplink traffic patterns that can efficiently be handled by a gateway-centric approach (star topology). In typical public large-scale LPWAN architectures data from end-devices will be pushed to Internet network servers, see Fig. 4, and dedicated application servers, that are normally managed by end-users, will later on get and decode the sensed data. While this architecture offers the highest data transparency level, it needs

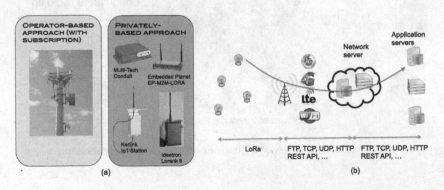

Fig. 4. (a) Gateway-centric deployment; (b) typical LPWAN architecture

various network elements and heavily relies on Internet connectivity. WAZIUP's approach is to prone a simpler approach for small, ad-hoc deployment scenarios such as those described in Fig. 2 where user's data servers or public IoT-specific cloud accounts will be accessed directly from the gateway.

3   Low-Cost LoRa IoT Platforms

3.1   Single-Connection Low-Cost LoRa Gateway

Under a full LoRaWAN specification [6], gateways must be able to simultaneously receive on several channels and LoRa settings, increasing dramatically the cost of the gateway's hardware. For developing countries, low cost and low complexity is more important to address small to medium size deployment scenarios for specific use cases instead of addressing large-scale, multi-purpose deployment scenarios. More than one gateway can deployed to serve several channel settings and this solution allows for incremental deployment as well as offering a higher level of redundancy.

Our LoRa gateway [7] is a so-called "single connection" gateway using the same simple radio module than for end-devices. Our communication library supports 7 radio models (the Libelium SX1272 LoRa, the HopeRF RFM92W/95W, the Modtronix inAir4/9/9B and the NiceRF SX1276) and most of SPI LoRa modules can actually be supported without modifications as reported by many users. The gateway is built on the well-known Raspberry PI (1B/1B+/2B/3B), see Fig. 5, and the cost of the entire gateway can be less than 45 euro.

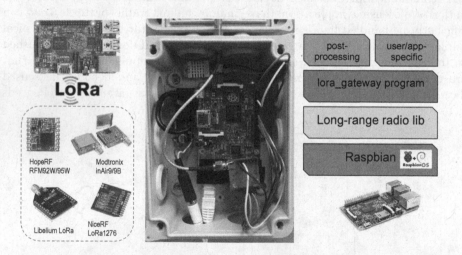

Fig. 5. Low cost gateway built from off-the-shelves components

The gateway's software is open-source running on top of a regular Raspberry Raspbian distribution. The original SX1272 communication library developed by the Libelium company has been greatly improved in many ways to provide enhanced radio channel access (CSMA-like with SIFS/DIFS) and support for both SX1272 and SX1276 chips that are used in most of radio modules available on the market.

The gateway has been tested in various conditions for several months while constantly monitoring the temperature and humidity level inside the case with a DHT22 sensor. Although the low-cost gateway is usually powered by a stable source of electricity, its consumption is low enough (about 400 mA for an RPIv3B with both WiFi and Bluetooth activated) to allow mobile applications with a high capacity battery pack offering more than 40 h of continuous operation.

3.2 Post-processing and Link with IoT Cloud Platforms

The gateway can be started in standalone mode as shown is Fig. 6a and packets received by the gateway are sent to the standard Unix-stdout stream.

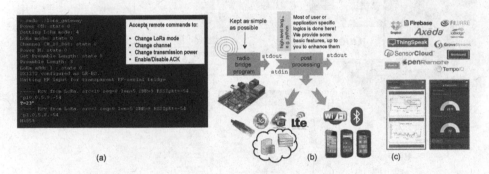

(a)   (b)   (c)

Fig. 6. Post-processing data from the gateway. (Color figure online)

All the added-value data post-processing tasks are performed after the low-level gateway stage with standard Unix redirection of low-level gateway's outputs as shown by the orange "post-processing" block in Fig. 6b. A `Python` high-level script implements all the data post-processing tasks such as access to IoT cloud platforms as well as AES encryption/decryption features. Various `Python` templates also show how to upload data on various publicly available IoT cloud platforms. Examples include `Dropbox`™, `Firebase`™, `ThingSpeak`™, `freeboard`™, `GrooveStream`™ & `FiWare`™, as illustrated in Fig. 6c.

With this architecture, WAZIUP clearly wants to decouple the low-level functionalities from the high-level features that mainly provide added-value data management facilities. With high-level languages for the data post-processing stage, the customization of data management tasks is made easier and quicker for third-parties. Therefore, the whole architecture and software stack offer either "out-of-the-box" utilization with the provided templates or quick appropriation & customization by third-parties. With the `ThingSpeak` template that WAZIUP is providing, a small farm can deploy in minutes a whole real-time remote sensing system with advanced visualization features.

3.3   Gateway Running Without Internet Access

Our low-cost gateway runs a MongoDB™ noSQL database to locally store received data, and a web server with PHP/jQuery to offer display of received data in graphic format. With the embedded web server, the gateway can therefore interact with the end-users' smartphone/tablet through WiFi or Bluetooth as depicted previously in Fig. 6b. Notification to users of important events can therefore be realized without the need of Internet access as this situation can clearly happen in very remote areas. Figure 7 shows for instance the web interface and an Android application using Bluetooth connectivity to demonstrate these local interaction models.

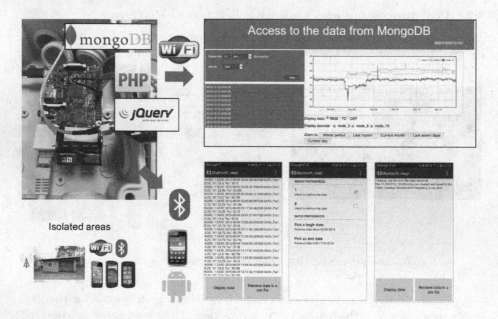

Fig. 7. Fully autonomous LoRa gateway

3.4   Low-Cost LoRa End-Devices

WAZIUP fully takes the "Arduino" philosophy for low-cost, simple-to-program yet efficient hardware platforms that is ideally well-suited for developing countries. It is also worth mentioning that these Arduino boards can be purchased quite easily world-wide. Our first experiences when transferring technical competencies in developing countries show that the issue of hardware availability should not be underestimated. The Arduino ecosystem is large and proposes various board models, from large and powerful prototyping boards to smaller and less energy-consuming boards for final integration purposes as illustrated in Fig. 8. The small form factor Arduino Pro Mini board that is available in the 3.3 V & 8 MHz version for much lower power consumption, can definitely be used

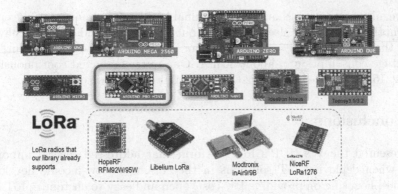

Fig. 8. Arduino low-cost ecosystem

to provide a generic IoT platform. The Pro Mini board if available for less than 2 euro from Chinese manufacturers.

WAZIUP develops and integrated building blocks for quick and easy new behaviour customization and physical sensor integration as shown in 9. Software building blocks provide security, transmission, activity & physical sensor management templates. Integration of new physical sensor can be realized without modifying the core template. Figure 9(right) also shows how the generic platform can be used to build a low-cost IoT device.

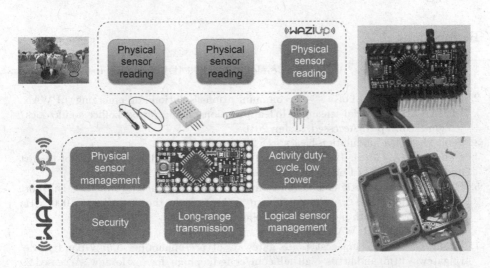

Fig. 9. Generic low-cost IoT platform and software building blocks

When deploying operational IoT application with low-power requirements, a deep-sleep mode is proposed in the example template. It is capable of running an Arduino Pro Mini for more than a year (assuming 1 measure/h) with

4 AA regular batteries without any additional hardware components. The energy consumption in this deep sleep mode is about $120\,\mu$A. Depending on the physical sensor that is needed, the activity time can be between 2 s to 8 s per hour, with an average consumption of about 50 mA. Our tests conducted continuously for the last 15 months demonstrates that Pro Mini clones are very reliable.

4   Conclusions

We presented the WAZIUP's IoT platform that addressed several important issues when deploying IoT solutions in the context of low-income developing countries. Focusing on providing low-cost, open and easy to customize IoT solutions, the WAZIUP IoT platform can provide quick and efficient answers for rural African application. The WAZIUP IoT platform framework is currently deployed in real cities, villages and farms test-beds. WAZIUP also supports a sustainable approach where the definitive target is to enable fast appropriation and new-market customized solutions. To do so, WAZIUP tightly involves end-users communities in the technical development and dissemination loop with frequent training and hackathon sessions organized in the sub-Saharan Africa region.

Acknowledgments. The WAZIUP project received funding from the European Union's Horizon 2020 research and innovation programme under grant agreement No 687607.

References

1. Zennaro, M., Bagula, A.: IoT for development (IOT4D). In: IEEE IoT Newsletter, 14 July 2015
2. Jeff McKeown, S.: LoRa^{TM}- a communications solution for emerging LPWAN, LPHAN and industrial sensing & IoT applications. http://cwbackoffice.co.uk/docs/jeff20mckeown.pdf. Accessed 13 Jan 2016
3. Semtech: LoRa modulation basics. rev.2-05/2015 (2015)
4. Goursaud, C., Gorce, J.: Dedicated networks for IoT : PHY/MAC state of the art and challenges. EAI Endorsed Trans. IoT **1**(1) (2015)
5. ETSI: Electromagnetic compatibility and Radio Spectrum Matters (ERM); Short Range Devices (SRD); radio equipment to be used in the 25 MHz to 1000 MHz frequency range with power levels ranging up to 500 mW; Part 1 (2012)
6. LoRaAlliance: LoRaWAN specification, v1.0 (2015)
7. Pham, C.: A DIY low-cost LoRa gateway. http://cpham.perso.univ-pau.fr/lora/rpigateway.html and https://github.com/congducpham/lowcostloragw. Accessed 29 Apr 2016

Design and Implementation of an Internet of Things Communications System for Legacy Device Control and Management

Martin Saint[1,2](✉), Aminata A. Garba[1], Audace Byishimo[1], and Rodrigue Gasore[1]

[1] Department of Electrical and Computer Engineering,
Carnegie Mellon University, Kigali, Rwanda
{msaint,aminata,abyishim,rgasore}@andrew.cmu.edu
[2] Interdisciplinary Telecommunications Program, College of Engineering and Applied Science, University of Colorado Boulder, Boulder, CO 80309-0530, USA
martin.saint@colorado.edu

Abstract. Applying the capabilities of the Internet of Things holds particular promise for advancing certain of the United Nations Sustainable Development Goals. For instance, citizens in many developing countries lack access to energy, and suffer from a lack of energy independence, scarcity, and high energy costs. Efforts are underway to make energy generation, transmission, and consumption more efficient via the application of modern communications and control. In this paper we focus on a communications and demand-side control application for legacy appliances. Instead of replacing existing devices with new "smart" devices with better communications capability, we integrate legacy devices into a centralized control system. We designed and implemented a communications system that allows control of infrared-enabled appliances over a network using wired or wireless communications. We designed a web application and user interface that can function remotely over the Internet, and use microcontrollers and infrared transmitters to communicate with infrared-enabled devices. We demonstrate a prototype of the system to control air conditioning units in a commercial building for energy management. The system uses open source hardware, software, and protocols. While we use energy management as an example, we focus on the general communications and control architecture, which is easily scalable and applicable to other devices and applications beyond those demonstrated here.

Keywords: Internet of Things (IoT) · Telecommunications · Wi-Fi · Internet · Pulse Width Modulation (PWM) · Infrared · Machine-to-machine · m2m · Energy management system · Smart building · Building automation system · eInfrastructure

1 Introduction

In most African countries electricity is scarce and expensive. In March 2016 the cost of electricity in Rwanda was US $0.22 per kilowatt-hour [1], compared to

© ICST Institute for Computer Sciences, Social Informatics and Telecommunications Engineering 2018
T.F. Bissyande and O. Sie (Eds.): AFRICOMM 2016, LNICST 208, pp. 145–154, 2018.
https://doi.org/10.1007/978-3-319-66742-3_14

an average cost in the US of US $0.126 for residential customers and US $0.101 for commercial use [2]. The United Nations Sustainable Development Goals call for affordable and clean energy for all, which serves as a foundation for other infrastructure and development [3]. Given limited resources in fossil fuels, the best solution to addressing global energy demand lies in renewable energy sources such as solar and wind, as well as various demand side management techniques that reduce energy consumption and increase efficiency [4]. Energy systems will benefit from applications of the Internet of Things to monitor, control, and manage generation, transmission, and energy demand [5].

In a small home it is easy to monitor and manage energy usage, and on a continent where the average income is not large, families are well aware of the financial impact of electricity usage. However, in large commercial buildings which lack any form of centralized energy management system, we observed ample opportunities for energy savings. Like similar buildings, our building was constructed to take advantage of natural light and ventilation where possible. During the day lighting was, in fact, seldom necessary. Ventilation, however, did not provide adequate cooling for most of the building, and therefore air conditioning units had been installed. On our campus, air conditioning was the largest consumer of electricity, and for this reason, we decided to focus our demand-side energy management efforts there.

In developed countries it is common for buildings to have central air conditioning, where cool air is delivered via ducts; or cold water or other refrigerant is delivered to individual fan-coil units distributed throughout the building. These systems depend on large centralized chillers or air conditioning units, and have electric or pneumatic controls which manage temperature and are often controllable from a remote central location. As is common in Africa, our building utilized a so-called *mini-split* or *ductless* system, which does not share any centralized components or control, and only serves one room per system. Mini-split systems have an air conditioning compressor and heat exchanger which is mounted on an exterior wall or balcony. The compressor serves a single fan-coil unit mounted in the room to be cooled, which is the component most users identify as the air conditioner, visible in Fig. 5. The compressor and fan coil unit are connected by refrigerant and electrical lines. The user can control functions such as temperature, fan speed, cooling mode, and blower vane direction via a keypad on the in-room unit, or with an infrared remote control. Our objective was to build an inexpensive communications system that can control infrared devices and centralize energy management using open source hardware and software. Our prototype focused on controlling air conditioning, but the approach is general and could apply to any other appliance which is infrared-enabled, such as floor fans or television monitors. It is also straightforward to retrofit infrared-enabled switches on lighting for a more comprehensive energy management system, but for this work we focus on air conditioning.

1.1 Other Work

Remotely monitored fire alarm systems date back to the 1870s, an example of an early building automation system [6]. Other building systems, such as elevators and heating/cooling, have had control systems for decades [7]. While not necessarily sophisticated or interconnected, they did provide a degree of automation and control for large buildings. The Internet of Things (IoT) provides new capabilities for smart buildings, and even smart homes. The International Telecommunication Union defines the Internet of Things as "a global infrastructure for the information society, enabling advanced services by interconnecting (physical and virtual) things based on existing and evolving interoperable information and communication technologies" [8]. The IoT enables better synergy between three functions that have traditionally been difficult to integrate in building automation: monitoring, communications, and computation [9]. The IoT also enables connecting a larger variety of devices at lower cost, more monitoring and control options, and offers the possibility of using open source hardware, software, and communication protocols.

With the continuing development of the Internet of Things, a larger number of "smart" appliances and devices are being manufactured. These include devices with embedded sensors, radio frequency identification (RFID) tags, microcontrollers, and wireless transmitters and receivers. This enables the devices to integrate into home or building networks, and allows users to control them even over the Internet. We wanted to achieve similar functionality, but with existing non-smart devices. Undertaking work similar to ours, applications have been developed for controlling devices in buildings and the home using a variety of universal input devices. The Remote Commander was an early application which enabled users to control a personal computer using a handheld device [10,11]. This work is cited by Nguyen et al. as an influence in their research developing appliance control systems using infrared and powerline communications [12]. Powerline communications were also used for controlling smart appliances via a network by Kim et al. [13] and Khan et al. [14]. Ballagas et al. were pioneers in using smart phones as input and control devices, and developed a number of user interface guidelines [15].

The user input devices, whether smartphones, PCs, 2000s-era personal digital assistants (PDAs), or proprietary controllers, must ultimately be able to communicate with the devices they are intended to control. This typically requires an adapter, also called a proxy or bridge. The input device communicates to the adapter, which either controls the device state directly, or translates between communication protocols in the input device and the device or appliance it is intended to control. One of the first widely used protocol and adapter families was X10, primarily for home automation applications. It uses a proprietary command module, the X10 powerline communications protocol, and various control modules such as switches and timers. It can be used to control devices such as lights and appliances, and later featured control software which could run on a PC. Device control is also possible via the IEEE 1394 protocol, which until recently was widely used in personal computers for a wired connection to peripheral devices, but also had wireless, coaxial, and fiber optic versions. Universal Plug and Play (UPnP) performs similar device-to-device communications for home use, but does not scale well to commercial applications. Commercial building automation is frequently accomplished via proprietary interface devices and protocols such as Modbus, LonWorks, and BACnet. For our application we wanted to use open source hardware, software, and protocols to the extent possible, and we wanted the system to be wireless. We wanted hardware which was inexpensive and readily available, and we wanted to build a system which was scalable and available from any user input device. In keeping with the *appropriate technology* for developing countries theme proposed by Schumacher [16], we wanted to create a solution which solved our problem and met our design goals as simply as possible, and was simple for the end user to understand and operate. This precluded the use of proprietary modules, protocols, and interfaces, and we needed a system which did not depend upon smart appliances. By utilizing the existing infrared control capability of the legacy air conditioners in our building we were able to design and implement a communications and control system for central energy management. The system uses infrared communications to control the air conditioners, and Wi-Fi and the Internet to permit the user to send commands from ordinary devices like smart phones or laptops from anywhere.

2   System Model and Design

The system architecture is shown in Fig. 1, which illustrates the web-based communications system designed for infrared appliance control. Details of the system are as follows.

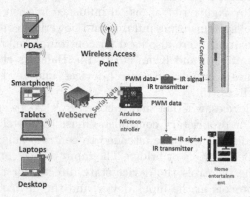

Fig. 1. The architectural view of the system.

2.1   System Components

The system is composed of:

1. A web server hosting a responsive web application. This provides the user with interface buttons rendered in software which control the same functions as the buttons available on the original factory remote control or on the air conditioner itself.

2. An Internet-enabled user interface device, such as a smart phone, tablet, laptop, or desktop computer. This permits access to the application on the web server.
3. An Arduino microcontroller and infrared control library, used to connect the web server hosting the control application to an infrared transmitter. The communication between the web server and the microcontroller can be via a wired or wireless connection.
4. Infrared transmitters, used to send control signals to the appliances as directed by the infrared control library on the Arduino.
5. Infrared-enabled target devices, such as building or home systems. In this case, air conditioners in individual rooms.

2.2 System Operation

To control the designated building or home devices, the application is opened by an authorized user on the desired user interface device, such as a smart phone. An Internet connection is established between the user interface device and the web server hosting the interface application. The user selects the device to be controlled, and is presented with a menu of control functions. For an air conditioner these consist of setting the cooling mode, temperature, the direction of airflow, or turning the device on or off. After the user selects the desired control function the web server sends an American Standard Code for Information Interchange (ASCII) text code corresponding to the instruction to the microcontroller. The microcontroller maps the ASCII code into an appropriate pulse width modulated (PWM) control command, and the PWM code is sent to the infrared transmitter(s). The infrared transmitter then sends the appropriate control command to the device being controlled, such as the air conditioner. In the next section we discuss the design considerations which were necessary to make the system operational.

2.3 User Interface Application

The user interface is a web application built using the HyperText Markup Language (HTML). To accommodate a variety of user interface devices we use responsive web design. As the user switches from one interface device to another, the interface application automatically adapts to the different device capabilities, such as for resolution, image size, and scripting language. This eliminates the need for the user to resize the application window, pan, or scroll in order to view the website on different devices. The user interface is composed of (1) the list of appliances to be controlled; and (2) the soft control keys that map to the control functions available for each device to be controlled. Each end device to be controlled must be preconfigured in the system so that it can be uniquely identified by the user and web application, and so that control functions appropriate for that device will appear in the user interface. For the system detailed in this paper we customized the interface application to control several Carrier brand air conditioner units in different rooms on our campus.

2.4 Web Server

The web server application was developed using the Node.js runtime environment, which is designed to build network applications with modules written in the JavaScript programming language [17]. It is an open source, cross-platform runtime for server-side programming that can run on all modern operating systems. As Node.js is non-blocking and utilizes JavaScript, an interpreted language, it responds to input in real-time and enables real-time communication [18]. After receiving user input, the web server sends an ASCII code that is specific for every instruction to an Arduino microcontroller.

2.5 Microcontroller

We used an Arduino UNO microcontroller for transmission of the signal from the web server to the end device to be controlled [19]. An Arduino program, or sketch, was written to transmit a signal corresponding to the user input command to the end appliance via an infrared transmitter connected to the board. Communication between the web server, microcontroller, and IR transmitter can be wired or wireless. With a wired connection cables are used between the web server, the microcontroller, and the IR transmitters. This option has the advantage of minimizing interference with other communications. However, to install the system for operation in multiple rooms would require installing cables to connect all devices, and likely a microcontroller per room. With a wireless connection, infrared modules are wirelessly connected to the microcontroller. This solution is easier to scale.

2.6 Infrared Transmitter

The infrared transmitter must be located within line of sight to the device it is intended to control and has a typical range of 10 to 15 m. The transmission pattern is relatively narrow, so for practical reasons this typically means one infrared transmitter for each end device to be controlled.

2.7 Control Commands

Every manufacturer and device model has its own set of control commands. Some manufacturers make these available on their official website. Another method of determining the appropriate commands is by capturing them from an existing infrared remote control transmitter supplied with the device to be controlled. We implemented a microcontroller program that listens to an infrared receiver connected to the Arduino and records the incoming set of commands from the manufacturer remote control. These commands are used later by a second programmed sketch that listens on a serial port for ASCII commands from the web server and communicates to the infrared transmitter in our system. The signal exchanged between the microcontroller/infrared transmitter and the infrared receivers is modulated using pulse width modulation (PWM), which is a technique of encoding a message into a pulsing signal [20].

3   Prototype and System Demonstration

We used our infrared receiver to capture control signals from the legacy remote control for the Carrier brand air conditioners used in our building, see Fig. 2. To assist with code capture we used the open-source IRremote Arduino library from Shirrif [21]. We modified the library to support the control commands required for our demonstration on different Carrier air conditioners. The commands captured by our infrared receiver are decoded by the library, and the corresponding voltages can be observed and saved into a text file, see Fig. 3. These commands are copied to the Arduino microcontroller sketch and can be transmitted using the infrared library. We designed and implemented the web server application and configured it to control the target Carrier air conditioners. Figure 4 shows a screenshot of the application running on a laptop PC. Via the desired user interface device and interface program we were able to successfully:

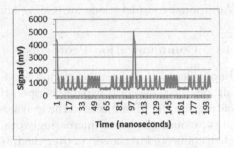

Fig. 2. Signal code capture from a legacy remote control via an infrared receiver.

Fig. 3. Voltage over time representation of the pulse width modulated *on* command for a Carrier air conditioner.

- Select the desired room or location.
- Select the desired device to control.
- Toggle the power on and off using the power control button.
- Change the cooling mode from the available options.
- Change the desired temperature set point within the range permitted by the manufacturer.
- Change the air direction and swing mode using the appropriate button.

The infrared transmitter and air conditioner being controlled are shown in Fig. 5. The air conditioner has a factory infrared receiver designed to accept commands from the factory remote control.

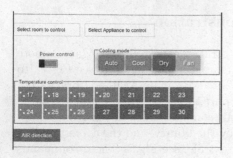

Fig. 4. Screenshot of the user interface.

Fig. 5. Infrared transmitter and air conditioner.

4 Discussion

Additional considerations for scaling and extending the project follow.

4.1 Communication Protocols

In our demo, the system operation was limited to the local area network (LAN), although the design is capable of operating over the Internet. This requires allocating a public IP address to the web server. The web server could also be hosted in the cloud, which is an increasingly practical option. The microcontroller unit is then connected to the server over the Internet, and wireless modules are mounted on the microcontroller for local connectivity. In addition to Wi-Fi, other communication protocols such as cellular wireless (GSM communication, 3G, 4G) can be used. The system could also be modified to incorporate other communication protocols for some functions under appropriate conditions, such as Bluetooth or ZigBee.

4.2 Device and Function Scalability

The proposed system is scalable to as many devices as desired as long as the initial commands are available from the manufacturer or can be captured using the legacy infrared remote control. Each time a new device is added, the web application is updated to support it and to present the device in the user interface. An interesting possibility is the idea of scaling the system to add new control functions beyond the ones initially programmed by the vendor. New functions can readily be created and communicated between the user interface device, interface application, web server, microcontroller, and infrared transmitter. Scaling the functionalities of a device becomes a question of envisioning the new functions and being able to successfully modify the device to support the new functions. Many devices already contain microprocessors, so they are limited only by their (current) inability to communicate.

4.3   Machine to Machine Communications

In the system demonstrated, integration of the infrared-enabled devices with the IoT is accomplished using a web application and a user interface. This human-to-machine communication model is extensible to enable machine-to-machine communication and control. For example, with smart grid communications, commands can be sent from a smart meter, energy controller, or an alternative energy system to appliances. The devices can be instructed to turn on or off, or to run with full or reduced functionality based on the availability or cost of energy. In such a case the proposed system runs an additional algorithm which takes as inputs the building energy information and control parameters and automatically sends the appropriate commands to the appliances. Similarly, the web application can send information to the home energy controller about the state of the appliances and their energy usage. This information could be utilized to construct a machine learning algorithm for forecasting and predictive control of energy generation and loads, enhancing capabilities for demand-side management.

5   Conclusion

In this paper we presented the design of a communications system for control of infrared-enabled appliances using a custom responsive web application. We demonstrated a working prototype of the system which controls air conditioners located in different rooms of a building. We showed that the proposed system does not require a line of sight between the user and the controlled appliance, and that it can work remotely. The communications and control system enables the integration of legacy infrared-enabled electrical and electronic devices into a building automation network using the Internet of Things. Significantly, it enables convenience and energy-savings without replacing existing appliances.

References

1. Economic Regulation Unit: Key statistics in electricity sub-sector as of March of the year 2016. Rwanda Utilities Regulatory Authority, Kigali, Rwanda, Report, March 2016
2. U.S. Energy Information Administration: Electric power monthly with data for. U.S. Department of Energy, Washington, DC, Report, March 2016
3. General Assembly: Transforming our world: the 2030 Agenda for sustainable development, United Nations, New York, Resolution A/RES/70/1, 25 September 2015
4. Suberu, M.Y., Mustafa, M.W., Bashir, N., Muhamad, N.A., Mokhtar, A.S.: Power sector renewable energy integration for expanding access to electricity in sub-Saharan Africa. Renew. Sustain. Energy Rev. **25**, 630–642 (2013)
5. Siano, P.: Demand response and smart grids-a survey. Renew. Sustain. Energy Rev. **30**, 461–478 (2014)
6. Moore, W.D.: Fire alarm system research-where it's been and where it's going, White Paper. Hughes Associates, Warwick, RI (2006)

7. Kastner, W., Neugschwandtner, G., Soucek, S., Newman, H.M.: Communication systems for building automation and control. Proc. IEEE **93**(6), 1178–1203 (2005)
8. Telecommunication Standardization Sector: Series Y: Global information infrastructure, Internet protocol aspects and next-generation networks-next generation networks-frameworks and functional architecture models-overview of the Internet of things. International Telecommunication Union, Geneva, Switzerland, Recommendation ITU-T Y.2060, June 2012
9. Dietrich, D., Bruckner, D., Zucker, G., Palensky, P.: Communication and computation in buildings: a short introduction and overview. IEEE Trans. Ind. Electron. **57**(11), 3577–3584 (2010)
10. Myers, B.A.: Using handhelds and PCs together. Commun. ACM **44**(11), 34–41 (2001)
11. Nichols, J., Myers, B.A.: Studying the use of handhelds to control smart appliances. In: Proceedings of 23rd International Conference on Distributed Computing System Workshops, pp. 274–279. IEEE, May 2003
12. Nguyen, T.V., Lee, D.G., Seol, Y.H., Yu, M.H., Choi, D.: Ubiquitous access to home appliance control system using infrared ray and power line communication. In: 3rd IEEE/IFIP International Conference in Central Asia on Internet (ICI 2007), Tashkent, pp. 1–4. IEEE, September 2007
13. Kim, D., Jun, T., Kwon, W.H.: Home network systems for networked appliances using power-line communication. In: 30th Annual Conference on IEEE Industrial Electronics Society (IECON), vol. 3, pp. 2394–2399. IEEE, November 2004
14. Khan, S., Islam, R., Khalifa, O.O., Omar, J., Hassan, A., Adam, I.: Communication system for controlling smart appliances using power line communication. In: 2nd International Conference on Information and Communication Technology, Damascus, vol. 2, pp. 2595–2600. IEEE (2006)
15. Ballagas, R., Borchers, J., Rohs, M., Sheridan, J.G.: The smart phone: a ubiquitous input device. IEEE Pervasive Comput. **5**(1), 70–77 (2006)
16. Schumacher, E.F.: Small is Beautiful: A Study of Economics as if People Mattered. HarperCollins, Scranton (1973)
17. Node.js Foundation: Node.js (2016). https://nodejs.org
18. Widman, J.: Overview of blocking vs non-blocking, GitHub Repository, March 2016. https://github.com/nodejs/node/blob/master/doc/topics/blocking-vs-non-blocking.md
19. Arduino.cc: Arduino UNO & Genuino UNO, n.d. https://www.arduino.cc/en/Main/ArduinoBoardUno
20. Hirzel, T.: PWM, Arduino Forum, n.d. http://www.arduino.cc/en/Tutorial/PWM
21. Shirriff, K.: IRremote Arduino library, GitHub Repository (2016). https://github.com/shirriff/Arduino-IRremote

Classification of Water Pipeline Failure Consequence Index in High-Risk Zones: A Study of South African Dolomitic Land

Achieng G. Ogutu, Okuthe P. Kogeda$^{(\boxtimes)}$, and Manoj Lall

Computer Science Department, Faculty of Information Communication Technology, Tshwane University of Technology, Private Bag X680, Pretoria 0001, South Africa
achienggrc8@gmail.com, {kogedaPO,lallM}@tut.ac.za

Abstract. Increasing numbers of pipeline breakdown experienced by utilities undoubtedly raise alarms concerning the anticipated failure consequences. Seemingly mild, these consequences can however, fluctuate to severe or fatal, especially in high risk locations. Utility personnel are therefore pressured to employ up-to-par operational policies in attempt to minimize possible fatalities. This however, may be overwhelming considering inherent uncertainties that make it difficult to understand and adapt these consequences into utilities' risk management structure. One way of handling such uncertainties is through the use of Bayesian Networks (BNs), which can comfortably combine supplementary information and knowledge. In this paper therefore, we present an overview of the causes and impacts of pipeline failure. We aggregate and classify failure consequences in a select high risk zone into four indexes; and finally, we outline how BNs can accommodate these indexes for pipeline failure prediction modeling. These indexes function as effective surrogate inputs where data is unavailable.

Keywords: Pipeline failure · Failure impacts · Consequence index · Dolomitic land · Predictive modeling · High-risk zones · Water leakage

1 Introduction

Pipeline systems are a fundamental division of the social infrastructure, considering their facilitation of material conveyance, supply and distribution to and from various locations [1]. With such a worthy responsibility, they are under constant performance and operational pressure [2], which in one way or another destabilizes their structural orientation leading to failure [2, 3]. Failures along pipelines transpire in different ways, and therefore have attracted an extended scope of definitions, largely based on suitability. In [4–7], failure is defined as the occurrence of bursts along a pipe or several other pipes in a network, while other research outputs [3, 8, 9] describe pipe breaks as a form of failure. In [10], cracks along the pipelines qualify them as failure candidates whereas in [11], an eventual pipe collapse due to continued exposure to several pipe deteriorative aspects is defined as failure. Regardless of the diversity in manifestation,

© ICST Institute for Computer Sciences, Social Informatics and Telecommunications Engineering 2018
T.F. Bissyande and O. Sie (Eds.): AFRICOMM 2016, LNICST 208, pp. 155–164, 2018.
https://doi.org/10.1007/978-3-319-66742-3_15

failure results to one uniform consequence (material loss). Therefore, *pipeline failure* can generally be defined as 'the unintended loss of pipeline contents' [12].

These failures are unavoidable [2], just as much as their unanticipated results are undesirable [2, 13–15]. For this reason, utilities are constantly on the lookout for better management and preventive tools in attempt to minimize extensive losses [2, 13, 16]. In oil and gas facilities, pipeline failures are undoubtedly hazardous and fatal [13] However, an almost equal level of fatalities should be expected in the case of water pipeline failure, because they are accompanied with exceedingly widespread impact index [2].

2 Causes of Water Pipe Failures

There exists a significant body of literature analyzing various aspects that directly or indirectly influence pipeline breakdown, for instance, in [2] factors causing failure in Pre-stressed Concrete Cylinder pipes (PCCP) and metallic pipes were examined. In both materials, corrosion was established as the highest failure contributor. An almost similar review conducted on waste water pipes indicated that construction dynamics and local external influence, as well as pipe age and other pipe characteristics and also contributed to failure [11]. In yet another study [17], pipe material, inappropriate pipe operation, earth movements and weather fluctuations were identified as possible threats on pipe integrity. To add to the list, improper pipe installation and water hammer surges were identified as possible failure threats in [9].

Identification of the factors influencing failure may be extracted with ease from the abovementioned articles [2, 9, 11, 17]; however, understanding how the different factors individually contribute to failure is of equal importance. An extensive research on corrosion effect was conducted in [9, 18, 19]. The respective studies adequately explained how corrosion affects failure in different pipe materials. Effects of pipe age on failure was also discussed in [3, 4, 8, 9, 18, 20], with [4, 9] also reporting on how pipe material influences failure. An aspect reported to highly test the strength of a pipe material however, was environmental fluctuations, especially temperature, given its ability to catalyze reactions, leading failure [9, 21]. Due to space limitations, a summary of influential factors, which in one way or another, contribute to pipeline failure, together with their possible nature of effect is given in Table 1.

Table 1. Summary of pipeline failure causes

Category	Individual factors	Mode of influence
Environmental factors	Corrosion	Causes loss of pipe mass through oxidation to soluble iron
	Ground movement	– Causes permanent ground damage – Affects pipe layout hence leads to breakages – Causes soil movement
	External load	– Increases the external stress level of the pipes – Exists in form of roads, railways, buildings, tunnels, excess soil, mud, dust, glaciers or frost

(continued)

Table 1. (*continued*)

Category	Individual factors		Mode of influence
	Temperature fluctuations		– Extremely cold temperature causes freezing, and at freezing point, water begins to expand forcing pipes to swell and break – High temperatures catalyses chemical reaction in water, hence propagating corrosion
	Soil acidity or alkalinity		Influences chemical reaction externally thereby propagating external corrosion
	Soil moisture content		Freezing of soil moisture content causes expansion of the soil hence creates vertical forces on pipes
Pipe properties	Static factors	Material	Depict pipe strength characteristics and also determines pipes corrosion characteristics
		Pipe joints	Are affected by external pressure and earth movements, hence prone to leakages
		Diameter	Small diameter pipes are identified to be more prone to failure than large diameter pipes
	Time dependent	Age	Indicates the length of time a pipe has been exposed to loading and the surrounding environment
		Break history	Clearly states the condition of a particular pipe, the more the breaks the poorer the condition
Poor installation/poor workmanship	Pipe embedment		Poor bedding deprives adequate support to the pipe leading to joint movements. Lack of uniformed bedding offers poor support
	Improper alignment		Causes longitudinal breaks in pipes, because of improper pipe gradient
	Poor backfilling		– Failure to remove rocks and trees from trenches or supporting pipe sockets on displaceable bricks or blocks leads to pipe breakage – Leaving decomposable materials can catalyze chemical decay and corrosion
	Damage due to improper handling		Poor handling of pipe during installation or manufacturing may result in cracks or other physical deformities
Manufacturing defects	Manufacturing defects are the largest contributors to pipes initial failures. Pipes should be carefully tested for cracks or any other possible defects before they are put to use, for instance, Cast Iron (CI) pipes should undergo "ring testing" after manufacturing and before installation to ensure its safety		

3 Consequences of Pipeline Failures

The impacts of pipeline failures, as described in [13] refer to the quantification of risk, which could be in the form of the number of affected individuals, damaged property, polluted environment, delayed missions and amount of product lost. These impacts materialize in different ways, directly and indirectly, and for this reason, there is a wide range of literature focusing on different failure consequences [2, 13, 16]. In [16], the financial impact of pipeline failure was analyzed and classified into three major categories: (i) value of product possibly lost, (ii) value of property damage (private, public and operator property) and (iii) the cost of recovery and cleanup.

Correspondingly, in [2], cost implications of failure were again studied and classified into direct, indirect and social costs. As one of the most critical social costs however, poor water quality resulting from contamination due to intrusion of particles into the pipe as a result of pressure reduction was also discussed. Among other effects of contamination, possible poisoning, illnesses as well as death of persons were identified. Similarly, another classification was done in [13], and failure consequences were organized into three general categories given as: (i) personnel, (ii) environmental and (ii) economic consequences.

Apart from the already identified consequences of pipeline failures, it was made clear in [2] that extensive research is still required so as to assist in the determination of the true magnitude of the indirect and the social consequences of pipeline failures. This would consequently enhance inclusion of these impacts in rehabilitation modeling. However, determination and quantification of some specific losses may be difficult, and utilities too may consider their information as confidential [2, 13]. It is important therefore, to classify some of these consequences in a way that makes them easily adaptable in the development of failure prediction models. This may as well accommodate the incorporation of non monetary consequences in modeling pipeline failure for extended decision making.

4 Failure in High Risk Zones

High risk zones in this context refer to areas that are underlain with naturally occurring or man-made grounds that are potentially challenging, and are commonly associated with structural damage [23]. Classification of a region as a high risk zone is however relative, given the severity of risk or consequences it may suffer from failure or by the different ways it is likely to contribute to failure. In a detailed report relayed in [23], potentially unsafe grounds were categorized into four categories; (i) expansive, (ii) collapsible, (iii) dispersive soils, as well as (iv) soft clays. Expansive soils were identified as those that have the potential to expand or shrink depending on variations in soil moisture conditions [9, 23]. Collapsible grounds were described as those that are likely to undergo abrupt volume reduction in the presence of sufficient triggering mechanisms. Soft clays and dispersive grounds, however, were said to be associated with extreme moisture contents and large volumes of Exchangeable Sodium Percentage (ESP) respectively [23, 37]. For an in-depth understanding of the problematic soils and the different mechanisms leading to hazardous events, a comprehensive review is done in [23, 37].

4.1   The Study Area

Situated in Gauteng, South Africa, Doringkloof region is a complete Dolomitic land. Dolomitic or dolomite land refers to regions underlain by dolomite rock, either directly or at shallow depths of possibly below 100 m [24, 26, 37]. The rocks are composed of a carbonate of magnesium and calcium; and are soluble in water [24, 25]. When these rocks dissolve in water, voids and cavities are created within the rocks, the upper soil cover may then collapse in to fill the void causing massive ground movement [24, 26, 37]. This qualifies the region to be categorized under collapsible soil [23]. Public works reports [25] as well as other research findings in [24, 26, 27] indicate that approximately 38 lives have been lost due to sinkhole formation in various regions including homes, entertainment and business premises. Sinkholes result from the collapse of surface soil into the hollowing underground rocks created as a result of rock solubility leading to formation of voids and cavities [24–26, 37].

An illustration of the process of sinkhole formation is shown in Fig. 1. Apart from the naturally occurring conducive underground activities; human activities also propagate the formation of sinkholes [25]. They may occur soon after installation of infrastructure due to poor workmanship or after some time due to material deterioration, which in this case, one major contributor is leakage from wet services like clean and waste water mains [25]. For this reason water leakage in such a risky environment should be treated with utmost urgency, and as much as possible, proactive measures should be put to place in attempt to capture failure possibilities before actual occurrence.

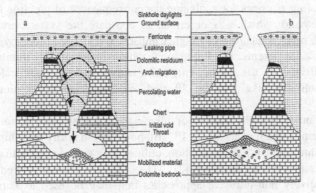

Fig. 1. Sinkhole formation mechanism [26]

5   Classification of Failure Consequence Index

The potential implication of failure in a given pipe section stands out as the most significant factor for the determination of the intensity and kind of effort that ought to be invested into collecting data about the water main [2]. In addition, it determines the level of prioritization of the water main for rehabilitation, repair or replacement [2, 22, 30]. For this reason, estimation of impending consequences from a pipe failure ought to address the questions: "What can be harmed by the failure? And how badly are they likely to be harmed?" [12]. Response to these questions consequently makes it possible to determine the water mains that have the most potentially severe outcomes in the event of failure, making it possible to exercise prioritization [22]. In addition, inclusion of the factors that addresses the said concerns in failure modeling would support the development of rehabilitation, replacement or condition assessment tools and programs using available limited resources [22, 30].

Following a rather satisfactory investigation, it was pointed out in [30] that apart from the general effects resulting from pipe failure, influential factors for failure modeling ought to address specific characteristics. These aspects include land use around the water main, population that might possibly be affected by the failure, the length and diameter of the water main. In a subsequent analysis conducted in [30] therefore, the consequences of pipeline failure were rated using three matrices given as: Land Use (LU), Pipe Diameter (PD) and the Population density (PP). Among all the classified consequences, pipe diameter was considered to hold the highest impact on the consequence level. This is largely due to the fact that pipe diameter dictates whether the pipe is a trunk main or an ordinary distribution main, which in turn quantifies the amount of loss that may be accumulated from a failure [2, 22, 30].

In yet another investigation, a model was developed in [5] to assist in determination of the risk of burst in trunk water mains. During the development of the consequence element of the model, the quantification was estimated by mainly considering repair and replacement costs and the costs of damage to private and commercial property. Other factors included were sensitive and key customers, which fit into the Land use category described in [30]. On the other hand, an almost similar analysis performed in [22] suggested four matrices for analyzing the consequences of pipeline failure. These included (i) demand; which was described to compare the system pressure against demand at each node, indicating that higher impacts were experienced by high-demand nodes during failure events. (ii) Population; which indicated the number of people likely to be affected by the failure. (iii) Land use and (iv) economic loss matrices, representing activities likely to be affected and financial implications of failure respectively.

Consideration of financial impacts of failure stands out as quite profound in almost all of the abovementioned analyses [2, 13, 16], however, majority of failure impacts are not easy to quantify [2, 31, 32]. In addition, utilities may not be willing to provide some financial details about their operations [21, 31], as they may be considered confidential. Therefore, relatively non-intrusive approaches that may be used as surrogate inputs should be embraced by researchers, developers and utilities at large. In Table 2, a classification of some of the consequences of failure; and respective inputs that they may represent are outlined. These surrogate inputs are none-intrusive and do not contain utilities sensitive information but are however, still adequate enough for failure modeling.

Table 2. Classification of the consequence index of pipeline failure

Index	Description	Represented inputs	Other possible representations
Pipe diameter (PD)	– Refers to the carrying capacity of the pipe – Commonly measured in millimeters (mm)	Amount/value of water loss, pipe usage/service level, environmental damage	Resistance to pressure – Construction standards – Manufacturing method – Pipe resilience
Activity Pressure (AP)	– Refers to the various activities carried out in the regions serviced by the pipe, commonly known as the degree of land usage around the pipe – Also quantified by the amount of commercial or agricultural premises served by a pipe	Activities likely to be affected by the failure, Sensitive or key customer base, secondary damage, service disruption cost, recovery cost	– Operating pressure – Pipe diameter – Private and public property damage – Service demand – Public image – Pipe use – Environmental damage
Population Pressure (PP)	– Refers to the number of persons served by a pipe section – Mostly quantified by the number of households surrounding the pipe segment or a rough estimate of a community's population density	Cost of service disruption, social costs, quantity of persons affected by failure, Health risks	– Pipe usage – Pipe diameter – Public health risk – Service demand – Operating pressure – Quality of life – Public image – Conceivable amount of fatalities
Operational pressure (OP)	Represents the weight of service demand from a pipe	Demand, pipe use, failure rate, amount of water loss	– Pipe pressure – Water velocity – Construction standards – Manufacturing method – Pipe resilience

6 Relevance of This Classification in Uncertainty Modeling

Pipeline failure process is a subject that is not fully comprehensible [21], given the level of complexities and uncertainties it is accompanied by. Likewise, availability of data regarding the failures and their subsequent consequences is daunting. Existing data therefore, tend to be either deficient or with defective information [3, 20]. Additionally, there is lack of a standard procedure for estimation, categorization and quantification of failure consequences. These challenges have, in a great way contributed to uncertainties in available data. However, availability dynamic models like Bayesian Networks (BNs), that are able to incorporate expert knowledge together with auxiliary information, make it possible to handle these inherent uncertainties, thereby enhancing precision in pipeline failure prediction [30, 33].

6.1 Overview of Bayesian Networks

BNs are graphical models used for reasoning under uncertainty. For this course, they depict a system as a network of interacting variables, with the variables presented as *nodes* and the interaction among them presented as *arcs* joining the nodes to indicate causal dependencies among them [33–35]. These interactions are the aspects used to determine the eventual behavior of a given system [35, 38], and are also instrumental for representation of uncertainty.

Uncertainty in this case, is determined by associating probabilities with the links between the variables [36]. These probabilities, however, must conform to three basic rules; (i) $P(A)$, the probability of an event A must be between 0 and 1. (ii) $P(A) = 0$ means that A is impossible, while $P(A) = 1$ means that A is definite. (iii) $P(A$ or $B) = P(A) + P(B)$, provided A and B are disjoint [36]. Conditional probabilities are then computed and later updated using the Bayes, theorem, as shown in Eq. (1). Given n number of mutually exclusive variables $X_{i \, (i = 1, 2, ..., n)}$ and observed data Y, updating of probabilities is done by:

$$P(x_i|Y) = [P(Y|X_i) \times p(X_i)]/[\Sigma_j p(Y|X_i)P(X_j)] \tag{1}$$

Where $p(X|Y)$ is the posterior occurrence probability of X on condition that Y occurs, $p(X)$ is the prior occurrence probability of X, $p(Y)$ for marginal (total) occurrence probability of Y which is considered constant given the data at hand, and finally $p(Y|X)$ representing the conditional occurrence probability of Y on condition that X occurs, also viewed as the likelihood distribution. These indexes can therefore, be plotted systematically to produce understandable causal dependencies in pipe failure. The classification also accommodates incorporation of non monetary consequences in modeling pipeline failure for extended decision making.

7 Conclusion and Future Work

In this paper, a review of the causes of failures along pipelines, as well as the associated consequences of these failures has been conducted. The causes of pipeline failure are found to be widely distributed and dependent on fluctuating natural and man-made conditions. Similarly, the consequences are just as diverse as the respective causes. An open classification of these consequences has also been done, indicating the different surrogate inputs that may be used in situations where availability of sensitive information may not be possible. These inputs however, may only be applicable when modeling techniques applied are fit enough to handle data uncertainty.

Therefore, following the above classification, BN models will be produced and computed accordingly for precise failure prediction. The classification of the failure consequences performed herein however is not exhaustive. Therefore, extended research focusing on the categorization of failure impacts is highly recommended. Additionally, further research that aims at possible quantification of these impacts is also necessary as this will in a point of fact; reveal the proper magnitude of pipeline failure.

References

1. Yoo, D.G., Kang, D., Jun, H., Kim, J.H.: Rehabilitation priority determination of water pipes based on hydraulic importance. Urban Water 6(12), 3864–3887 (2014)
2. Makar, J.M., Kleiner, Y.: Maintaining water pipeline integrity, Baltimore, Maryland (2000)
3. Kleiner, Y., Rajani, B.: Considering time dependent factors in the statistical prediction of water main breaks. In: American Water Works Association: Infrastructure Conference (2000). Accessed 2015
4. Boxall, J., O'Hagan, A., Pooladsaz, S., Saul, A., Unwin, D.: Estimation of burst rates in water distribution mains. Inst. Civil Eng. Water Manage. 160(2), 73–82 (2007)
5. Cooper, N., Blakey, G., Sherwin, C., Ta, T., Whiter, J., Woodward, C.: The use of GIS to develop a probability-based trunk main burst risk model. Urban Water 2(2), 97–103 (2000)
6. Mounce, S.R., Khan, A., Wood, A.S., Day, A.J., Widdop, P.D., Machell, J.: Sensor-fusion of hydraulic data for burst detection and location in a treated water distribution system. Inf. Fusion 4(3), 217–229 (2003)
7. Mounce, S.R., Machell, J.: Burst detection using hydraulic data from water distribution systems with artificial neural networks. Urban Water J. 3(1), 21–31 (2006)
8. Kettler, A., Goulter, I.: An analysis of pipe breakage in urban water distribution networks. Can. J. Civ. Eng. 12(2), 286–293 (1985)
9. Morris, R.: Principal causes and remedies of water main breaks. J. Am. Water Works Assoc. 59(7), 782–798 (1967)
10. Iyer, S., Sinha, S.K.: A robust approach for automatic detection and segmentation of cracks in underground pipeline images. Image Vis. Comput. 23(10), 921–933 (2005)
11. Davies, J., Clarke, B., Whiter, J., Cunningham, R.: Factors influencing the structural deterioration and collapse of rigid sewer pipes. Urban Water 3(1), 73–89 (2001)
12. Muhlbauer, W.K.: Pipeline Risk Management Manual: Ideas, Techniques, and Resources. Gulf Professional Publishing, Houston (2004)
13. Bai, Y., Bai, Q.: Subsea Pipeline Integrity and Risk Management. Gulf Professional Publishing, Houston (2014)
14. Tabesh, M., Soltani, J., Farmani, R., Savic, D.: Assessing pipe failure rate and mechanical reliability of water distribution networks using data- driven modeling. J. Hydro Inform. 11(1), 1–17 (2009)
15. Yamijala, S.: Statistical estimation of water distribution system pipe breaks risk. Master of Science, Texas A&M University (2007)
16. Restrepo, C.E., Simonoff, J.S., Zimmerman, R.: Causes, cost consequences, and risk implications of accidents in US hazardous liquid pipeline infrastructure. Int. J. Crit. Infrastruct. Prot. 2(1), 38–50 (2009)
17. Kishawy, H.A., Gabbar, H.A.: Review of pipeline integrity management practices. Int. J. Press. Vessels Pip. 87(7), 373–380 (2010)
18. McNeiill, L.S., Edwards, M.: Iron pipe corrosion in distribution systems. J. Am. Water Works Assoc. 93(7), 88–100 (2001)

19. Revie, R.W., Uhlig, H.H.: Corrosion and Corrosion Control, 4th edn. Wiley, Hoboken (2008)
20. Mailhot, A., Poulin, A., Villeneuve, J.: Optimal replacement of water pipes. Water Resour. Res. **39**(5), 11–36 (2003)
21. Rajani, B., Kleiner, Y.: Comprehensive review of structural deterioration of water mains: physically based models. Urban Water **3**(3), 151–164 (2001)
22. Giangrande, V.E.H.: Trunk water main failure consequence modelling during normal, peak and fire flow conditions. Masters of Applied Science, Kingston, Ontario, Canada Queen's University (2014)
23. Diop, S., Stapelberg, F., Tegegn, K., Ngubelanga, S., Heath, L.: A review on Problem Soils in South Africa. Western Cape, South Africa: Council for Geoscience (2011)
24. Buttrick, D.B., Trollip, N.Y., Watermeyer, R.B., Pieterse, N.D., Gerber, A.A.: A performance based approach to dolomite risk management. Environ. Earth Sci. **64**(4), 1127–1138 (2011)
25. Department of Public Works: Appropriate development of Infrastructure on dolomite: Manual for consultants (2010)
26. Buttrick, D., van Schalkwyk, A.: Hazard and risk assessment for sinkhole formation on dolomite land in South Africa. Environ. Geol. **36**(1–2), 170–178 (1998)
27. Kleywegt, R., Watermeyer, R., Trollip, N., Buttrick, D., Van Schalkwyk, A.: Proposed method for dolomite land hazard and risk assessment in South Africa. J. S. Afr. Inst. Civil Eng. **43**(2), 27–36 (2002). Discussion. Journal of the South African Institution of Civil Engineering = Joernaal van die Suid-Afrikaanse Instituut van Siviele Ingenieurswese, 44(3), pp. 25–30 (2001)
28. Clair, A.M.S., Sinha, S.: State-of-the-technology review on water pipe condition, deterioration and failure rate prediction models. Urban Water **9**(2), 85–112 (2012)
29. Makar, J., Chagnon, N.: Inspecting systems for leaks, pits, and corrosion. J. Am. Water Works Assoc. **91**(7), 36 (1999)
30. Kabir, G., Tesfamariam, S., Francisque, A., Sadiq, R.: Evaluating risk of water mains failure using a Bayesian belief network model. Eur. J. Oper. Res. **240**(1), 220–234 (2015)
31. Kleiner, Y.: Water distribution network rehabilitation: selection and scheduling of pipe rehabilitation alternatives. Doctor of Philosophy, Ottawa. Canada, University of Toronto (1997)
32. Shamir, U., Howard, C.D.D.: An analytic approach to scheduling pipe replacement. J. Am. Water Works Assoc. **71**(5), 248–258 (1979)
33. Margaritis, D.: Learning Bayesian Network Model Structure from Data. Doctor of Philosophy, Pittsburgh, Carnegie Mellon University (2003)
34. Ben-Gal, I., Ruggeri, F., Faltin, F., Kenett, R.: Bayesian Networks. In: Encyclopedia of Statistics in Quality and Reliability (2007)
35. Doguc, O., Ramirez-Marquez, J.E.: A generic method for estimating system reliability using Bayesian networks. Reliab. Eng. Syst. Saf. **92**(2), 542–550 (2008)
36. Fenton, N., Krause, P., Neil, M.: Software measurement: uncertainty and causal modeling. IEEE Softw. **10**(4), 116–226 (2002)
37. Ogutu, A.G., Kogeda, O.P., Lall, M.: Decoding leakage tendencies of water pipelines in dolomitic land: a case study of the city of Tshwane. In: Proceedings of The World Congress on Engineering and Computer Science 2016. Lecture Notes in Engineering and Computer Science, 19–21 October, 2016, San Francisco, USA, pp. 931–936 (2016)
38. Kogeda, O.P., Agbinya, J.I., Omlin, C.W.: A probabilistic approach to faults prediction in cellular networks. In: The Proceedings of the 5th International Conference on Networking, ICN 2006, Mauritius, 23–28 April 2006 (2006)

Exploring Crowdfunding Performance of Agricultural Ventures: Evidence from FlyingV in Taiwan

Wen-I Chang[✉]

Department of Agribusiness Management, National Pingtung University
of Science and Technology, 1 Hseuh-Fu Rd., Nei-Pu Hsiang,
Pingtung 91201, Taiwan
lorna@mail.npust.edu.tw

Abstract. Crowdfunding has been growing rapidly as a new financing source for ventures. To support the application of crowdfunding for the agricultural sector, this study explored the characteristics and crowdfunding performance of agricultural projects. A total of 112 projects were selected from one of the largest crowdfunding platforms in Asia. The results showed most of the agricultural projects were grouped under the categories of leisure, public, or local. Within two months of the funding duration, each of these agricultural projects pledged an average of 6,880.9 USD from 123 contributors. But the total share and the overall success rate of agricultural projects remained low. Furthermore, project category, funding target, and number of contributors had significant effects on the crowdfunding performance of the agricultural projects. The findings suggest project initiators may need to diversify project categories, set a relatively low funding target, and expand social network to increase number of contributors.

Keywords: Crowdfunding performance · Reward-based crowdfunding · Alternative financing · FlyingV · Agricultural development · Innovative ventures

1 Introduction

In recent years, crowdfunding has emerged as a new approach for individuals and teams to obtain financial support from people across the world through online platforms. Many start-ups and innovative ventures are able to apply for funds from end customers or potential sponsors in the online community rather than from banks or other traditional funding systems. Since its first platform launched in 2001, crowdfunding has been growing rapidly [1]. In 2014, there were 1,250 platforms which collectively raised $16.2 billion worldwide. The estimated funding volumes had even doubled in 2015 and reached to $34.4 billion, particularly because of the expansion in Asia [2]. Through these online platforms, numerous project categories, including real estate, sports, entertainment, art, and healthcare, have been financially supported [3]. Crowdfunding substantially enables access and opportunities for entrepreneurs and contributors to meet their needs.

© ICST Institute for Computer Sciences, Social Informatics and Telecommunications Engineering 2018
T.F. Bissyande and O. Sie (Eds.): AFRICOMM 2016, LNICST 208, pp. 165–173, 2018.
https://doi.org/10.1007/978-3-319-66742-3_16

In many developing countries, the agricultural sector is the core economy. But capital is often not accessible for small-scaled agricultural ventures. With the rising trend of crowdfunding, it may serve as an alternative channel to bring capital and resources for agricultural development and stimulate industry innovations. Many micro-financing projects also proved small amount of credit may effectively reinforce entrepreneurship and improve community income in rural areas and developing countries [4–6]. Nevertheless, the understanding of crowdfunding adoption in the agricultural sector is limited. Current studies mainly focus on the funding system itself rather than the venture aspect of various industries. To gain progressive insight of how this new online mechanism may benefit agriculture, this study seeked to answer the following questions: (1) What were the funding characteristics set in agricultural projects for crowdfunding? (2) How successful were agricultural projects in crowd-funding? (3) What was essential in agricultural projects to succeed in crowdfunding?

To support the crowdfunding adoption of agricultural ventures, this study targeted one of the largest crowdfunding platforms in Asia to investigate the features and crowdfunding performances of agricultural projects. The relationship between funding characters of agricultural projects and their crowdfunding performances would also be explored. The results may provide valuable knowledge of how agricultural ventures can succeed in crowdfunding.

2 Literature Reviews

2.1 Crowdfunding

Crowdfunding is a new form of finance sources for entrepreneurial individuals and groups to draw relatively small contributions of funds from a relatively large number of audience using the Internet [7]. The concept of crowdfunding originated from crowd-sourcing, which gathers ideas, feedback, and solutions from the crowd to create enterprise activities [8]. There are four major models of crowdfunding: donation, lending, reward, and equity crowdfunding. The donation crowdfunding can be regarded as the most traditional form of crowdfunding. Contributors do not receive any reward for their donations. But with the increasing competition for funds, some proposers of free donation projects also start to provide incentives for their contributors. With the second type, lending crowdfunding, contributors receive monetary compensation, such as profit sharing. The reward crowdfunding, on the other hand, offers non-monetary compensations. This is also the most prevalent approach and frequently operationalized using a kind of pre-selling or pre-ordering of the final product or service. As for the equity crowdfunding, contributors receive shares or similar rights in return for their contribution. Moreover, contributors may not only support the project financially but also participate in further aspects of the projects, e.g., designing products [7].

In addition to the primary role for financing ventures, crowdfunding can also serve for multiple purposes, including the marketing function to raise public awareness of the products, the testing function to validate market potentials of the products, and the legitimizing function to obtain public approval of the products through early societal interaction [7, 9, 10]. These functions of crowdfunding not only help the cost sharing of the commercialization of innovation, but also reduce the risk of launching wrong products and services that lead to failure. The nature that anyone can be an investor or a project initiator of crowdfunding without requiring large capital or high profit [11] also facilitates the realization of creative ventures. Many small and medium-sized enterprises (SMEs) have obtained financing through crowdfunding since the global financial crisis [12]. Crowdfunding is also regarded as a potential trigger for the economic growth and social advancement in developing countries.

The high expectation comes along with the impressive expansion of crowdfunding in recent years. An industry report showed crowdfunding increased 166% from $6.1 billion USD in 2013 to 16.2 billion USD in 2014, and then achieved $34.4 billion USD, another remarkable increase of 112%, in 2015 [2]. While North America remains leading, and accounts for half of the crowdfunding market with 17.2 billion USD, Asia has overtaken Europe (6.5 billion USD and 19%) as the second largest market with 10.5 billion USD and a share of 31% in 2015. The funding volume of South America, Oceania, and Africa, on the other hand, reached 85.7, 68.6, and 24.1 million USD, respectively.

The growing crowdfunding movement has attracted research on the behavior of crowdfunding communities and the determinants of crowdfunding success. A study indicated the motivations of entrepreneurs to engage in crowdfunding are not merely for capital, but also for awareness, connection, approval, control, and learning [1]. On the other hand, contributors are propelled not simply by rewards, but also by charity, ideals, and community identification. Nevertheless, fear of failure can be a deterrent of crowdfunding participation to project initiators as lack of trust can be another one to contributors. Additionally, other studies have found the success of crowdfunding campaigns can be related to several factors, and the main ones which have been repeatedly highlighted include the scale of funding targets, minimum funding amount, days of campaign duration, and number of contributors [7, 13–18]. After the fundraising targets are achieved, contributors' satisfaction in the implementation process of crowdfunding projects may still be affected by entrepreneur activeness, contributor participation, project novelty, delivery timeliness, and product quality [19].

2.2 FlyingV

FlyingV, founded in April 2012, is a rewards crowdfunding platform registered in Taiwan. To be launched on FlyingV, each project needs to be registered with a heading, fundraising goal, an abstract within 100 words, a start date, a cover picture, a short campaign video, a brief proposal within 2,000 words, and reward items with the expected delivery dates for contributors [20]. In accordance with their features, the projects would also be classified into twelve categories, including design, music, film, technology, art, leisure, public, local, sport, game, publishing, and travel.

With an all-or-nothing model, FlyingV charges an 8% fee for successful campaigns. If the goal is not met, the collected money is refunded to contributors. The minimum funding goal of a project is 5,000 NTD (about 160 USD) within a time limit from 7 to 60 days. It is estimated that a project lasting 45–60 days on FlyingV would have between 6,000 and 10,000 views [20]. Most of the contributors are young people with an average age of 30 years old.

By June 2016, 785 projects have successfully achieved their fundraising goals which collectively solicited over 326 million NTD (approximately 10 million USD) on FlyingV [21]. The highest funding was 25.9 million NTD (about 0.8 million USD) for a font design project, which largely surpassed its setting goal of 1.5 million NTD. The top three categories of successful projects with the highest funds accumulated were public, design, and technology, and they accounted for 30.3%, 23.8%, and 8.2% of the total funds raised, respectively. The entire success rate among the 1,700 launched projects was about 46%. In addition, projects of music (72.7%), local (64.6%), and game (56.9%) had the highest success rates.

Currently, FlyingV is also planning to gather ended projects to curate online exhibitions with different themes, such as agriculture [22]. Project initiators will have opportunities to share their crowdfunding experiences, which may not only deepen the relationship between initiators and contributors, but also provide references for future project initiators.

3   Research Methods

3.1   Research Framework

To support agricultural ventures through crowdfunding, this study attempted to identify the characteristics of agricultural projects on a crowdfunding platform. Furthermore, the influences of project category, funding target, funding duration, and number of contributors on the crowdfunding performance of these agricultural projects were also explored. The findings may help develop strategies for agricultural ventures to successfully pledge required capital on crowdfunding platforms (Fig. 1).

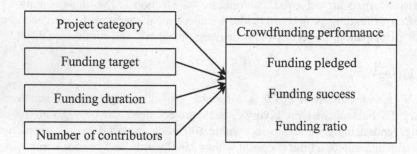

Fig. 1. Research framework and key variables of this study.

3.2   Data Collection and Analyses

The crowdfunding campaigns of agricultural projects between April 2012 and June 2016 on the crowdfunding platform FlyingV were targeted in this study. A total of 112 agricultural projects were identified from 1,693 crowdfunding projects. Quantitative data of the key variables were individually obtained from the text content of crowdfunding campaigns of these agricultural projects on FlyingV. Table 1 displays the measurement descriptions of the variables. The project category and funding success, in particular, were measured using dummy variables. In addition, the SPSS 18.0 statistical software was adopted in this study to display descriptive statistics, linear regression models for funding pledged and funding ratio as well as a binary logistic regression model for funding success.

Table 1. Measurement descriptions of variables collected in the study.

Variables	Measurement descriptions
Project category	Dummy = 1 if project category is one of the major three categories of the agricultural projects; 0 otherwise
Funding target (1,000 NTD)	The total amount of capital that project initiators aimed to raise from the crowdfunding campaign
Funding duration (days)	The number of days from the start to the end of the crowdfunding campaign
Number of contributors (persons)	Number of people provided fund to the project
Funding pledged (1,000 NTD)	The total amount of capital raised by the end of the crowdfunding campaign
Funding success	Dummy = 1 if funding pledged is greater than or equal to funding target; 0 otherwise
Funding ratio	The ratio of funding pledged over funding target

4 Results and Discussion

4.1 Profile Analysis of the Agricultural Projects

Table 2 shows the descriptive statistics of the 112 targeted agricultural projects on FlyingV. Three categories, leisure (46.4%), public (20.5%), and local (8.9%) accounted for the majority of these projects. The average amount of funding targets was 262,959.9 NTD. Their funding duration tended to be long with a mean of 52.9 ± 14.1 days, relatively close to the top limit of two months set by FlyingV. Each project attracted 123.0 contributors and pledged 215,026.8 NTD on average. But the results indicated most of the agricultural projects were unsuccessful (56.3%). The funding ratio of pledge over target was merely 0.82.

Table 2. Descriptive statistics of the agricultural projects on FlyingV from April 2012 and June 2016.

Characteristic	N	%	Sum	Mean	SD
Project category	112	100.0	–	–	–
• Public	23	20.5	–	–	–
• Design	9	8.0	–	–	–
• Art	0	0.0	–	–	–
• Technology	5	4.5	–	–	–

(*continued*)

Table 2. (*continued*)

Characteristic	N	%	Sum	Mean	SD
• Publication	7	6.3	–	–	–
• Film	4	3.6	–	–	–
• Leisure	52	46.4	–	–	–
• Travel	1	0.9	–	–	–
• Local	10	8.9	–	–	–
• Game	1	0.9	–	–	–
• Sport	0	0.0	–	–	–
• Music	0	0.0	–	–	–
Funding target (1,000 NTD)	112	–	29,451.5	263.0	293.2
Funding duration (days)	112	–	–	52.9	14.1
Number of contributors (persons)	112	–	13,771	123.0	490.4
Funding pledged (1,000 NTD)	112	–	24,083.0	215.0	644.7
Funding success	112	–	–	–	–
• Unsuccessful	63	56.3	–	–	–
• Successful	49	43.8	–	–	–
Funding ratio	112	–	–	0.82	1.18

4.2 Factors to Funding Pledged of Agricultural Projects

The results of the linear regression analysis (see Table 3) showed project category, funding target, and number of contributors would significantly affect the funding pledged of the agricultural projects ($R^2 = 0.937$, $p < .001$). The projects with higher funding targets or number of contributors tended to have higher amount of funding pledged. But the projects grouped into the three major categories, namely "leisure", "public", and "local" seemed to pledge less amount of funding than projects in other categories.

Table 3. Linear regression model for funding pledged of the agricultural projects.

Variable	B	S.E.	R^2	F	Significance of the model
Constant term	29.629	38.287	0.937	533.202[***]	<.001
Project category	−13.249[*]	5.713			
Funding target (1,000 NTD)	0.426[***]	0.057			
Number of contributors	1.167[***]	0.034			

[*]$p < .05$, [**]$p < .01$, [***]$p < .001$; n = 112

4.3 Factors to Funding Success of Agricultural Projects

Table 4 shows that the binary logistic regression model for funding success of the agricultural projects was significant ($\chi^2 = 87.261$, $p < .001$). The model explains 72.5% of the variation of the funding success. Projects with higher number of contributors were more likely to be successful. But higher funding targets, on the other hand, decreased the likelihood of funding success of the agricultural projects.

Table 4. Binary logistic regression model for funding success of the agricultural projects.

Variable	B	S.E.	Nagelkerke's pseudo R^2	Chi^2	Significance of the model
Constant term	−0.894	1.046	0.725	87.261***	<.001
Project category	0.988	0.722			
Funding target (1,000 NTD)	−0.003*	0.002			
Funding duration (days)	−0.029	0.021			
Number of contributors	0.070***	0.015			

$^*p < .05,$ $^{**}p < .01,$ $^{***}p < .001$

4.4 Factors to Funding Ratio of Agricultural Projects

The third model using funding ratio as the dependent variable was also found significant ($R^2 = 0.325$, $p < .001$). The results showed funding target was negatively affecting funding ratio of the agricultural projects while number of contributors remained a positive factor to the crowdfunding performance (see Table 5).

Table 5. Linear regression model for funding ratio of the agricultural projects.

Variable	B	S.E.	R^2	F	Significance of the model
Constant term	0.855***	0.124	0.325	26.293***	<.001
Funding target (1,000 NTD)	−0.001*	0.000			
Number of contributors	0.001***	0.000			

$^*p < .05,$ $^{**}p < .01,$ $^{***}p < .001$

5   Conclusions

Overall, this study aims to reveal the potential of crowdfunding for agricultural ventures. Since crowdfunding has grown rapidly in developing regions, it may serve as a supportive financing system for small-scaled innovative agricultural ventures. Using the existing agricultural projects from one of the largest crowdfunding platform in Asia, this study conducted an empirical approach to identify the characteristics of agricultural projects and relevant factors of crowdfunding performances. The major findings are summarized as follows:

First, agricultural projects did not have a specific category in the crowdfunding platform, but grouped into diverse categories, mostly "leisure", "public", and "local" categories. So far these projects only accounted for a small share of the total projects proposed (6.6%) and succeed (6.3%) as well as the total funding pledged (6.9%). Furthermore, their funding duration tended to be as long as the default days of top limit, but the crowdfunding success rate (43.8%) and funding ratio (0.82) of the agricultural projects still needs to be improved.

Second, project category, funding target, and number of contributors were found to have significant effects on the crowdfunding performance of the agricultural projects. The findings imply project initiators may diversify and group their projects into other categories, rather than "leisure", "public", and "local" categories. The funding target should also be reasonable and relatively low. Also, project initiators may use multiple media effectively to extend the social network and increase the number of contributors. To fulfill the promising potential of crowdfunding for agricultural ventures, further researches are encouraged.

Acknowledgments. The author thanks Edgardo Reyes, Dr. Angel Amed Duron Benitez, and Meidiana Purnamasariand for their thoughtful feedback on the manuscript. The research suggestions of Dr. Ru-Mei Hsieh and Dr. Grace Yueh - Hsiang Tsay are also highly appreciated.

References

1. Gerber, E.M., Hui, J.: Crowdfunding: motivations and deterrents for participation. ACM Trans. Comput. Hum. Inter. (TOCHI) **20**(6), 1–32 (2013). Article 34
2. Massolution: 2015 CF Crowdfunding Industry Report. Los Angeles CA, USA (2015)
3. PENSCO Trust Company: 2015 PENSCO Crowdfunding Report. Denver, CO, USA (2015)
4. Olu, O.: Impact of microfinance on entrepreneurial development: the case of Nigeria. In: The International Conference on Economics and Administration, Faculty of Administration and Business, University of Bucharest, Romania, ICEA – FAA, Bucharest, 14–15 November 2009
5. Ghalib, A.K., Malki, I., Imai, K.S.: Microfinance and household poverty reduction: empirical evidence from rural Pakistan. Oxford Dev. Stud. **43**(1), 84–104 (2015)
6. Lopatta, K., Tchikov, M.: Do microfinance institutions fulfil their promise? Evidence from cross-country data. Appl. Econ. **48**(16–18), 1655–1677 (2016)
7. Hörisch, J.: Crowdfunding for environmental ventures: an empirical analysis of the influence of environmental orientation on the success of crowdfunding initiatives. J. Cleaner Prod. **107**, 636–645 (2015)
8. Belleflamme, P., Lambert, T., Schwienbacher, A.: Crowdfunding: tapping the right crowd. J. Bus. Ventur. **29**(5), 585–609 (2014)
9. Lambert, T., Schwienbacher, A.: An empirical analysis of crowdfunding. University de Louvain France, Louvain (2010)
10. Lehner, O.M., Nicholls, A.: Social finance and crowdfunding for social enterprises: a public–private case study providing legitimacy and leverage. Ventur. Cap. **16**(3), 271–286 (2014)
11. Berglin, H., Strandberg, C.: Leveraging Customers as Investors: The Driving Forces behind Crowdfunding. http://uu.diva-portal.org/smash/get/diva2:604272/FULLTEXT01
12. Therriault, K.: What is the Size of the Crowdfunding Industry? http://www.crowdcrux.com/size-of-crowdfunding-industry/
13. Frydrych, D., Bock, A.J., Kinder, T., Koeck, B.: Exploring entrepreneurial legitimacy in reward-based crowdfunding. Ventur. Cap. **16**(3), 247–269 (2014)
14. Mollick, E.: The dynamics of crowdfunding: an exploratory study. J. Bus. Ventur. **29**(1), 1–16 (2014)

15. Pitschner, S., Pitschner-Finn, S.: Non-profit differentials in crowd-based financing: evidence from 50,000 Campaigns. Econ. Lett. **123**(3), 391–394 (2014)
16. Zheng, H., Li, D., Wu, J., Xu, Y.: The role of multidimensional social capital in crowdfunding: a comparative study in China and US. Info. Manage. **51**(4), 488–496 (2014)
17. Calic, G., Mosakowski, E.: Kicking off social entrepreneurship: how a sustainability orientation influences crowdfunding success. J. Manage. Stud. **53**(5), 738–767 (2016)
18. Yang, Y., Wang, H.J., Wang, G.: Understanding crowdfunding processes: a dynamic evaluation and simulation approach. J. Electro. Com. Res. **17**(1), 47–64 (2016)
19. Xu, B., Zheng, H., Xu, Y., Wang, T.: Configurational paths to sponsor satisfaction in crowdfunding. J. Bus. Res. **69**(2), 915–927 (2016)
20. FlyingV. https://www.flyingv.cc/
21. Taiwan Institute of Economic Research, Small and Medium Enterprise Administration of Taiwan Ministry of Economic Affairs: 2016 Second Quarterly of Global Early Fund Trend Observation (in Chinese). http://findit.org.tw/upload/news/news_20160711001.pdf
22. Lai, Z.X.: Crowdfunding is More than Collecting Money - Taiwan Crowdfunding is Turning Mature (in Chinese). https://www.twreporter.org/a/2016-crowdfunding-future

An Integrated RoIP Communication Network for Effective Collaboration During Emergency and Disaster Management

Quist-Aphetsi Kester[1,2,3,4(✉)]

[1] Ghana Technology University, Accra, Ghana
[2] Lab-STICC (UMR CNRS 6285), University of Brest, Brest, France
`kester.quist-aphetsi@univ-brest.fr, kquist@ieee.org`
[3] Department of Communications and Computer Networks,
CRITAC, Accra, Ghana
[4] Directorate of Information Assurance and Intelligence Research,
CRITAC, Accra, Ghana

Abstract. Disaster and emergencies are sometimes difficult to manage in terrains where there are limited communications. Some geographical areas can prove to be difficult during disaster areas to reach. During disasters, lack of communications infrastructure can hinder operations involving coordination, effective reporting and communications of events on the grounds for delivery of services such as food, medicine, etc. In this paper we proposed and developed an integrated radio over Internet Protocol Network for easy integration into other networks for effective communications, deployment and management of information. We integrated the system over satellite, phone and other alert voice systems for effective disaster management. Results showed ease of usage was effective and it is suitable for easy deployment and management of disaster and emergencies.

Keywords: Disaster management · Communications network · Radio over internet protocol · Satellite communications

1 Introduction

The success of personal mobile communication technologies has led the emergence of mobile telephony and communication technologies involving identity calling and unicasting capabilities with privacy enhancement technologies. These technologies have made communications easier across geographical locations in real-time. An emerging expansion of the telecommunication infrastructure led explosion of mobile broadband data traffic as more and more people completely rely on their mobile devices, either for work or entertainment etc. [1]. With massive telecommunications infrastructure and wide range network, communications involving, text, voice, image and video becomes a daily part of one's digital life. The widespread of the internet has made access to information more open and easier. Integrating devices over the internet and the developments in internet of things are creating endless intercommunications and monitory systems ranging from home automation, sensor networks [2] etc.

T.F. Bissyande and O. Sie (Eds.): AFRICOMM 2016, LNICST 208, pp. 174–185, 2018.
https://doi.org/10.1007/978-3-319-66742-3_17

During disaster and emergency, communications have to be broadcasted to teams on the grounds over radio communications systems for an effective collaboration. This is where several teams of intervention need to be coordinated with different teams. Integration of different radio networks such as fire fighters, police, ambulance services radio communications etc. can be better used in coordination in the presence of interoperable communications system. This will make situational awareness of events for effective. In this paper, we proposed and developed an integrated radio over Internet Protocol Network for easy integration into other networks and an effective interoperable communications to aid coordination and management of disaster events.

2 Radio Communications and the Internet Protocol

A radio communications uses a radio wave which is a signal with characteristics such as phase, amplitude and frequency [3]. It may be simplex which a one-way communication is where there is no reply channel provided; e.g. radio and television broadcasting. There is also a Half-duplex which is a two-way service with transmission over a circuit capable of transmitting in either direction but with only one direction at a time. The other one of a half-duplex is Full duplex or just duplex defines simultaneous two-way independent transmission on a circuit in both directions [4] (Fig. 1).

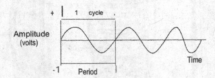

Fig. 1. A graph of amplitude, period and cycle of a pure radio wave in time

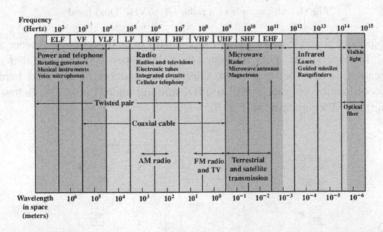

Fig. 2. Electromagnetic Spectrum for Telecommunications LF Extremely low frequency VF Voice frequency, VLF Very low frequency, LF Low frequency, MF Medium frequency, HF High frequency, VHF Very high frequency, UHF Ultra high frequency, SHF Super high frequency, EHF Extremely high frequency [4]

We have several part of the electromagnetic spectrum engaged in communications at different levels of communications. Above in the Fig. 2 is the ranges used in telecommunications. In our work, we considered the devices in the VHF and UHF frequency range used for a two-way half duplex radio communications system. Below in Fig. 3 is a block diagram and example of the radio in Fig. 4.

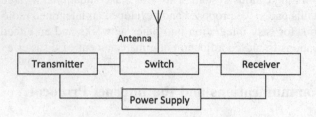

Fig. 3. An amateur radio block diagram

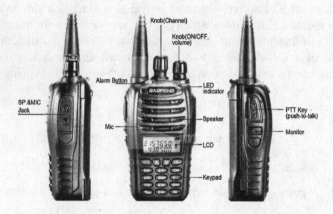

Fig. 4. An example of a radio UHV/VHF Dual band

Tabsombat et al. presented a Linux-based Radio over IP system and were able to achieve IP interoperability. They integrated their developed system with other mobile communication devices and also with a telephone network. They used hardware-software coordination on asterisk SIP IP-PBX running under Linux OS. Below is the block diagram of their system [5] (Fig. 5).

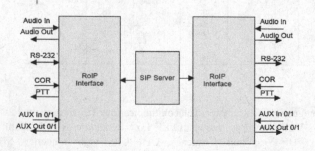

Fig. 5. Block diagram of radio over IP system

The system can enable the interconnection between many different kinds of equipment such as cell-phones, 2-way radio, PSTN, Internet phones, VoIP phones, etc. and it can be readily deployed to use as a backup communication system in both urban and remote area.

There have been other integrated approaches where integration of other systems have been successful such as remote microwave observation systems over optical IP networks using a Digitized Radio-over-Fiber technique by Shoji et al. [6] based on the concept in Fig. 6.

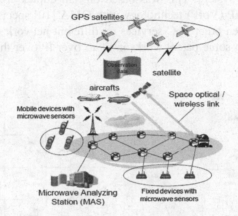

Fig. 6. A basic concept of remote microwave observation systems

They have considered a concept where aircrafts, mobile devices, satellites and other stationary devices that have microwave sensors and network interfaces can be connected to IP-based networks as shown in the figure above. Their approach was effective in analyzing remote microwave conditions at multiple places.

There have been some works in push to talk mobile communications over IP such as with JAIN SIP Object Architecture [7] as shown in Fig. 7 below, Voice Communication Systems with Session Initiation Protocol [8] as shown in Fig. 8 and Push-To-Talk in IP Multimedia Subsystem Mobile Environment [9] as in Fig. 10 and with PTT components as specified by OMA as shown in Fig. 9.

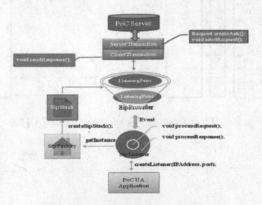

Fig. 7. JAIN SIP Object Architecture

In Fig. 7, JAIN Session Initiation Protocol Application Programming Interfaces were to used to create services using high-level methods that were not independent of the underlying network technology. This made it possible to manage multiple tasks. This can support RTP and RTCP, SIP-based Push to talk over Cellular PoC service. The SIP-based Voice Communication System (VCS) in Fig. 8 can provide phone and radio services different communication standards which may consists of multi-feature operator positions as well as standard IP-phones, which were connected peer to peer in the LAN. In Fig. 10, the Push To Talk service has a relation of one-to-one and one-to-many voice communication system. This was based on half-duplex communications mode based on Voice over IP (VoIP) technology with OMA [10] specifications. This made interoperability between other PoC services on different network operators more possible. There have been some patent works in radio over IP over the years [12–15].

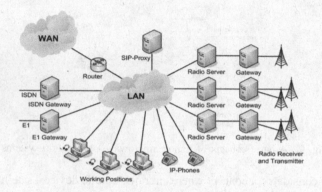

Fig. 8. SIP-based Voice Communication System

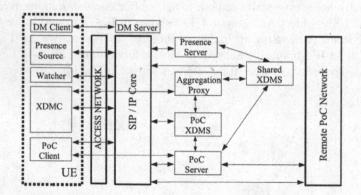

Fig. 9. PTT components as specified by OMA [10].

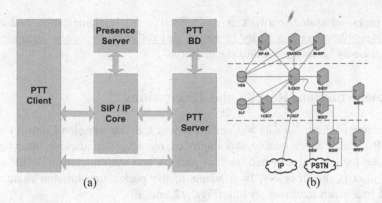

Fig. 10. PTT on IMS solution (a) and Simplified IMS architecture (b)

3 The Approach

The proposed approach was based on VoIP in accomplishing the sending and receiving audio data over TCP/IP protocol. The radio 1, 2, 3...n can communicate among themselves and radio 3 is connected to the server A which then relay the voice communication via IP to Node A and Node B. Mobile A can also tap into the same system and listen to communications over the radio network. Node A, node B and Mobile A can also communicate over back to the radio 1, 2, 3...n via the server. This made it effective for interoperability to be possible with disparate communication devices over the network making integration more easy and deployment more possible over satellite communications and the internet (Fig. 11).

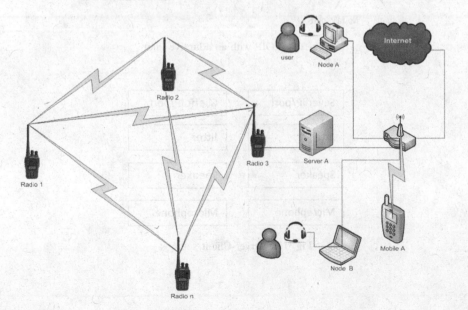

Fig. 11. The proposed system network

The proposed system network is cost effective for implementation and easy to deploy. New Networks can easily be added and different frequency communicating radios can easily be integrated into the platform.

4   Implementation, Results and Discussions

The streaming of the audio data was streamed over the Transmission Control Protocol. The RoIP systems voice quality was improved by using an adaptive jitter buffer to compensate for late, misarranged, or loss packets and the diagram of VOIP with an adaptive jitter is shown below. Jitter adapts to the packet transmission characteristic observed in a given transmission link (Figs. 12 and 13).

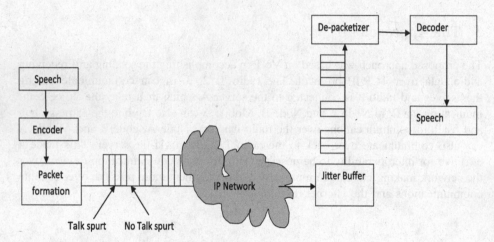

Fig. 12. VOIP with an adaptive jitter

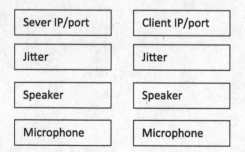

Fig. 13. Server-Client settings

Below are code snippets that are used to start the server and also connect the client. The client and server configuration involves the setting of the IP, choosing of jitter value and communication port. The microphones and speakers are also enabled for communications (Figs. 14, 15 and 16).

```
Server_connect(object sender, EventArgs e)
         {try
               {FormToConfig();
                     if (IsServerRunning)
                     {StopServer();
         StopRecordingFromSounddevice_Server();
                          StopTimerMixed();
                     }else {
                          StartServer();
if m_Config.ServerNoSpeakAll == false)
         {StartRecordingFromSounddevice_Server();
         }StartTimerMixed();
                     }}catch (Exception ex){
    ShowError(LabelServer, ex.Message);
               }
         }
```

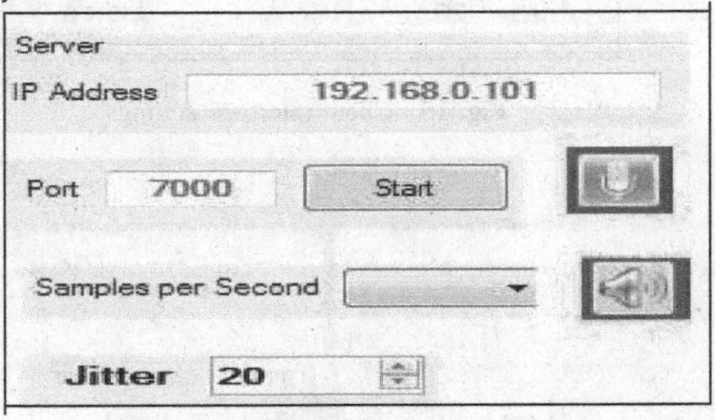

Fig. 14. Server interface settings

The radio used was UV-B5 Dual Band UHF VHF Two way radio with its specifications below and the setup was done as shown in Fig. 17 and performance analysis was done on the TCP IPV4 protocol as shown in the graph above in Fig. 18. The drop in graph shows no communications and the measure in high peaks showed commu-

```
Client_Connect(object sender, EventArgs e)
          {try{ FormToConfig();
                    if (IsClientConnected)
                    {DisconnectClient();
               StopRecordingFromSounddevice_Client();
                    }else{
                              ConnectClient();
                    }
     System.Threading.Thread.Sleep(100);
               }
               catch (Exception ex)
               {
ShowError(LabelClient, ex.Message);
               }
          }
```

Client		
IP Address	192.168.0.101	
Port	7000	Speak
Jitter	20	Listen

Fig. 15. Client interface settings

Fig. 16. BAOFENG UV-B5 Dual Band UHF VHF two way walkie radio

nications. The tested system performed effectively over the designed network and it was effective. Different radio frequency channels were able to interoperate on the system (Table 1).

Fig. 17. System setup of the communication system

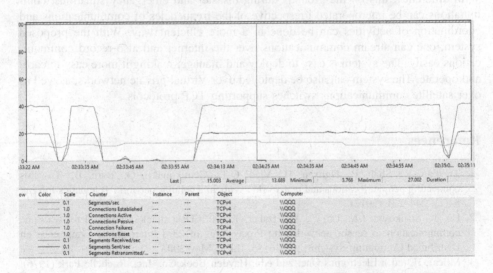

Fig. 18. System setup of the communication system

Table 1. Specifications of the BAOFENG UV-B5 dual band UHF VHF two way walkie radio

Specification	Description
Brand	Baofeng/Pofung
Model	UV-B5
Features	Built-in VOX Function, 50 CTCSS, 104 CDCSS, 1750 Hz Brust Tone, LED Flashlight, Large LCD Display, Hight/Low RF Power Switchable, Emergency Alert, Low Battery Alert, Battery Saver
Number of channels	128
Type	Portable/Handheld
Frequency range (FM)	65–108 MHz (FM Receive only)
Frequency range	VHF136–174 MHz UHF 400–520 MHz

5 Conclusions

With different teams on the grounds during disaster and emergency situations, commutations can be interoperated irrespective of the frequencies of communications and coordination of activities can be done in a more efficient way. With the proposed system, one can stream communications over the internet and also record communications easily. The system is easy to deploy and manage, making it more easy to carry and operate. The system can also be deployed over Virtual private networks, as well as over satellite communications switches supporting TCP protocols.

References

1. Trestian, R., Shah, P., Nguyen, H., Vien, Q.T., Gemikonakli, O., Barn, B.: Towards connecting people, locations and real-world events in a cellular network. Telematics Inform. **34**(1), 244–271 (2017)
2. He, T., Stankovic, J.A., Lu, C., Abdelzaher, T.: SPEED: a stateless protocol for real-time communication in sensor networks. In: Proceedings of 23rd International Conference on Distributed Computing Systems, pp. 46–55. IEEE, May 2003
3. Mileaf, H. (ed.): Electronics One, 2nd edn. Hayden Book Co., Inc., Rochelle Park (1976). U.S. Congress, Office of Technology Assessment
4. Stallings, W.: Data and Computer Communications. Pearson/Prentice Hall, Upper Saddle (2007)
5. Tabsombat, S., Pimpuch, N., Hiranya-ekaparb, A., Raksapatcharawong, M., Yamaoka, K., Phatrapornnant, T., Duangtanoo, P.: Radio over IP prototyping: a communication system for emergency response. In: 2010 7th International Conference on Service Systems and Service Management, pp. 1–5. IEEE, June 2010
6. Shoji, Y., Takayama, Y., Toyoshima, M., Ohta, H.: Remote microwave observation systems over optical IP networks using a digitized radio-over-fiber technique. In: Asia-Pacific Microwave Conference, Yokohama, pp. 330–333 (2010)

7. Cho, J.H., Lee, J.H., Yu, B.F., Lee, J.O.: Push-to-Talk service investigation and improvement. In: WRI International Conference on Communications and Mobile Computing, CMC 2009, Yunnan, pp. 167–171 (2009). doi:10.1109/CMC.2009.277
8. Kurth, C., Prinz, J., Kampichler, W.: Evaluation of SIP signaling usability in networked operations. In: IEEE Aerospace Conference, Big Sky, MT, pp. 1806–1815 (2005)
9. Cruz, R.S., Nunes, M.S., Varatojo, G., Reis, L.: Push-to-Talk in IMS mobile environment. In: Fifth International Conference on Networking and Services, ICNS 2009, Valencia, pp. 389–395 (2009)
10. Push to talk over Cellular (PoC) - Architecture, Open Mobile Alliance (OMA) Specification Approved (2006)
11. Rosenberg, J., Schulzrinne, H., Camarillo, G., et al.: RFC3261 - SIP: Session Initiation Protocol, Internet Engineering Task Force (IETF), Technical report RFC 3261, August 2004
12. Bao, D.H., Rawat, V.: U.S. Patent No. 7,260,087. U.S. Patent and Trademark Office, Washington, D.C. (2007)
13. Chow, A.T., Robert, R.M.I., Murray, J.F., Rice, C.W.: U.S. Patent No. 7,738,407. U.S. Patent and Trademark Office, Washington, D.C. (2010)
14. Ekström, H., Wiemann, H., Schieder, A.: U.S. Patent No. 7,292,564. U.S. Patent and Trademark Office, Washington, D.C. (2007)
15. Ehlers, D., Howell, P., Marsh, D.: U.S. Patent Application No. 10/950,619 (2004)

Head to Head Battle of TV White Space and WiFi for Connecting Developing Regions

David Johnson[1](✉), Natasha Zlobinsky[1], Albert Lysko[1],
Magdeline Lamola[1], Senka Hadzic[2], Richard Maliwatu[2],
and Melissa Densmore[2]

[1] Meraka, CSIR, Pretoria, South Africa
{djohnson, nzlobinsky, alysko, mlamola}@csir.co.za
[2] Computer Science Department, UCT, Cape Town, South Africa
{shadzic, rmaliwatu, mdensmore}@cs.uct.ac.za

Abstract. TV White Space networks are gaining momentum worldwide as an important addition to the suite of wireless protocols available for connecting developing regions. However, there has been no thorough investigation of scenarios where TV White Space performs better or worse than alternative low-cost wireless technology such as WiFi. This paper analyzes the performance of 5 GHz WiFi links and TV White space links using down-converted WiFi, typically used as wireless backhaul for poorly connected regions, in different scenarios including line-of-sight links and links obstructed by trees and structures. The experiments make use of 802.11a/b/g WiFi and TV White Space equipment that downconverts standard 802.11 a/b/g WiFi from the 2.4 GHz band into the UHF band. The paper finds that 5 GHz links outperformed TVWS where clear line-of-sight is available and point-to-point links are required. TVWS however is a clear choice where there are obstructions and where wider coverage is needed. Some interesting observations on the negative effect of TV transmissions in adjacent channels a few channel-hops away from the channel being used for TVWS are also provided.

Keywords: TV white space · 802.11 · Rural connectivity

1 Introduction

According to www.internetworldstats.com [1] as well as other sources [1–3], the African continent has the lowest internet penetration rate of all, with a mere 28.6% of the population having internet access compared to the world average of 46.4% [2, 3]. The second lowest is Asia with 40.2%. By far the main contributors to low access rates are rural areas. For example, the ITU research found that in Africa the 3G coverage of the rural population was 29% while the coverage in urban areas was a significantly higher 89% [4]. Statistics South Africa also found in 2014 that 27.5% of households with internet access were in metropolitan and urban areas while only 2.4% were in rural areas [5]. The reason for the persistently low rates is that internet access is not affordable for a large portion of the population.

© ICST Institute for Computer Sciences, Social Informatics and Telecommunications Engineering 2018
T.F. Bissyande and O. Sie (Eds.): AFRICOMM 2016, LNICST 208, pp. 186–195, 2018.
https://doi.org/10.1007/978-3-319-66742-3_18

Expanding access in rural areas has been typically achieved using a mix of commercial mobile operators, satellite and licence-free WiFi backhaul and access networks [6, 7] Internet access offered by mobile operators and satellite is usually very costly and only allows limited Internet to be used. WiFi access is far more cost-effective as no licence fees are required for access to spectrum and low-cost equipment is readily available. Many of these WiFi networks are adapted for long distances using high-gain antennas and a modified MAC to handle long distances [8]. However, WiFi only works well when line-of-sight is available.

TV White spaces is an emerging communication technology that offers many of the low-cost benefits of WiFi but with improved coverage - especially in mountainous areas and areas with vegetation that require very high masts to achieve line-of-sight. Early trials of TVWS show that respectable throughput (up to 12 Mbps) can be achieved at distances of 6 km [9] with 802.22 promising speeds up to 22.69 Mbps and a maximum distance of 100 km [10]. 802.11af-based equipment, due for release this year, can achieve rates up to 569 Mbps when used with four spatial streams and four bonded 8 MHz channels [11]. TV White spaces can only use spectrum not used by TV broadcasters and the performance of the link will also be related to the amount of available spectrum.

The performance of WiFi and TV White space is linked to a number of factors: the amount of available spectrum, the level of interference for a specific chosen channel, the antennas being used and the propagation environment. The choice between TV white space and WiFi is not always obvious; if no interference is present, WiFi will usually be best for line-of-sight links with clear Fresnel zones and TV white space will usually provide better performance than WiFi where there is not clear line-of-sight. But there are various shades in-between these extremes once interference from TV transmitters in adjacent channels, different antenna types, multi-path and degree of Fresnel zone obstruction are factored in.

This paper uses a set of theoretical predictions and real-world measurements in different environments to illuminate the subtle shift between the choice of TVWS and WiFi for a specific link. We also show how well the theory correlates to what could actually be expected by users in terms of throughput and propagation. In Sect. 3 we discuss popular simplified propagation models and the results that can be expected from these. The following sections show both idealized laboratory testing results and outdoor "real-world" test results, together with analysis and recommendations based on our discoveries.

2   Related Work

In order to keep deployment costs low, most alternative rural networks rely on license free or license exempt frequency bands, such as the 2.4 GHz ISM band or 5 GHz U-NII band. Wireless Mesh Networks (WMNs) are often seen as an affordable solution to bring wireless connectivity into rural and remote regions [6]. Several deployments using long range IEEE 802.11 links have been rolled out in sub-Saharan Africa using WiBACK technology [12, 13].

Low-cost WiFi-based Long Distance (WiLD) networks have been deployed in India, Ghana and the San Francisco Bay area [8]. With links up to 100 km, WiLD networks seemed a promising connectivity solution for rural areas. However, real-world deployments of such networks showed very poor end-to-end performance, thus the same authors proposed WiLDNet – a system with modified 802.11 MAC protocol and an adaptive loss-recovery mechanism for improved link utilization [14]. In [7] a multi-hop long-distance WiFi network has been designed, and the solar-powered system deployed in a remote village in Borneo, connecting six nearby villages to the telecentre for Internet access. An important aspect of long-distance WiFi deployments is the low cost due to the use of off-the-shelf devices.

Cognitive radio technology enables utilization of unused UHF frequencies originally assigned to TV broadcast, referred to as TV white spaces (TVWS). TVWS based last mile access has received a lot of attention in the research community and several systems have been deployed in rural areas and developing countries such as India [15], Malawi [16], Southern Africa [17] and rural Malaysia [10]. Preliminary results of a TVWS deployment in rural Malawi report coverage distances of up to 7.5 km, maximum throughput of 2 Mbps and average latency of 120 ms [16]. Wide coverage and availability of white spaces particularly in sparsely populated regions make this technology an attractive solution for last mile access in rural areas. While deployments in cities and densely populated areas inevitably depend on geolocation spectrum databases, in rural areas most of the spectrum is underutilized. Therefore, a spectrum database is not technically essential. Furthermore, spectrum mask requirements for the low cost equipment can be looser, since there are usually only few TV stations deployed in rural areas in developing countries, leading to very low channel occupancy [18].

However, trials performed in one of the suburbs of Cape Town, South Africa showed that TVWS can provide interference free Internet even in urban areas, with speeds up to 12 Mbps for downlink and 5 Mbps for uplink, and average latency 120 ms [9].

An overview of deployment trends for last-mile connectivity in rural areas is given in [19]. To the best of our knowledge, there is no reported performance comparison between long-distance WiFi and TVWS in terms of throughput and propagation characteristics.

3 Background

WiFi and TVWS spectrum have different advantages and disadvantages that make it relatively difficult to select one or the other technology. TVWS has the obvious technical advantage of wider coverage (up to 30 km [13]) which means fewer radio devices are required per unit area than in the case of shorter range equipment, and make TVWS particularly suitable to rural backhaul applications. Greater penetration and less absorption by buildings, trees and other obstacles are further technical advantages, enabling a signal to be received even in non-line of sight situations. TVWS is well suited to areas with low population densities [13]. On the other hand, the greater propagation range and penetration could also result in higher interference effects between TVWS nodes. TVWS is also a comparatively immature technology in the market. In contrast the WiFi properties of shorter propagation range and higher sensitivity to obstacles result in less interference, but the consequence is that the technology requires more nodes per unit area as well as line-of-sight. A further technical advantage is that Fresnel zones have smaller radius so less clearance (height) is required to avoid attenuation. Additionally, WiFi is a mature and well known technology that is readily available, and high gain WiFi antennas up to 30 dBi are common.

It is generally assumed that operating WiFi in TV bands would provide reliable connections with greater speeds. In free space, in the absence of other impairments, the main effect on the performance from a theoretical perspective is path loss. Using the Friis path loss equation where P_r is receive power, P_t is transmit power, G_t is transmit antenna gain, G_r is receive antenna gain, d is distance between antennas and f is frequency:

$$\frac{P_r}{Pt} = G_t G_r \left(\frac{c}{4\pi df}\right)^2$$

If the TVWS frequency (f_{TV}) is set to 700 MHz and the 5 GHz WiFi operating frequency (f_{WF}) is set to 5600 MHz then $f_{WF} = 8f_{TV}$.

The change in path loss in dB when moving from 5 GHz WiFi to TVWS with the same receive and transmit antenna gains and the same transmit power and distance is

$$10\,Log\left(\frac{P_{rtv}}{P_{rWF}}\right) = 10\,Log\left(\frac{G_t G_r \left(\frac{c}{4\pi df TV}\right)^2 P_t}{G_t G_r \left(\frac{c}{4\pi df TV}\right)^2 P_t}\right) = 10\,Log\left(\frac{\frac{1}{f_{TV}}}{\frac{1}{f_{WF}}}\right)^2$$

$$= 20\,Log\left(\frac{\frac{1}{f_{TV}}}{\frac{1}{8f_{TV}}}\right) = 18.06\,dB$$

Hence TVWS would generally have approximately an 18 dB advantage compared to 5 GHz WiFi when using exactly the same RF parameters. The reality, however, is that 5 GHz WiFi antennas can be built with a gain of up to 30 dBi whereas UHF antennas usually have a gain of no more than 12 dBi. When the transmit and receive gains of these maximum gain antennas are combined, TVWS has a combined maximum antenna gain of 24 dBi and UHF has a combined maximum antenna gain of 60 dBi. For the same distance TVWS will now be 18 dB weaker when building point to point links with high gain antennas. This is the reality for narrow-beam point-to-point links; however if point-to-multipoint links are required TVWS is more ideal as its lower gain antennas have a wider beam width. The antennas we use in our experiments (22 dBi 5 GHz WiFi antennas and 12 dBi UHF antennas) result in similar received signal strengths for line-of-sight links with antennas pointed directly at each other. However, the TVWS antennas will have a wider horizontal beam width and coverage and provide better links in a point-to-multipoint scenario. Multipath fading will also result in variation of the received signal and this paper makes use of real world experiments to compare TVWS and WiFi more accurately.

4   Methodology

4.1   Description of Equipment Used

The measurements made use of the Meraka White Space Mesh Node (WSMN) which consists of a Mikrotik Routerboard RB435 running OpenWRT and Atheros-based 802.11 a/b/g mini PCI adapters as well as a Doodle labs DL509-78 Broadband Radio Transceiver for the 470–784 MHz TV band.

The WSMN setup used the following antennas

- 22 dBi 5 GHz Panel antenna (connected directly to enclosure with pigtail)
- Static unit: 13 dBi MaxView MXR0025 Yagi TV antenna (connected via LMR400 1.5 m low-loss cable)
- Mobile unit: 10 dBi Ellies AA15EE4/69 15 Element VHF/UHF Yagi TV antenna
- The WSMN also has two 8 dBi omnidirectional antennas for 2.4 GHz and 5 GHz bands but these were not used.

The Doodle lab transceiver uses a transverter that down-converts the 2.4 GHz WiFi band to the UHF band (550 MHz to 650 MHz).

4.2   Measurement Process

Before carrying out the measurements, scans were carried out in the 5 GHz WiFi band and the UHF band. We selected a channel in WiFi and TVWS which resulted in the lowest noise level in the channel or lowest level of interference. To test the performance of the links the *iperf* tool was utilized to test the TCP throughput in both directions. Three measurements over 60 s were taken to ensure that variability in the channel is captured. To test the latency and packet loss we make use of the *ping* tool and again take three 60 s measurements. Performance of the radios for different channel widths (5, 10, 20 MHz) was tested to check if interference in neighboring channels was having any effect on the performance.

4.3   Setup for Cabled Measurements

Baseline experiments were conducted to determine the best performance possible on the TVWS and WiFi radios, in the absence of the effects of the wireless channel (e.g. noise, interference, fading). For the baseline experiments the network card of one interface was physically connected to the network card of a similarly kitted board through each board's antenna pigtail, RF cable, two 30 dB attenuators and appropriate connectors. (This is illustrated in Fig. 1 above for clarity.)

Fig. 1. Cabled measurement setup using 60 dB of attenuation and a splitter to check performance of devices without interference and with various levels of attenuation

4.4   Setup for Outdoor Measurements

For outdoor measurements, one WSMN was statically mounted at the apex of the roof of a house in Fish Hoek, Cape Town (shown in Fig. 2(a)) and another WSMN was a mobile device powered by an uninterruptible power supply and placed at various points to test specific scenarios (shown in Fig. 2(b, c, d)) below.

Fig. 2. Outdoor measurements setup: (a) Static installation on roof (b, c) Mobile installation 500 m up the road (d) Mobile installation 2.2 km away behind a tree

The 5 GHz WiFi and TVWS antennas of the static WSMN were 5 m above ground level. The antennas of the mobile unit were 1.5 m above ground level. Two outdoor scenarios (shown in Fig. 3) were tested (1) a line-of-sight test 500 m from static site shown in Fig. 2(b, c), and (2) a longer range 2 km test with line-of-sight and a 2.2 km non-line-of-sight test obstructed by a tree shown in Fig. 2(d).

Fig. 3. Location of outdoor test sites in Fish Hoek, Cape Town

5   Results and Analysis

In this section we summarize all the measurements taken with respect to distance and environment. Take note of the following abbreviations used:

- S/N: Signal to Noise Ratio
- M→S: Mobile Node-to-Static Node
- S→M: Static Node-to-Mobile Node

5.1   Baseline Cabled Measurements

A summary of the baseline results is shown in Table 1. There is a fairly linear average throughput relationship as channel width increases, which is to be expected. WiFi has a slightly higher throughput than TVWS in the absence of environmental effects, with a difference of about 1.7 Mbps. The latency variation is insignificant. The slightly worse throughput of TVWS is most likely due to the extra distortion added by the transverter of the TVWS radio.

Table 1. Cabled measurements results for establishing baseline performance

	Wi-Fi		TVWS	
Channel width	Throughput (Mbps)	Latency (ms)	Throughput (Mbps)	Latency (ms)
	Min/Avg/Max	Min/Avg/Max	Min/Avg/Max	Min/Avg/Max
5 MHz	1.2/6.1/7.3	1.1/1.3/4.0	2.8/4.4/5.1	1.1/1.5/5.0
10 MHz	6.9/11.8/13.0	0.8/1.0/3.7	6.0/9.8/11.4	0.8/1.1/4.5
20 MHz	13.6/22.4/24.6	0.7/0.8/3.3	18.1/20.6/22.5	0.7/0.8/2.7

5.2   Short-Range 500 m Line-of-Sight Measurements

Spectrum scans revealed that channel 36 (5180 MHz) was the best WiFi channel to use and 575 MHz was the best frequency to use for TVWS. The SNR for WiFi was −52/ −102 dBm for all channel widths and the signal strength of TVWS was −44/−93 dBm, −44/−90 dBm and −46/−89 dBm for 5, 10 and 20 MHz respectively. The latency variation was insignificant and averaged between 1.1 and 1.2 ms for WiFi and 1.1 and 1.7 ms for TVWS. The throughput variation is shown in Fig. 4 below. TVWS performance followed the same trend as the cabled measurements for 5 MHz and 10 MHz, where its performance was slightly poorer than WiFi but at 20 MHz, the interference from a strong DTV transmission in a nearby adjacent channel caused the performance to degrade significantly due to the weak input filter of the Doodle lab radio.

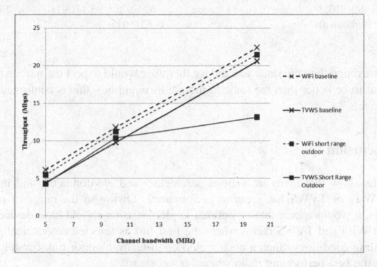

Fig. 4. Comparison of average throughput of WiFi and TVWS for baseline and outdoor measurements

5.3 Long Range Measurements with and Without Obstructions

The results of the long range measurements are given in Table 2. For this experiment, spectrum scans also revealed that WiFi channel 36 (5160 MHz) and 575 MHz for TVWS had the least amount of interference. These experiments were only carried out with 20 MHz channel width. We obtained significantly higher throughput for the TVWS link compared to WiFi. In case of a 2.2 km NLOS link, the SNR of the WiFi link was too low to establish connectivity between the two nodes. For the TVWS link we were able to achieve 5.18 Mbps throughput even with a tree obstructing line-of-sight.

In the line-of-sight case, the WiFi performance was also weaker than the TVWS. We would have expected the WiFi to perform better in this scenario but this may be due to us not being able to perfectly align the panel antennas which had a much narrower beam width than the TVWS antennas. This may also have been due to some intermittent WiFi interference in the 5 GHz band.

Both the static to mobile and mobile to static throughput is captured as this is often not symmetrical. The lack of symmetry is due to different noise levels at each site. Typically, higher sites experience more noise. In this experiment, the mobile site was at

Table 2. Long range outdoor measurements

Scenario	Wi-Fi 5180 MHz M → S(S → M)			TVWS 575 MHz M → S(S → M)		
	RSSI	Throughput Avg (Mbps)	Latency (ms)	RSSI	Throughput Avg (Mbps)	Latency (ms)
	S/N: M→S (S→M)	M→S(S→M)	Avg	S/N: M→S (S→M)	M→S(S→M)	Avg
2.2 km LOS	−72/−102 (−74/−103)	1.45(1.52)	1.804	−50/−89 (−49/−91)	7.26(6.85)	1.043
3 km NLOS	−99/−102 (unknown)	none	none	−62/−92 (−61/−91)	5.18(3.1)	2.175

a higher elevation than the static site and we therefore would expect the mobile to static throughput to be better than the static to mobile throughput – this is confirmed by the measurements.

6 Conclusion

The results show that there are various parameters and environments that influence whether WiFi or TVWS has superior performance. Owing to the range of possible conditions, it would appear that an optimal implementation should have devices fitted with both WiFi and TVWS radios where the best link is selected automatically based on prevailing conditions. Such a node would continually monitor link conditions and switch to the best performing radio whenever necessary.

From our analysis so far, WiFi performs better in short-range line-of-sight scenarios and our theoretical analysis shows that for very long range point-to-point links they will outperform TVWS but antenna alignment is challenging. TVWS performs best in NLOS scenarios and is well suited to point to multi-point scenarios where wider coverage is required. TVWS can however be negatively affected by strong TV signals even in adjacent bands a few channel hops away.

References

1. Internet World Stats: Africa Internet users, Facebook and 2015 population statistics (2015)
2. Neto, I., Best, M.L., Gillett, S.E.: License-exempt wireless policy: results of an African survey. Inf. Technol. Int. Dev. **2**(3), 73–90 (2005)
3. Thanki, R.: The Economic Significance of Licence-Exempt Spectrum to the Future of the Internet, June 2012
4. Sanou, B.: ICT facts & figures: the world in 2015. Itu 150 Años (1865 - 2015), p. 6 (2015)
5. Office for National Statistics: "Census 2013", General Household Survey, p. 78, May 2013
6. Kretschmer, M., Niephaus, C., Horstmann, T., Jonas, K.: Providing mobile phone access in rural areas via heterogeneous meshed wireless Back-Haul networks. In: 2011 IEEE International Conference on Communications Workshops (ICC), Kyoto, pp. 1–6 (2011)

7. Ab-Hamid, K., Tan, C.E., Lau, S.P.: Self-sustainable energy efficient long range WiFi network for rural communities. In: 2011 IEEE GLOBECOM Workshops (GC Wkshps), Houston, TX, pp. 1050–1055 (2011)
8. Subramanian, L., Surana, S., Sheth, A., Nedevschi, S., Patra, R., Ho, M., Brewer, E.: Re-thinking wireless for the developing world. In: ACM Hotnets (2006)
9. Lysko, A.A., et al.: First large TV white spaces trial in South Africa: a brief overview. In: 2014 6th International Congress on Ultra Modern Telecommunications and Control Systems and Workshops (ICUMT), St. Petersburg, pp. 407–414 (2014)
10. Omar, M.H., Hassan, S., Shabli, A.H.M.: Feasibility study of using IEEE 802.22 wireless regional area network (WRAN) in Malaysia. In: Network Applications Proto- cols and Services (NETAPPS) (2010)
11. Lee, W., et al.: TGaf PHY proposal. In: IEEE P802.11. Accessed 29 Dec 2013
12. Kretschmer, M., Niephaus, C., Henkel, D., Ghinea, G.: QoS-aware wireless back-haul network for rural areas with support for broadcast services in practice. In: 2011 IEEE Eighth International Conference on Mobile Ad-Hoc and Sensor Systems, Valencia, pp. 758–764 (2011)
13. Henkel, D., Engländer, S., Kretschmer, M., Niephaus, C.: Connecting the unconnected - economic constraints and technical requirements towards a back-haul network for rural areas. In: 2011 IEEE GLOBECOM Workshops (GC Wkshps), Houston, TX, pp. 1039–1044 (2011)
14. Patra, R., Nedevschi, S., Surana, S., Sheth, A., Subramanian, L., Brewer, E.: WiLdnet: design and implementation of high performance wifi based long distance networks. In: Proceedings of the 4th USENIX Conference on Networked Systems Design & Implemen- tation (NSDI 2007), p. 7, USENIX Association, Berkeley, CA, USA
15. Naik, G., Singhal, S., Kumar, A., Karandikar, A.: Quantitative assessment of TV white space in India. In: Twentieth National Conference on Communications (NCC), Kanpur, pp. 1–6 (2014)
16. Mikeka, C., et al.: Preliminary performance assessment of TV white spaces technology for broadband communication in Malawi. In: Humanitarian Technology: Science, Systems and Global Impact 2014, HumTech2014, vol. 78, pp. 149–154 (2014)
17. Masonta, Moshe T., Johnson, D., Mzyece, M.: The white space opportunity in Southern Africa: measurements with Meraka cognitive radio platform. In: Popescu-Zeletin, R., Jonas, K., Rai, Idris A., Glitho, R., Villafiorita, A. (eds.) AFRICOMM 2011. LNICSSITE, vol. 92, pp. 64–73. Springer, Heidelberg (2012). doi:10.1007/978-3-642-29093-0_6
18. Zennaro, M., Pietrosemoli, E., Sathiaseelan, A.: Architecting a low cost television white space network for developing regions. In: Proceedings of the Fifth ACM Symposium on Computing for Development (ACM DEV-5 2014), pp. 113–114. ACM, New York
19. Nandi, S., et al.: Computing for rural empowerment: enabled by last-mile telecommuni- cations. IEEE Commun. Mag. 54(6), 102–109 (2016)

Networks, TVWS

Comparison of Different Antenna Arrays with Various Height

Chien-Hung Chen[1], Chi-Jie Hung[2], Chien-Ching Chiu[2(✉)], and Shu-Han Liao[3]

[1] Taipei College of Maritime Technology, New Taipei City, Taiwan, R.O.C.
fl092@mail.tcmt.edu.tw
[2] Tamkang University, New Taipei City, Taiwan, R.O.C.
chiu@ee.tku.edu.tw
[3] Smart and Network System Institute, Institute for Information Industry,
Taipei, R.O.C.
shliao@iii.org.tw

Abstract. In this paper, we use the shooting and bouncing ray/image (SBR/Image) method to compute the path loss for different outdoor environments in the residential area. Their corresponding path loss of the outdoor environment for the non-line-of-sight (NLOS) cases are calculated. Numerical results show that the performance in reduction of path loss by DDE algorithm is better than that by GA. Besides, the path loss for the circular shape antenna is lower than that for the cross shape antenna array both in NLOS case.

Keywords: SBR/image method · Antenna height · Antenna patterns

1 Introduction

In recent years, the development in the wireless communication is promising. In the wireless outdoor communication [1–3], the heights of buildings are tall in modern cities to make the outdoor communication more difficult and complex. Obstructions by the buildings in outdoor environments will reduce the received power. Various heights of transmitting antenna will lead different path loss [4, 5], due to the different reflection and the diffraction of waves [6, 7]. To reduced the path loss, antenna arrays are usually employed for transmitters. Applying GA to reduce signal path loss for the array in outdoor communication has been presented in the references [8–10].

Section 2 describes the pattern synthesis by the algorithms. The simulating environment and the design of the proposed arrays are also described. Section 3 shows the numerical results. Finally, some conclusions are drawn in Sect. 4.

© ICST Institute for Computer Sciences, Social Informatics and Telecommunications Engineering 2018
T.F. Bissyande and O. Sie (Eds.): AFRICOMM 2016, LNICST 208, pp. 199–205, 2018.
https://doi.org/10.1007/978-3-319-66742-3_19

2 Antenna Pattern Synthesized by the Dynamic Differential Evolution Algorithm

2.1 Calculation of Antenna Current and Pattern

N dipole elements excited by a voltage source are used to form an antenna array. Let V_m and ϕ_m be the amplitude and phase of excitation voltage of the m-th element respectively. Then the total current distribution of N antennas can be calculated by the following equation.

$$\sum_{n=1}^{N} \int_0^{l_n} I_n\left(z'\right)\left[K_{mn}\left(z,z'\right) + K_{mn}\left(z,-z'\right)\right] dz = \frac{j4\pi}{\eta_0}\left[c_m \cos \phi_m + \frac{V_m}{2} \sin \phi_m\right] \quad (1)$$

$$0 \le z \le l_m \quad m = 1, 2, \ldots, N$$

$$K_{mn}\left(z,z'\right) = \frac{e^{-jkR_{mn}(z,z')}}{R_{mn}\left(z,z'\right)} \quad (2)$$

2.2 SBR/Image Method

The SBR/Image method is used to calculate the path loss for any given antenna pattern. The SBR/Image method can deal with radio wave propagation in the outdoor environments. It conceptually assumes that many ray tubes are shot from the transmitting antenna and each ray tube bouncing and penetrating in the environments is traced. If the receiving antenna is within a ray tube, the ray tube will contribute to the received field and the corresponding equivalent source (image) can be determined. By summing all contributions of these images, we can obtain the total received field at the receiver. As the result, we can calculate the path loss. GA and DDE are used to find the excitation voltages and phases to minimize the path loss.

2.3 Dynamic Differential Evolution (DDE)

DDE algorithm starts with an initial population of potential solutions that is composed by a group of randomly generated individuals which represents excitation voltages and phases. Each individual in DDE algorithm is a D-dimensional vector consisting of D optimization parameters. The initial population may be expressed by $\{x_i : i = 1, 2, \cdots, Np\}$, where Np is the population size. After initialization, DDE algorithm performs the genetic evolution until the termination criterion is met. DDE algorithm, like other EAs, also relies on the genetic operations (mutation, crossover and selection) to evolve generation by generation.

3   Numerical Results

The layout of the buildings in the residential area is shown in Fig. 1. There are nine buildings from A to I in this area. The height of these buildings are all in 10 m and the wall thickness is 30 cm. Cross shape and circular shape arrays consisted of 8 short dipoles are used for transmitting antenna arrays. The proposed transmitting antenna arrays are set for six different height at the position by triangle mark. The receiving antenna is a short dipole antenna with the height of 1.5 m. There are 36 receiving points distributed with equal space in NLOS area. Each transmitting height has 36 receiving point in the area. The final path loss of each height is the average value of total receiving data. The searching ranges of excitation voltage and phase are 0–1 V and 0–360°, respectively. The operation frequency is 5.9 GHz. For fair and comparison, GA and DDE algorithm's cross over probability (0.6), mutation probability (0.025), population size (30) and termination generation (700) are the same. Note that the total number of generations is set equal to 700. i.e., $g_{max} = 700$. NLOS case are considered respectively in the followings:

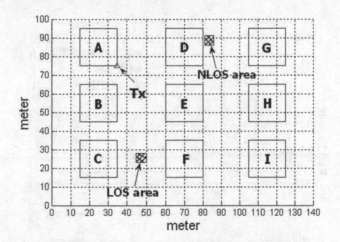

Fig. 1. The simplified layout geometry for simulation

NLOS case:
There is an obstruction between the transmitter and receiver for NLOS case. Some transmitting ray is diffracted by different way in various transmitting height. The path losses with GA and DDE, and without algorithms for the cross and circular shape arrays are shown in Figs. 2 and 3 respectively. In Fig. 2, it is observed that path losses of cross shape arrays for transmitting antenna height of 1.5, 5, 10, 12, 15 and 20 m by GA are lower 1.6, 4.3, 2.9, 2.5, 4.6 and 4.7 dB than the case without the algorithm, respectively. The path loss by DDE for transmitting antenna height of 1.5, 5, 10, 12, 15

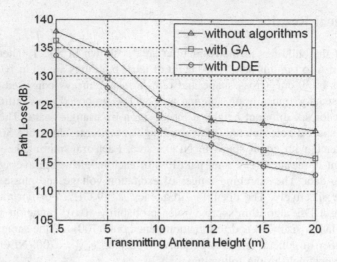

Fig. 2. Path loss of cross shape array with different algorithms in NLOS case

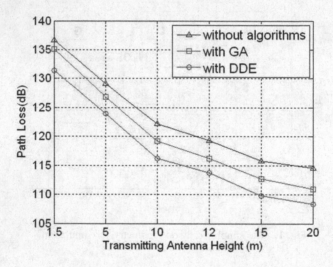

Fig. 3. Path loss of circular shape array with different algorithms in NLOS case

and 20 m are lower 4.2, 6, 5.4, 4.1, 7.4 and 7.5 dB than the case without the algorithm. In Fig. 3, path losses of circular shape arrays for transmitting antenna height of 1.5, 5, 10, 12, 15 and 20 m by GA are lower 1.5, 2.2, 2.9, 3, 3 and 3.6 dB than the case without the algorithm. The path loss by DDE for transmitting antenna height of 1.5, 5, 10, 12, 15 and 20 m are lower 5.2, 5.2, 5.9, 5.5, 5.9 and 6.1 dB respectively than without algorithm. It is clear that the path loss by the DDE algorithm is lower than

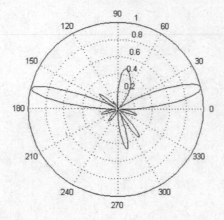

Fig. 4. Radiation pattern of cross shape array of transmitting height at 20 m by the GA algorithm in the NLOS case

those by GA. It is also seen that the path loss for the circular shape array are better than that for the cross shape array in NLOS case. Figure 4 shows the radiation patterns of cross and circular shape arrays by GA and DDE at transmitting height 20 m. In the NLOS case, the transmitting signal can't propagate directly to the receiver. Nevertheless, it is seen that antenna patterns by algorithms can find the route with the lowest path loss by reflection and diffraction. The radiation pattern by DDE is more directional than that by GA. Moreover, the power for circular shape antenna array is more focused than that by cross shape antenna array (Figs. 5, 6 and 7).

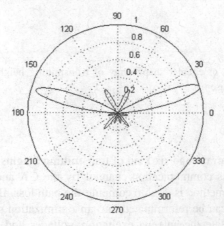

Fig. 5. Radiation pattern of cross shape array of transmitting height at 20 m by the DDE algorithm in the NLOS case

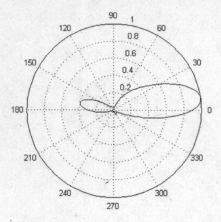

Fig. 6. Radiation pattern of circular shape array of transmitting height at 20 m by the GA algorithm in the NLOS case

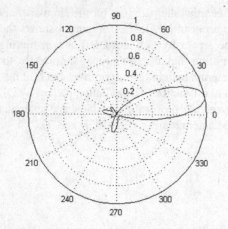

Fig. 7. Radiation pattern of circular shape array of transmitting height at 20 m by the DDE algorithm in the NLOS case

4 Conclusion

Two different antenna arrays and six kind of transmitting heights for reducing the path loss in outdoor wireless communication channel by the GA and DDE algorithm are presented. SBR/Image method is used to compute the path loss. Based on the path loss, the synthesis problem can be reformulated into an optimization problem. The GA and DDE are used to regulate the antenna excitation voltages and phases of each array element to minimize the path loss. Numerical results show that path loss in LOS case can be reduced 3–6 dB by using algorithm. The path losses for the NLOS cases can be reduced about 3–7 dB by using algorithm. It is also found that the path loss reduction by DDE is better than that by GA. Two algorithms in same condition (cross over, mutation, population and generation) shows that DDE's optimization is better than GA. It is found the path loss for circular antenna array is lower than that for cross antenna array. It is worth noting that in these cases the present work provides not only comparative information but also quantitative information on the performance reduction.

References

1. Alexander, P., Thomas, Z., Laura, B.: Non-WSSUS vehicular channel characterization in highway and urban scenarios at 5.2 GHz using the local scattering function. In: International ITG Workshop on Smart Antennas, pp. 9–15. (2008)
2. TGa modelling group: IEEE 802.15.4a channel model-final report on wireless personal area network, September 2004. Molisch, A.F. (Chiarman)
3. Rappaport, T.S.: Wireless Communications: Principles and Practice. Prentice-Hall, Upper Saddle River (1996)
4. Sasaki, M., Yamada, W., Kita, N., Sugiyama, T.: Applicability to different environment of path loss model with low antenna height in residential area. In: Proceedings of ISAP2012, Nagoya, Japan (2012)
5. Ghassemzadeh, S.S., Worstell, H.R., Miller, R.R.: Wireless neighborhood area network path loss characterization at 5.7 Ghz. In: 72nd IEEE Vehicular Technology Conference Fall (2010)
6. Chen, C.M., Chiu, Č.C., Chen, C.H., Chen, Y.C.: A novel propagation-prediction model for small rooms with metallic furniture. Microw. Opt. Technol. Lett. **44**(3), 281–284 (2005)
7. Chiu, C.C., Chen, C.H., Liao, S.H., Tu, T.C.: Ultra-wideband outdoor communication characteristics with and without traffic. EURASIP J. Wirel. Commun. Netw. (EI) (SCI) **2012**, 92 (2012)
8. Tu, T.C., Chiu, C.C.: Path loss reduction in an urban area by genetic algorithms. J. Electromagn. Waves Appl. **20**(3), 319–330 (2006)
9. Polpasee, M., Homsup, N., Virunha, P.: Optimize directivity pattern for arrays by using genetic algorithms based on planar fractal arrays. In: International Symposium on Communications and Information Technologies, pp. 28–31 (2006)
10. Chiu, C.C., Cheng, Y.T., Chang, C.W.: Comparison of particle swarm optimization and genetic algorithm for the path loss reduction in an urban area. J. Appl. Sci. Eng. **15**(4), 371–380 (2012)

A Priority-Based Service Discovery Model Using Swarm Intelligence in Wireless Mesh Networks

Lungisani Ndlovu[✉], Manoj Lall, and Okuthe P. Kogeda

Department of Computer Science, Faculty of Information Communication Technology, Tshwane University of Technology, Private Bag X680, Pretoria 0001, South Africa
{ndlovul,lallm,kogedapo}@tut.ac.za

Abstract. The ever increasing number of users in Wireless Mesh Networks (WMNs) setups consequently represents an upsurge in competitions for available services. Consequently, services are clogged and ran over WMNs, which further leads to poor Quality of Service (QoS). Quick and timely discovery of available services becomes an essential parameter in optimizing performance of WMNs. In this paper therefore, we present a Priority-based Service Discovery Model (PSDM) using Swarm Intelligence in WMNs. We use the Particle Swarm Optimization (PSO) algorithm to dynamically define and prioritize services supported by the network. Additionally, the Ant Colony Optimization (ACO) algorithm is used to choose the shortest path when each transmitter has to be searched to identify if it possesses the requested services. We have designed and implemented the PSDM using Network Simulator 2 (NS-2) tool. Consequently, we realized throughput of 80%, service availability of 96% in some instances, and an average delay of 1.8 ms.

Keywords: Services · Service discovery models · Optimization · ACO · PSO · QoS · WMNs

1 Introduction

In all of human history, Information Technology (IT) has brought a tremendous change in our lives especially the introduction WMNs in places such as offices, campuses, government institutions, military bases, etc. Consequently, WMNs have become increasingly popular in recent years. This is primarily because of their availability of resources and services. Currently, there are three types of WMN topologies which are known as infrastructure\backbone, client and hybrid. WMNs consist of Mesh Routers (MRs), Mesh Clients (MCs), and Mesh Gateways (MGs). In most cases, each MR has limited mobility which eventually forms a multi-hop wireless mesh backbone between MCs and MGs [1]. The responsibility of MRs is to interconnect other nodes in the network. On the other hand, MGs provide access to the internet and/or other networks. The research in [2] stated the attractive qualities of WMNs as low-cost deployment, robustness and its inheritance of useful characteristics from both the ad-hoc networking paradigm and traditional wired infrastructure paradigm.

© ICST Institute for Computer Sciences, Social Informatics and Telecommunications Engineering 2018
T.F. Bissyande and O. Sie (Eds.): AFRICOMM 2016, LNICST 208, pp. 206–216, 2018.
https://doi.org/10.1007/978-3-319-66742-3_20

However, the work in [3] analysed and discussed service discovery as a challenge in WMNs. Service discovery refers to the process whereby devices whether mobile or stationary are able to discover appropriate services as requested by users without any intervention [4]. It consists of three components, known as services, service registries, and clients. The work in [5] defined a service as any tangible or intangible facility a device provides to other devices that can be useful. Furthermore, there are two types of services, known as software and hardware services. On the other hand, service registries are entities to store information about available services. Clients represent both service receivers and service providers. They provide services to other clients or discover services from other clients.

Currently, there are three types of service discovery approaches for flooding information to the network. These are known as directory-based, non-directory based, and hybrid approaches. The most suitable one for WMNs is the directory-based approach. However, recent approaches perform broadcasting or multicasting for flooding messages in the network which leads to network overhead [3]. On the other hand, users continue to join WMNs, which has led to a competition of available services and resources. This further leads to clogging [4]. In this paper therefore, we present a Priority-based Service Discovery Model (PSDM) that optimizes the performance of WMNs and eradicates the various gaps available in the existing models. We have incorporated Particle Swarm Optimization (PSO) and Ant Colony Optimization (ACO) algorithms. PSO algorithm is used to define and prioritize services supported by the network. On the other hand, ACO is used to choose the shortest path whenever each transmitter has to be searched to identify if it possesses the requested service. We have demonstrated that our model provides the throughput of 80%, service availability of 96% in some instances, and an average delay of 1.8 ms.

The remainder of this paper is organized as follows: In Sect. 2, related is presented. In Sect. 3, we provide an overview of PSO and ACO algorithms. In Sect. 4, we present the system design and architecture. In Sect. 5, we present system implementation. In Sect. 6, we present simulation results and discussions. Finally, we present conclusion and future in Sect. 7.

2 Related Work

Over the past few years a lot of work has been presented in the field of service discovery in computer networks. However, most of the models were designed for home or enterprise environments [3, 6–8]. Additionally, other models were developed for Mobile ad-hoc Networks (MANETs) wherein the focus is energy consumption and message dissemination. Consequently, these models do not scale well in WMNs [6, 7]. This is because in MANETs flooding techniques are applied as there are no dedicated servers [6]. This leads to network overhead. Additionally, flooding of query messages consumes a lot of bandwidth, computation and battery resources [9].

A service discovery model that assured certain levels of QoS was presented in [3]. In the model, a combination of Fisheye State Routing (FSR) and Optimized Link State Routing (OLSR) were used to minimize flooding and broadcasting of packets. Also, the model used Normalized Link Failure Frequency (NLFF) metric to randomly select backbone nodes as service directories based on the networks' stability constraints. This reduced network load and power consumption; reasonable mean time delay, great average hit ratio. However, factors such as service response and availability were not considered.

An Ant Colony based-multi constraints QoS aware service selection (QSS) model was developed in [10]. In the model, services were discovered based on a defined metric developed to guide ants regarding the shortest path between the source and destination. The metric guides the ants to choose a cost effective path in the presence of constraints such as delay, jitter, and service availability. The model increased service availability and reduced end-to-end delay as compared to other models.

A FLEXIble Mesh Service Discovery (FLEXI-MSD) model was developed in [6]. The model used OLSR and Domain Name System Service Discovery (DNS-SD). OLSR helped in finding routes. DNS-SD provided an opportunity to discover a list of named instances of the requested service by using standard DNS-messages. The model realized that an adaptive (hybrid) service discovery mechanism which switches between ad-hoc and supernode-based backbone system outperforms a static operation mode system. This was because WMNs vary in network stability, device capabilities and different mobility patterns.

Unfortunately, various existing models were more concerned about energy consumption and message dissemination. Additionally, these models applied flooding and broadcasting approach which led to network overhead. Furthermore, in these models, services were not given different priorities in order to improve QoS. On the other hand, there was no maximum number of receivers to be given access to services. These challenges led to poor QoS.

3   Overview of ACO and PSO Algorithms

As discussed in [11], PSO algorithm was proposed for the optimization of continuous nonlinear functions. PSO defines three behaviours of flocks in swarm: cohesion – sticking together, separation – do not come too close and alignment – follow the general heading of the flock. The implementation of PSO algorithm was based on two paradigms that are known as one globally oriented (GBEST) and one locally oriented (LBEST). The PSO algorithm can also be used to solve same kinds of problems as Genetic Algorithms (GAs). However, it has memory which GAs do not have [11].

On the other hand, ACO algorithm was proposed as a multi-agent approach to difficult combinatorial optimization problems such as the traveling salesman problem (TSP) and the quadratic assignment problem (QAP) [12]. The ACO algorithm is based on the cooperative behaviour of real time ant colonies, which are able to find the shortest path from their nest to a food source.

The benefits of PSO is that it is based on intelligence and it can be applied into both scientific research and engineering use [13]. On the other hand, ACO provides positive feedback accounts for rapid discovery of good solutions [13].

4   System Design and Architecture

In general, WMNs can be mathematically modelled by a directed graph which can be represented by $G = (V, E)$ wherein $V = (v_1, v_2, \ldots, v_n)$ represents the number of mesh nodes (both routers and gateways) in the network. Whereas, $E = (e_1, e_2, \ldots, e_n)$ represents the number of both wired and wireless links for communication within and outside the network i.e., internet. MGs are used for the internet or outside communications. As a result, amongst the V nodes, J would represent the MGs. Therefore $|V| - J$ would be regarded as ordinary MRs. This is because MRs could also provide routing capability for gateway/bridge functions.

As illustrated in Fig. 1, each MR relays data traffic across the network (between MCs and to the internet via MGs in a single hop or multi-hop manner. MCs may be any end-user i.e., desktop computers, laptops, PDAs, mobile phones, etc., sharing services in the network. In this work, MCs are representing both service requesters and providers. Therefore, it is very crucial that service requesters get access to available services without any obstruction. As a result, service requesters expect the network to have n services available thus $s = (s_1, s_2, \ldots, s_n)$ whereby s represents each service and $s_n \in s$ and $n = 1, 2, 3, \ldots, \infty$. Additionally, different services have varied workflow procedures, which can be represented by $s_n > s_{n-1} > s_{n-2} > \ldots > s_1$ during service discovery in the network.

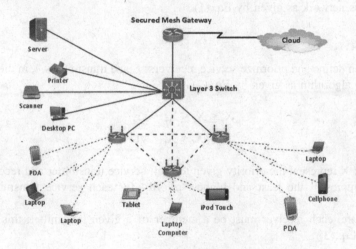

Fig. 1. WMNs system architecture.

Based on Fig. 1, the proposed architecture has been set up through pooling together various components such as Layer 3 switch, secured MG, server, and wireless MRs. The network consists of 3 MRs interconnecting the clients to the network. These 3 MRs are connected to the Layer 3 switch, which represents the transmitter and works at a distribution layer of the network. The transmitter provides centralized network management and configurations. Also, it interconnects MRs, server, and internet. Its' responsibility is to provide the communication between service transmitters and receivers. The advantage is that it incorporates routing and bridging simultaneously. Also, it has multiple Ethernet interfaces, easier to configure, able to handle large amount of traffic, and less expensive as compared to other routers. Furthermore, it supports advanced QoS features which include prioritization, classification, policing, marking, queuing, and scheduling of packets. Hence, it is responsible for the prioritization of services according to their varied workflow procedures. We also included a secured MG, which is statistically configured with an Internet Protocol (IP) address. The MG connects to remote sites and\or other networks. Also, we have a server that has been configured with a static IP address, which is used as a Domain Name System (DNS) address. The server hosts files, databases, configurations and security. Additionally, the server stores information about available services. Moreover, we have statistically configured the MRs with unique IP address. Lastly, MCs have been configured with dynamic IP addresses using Dynamic Host Configuration Protocol (DHCP).

5 System Implementation

The goal of the proposed PSDM is to reduce clogging as it leads to link congestions, data collisions, interferences, etc. The proposed PSDM is based on two theories, known as, PSO proposed in [11] and ACO proposed in [12].

We initially determine and define numbers of Transmitters, T_x and Receivers, R_x in the wireless network as given by Eq. (1).

$$R_x \geq T_x. \tag{1}$$

We then define and prioritize service receivers, r, and transmitters, t, in the network using PSO algorithm as given by Eq. (2).

$$X_r^l \leq X_r \leq X_r^u \quad \forall r.$$
$$X_t^l \leq X_t \leq X_t^u \quad \forall t. \tag{2}$$

Where: X represent the priority given to each service transmitter and receiver. But L and U represent the least and highest priority for each service transmitters and receivers.

Therefore, each receiver must be a member of a given transmitter; this is represented by Eq. (3):

$$r_n \in t. \tag{3}$$

We then define and prioritize services supported by the network using PSO algorithm as given by Eq. (4).

$$X_s^l \leq X_s \leq X_s^u \quad \forall s. \tag{4}$$

Where: X represents the priority given to each service. But L and U represent the least and highest priority for each service.

Each transmitter and receiver must be able to receive or send a service request or acknowledgement. This is represented by:

$$s_n \exists t \ \& s_n \exists r. \tag{5}$$

Thereafter, we make sure that during service requesting by receivers, a single receiver cannot request for more services than what is within the network.

Also, we make sure that a shortest path is chosen when each transmitter has to be searched to identify if it possess the requested service. ACO algorithm is used in aiding this, in which:

$$P_{t_1 t_n}^{(r)} = \begin{cases} \dfrac{\tau_{t_1 t_n}^{\alpha}}{\sum_{t_n \in N_{t_1}^{(r)}} \tau_{t_1 t_n}^{\alpha}} & \text{if } t_n \in N_{t_1}^{(r)} \\ 0 & \text{if } t_n \not\exists N_{t_1}^{(r)} \end{cases} . \tag{6}$$

Any receiver/requester, r, located at transmitter t_1, uses pheromone trail $\tau_{t_1 t_n}^{\alpha}$. to compute the probability, P, of choosing t_n as the next transmitter. While α denotes the degree of importance of the pheromones and $N_{t_1}^{(r)}$ indicates the set of neighbourhood transmitters of receiver when located at transmitter t_1. The neighbourhood of transmitter t_1 contains all the transmitters directly connected to transmitter t_1 except the predecessor transmitter. This limits the receiver from returning to the same transmitter visited immediately before transmitter t_1. A given receiver travels from one transmitter to the next in search of services.

Before returning to the home transmitter, the *nth* receiver deposits $\Delta\tau^r$ of pheromone on arcs it has visited. The pheromone value $\tau_{t_1 t_n}$ on the arc (t_1, t_n) traversed is updated as follows:

$$\tau_{t_1 t_n} \leftarrow \tau_{t_1 t_n} + \Delta\tau^{(r)}. \tag{7}$$

Therefore, because of the increase in the pheromone, the probability of this arc being selected by the forthcoming receivers in the network increases.

Whenever a receiver moves to the next transmitter in search of services, the pheromone evaporates from all the arcs according to the relation:

$$\tau_{t_1 t_n} \leftarrow (1 - p)\tau_{t_1 t_n}; \forall (t_1, t_n) \in A. \tag{8}$$

Where: $p \in (0, 1)$ is a parameter and A denotes the segments/arcs travelled by receiver, r in its path from home to destination. A decrease in pheromone intensity favours the exploration of different paths during the search process. This in return favours elimination of poor choices made in the path selection. Iteration, therefore, is a complete cycle involving receiver's movement, pheromone evaporation and pheromone deposit.

After all the receivers have returned to the home transmitter, the pheromone information is updated using the relation:

$$\tau_{t_1 t_n} = (1-p)\tau_{t_1 t_n} + \sum_{r=1}^{N} \Delta\tau_{t_1 t_n}^{(r)}. \tag{9}$$

Where: $p \in (0,1)$ represents the evaporation rate (pheromone decay factor) and $\Delta\tau_{t_1 t_n}^{(r)}$ is the amount of pheromone deposited on arc $t_1 t_n$ by the best receiver.

The major goal of pheromone update is to increase the pheromone value associated with good or promising paths. The pheromone deposited on arc $t_1 t_n$ by the best receiver is:

$$\Delta\tau_{t_1 t_n}^{(r)} = \frac{Q}{L_r}. \tag{10}$$

Where: Q represents a constant and L_r is the length of the path travelled by the receiver.

However, for every service request, a maximum of 5 receivers are allowed to request services simultaneously and then leaves the media for the next receivers.

```
Do
        If number of waiting receivers > 4 Then
            For r = 1 to 5 Do
                Discover the requested services within the network.
            End For
            Allow the next 5 receivers in the media to make their requests.
        Else
                Discover the requested services within the network.
    While (number of waiting receivers > 0)
```

The above iterations are repeated until all the receivers in the network get their requests submitted to the available services.

Finally, a maximum of ten services, in priority order, can be requested at any particular time by the receivers. This aids in reducing link congestions, data collisions, and interferences, which increases service discovery throughput, service availability, and reduces service discovery delay.

6 Performance Analysis

We performed the simulations in NS-2, using a developed model of IEEE 802_11b/g. We had 30 mobile nodes (service receivers) randomly placed in a network and numbered 13–43. Also, we had 3 T_x (s) labelled Transmitter and each with 600 m coverage area. Furthermore, we also had 10 services labelled with service names such as Voice-on-Demand, etc. These services were randomly placed nearby each T_x. We ran the simulations for 100 s. The simulation parameters are given in Table 1.

Table 1. Simulation parameters.

Parameters	Values
Routing protocol	AntNet
Simulation area	1800×840
Number of nodes	43
Mobility model	Random waypoint
Message size	64 bytes

We evaluated the proposed PSDM against QSS and FLEXI-MSD models. The two models were chosen mainly because QSS support the shortest path communication between sources and destinations. On the other hand, FLEXI-MSD supports DNS-SD, which offers an opportunity to discover a list of named instances of the requested service by using standard DNS-messages. However, both QSS and FLEXI-MSD models did not have a definite number of receivers to be given access to services, which leads to clogging. Additionally, both QSS and FLEXI-MSD models did not give different priorities to different services in order to guarantee a certain level of performance to data flows during service discovery. Furthermore, FLEXI-MSD did not support the shortest path communication between two nodes which resulted to service discovery delays.

The performance metrics considered include:

(1) Throughput – the amount of requests that can be transmitted in a given time.
(2) Service availability – the availability of services during service discovery.
(3) Delay – measurement of the delay it takes a request to reach its destination.

Throughput
Looking at Fig. 2, we realized an improved throughput in PSDM as compared to QSS and FLEXI-MSD models. This is because PSDM permits a maximum number of receivers to requests services simultaneously and then leaves the media for the next receivers. Additionally, PSDM permits a maximum number of services, in priority order, to be requested at a time which reduces link congestions, data collisions, interferences, etc. This resulted to an improved average throughput.

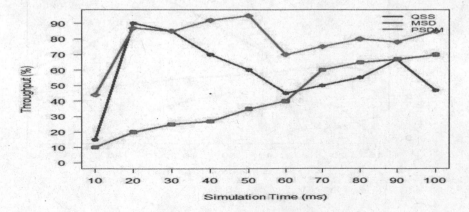

Fig. 2. Average throughput.

Service Availability

On the other hand, we realized that PSDM outperforms QSS and FLEXI-MSD models. However, as shown in Fig. 3, we observed service availability rate dropping in some instances. The is primarily because PSDM applied a queuing mechanism whereby a maximum number of receivers are given access to request available services simultaneously and then leaves the media for the next receivers. This was meant for reducing factors such as link congestion, which affects QoS.

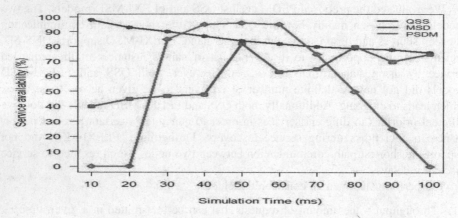

Fig. 3. Average service availability.

Service Discovery Delay

Looking at Fig. 4, PSDM reduced service discovery delay as compared to QSS and FLEXI-MSD models. Therefore, the proposed model outperforms both QSS and FLEXI_MSD models. This is because PSDM permits a maximum number of receivers to requests services simultaneously and then leaves the media for the next receivers. This is meant for collision reduction in order to minimize delay.

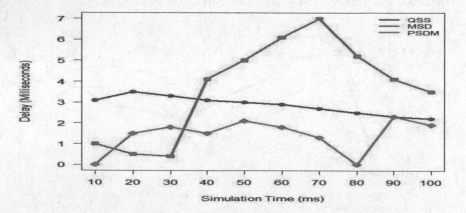

Fig. 4. Average delay.

7 Conclusion and Future Work

In this paper, we presented the design and implementation of the proposed PSDM that optimizes the performance of service discovery in WMNs. This model relies on PSO and ACO in order to reduce link congestions, data collisions, interferences, etc. We have used PSO algorithm in order to define and prioritize services in the network. This was done to provide different priorities to services in order to guarantee a certain level of performance to data flow during service discovery. On the other hand, we have used ACO algorithm in order to choose the shortest path when each transmitter has to be searched to identify if it possess the requested service. The results demonstrated that the proposed PSDM improved throughput, service availability, also reduced average delay than QSS and FLEXI-MSD. This further led to an improved QoS.

The possible future direction of this work will be considering Accelerated Particle Swarm Optimization (APSO) algorithm for the prioritization of services. Additionally, we will also focus on security issues during service discovery in WMNs. Finally, we recommend these finding for enterprise telecommunication and networking industries.

Acknowledgments. We would like to give thanks to Tshwane University of Technology for financial support.

References

1. Komba, G.M., Kogeda, O.P., Zuva, T.: A new gateway location protocol for mesh networks. In: Proceedings of the World Congress on Engineering and Computer Science, San Francisco, USA, pp. 713–718 (2014)
2. Pathak, P.H., Dutta, R.: A survey of network design problems and joint design approaches in wireless mesh networks. IEEE Commun. Surv. Tutorials 3(13), 396–428 (2011)
3. Ahmad, F., Khalid, S.: Scalable design of service discovery mechanism for Ad-Hoc network using wireless mesh network. Int. J. Smart Sens. Ad Hoc Netw. 4, 1 (2012)
4. Ndlovu, L., Lall, M., Kogeda, O.P.: A review of service discovery schemes in wireless mesh networks. In: Proceedings of IST Africa, Durban, South Africa (2016). ISBN 978-1-905824-54-0
5. Mian, A.N., Baldoni, R., Beraldi, R.: A survey of service discovery protocols in multi-hop mobile Ad Hoc networks. IEEE Pervasive Comput. 1536–1268, 66–74 (2009)
6. Krebs, M.: Dynamic virtual backbone management for service discovery in wireless mesh networks. In: Proceedings of Wireless Communications and Networking Conference, Budapest, pp. 1–6 (2009). ISBN 978-1-4244-2948-6
7. Krebs, M., Krempels, K.H.: Optimistic on-demand cache replication for service discovery in wireless mesh networks. In: Consumer Communications and Networking Conference, Las Vegas, NV, pp. 1–5 (2009). ISBN 978-1-4244-2309-5
8. Zhu, F., Mutka, M.W., Ni, L.M.: Service discovery in pervasive computing environments. IEEE Pervasive Comput. 4(4), 81–90 (2005)
9. Zakarya, M., Rahman, I.: A short overview of service discovery protocols for MANETs. VAWKUM Trans. Comput. Sci. 2, 1–6 (2013)
10. Kumar, N., Iqbal, R., Chilamkurti, N., James, A.: An ant based multi constraints QoS aware service selection algorithm in wireless mesh networks. Simul. Model. Pract. Theor. 9, 1933–1945 (2011)

11. Eberhart, R.C., Kennedy, J.: A new optimizer using particle swarm theory. In: Proceedings of the Sixth International Symposium, Nagoya, Japan, pp. 39–43 (1995)
12. Dorigo, M., Di'Caro, G., Gambardella, L.M.: Ant algorithms for discrete optimization. Artif. Life 5(2), 137–172 (1999)
13. Selvi, V., Umarani, D.R.: Comparative analysis of ant colony and particle swarm optimization techniques. Int. J. Comput. Appl. 5, 4 (2010)

Innovating Based on R tree and Artificial Neural Network for Hierarchical Clustering in Order to Make QoS Routes in MANET

Nguyen Thanh Long[1(✉)], Nguyen Duc Thuy[2],
and Pham Huy Hoang[3]

[1] Software Development Division III, Informatics Center of Hanoi
Telecommunications, Hoan Kiem, Hanoi, Vietnam
Ntlptpml@yahoo.com
[2] Center for Applied Research and Technology Development,
Research Institute of Posts and Telecommunications, Hanoi, Vietnam
Nguyenducthuy07@gmail.com
[3] Information Technology Institute, Hanoi University of Science Technology,
Hanoi, Vietnam
Hoangph@soict.hut.edu.vn

Abstract. The advanced routing protocol not only operates on lower levels of a network protocol, but it also operates on upper layers such as the application layer of OSI model. The routing task can be operated on a wider scale. It can process based on results of some other protocols for example service based protocol can be operated based on the service discovery protocol. So this kind of routing protocols may be determinized as upper layer routing protocols. Such as the service based routing protocol can operate based on content based protocol and combines some service filters. In service based routing protocol as well as content based routing protocol, subscriber and publisher can communicate with each other but they don't know the other's address. So it is more flexible in processing and more comfortable for mobile ad-hoc network. In mobile ad-hoc networks, nodes usually move, so bandwidth of connection between them may be not stable. Therefore transmission delay, overhead and packet loss may be larger than other kinds of networks. The paper aims at purpose to increase QoS of routing by hierarchical clustering routing by using R^+ tree in addition with some advanced techniques such as multicast routing, multiple paths, use can ACO to optimize routes to transmit data. By using R tree structure, the network topology are managed by bottom-up model from leaf level to root of the tree. All the leaf nodes, inner nodes and root of this tree have two roles: (i) Manage a cluster that consisting all nodes that have direct connections with this node; (ii) Operate as a normal node. The paper introduces and analyzes: (i) Establish hierarchical clustering network by using R tree structure; (ii) Make multicast tree from some cluster heads for fast routing; (iii) Make optimized route by Ant Colony Optimization. The paper also uses the Artificial Neural Network to choose optimal cluster head and members for cluster of network.

Keywords: MANET · R^+ · Service · Routing · Multi-paths · Bandwidth · Cluster · Tree · Multicast · QoS · Overhead · Ant · ACO · ANN

© ICST Institute for Computer Sciences, Social Informatics and Telecommunications Engineering 2018
T.F. Bissyande and O. Sie (Eds.): AFRICOMM 2016, LNICST 208, pp. 217–231, 2018.
https://doi.org/10.1007/978-3-319-66742-3_21

1   Introduction

1.1   History of R tree Applications

R-tree are tree data structure used for spatial access methods, for example, it can used for indexing multi-dimensional information such as geographical coordinates, rectangles or polygons [12]. The R-tree was invented by Guttman in 1984, focuses on handling geometrical data, such as points, line segments, surfaces, volumes, and hyper volumes in high-dimensional spaces [11]. R-trees are accepted as an additional access method to process multi-dimensional data. Today, spatial databases and geographical information systems have been established as a mature field, spatiotemporal databases and manipulation of moving points and trajectories are being studied extensively, and finally image and multimedia databases able to handle new kinds of data, such as images, voice, music, or video, are being designed and developed. An application in all these cases should rely on R-trees as a necessary tool for data storage and retrieval.

1.2   Main Features of R tree

The key idea of the data structure is to group nearby objects and represent them with their minimum in the next higher level of the tree; the "R" in R-tree is for rectangle. Since all objects lie within this bounding rectangle, a query that does not intersect the bounding rectangle also cannot intersect any of the contained objects. At the leaf level, each rectangle describes a single object; at higher levels the aggregation of an increasing number of objects. This can also be seen as an increasingly coarse approximation of the data set [12].

R tree has a typical feature that is each leaf/inner/root node has number of children in the predefined range [m, M].

In this paper, we may utilize the R^+ to organize the network topology in hierarchical clustering model. The procedures for processing R^+ tree is already defined in some previous papers. The R^+ can be expressed by the recursive formula:

$$R^+ = \text{Root} \cup R^+(C_1) \cup R^+(C_2) \cup \ldots \cup R^+(C_n). \tag{1}$$

The root of the R^+ tree has n children: $C_1, C_2, \ldots, C_n$. In which, every C_i is a child that has direct link to the root of R^+. In R^+ tree, every inner and leaf node can connect directly to a rather stable number of children that is belonged to predefined range [m, M], m, M are lower and upper bound of this range respectively. The lower bound m is usually belonged to the range $(0, \lfloor M/2 \rfloor]$. When number of nodes is increased and the overhead also increases very fast. The normal topologies are not effectively, they must be innovated by some artificial algorithms. For example, OLSR protocol uses MPR to reduce overhead, control packet flooding and route loop. In the recent time the multicast topology is usually used to reduce delay and transmit packet to all destinations at the same time. Especially, on a larger network we may use hierarchical clustering model to organize the network topology to reduce overhead and easily to apply artificial algorithms to find optimal routes to control packets and transmit data. In the R^+ tree, the network nodes in a level and are managed by a local root that are called a cluster. The network of some cluster heads may cooperate to establish an upper cluster. In that way, the root node manages to highest level cluster of the network.

$$\text{Upper}(\text{Cluster}) = \text{NETWORK}(U(CH_i)) = CH_1 \, U \, CH_2 \, U \, CH_3 \, U \ldots U \, CH_n \qquad (2)$$

This NETWORK(U(CH$_i$)) is established that is called the upper level cluster, as lower level cluster that choose a node to manage this cluster which is called cluster head. In this way, up to the root we have the root cluster that has root of tree is the cluster head of the highest level cluster of the whole network. At the first time, the root cluster has only three nodes, the root of tree that manages two cluster heads of two one level lower clusters that are just established by dividing original cluster into two parts when the number of nodes of this cluster reaches M. Therefore, it is easy to realize that in the leaf level, there are some basic clusters, in which each cluster has some nodes that are only managed by a cluster head; they don't manage any other node. The cluster head of each leaf cluster is a leaf node of the R tree. The member nodes communicate with their cluster head for receiving and sending data and control information in this cluster and from outside networks. In R tree, we define a level of the tree is collection of nodes that have the same height to the root of the tree. The zero level consists of nodes are managed by leaf nodes, the first level contains leaf nodes, the root level contains only root of the tree. The number of levels of tree is equal to the height of tree plus one. Therefore, it is easy to realize that the root of an upper level cluster manages all nodes of all branches that connect to this local root. Then it is also the cluster head of this upper level of some cluster heads of one level lower some clusters.

2   Use R^+ tree for Hierarchical Cluster Routing

The algorithms are used for making, updating, deleting, regulating, cluster dividing … of R^+ tree is introduced in previous papers. This paper introduces technical specification details on using this tree to make hierarchical clustered routing. R tree can be defined by a four items tuple:

$$R = \{m, \ M, \ root, \ \{F\}\} \qquad (3)$$

{F} is the set of functions to insert, update, delete and regulate R tree.

The root often transmits control messages to their children to coordinate its cluster. If root stops then the tree will be must to renew. In that way these child members also manage their clusters by periodically sending controlling messages. So the overhead for transmitting one control message is:

$$\text{Overhead}(\text{Control}) = \prod_{i=1}^{h} n_i \qquad (4)$$

It is approximate overhead to transmit a control packet to each node in the network. In that h is number of levels, n_1 is average number of nodes of each cluster in level 1 of R^+ tree, n_2 is average number of children nodes of each cluster in level 2…, level h has only root node. As mention above, $n_i \in [m, M]$, with one level of the tree, h is usually not large because number of nodes of the tree is less than M^{h-1}. For example, with network, choose m = 5, number of nodes is 100000, h is less than or equal to 7. Especially controlling messages are sent simultaneously from a cluster head to all its child nodes. So its delay is reduced and all managed nodes can receive at one time, satisfies the QoS request. Beside requested bandwidth is reduced significantly because at one time all child nodes can receive a control packet from their cluster head. Cluster head can transmit data by multicast protocol, it can decrease flood of data over the network. When a node is covered by a cluster head with satisfied bandwidth, it may join this cluster by receiving one invitation message of this cluster head. Then all of this network local change is spread over network locally in its managed region by multicast tree of combination of some clusters to reduce packet loss. At first, this control message (M) is transmitted to the cluster head (CH) of parent cluster (PC) of the cluster head of current cluster. The cluster head of PC transmits this M to all members of PC and to CH of its cluster. By this way, any change of network configuration is very fast to be notified to all CHs. On the other hand, all child nodes of network leaf nodes or managed nodes don't need to receive this information, for example, some network policy information only are needed by cluster heads, so it reduces much of required bandwidth.

Each cluster has to store two main kinds of connections: (i) one to the cluster head of cluster that it is belonged; (ii) one to all its cluster members. This number of connections is approximate to: $n_i + 1$.

The algorithm for choosing cluster head as introduced by our previous papers [1–7]. In fact, a node may be accepted to some clusters simultaneously because all connections to these clusters also satisfy bandwidth request. So it may be reasonable to use an ANN for choosing the best cluster to accept this node. Exceptionally, at the time to join network with very high density of nodes. For example, many upper levels of clusters may accept this node at a very short time duration. If this node stores all connections to these cluster heads then the time to update network topology is reduced by multicast tree from this node to all these CHs. In this way the root of R^+ can be connected to some another trees easily. It establishes a daisy chain R^+ trees. Because this model of networks can avoid the constraint of [m, M] in each level of R^+.

3   Find the Optimized Route by Multiple Paths and Multicast Routing

The temporary backbone of network of R^+ daisy chain can be established, so some multicast trees or meshes of cluster heads of some clusters of this network can established for data transmission. Therefore it overcomes constraint of R^+ structure in some critical circumstances to directly transmitting data from a source node to many destinations. This concept is very comfortable on upper layer routing protocol in advanced networks. The algorithms to establish multiple optimal multicast trees and optimal multiple paths routes that are found by GEN/ACO are introduced in [3, 4].

4 Acceptance of a Node

As any normal wireless routing protocol, when a node wants to join a network, it has to create HELLO packet to broadcast over network. When a cluster head receives this packet, it checks some context aware conditions and node's capabilities. In a general circumstance, these conditions are node's energy, strength of signal, processing capacity, CPU usage, and network bandwidth. CH will make a join invitation to send to this node. This node will send this CH its authentication information to join this cluster. As it is introduced in [6], this node information is processed and it will be propagate to a basically cluster from this cluster. When the best congruous cluster accepts this node, all needed changes will be processed on this cluster to propagate to the root of R^+ tree, after that the changes of network are transmitted to all CH in the network. Because every CH also receives these changes so it can manage its cluster better. So the new node may be cluster head based on its capability and the procedures for accepting this node as the new cluster head of this cluster is carried out. Hence at first it will be cluster of current cluster. If new node is chosen as CH then this node's information is processed by upper level clusters. This process is executed until the new node will not be accepted as CH on any upper cluster. The some cluster heads with the same level with this cluster head will vote new cluster head for the next level of clusters. The new node may be root of R^+ tree, if it satisfies the conditions.

4.1 Procedure for Accepting Node

When a node is invited to join R^+ tree or the root of an R^+ that can be a branch of the large R^+ to receive the HELLO message of this node. The node's information is spread back to the root of the R^+ tree. The node's information is processed that begins from root node to choose the best child node to transmit node information to. The child node continuously processes node information to choose the best grandchild to relay node information to. This process executes continuously until it reaches leaf node. The leaf node processes the node information by the same algorithms or any optimal algorithm such as an artificial algorithm. If the node is accepted by this CH to join its cluster then this cluster has to regulate to follow R tree structure. The regulation processing begins from current CH up to the root, until there is no change to the structure or cluster head of the processing cluster. The algorithm is used to evaluate a node for a CH to accept a node based on some context conditions and candidate node's information. For example, it can use fuzzy logic controller to decide, these parameters of candidate node are fuzzed to be put into a fuzzy logic controller to get the fuzzed output result to make the decision. Besides, it may use ANN to process the parameters of node with condition is that ANN has been trained to choose the best result.

4.2 Procedure for Choosing Cluster Head

The procedure is used to choose a cluster head that depends on some metrics of nodes in each cluster. After a cluster is formed, it have to choose a node that has strong capacity and/or many good characteristics and fit best to context conditions to manage the cluster that is called cluster head. Then we can use a neuron network or fuzzy logic controller to choose the cluster head or a range of several cluster heads. After that, the network established by found cluster heads of R^+ tree is optimized by GENETIC algorithm or some other algorithms.

5   Artificial Neural Network

5.1   Basic Concepts

The Artificial Neural Network (ANN) has some layers, which are input layer, hidden layers and output layer (Fig. 1).

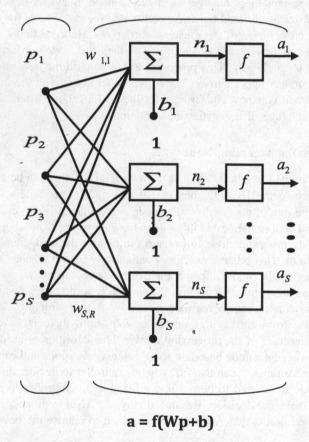

$$a = f(Wp+b)$$

Fig. 1. ANN model with one layer.

The input data is executed by the input layer, each data of input is received by a neuron of input layer (Fig. 2).

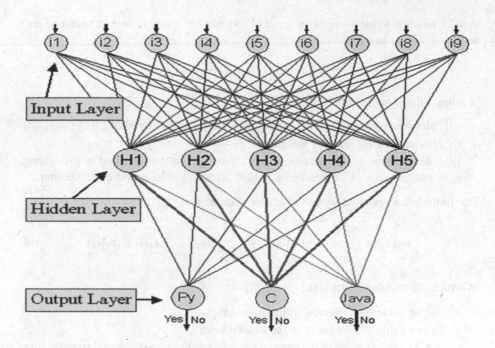

Fig. 2. ANN model with multiple layers.

These data of neurons of input layer are the inputs of the first hidden layer; each input is multiplied with a weight value. So each neuron stores a weight vector, we get the sum of weighted input data with a bias of each layer to get a sum:

$$S = \sum_{i=1}^{n} I_i W_i + B \qquad (5)$$

The transfer function is used for this sum to get a result of each neuron:

$$R = \text{Transfer Function}(S) \qquad (6)$$

The results of each hidden layer are inputs for the next hidden layer. Finally, the results of the last hidden layer are inputs for the output layer. The output layer calculates the output vector for the neural network. In order to tune the result of the neural network in the training stage for the ANN, We calculate the error vector by subtracting the desired vector to result vector. We use the error vector to tune the weight vector of hidden layers individually from the last hidden layer to the first hidden layer. After some predefined steps or the output vector is converged we stop the training process to get neural network to use for clustering network as the next section will introduce. We must use a transfer function that can be derived. So we can use derivation of the transfer function to tune weight vector. The formula for updating weight vector of each neuron in output layer is:

$$w_{ij}(1+1) = w_{ij}(1) + \eta.e_i(1).y_j.f'(y_i(1)) \tag{7}$$

In which: η: training coefficient,

$e_i(1)$: deviation value of ith neuron in output layer in lst round of processing.
f': derivation of the transfer function, $f' = \frac{1-x^2}{2}$.
$y_i(1)$: output value of ith neuron in the output layer in the lst round of processing.
$y_j(1)$: output value of jth neuron of hidden layer in the lst round of processing.

The formula for updating weight vector of each neuron in the hidden layer is:

$$w_{ij}(1+1) = w_{ij}(1) + \eta.x_j.f'(y_i). \sum_{k=1}^{m} w_{ki}(l+1).e_k(l).f'(y_k(l)) \tag{8}$$

In which: η: training coefficient,

x_j: output value of jth neuron of the input layer.
y_i: output value of ith neuron in the hidden layer.
$w_{ki}(1 + 1)$: weight value of the connection between the kth neuron in the output layer and the ith neuron in hidden layer in the $(l+1)^{th}$ round of processing.
$y_k(1)$: output value of the kth neuron of output layer in the lth round of processing.

5.2   Apply Artificial Neural Network to Cluster Network

The network is clustered by two processes stages: the first step is for choosing a cluster head for each cluster. The second stage is for choosing cluster members for each cluster. We use ANN concepts as analyzing above for training an ANN for each cluster head. After that we use found ANNs for accepting cluster member for each cluster. We use back propagation algorithm to update weight matrix of ANN. The algorithm consist of two steps: (i) At the first step: starting from output layer, the output value (OVE) error is used to update weight matrix of the previous layers:

$$[OVE] = [Desired\ Output\ Value] - [Calculated\ Output\ Result] \tag{9}$$

We calulate the delta for each neuron in hidden layers and input layer by summing the multiple of weight vector of the current neuron and delta of each neuron in the next layer:

$$Delta_j^i = \sum_{k=1}^{n} w_k^{ij} Delta_k^{i+1} \tag{10}$$

In which: Delta is the deviation between desired result and real got result, $Delta_k^{i+1}$ is delta of neuron k in the layer $i + 1$, w_k^{ij} is the weight kth in the weight matrix of neuron j of layer i; (ii) At the second step, we start at the input layer to the last hidden layer. The weight matrix of each neuron of each layer is added by summing the multiplication of three items: the learning rate of the current neuron, the delta of respective neuron with current weight in the next layer and result of the neuron:

$$w_k^{ij} = w_k^{ij} + \sum_{k=1}^{n} LR_i^j * Delta_k^{i+1} * NR_j^i \qquad (11)$$

In this formula, n is number of neurons in the next layer $i + 1$, w_k^{ij} is the kth weight in of weight vector of the neuron j in the layer i, LR_i^j is learning rate of this neuron, $Delta_k^{i+1}$ is delta of the neuron k of the layer $i + 1$, NR_j^i is result of this neuron. We also update weight vector for bias in each layer:

$$w_k^i = w_k^i + \sum_{k=1}^{n} B_i * Delta_k^i * LR_k^i \qquad (12)$$

In which, B_i is bias of the layer i, n is number of neurons of this layer. $Delta_k^i$ is delta of the neuron k^{th} of the layer i, LR_k^i is learning rate of the neuron k in the layer i.

5.3   Use the Genetic Algorithm to Innovate the Weight Updating Algorithm

In order to update weight matrices of layers of ANN fast, we use the Genetic (GEN) algorithm. In particular, we use the crossover operator to update weight matrices of ANN. The crossover operator is:

We assume each neuron network after training is a solution in the population. We interchange weight vector of neurons between two networks randomly, with condition, two neurons have the same position in each network (the layers and position in each layer). We change weights for each neuron respectively. By simulations, we see that the training process is improved with time required is reduced.

6   Selection of QoS Route by ACO

The paper introduces an algorithm to find QOS routes based on ACO which consists of two phases: (i) route discovery; (ii) route maintenance. In the discovery phase, it uses two kinds of packets that like route request and route reply as used in DSR protocol which are Ant_Route_Request and Ant_Route_Reply packets. Some QOS demands are stored in Ant_Route_Request in combination with visited node's list field, this field stores nodes that are visited by this packet.

6.1   Introduction

Pheromone evaporation is some condition to assess the probability to choose the optimal route. On the route to find food, ants emit pheromone evaporations to sign routes which are traversed. So other ants easy to find and focus to the food source very fast.

6.2   Discovery Process

The Ant_Route_Request is broadcasted to 1-hop neighbors of the source node like a HELLO packet of OLSR. In each neighbor node: (i) node has to maintain its link quality table $\{L_{i \to j}\}$ of 1-hop distance nodes based on the accessing pheromone evaporation, it calculates the preference probability (P_{pref}) of each link based on information of routing table on this node. If P_{pref} is more than predefined threshold preference probability, then this link is selected for forwarding Ant_Route_Request on the network; (ii) Select a 1-hop distance node among 1-hop distance nodes that is MPR, that has connections to almost 2-hop distance nodes of this node. So in selecting MPR being next hop on the route to the destination. Obvious MPR functions as source node, it carries out the same functions: broadcast Ant_Route_Request to its 1-hop distance nodes. When packet for finding a route arrives at a destination node. The destination node instantly makes Ant_Route_Reply packet to transmit back to the source node. The Ant_Route_Reply stores the route that has just been detected by the unicast protocol.

6.3   Maintenance Process

Some routes may be discovered by discovery process, but we select the optimal route by Genetic algorithm to transmit data. The other routes may be cached in the buffer of the source node for multiple path routing purpose; they may be used for alternating or replacing route in the case of main route hasn't existed because of topology changes. But these routes are periodically updated their status for checking existence state.

7   Hidden Markov Model

We assume a node in a hierarchical network can belong to N clusters in M times. In each time t, this node can be in cluster i (i = 1..N) with probability P_i. The purpose is to find the route that passes through some member nodes which belonged to these clusters. In which each node is belonged to one cluster. The host can be the member node of one of N clusters. Applying the HMM to this problem:

N states are N cluster heads of N clusters that are established before. In which each cluster (i) connects to some cluster member (j) with some probability existence that is called A_{ij};

M outputs are M node members of N clusters that are hops on finding route from the source S. So the finding route can be denoted by:

$$R = (S, R_1, R_2, \ldots, R_{m-2}, D);$$

A node of this hierarchical cluster network that needs to find routes R that passes through M nodes. At each step we have to find a cluster that has connection to recent selected cluster. This may be known as state transition. At each state i or cluster C_i which must to choose one or more cluster members connected this cluster which are belonged to the finding route.

From these assumptions, we establish a HMM with probabilities for transitions and connection choosing between nodes are calculated by ACO as mentioned above. The transition probability is the probability of connection between two cluster heads of this network is also defined by ACO. So applying HMM formulas that are easy to get the probability to select a route from these member nodes [10].

We define probability model of HMM model system:

Transition probability from state i (cluster i) to state j (cluster j) is probability of existance of connection between cluster i and j $(i, j \in \overline{1..N})$:

$$P_{ij} = \text{probability}(\text{existance}(i, j)) \tag{13}$$

The probability to generate observed output j $(j \in \overline{1..M}))$ from a state i $(i \in \overline{1..N}))$:

$$A_{ij} = \text{probability}(\text{existance}(i, j)) \tag{14}$$

At first, the source node can be connected to one of clusters with some probability. So if this node is connected to cluster C_i then the probability to get the first state is the existance probability of the connection between the source node and C_i.

At the state i, with accumulation probability to reach cluster C_i is P_i, so the for reaching to cluster j P_{i+1} that has probability is:

$$P_{i+1} = P_i * P_{C_i C_j} * \prod_{k=j}^{t} A_{C_i M_k} \tag{15}$$

In which, $k \in \overline{j..t}$ is the range of cluster members that are connected to C_i.

Apply the formula (16) for all related cluster heads to get the result.

8   Assessments

8.1   Use ANN for Choosing Cluster Member for Each Cluster

As analyzing above about ANN, We make ANN for each cluster head. We have to choose model for each ANN, the number of layers, the number of neuron of each layer. The weight vector is made randomly, and then it is tuned by the back propagation process. The formulas for tuning weight vector are calculated:

The code is written in C# as follow:

```
public void Correct_weight()
    {
        double ws = 0;
        int iCount = 0;
        for (int k = ls_Layer.Count - 2; k > 0; k--)
        {
            iCount = ls_Layer[k + 1].ds_Neural.Count;
            for (int j = 0; j < ls_Layer[k].ds_Neural.Count;
j++)
            {
                ws = 0;
                for (int i = 0; i < iCount; i++)
                {
                    ws +=
ls_Layer[k].ds_Neural[j].weight_vector[i] * ls_Layer[k +
1].ds_Neural[i].delta;
                }
                ls_Layer[k].ds_Neural[j].delta = ws;
            }
        }
        for (int k = 0; k < ls_Layer.Count - 1; k++)
        {
            for (int i = 0; i < ls_Layer[k].ds_Neural.Count;
i++)
            {
                for (int j = 0; j < ls_Layer[k +
1].ds_Neural.Count; j++)
                {
                    ls_Layer[k].ds_Neural[i].weight_vector[j]
+= ls_Layer[k].ds_Neural[i].hs_run * ls_Layer[k +
1].ds_Neural[j].delta *
                        ls_Layer[k].ds_Neural[i].neural_res;
                }
                ls_Layer[k].weighted_vector[i] +=
ls_Layer[k].bias *
                    ls_Layer[k].hs_run *
ls_Layer[k].ds_Neural[i].delta;
            }
        }
    }
```

The simulation data is collected consisting of three dimensions that are number of layers, number of neurons of the first hidden layer and the time required for execution. The execution time consists time for training and time to recognize or detect a member. The diagram is drawn from the simulation data below indicates that the time is not increased fast when the number of layers and number of neurons increasing (Fig. 3).

8.2   Assessment of Using Genetic Algorithm to Train Neural Network

In order for training artificial neural network, as mentioned above we can use Genetic algorithm by crossover operator. We assume a neural network as a solution in each round that it is a gene of genetic population, so we can crossover between these genes.

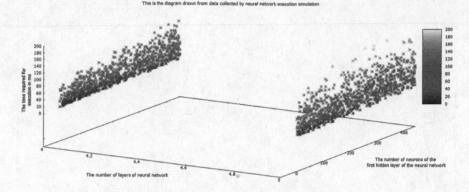

Fig. 3. Assessing results of applying ANN to get a node for a network cluster.

Each gene has some layers; each layer has some nodes, each node has some weight inputs. The procedure to apply the crossover operator as below:

```
public void crossover_2(cNeural_Network gen_1, cNeural_Network
gen_2, int iLayer)
        {
            int iPos = -1;
            double weight = 0;

            try
            {
                rand = new Random();
                iPos =
rand.Next(gen_1.ls_Layer[iLayer].neural_count);
                weight = 0;

                for (int i = 0; i <
gen_1.ls_Layer[iLayer].prev_layer.ds_Neural.Count; i++)
                {
                    weight =
gen_1.ls_Layer[iLayer].prev_layer.ds_Neural[i].weight_vector[iPos];

gen_1.ls_Layer[iLayer].prev_layer.ds_Neural[i].weight_vector[iPos] =
gen_2.ls_Layer[iLayer].prev_layer.ds_Neural[i].weight_vector[iPos];

gen_2.ls_Layer[iLayer].prev_layer.ds_Neural[i].weight_vector[iPos] =
weight;
                }
            }
            catch { }
        }
```

In the following graph, we compare the time required to training ANN in two cases: (i) case 1: training ANN normally; (ii) case 2: training ANN using Genetic's crossover operation:

We try to test the algorithms to train ANN in 280 times, we calculate two factors: (i) Average time required to train; and (ii) the time required for normal training and training with Genetic's crossover operation. The average time of Genetic (T(Gene)) is rather lower than in normal training (T(Norm)) (Fig. 4).

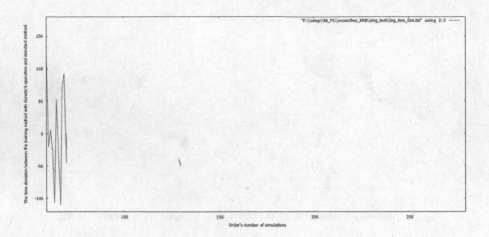

Fig. 4. Simulation results of training ANN with genetic's operation.

According the above graph, we can see that in common:

$$T(Gene) < T(Norm) \tag{16}$$

From the last point in the graph, we can see that:

$$Average(T(Gene)) - Average(T(Norm)) < 0 \tag{17}$$

So we can apply Genetic's operation for training process of ANN.

9 Assessing Results

In combination of some advanced technologies as introduced above of the paper to make MANET operating better and reduce overhead. We can use R tree to cluster network hierarchically effectively. ANN can be used to choose CH to manage cluster and choose child node of CH. In each cluster, We can use multicast tree to transmit information from CH to its child nodes. Besides, We can use ACO, HMM to find optimal route to transmit data.

References

1. Long, N.T., Thuy, N.D., Hoang, P.H.: Research on applying hierarchical clustered based routing technique using artificial intelligence algorithms for quality of service of service based routing. IoT Cloud Comput. **3**, 14–21 (2015). doi:10.11648/j.iotcc.s.2015030601.11. Special Issue: Quality of Service of Service Based Routing

2. Long, N.T., Thuy, N.D., Hoang, P.H.: Research on innovating and applying evolutionary algorithms based hierarchical clustering and multiple paths routing for guaranteed quality of service on service based routing. IoT Cloud Comput. **3**, 9–15 (2015). doi:10.11648/j.iotcc.s. 2015030601.12. Special Issue:Quality of Service of Service Based Routing
3. Srungaram, K., Krishna Prasad, M.H.M.: Enhanced cluster based routing protocol for MANETS
4. Ferreira, C.: Gene expression programming: a new adaptive algorithm for solving problems
5. Roy, B.: Ant Colony based Routing for Mobile Ad-Hoc Networks towards Improved Quality of Services
6. Long, N.T., Thuy, N.D., Hoang, P.H., Chien, T.D.: Innovating R tree to create summary filter for message forwarding technique in service-based routing. In: Qian, H., Kang, K. (eds.) WICON 2013. LNICSSITE, vol. 121, pp. 178–188. Springer, Heidelberg (2013). doi:10.1007/978-3-642-41773-3_19
7. Long, T.N., Tam, N.T., Chien, T., Thuy, N.D.: Research on innovating, applying multiple paths routing technique based on fuzzy logic and genetic algorithm for routing messages in service - oriented routing. J. Scalable Inf. Syst. EAI **15**, e2 (2015)
8. Chen, K.-T., Fan, K., Dai, Y., Baba, T.: A particle swarm optimization with adaptive multi-swarm strategy for capacitated vehicle routing problem. EAI Endorsed Trans. Ind. Netw. Intell. Syst. **15**, e3 (2015)
9. Long, N.T., Thuy, N.D., Hoang, P.H.: Research on innovating, evaluating and applying multicast routing technique for routing messages in service-oriented routing. In: Vinh, P.C., Hung, N.M., Tung, N.T., Suzuki, J. (eds.) ICCASA 2012. LNICSSITE, vol. 109, pp. 212–228. Springer, Heidelberg (2013). doi:10.1007/978-3-642-36642-0_22
10. Newson, P., Krumm, J.: Hidden Markov Map Matching Through Noise and Sparseness. Microsoft Research, Redmond (2009)
11. http://www.bowdoin.edu/~ltoma/teaching/cs340/spring08/Papers/Rtree-chap1.pdf
12. https://en.wikipedia.org/wiki/R-tree

DNS Lame Delegations: A Case-Study of Public Reverse DNS Records in the African Region

Amreesh Phokeer[1]([✉]), Alain Aina[2], and David Johnson[3]

[1] AFRINIC, Ebene, Mauritius
amreesh@afrinic.net
[2] WACREN, Accra, Ghana
alain.aina@wacren.net
[3] CSIR, Pretoria, South Africa
djohnson@csir.co.za

Abstract. The DNS, as one of the oldest components of the modern Internet, has been studied multiple times. It is a known fact that operational issues such as mis-configured name servers affect the responsiveness of the DNS service which could lead to delayed responses or failed queries. One of such misconfigurations is lame delegation and this article explains how it can be detected and also provides guidance to the African Internet community as to whether a policy lame reverse DNS should be enforced. It also gives an overview of the degree of lameness of the AFRINIC reverse domains where it was found that 45% of all reverse domains are lame.

Keywords: Reverse DNS · Misconfigurations · Lame delegation · Non-authoritative nameservers

1 Introduction

The Domain Name System (DNS) is a core functionality of the Internet which allows the translation of domain names into IP addresses i.e. from human-readable host names to machine-interpretable addresses. The DNS has become popular thanks to its distributed architecture which provides a very convenient way for users to publish and propagate their DNS information to the world.

On the Internet today, besides web browsing which involves lots of DNS queries, many applications such as content distribution through CDNs, email, spam filtering, Voice Over IP (VOIP) and telephone number mapping (ENUM), rely heavily on the availability of the DNS service [12]. However, when DNS was designed in the 1980's, engineers focused mainly on making the system scalable rather than secure, a requirement which only came much later.

As the DNS became an indispensable function of the Internet, questions pertaining to security and high availability became very relevant. The critical nature of the DNS makes it prone to multiple types of attack such as cache poisoning [8] and DDoS on DNS servers [10]. Besides the inherent security vulnerabilities,

© ICST Institute for Computer Sciences, Social Informatics and Telecommunications Engineering 2018
T.F. Bissyande and O. Sie (Eds.): AFRICOMM 2016, LNICST 208, pp. 232–242, 2018.
https://doi.org/10.1007/978-3-319-66742-3_22

the reliability of DNS services is also affected by different configuration errors as explained by Pappas et al. in their study on the impact of misconfiguration on the robustness of the DNS [6].

In this paper, we will look at one particular type of error called lame delegations on a subset of publicly DNS records, more specifically, the public DNS records of the AFRINIC[1] reverse tree.

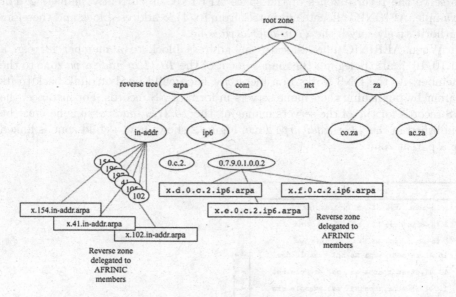

Fig. 1. DNS tree showing reverse delegations to AFRINIC members.

2 Background

AFRINIC manages reverse delegations for the IPv4 and IPv6 address space delegated by IANA. The resources currently managed by AFRINIC are listed on the IANA website[2,3]. The aim of Reverse DNS entries is to allow applications on the Internet to map an IP address to its host, as opposed to forward DNS entries that map a domain to an IP. An example of a reverse DNS entry is a pointer record (PTR) that maps an IP address to a hostname. PTR records are very important for the many applications on the Internet. For example, some mail servers would enforce the check on reverse entries to make sure the originating IP of a incoming email transfer request is legitimate [7].

---

[1] The African Network Information Centre (AFRINIC) is the Regional Internet Registry (RIR) for Africa and the Indian Ocean. AFRINIC allocates Internet number resources i.e. IPv4, IPv6 and Autonomous System (AS) numbers to network operators in its constituency.

[2] http://www.iana.org/assignments/ipv4-address-space/ipv4-address-space.xhtml.

[3] http://www.iana.org/assignments/ipv6-unicast-address-assignments/ipv6-unicast-address-assignments.xhtml.

> 6.2.216.196.in-addr.arpa domain name pointer www.afrinic.net.

Similarly as any other Top Level Domain (TLD), the DNS reverse tree is managed under the .ARPA zone as shown in Fig. 1. The subdomain for the IPv4 number space is the *in-addr.arpa* and *ip6.arpa* for IPv6. As registry of the IANA allocated space, AFRINIC needs to host an authoritative[4] DNS server to serve the reverse zones of the space AFRINIC is currently managing. For example, AFRINIC allocates resources from its 41/8 address block and therefore authoritatively serves the *41.in-addr.arpa* zone.

When AFRINIC now allocates an address block to a member for e.g. a 41.10/16, it also delegates the management of the *10.41.in-addr.arpa* zone to the member. As the DNS works in a hierarchy, each child needs to link back to its parent by publishing their name servers in form of NS records. For instance, the NS records for the of the servers managing the *10.41.in-addr.arpa* zone must be published in the *41.in-addr.arpa* zone. Figure 2 shows how a child zone is linked to a parent zone.

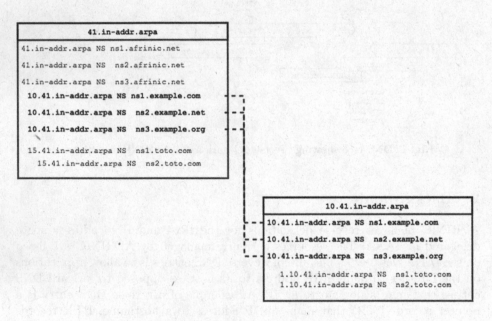

Fig. 2. NS records linking child and parent zones.

All the zones managed by AFRINIC are publicly available data and published on the AFRINIC public repository[5]. By analysing this data set, it gives us an idea of how well reverse delegations are configured in the African region.

---

[4] An authoritative name server holds the actual records (A, AAAA, CNAME, PTR, etc.) of the zones, as opposed to a recursive server or resolver that needs to query an authoritative name server to resolve a domain/address.

[5] ftp://ftp.afrinic.net/pub/zones.

3   Definitions and Related Work

In this section, we will provide a definition for lame delegations and give an insight on how other RIRs have dealt with this issue. We shall also provide some insight on the findings of two scientific studies on DNS availability.

3.1   What Is a Lame Delegation?

RFC1912 defines a delegation to be lame when a name server is delegated the responsibility for providing a name service for a zone (via NS records) but it is not actually doing it i.e. the name server is neither set up as a primary nor as a secondary server [2]. This is a classic example of a lame delegation, however there are some more granular cases as described in Sect. 4. A very common example of lame delegation is when a network administrator recently added a new resource record for e.g. *newdomain.example.org* with an NS record pointing to *new-name-server.example.org* in the parent zone, but no name service has yet been deployed on the host.

Basically, if the server does not respond to DNS queries, it is considered lame. Lame delegation is considered as a bad practice as it increases the load on the parent name servers and consequently increases the delay in DNS responses. Many commercial DNS servers now have in-built mechanism to check for lame delegations such as BIND [4]. CISCO Prime Network Registrar, which includes a DNS server, can detect lame delegation by reporting non-matching or missing NS records in the parent zone [3].

3.2   Lame Delegation Policies at Other RIRs

All RIRs run authoritative name servers to serve the reverse zones of the IANA delegated space they manage. LACNIC[6] and ARIN[7] have implemented a "Lame delegation policy" which enforces the DNS best practices against lame entries. The APNIC[8] and the RIPE[9] community made proposals but have not adopted a lame delegation policy. However, they have implemented checks on their reverse DNS system precluding lame entries [11]. AFRINIC has no lame delegation policy on reverse delegation.

LACNIC periodically revises their *in-addr.arpa* and *ip6.arpa* zones and checks for lame delegation. Their methodology is to check whether a query of a SOA record on a selected server is returned as an authoritative response by the server. If not, the reverse DNS entry is considered as lame and the zone operator is contacted. LACNIC has implemented a "Lame delegation policy" which has helped to curb the number of lame delegations and now has a DNS success rate of 96.80% [9]. Figure 3 shows how the percentage of lame delegation which consistently dropped after implementation of the lame delegation policy in around 2003.

---

[6] http://www.lacnic.net/en/web/lacnic/manual-6.
[7] https://www.arin.net/policy/proposals/2014_5.html.
[8] https://www.apnic.net/policy/proposals/prop-004.
[9] https://www.ripe.net/ripe/mail/archives/dns-wg/2005-May/001493.html.

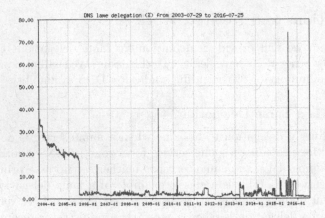

Fig. 3. Percentage of lame delegations in LACNIC database since 2004 [9].

APNIC proposed a slightly different taxonomy of lame delegations in four categories, where a delegation is considered lame if any of the following is true (1) a listed DNS server is unreachable, (2) a listed DNS server is reachable but not responsive on port 53, (3) a listed DNS server is reachable and responds on port 53, but it is not able to answer for the domain, (4) a listed DNS server is reachable and responds on port 53 but serves incorrect data for the domain [1].

3.3   Previous Studies

Pappas et al. conducted passive and active measurements on a university network [6]. They first analyzed DNS traffic exchanges from the university network to external websites and also implemented a specialized resolver to perform DNS queries to a randomly selected list of destinations. They found out that DNS configuration errors are widespread, with more than 15% of delegation being lame, 22% of zones with inconsistency and 2% affected by cyclic dependency [5]. They classified lame delegations in three different categories, depending on the type of error found:

- Type 1: Non responding server
- Type 2: DNS error indication
- Type 3: Non-authoritative answer

Redundancy is another important aspect of availability. A zone can authoritatively be served by multiple redundant name servers. DNS best practices stipulate that it is preferable to have name servers, serving the same zone, spread geographically (both in terms of location and network) [2]. Although Deccio et al., were not specifically targeting lame delegations, they discovered that 14% of DNS entries experience "false redundancy", meaning that either there is no redundant server (different NS records pointing to the same name server) or the supposedly redundant servers reside on the same network.

4   Methodology

In this section, we will explain how the DNS data was collected and how lame delegations were detected and classified.

4.1   Data Collection

The AFRINIC database contains around 30000 domain objects. Each domain object is associated with at least two name servers. For the purpose of this experiment, we took the whole set of reverse domains and run the experiment against each domain and name server (NS) tuple. A domain can have multiple NS records and each record is considered as an entry in DNS for which we have verified its validity. All the reverse zones were obtained from ftp://ftp.afrinic.net/pub/zones. Table 1 shows the breakdown between IPv4 and IPv6 reverse zones and gives the total number of NS records.

Table 1. Total registered domains and corresponding number of NS entries

Type	Domains	NS records
IPv4	29894	72341
IPv6	196	550
Total	29986	72891

As DNS query tool, we used "dig" (Domain information groper) which is commonly found on all Unix machines. It basically performs DNS lookups and returns the answers from the server that has been queried. In our case we used the option *+norec* which instructs the server queried not to retrieve DNS data from "recursive servers" but instead to get the answer from the name server that have been specified or from an authoritative source.

We paid attention to three main elements in the query response: **STATUS**, **FLAGS** and **ANSWER**. The different type of statuses are described in RFC6895[10]. In our case, a query is considered "successful" if the STATUS is *NOERROR*, the FLAGS section contains AA[11] and the ANSWER section is not null (a query is actually also technically "successful" for example if it returns an **NXDOMAIN** with **ANSWER: 0**, however for us here, it would be considered as a "failure", the domain not being found). Table 2 gives a breakdown of some of the main statuses. Below is example of a dig query and response asking for NS records of the afrinic.net domain from ns1.afrinic.net without recursion:

---

[10] https://tools.ietf.org/html/rfc6895.
[11] AA means Authoritative Answer.

```
$ dig NS @ns1.afrinic.net afrinic.net +norec

; <<>> DiG 9.8.3-P1 <<>> NS afrinic.net @ns1.afrinic.net +norec
;; global options: +cmd
;; Got answer:
;; ->>HEADER<<- opcode: QUERY, status: NOERROR, id: 12713
;; flags: qr aa ra; QUERY: 1, ANSWER: 7, AUTHORITY: 0, ADDITIONAL: 12

[...]

;; Query time: 155 msec
;; SERVER: 196.216.2.1#53(196.216.2.1)
;; WHEN: Mon May  2 21:07:13 2016
;; MSG SIZE  rcvd: 447
```

Table 2. Meaning of STATUS response (extract)

Status	Description
NOERROR	Domain exists
NXDOMAIN	Domain does not exists
REFUSED	Server refuses to perform query
SERVFAIL	Something went wrong

4.2 Error Classification

We run the experiment on each and every delegation from two different locations (Mauritius and Johannesburg). It is important to use two geographically spread locations to cater for failed queries that may occur due to congestion on the network or due to firewall restrictions. A delegation is considered lame if it fails from both sites. If a query positively responds from one site or the other, we would consider the NS to be successful and if fails on both sites, NS is tagged as erroneous. To simplify the representation of the results, we decided to classify them in four categories as shown in Table 3. The first category is CASE_0 is the null case which means that the NS record is OK.

We developed a simple algorithm to classify the dig results of each delegation found on the public reverse zones of AFRINIC, as per the criteria in Table 3. The algorithm below makes provision for more granular types of lame delegation but in the results section, only the four main categories have been considered.

Query: dig domain @nameserver for NS record (without recursion)

```
begin
    if output = any_of_CASE_1_errors
        then z = CASE_1;
    fi
    if status = (REFUSED||SERVFAIL||NXDOMAIN)
        then z = CASE_2;
    fi
    if status = NOERROR
        if answer = 0
            then z = CASE_2(NO_ANSWER);
        fi
        if flag1 = AA
            if flag2 = RA
                then z = CASE_2(RECURSIVE);
                else
                    then z = CASE_3(AUTHORITATIVE)
            fi
        fi
    fi
    if status = NOERROR
        if RAflagispresent
            then z = CASE_0(RECURSIVE);
            else
                then z = CASE_0(AUTHORITATIVE);
        fi
    fi
print(z)
```

5   Results and Observations

5.1   Valid Versus Lame

We found that approximately 55% of IPv4 domain registered in the AFRINIC database do not have any issue and can be considered as valid. For the other 45% considered as lame, it means that at least one of the NS records for the domain is actually lame. For IPv6 domains, 32% is found to be lame. Table 4 gives the number of IPv4 and IPv6 domains that passed the test i.e. tagged as CASE_0.

Table 3. Classification of delegation into different categories

Category	Error response
CASE_0	All of: — NS is responsive — NS serves the domain — NS is authoritative — Response status is NOERROR *Flag: AUTHORITATIVE(AA)*
CASE_1	Either of: — Connection timed out — Name or service not known — Connection refused — Network unreachable — Host unreachable — End of file — Communications error — Couldn't get address
CASE_2	Response status is either: — REFUSED — SERVFAIL — NOERROR without response from server i.e. ANSWER: 0 *Flag: AUTHORITATIVE(AA) or RECURSIVE(RA)*
CASE_3	All of: — NS is responsive — NS serves the domain — NS is authoritative — Response status is NOERROR *Flag: RECURSIVE(RA)*

Table 4. Percentage of lame versus non-lame domains

Type	VALID	%	LAME	%	Total
IPv4	39439	54.5	32970	45.5	72409
IPv6	369	68	174	32	543

5.2 Breakdown by Error Type

We classified the 45% of lame delegations found into the three error categories which are CASE_1, CASE_2 and CASE_3. From the results in Table 5, we observed that 75.5% are actually CASE_2 (responsive servers but not serving the zone). Most probably, the name servers that were recorded have been decommissioned by the operators. 23.5% of errors are CASE_1, meaning that the servers are not even reachable, and finally, only 1% of faulty domains have been tagged as CASE_3, meaning that more 99% of all servers queried are authoritative.

Table 5. Percentage of error type vs. address type

Type	CASE#1	CASE#2	CASE#3	Total
IPv4	7803	24941	314	32970
IPv6	19	155	0	174
Total	7822	25096	314	33144
%	23.5	75.5	1	

6 Conclusion

We found that a big chunk (45%) of reverse domains registered at AFRINIC is lame and the predominant cause of lame delegation (more than 75%) is the CASE_2 which means that servers are proper DNS servers and are responsive but they are not serving the zone as indicated by the DNS operator. One reason which could explain this situation is that in our region where resources are constrained, operators do not have the facility of hosting additional servers to ensure redundancy of their name servers. They would therefore register an ad-hoc or sometimes non-operational name server as secondary entry for their zones. Another reason could be a lack of continuity of service for a domain where the server has been recycled to serve another domain. This contributes to pollute the African reverse DNS ecosystem and must definitely have a negative impact on query time, affecting latency of services in general. It is therefore important for AFRINIC to fix those issues and provide a clean and reliable DNS service to the African operators and users on the Internet. It has become clear that to curb the number of lame delegation, AFRINIC needs to come up with a policy or implement stringent operational checks to (1) clear all existing lame delegations and (2) prevent any new lame delegation to be inserted in AFRINIC's database.

7 Future Work

Lame delegation is only a subset of DNS misconfiguration. To ensure full availability, name servers should be truly redundant. By truly redundant, we mean that primary and secondary name servers should be geographically spread and not found on the same host and as far as possible, not on the same network (i.e. on different ASes). In the event of a routing outage and one network is unavailable, the other network would still be reachable. This ensures full redundancy. Furthermore, it would be interesting to see where African network operators are hosting their DNS servers. Mapping the servers by location would give us an indication whether African operators are using local or offshore services, usually reachable on expensive international links. Cyclic zone dependency [6] is another issue that is less known but yet important to tackle as they create dependency loops between DNS servers. The impact is the addition of unnecessary load on those servers ultimately affecting availability on the overall.

References

1. APNIC's operational response to lame delegations. https://www.apnic.net/manage-ip/manage-resources/reverse-dns/lame-dns-reverse-delegation/apnics-operational-response
2. Barr, D.: Common DNS Operational and Configuration Errors (1996)
3. CISCO.   http://www.cisco.com/c/en/us/td/docs/net_mgmt/prime/network_registrar/8-2/user/guide/CPNR_8_2_User_Guide/UG16_Zon.html
4. Albitz, P., et al.: DNS and BIND, 5th edn. O'Reilly, Sebastopol (2006)
5. Pappas, V., et al.: Distributed DNS troubleshooting. In: Proceedings of the ACM SIGCOMM Workshop on Network Troubleshooting Research, Theory and Operations Practice Meet Malfunctioning Reality - NetT 2004, p. 265 (2004)
6. Pappas, V., et al.: Impact of configuration errors on DNS robustness. IEEE J. Sel. Areas Commun. **27**(3), 275–290 (2009)
7. Phokeer, A., et al.: A survey of anti-spam mechanisms from an RIR's perspective. In: Proceedings - IST-Africa (2016)
8. Trostle, J.B., et al.: Protecting against DNS cache poisoning attacks. In: 2010 6th IEEE Workshop on Secure Network Protocols, NPSec 2010, pp. 25–30 (2010)
9. LACNIC. http://lacnic.net/en/lame_delegation.html
10. Wei, M.L., Lu, Y.C., Zhen, M.L.: Alleviating the impact of DNS DDoS attacks. In: NSWCTC 2010 - The 2nd International Conference on Networks Security, Wireless Communications and Trusted Computing, vol. 1, pp. 240–243 (2010)
11. RIPE-NCC.   https://www.ripe.net/manage-ips-and-asns/resource-management/assisted-registry-check
12. van Adrichem, N.L.M., et al.: A measurement study of DNSSEC misconfigurations. Secur. Inf. **4**(1), 8 (2015)

A Correlation Between RSSI and Height in UHF Band and Comparison of Geolocation Spectrum Database View of TVWS with Ground Truth

Richard Maliwatu[1]([✉]), Albert Lysko[2], David Johnson[2], and Senka Hadzic[1]

[1] Computer Science Department, University of Cape Town, Cape Town, South Africa
{rmaliwatu,shadzic}@cs.uct.ac.za
[2] CSIR, Meraka Institute, Pretoria, South Africa
{alysko,djohnson}@csir.co.za

Abstract. An investigation into the Received Signal Strength Indicator (RSSI) dependency on receiver antenna height in UHF band is conducted. The results show a high correlation between RSSI and height on channels with high signal strength. There is approximately 2.5 dBm RSSI gain per 1 m increase in height above ground up to 8.5 m. From 8.5 m to 12 m, there is no consistent observable increase in RSSI. Furthermore, the geolocation spectrum database's (GLSD) view of white space in the television band is compared with the ground truth. Results show signal presence on some of the channels indicated free by the spectrum database. These findings imply that an increase in transmission range of UHF links can be achieved by increasing receiver height. White space devices using A GLSD should additionally require spectrum scanning to determine clear channels.

Keywords: UHF television white space · RSSI vs. antenna Height · Geolocation spectrum database · Received signal

1 Introduction

The 470–890 MHz frequency range has historically been used for television broadcast. Traditionally protection of primary transmitters has been achieved through strict frequency assignment. However due to the increase in wireless applications, the spectrum assignment paradigm is shifting towards the adoption of technologies such as smart antennas, cognitive radios, adaptive coding, etc. that allow efficient utilisation and reuse of spectrum [1]. While these ideas have been around for quite some time, the technical details of dynamically allocating and sharing spectrum without interference among users are yet to be fully addressed.

This study is motivated by the ever increasing relevance of wireless communication and the particular interest in *television white space* (TVWS) based communication. The implementation of TVWS based communication might vary from application to application but, the general requirement is for the device to know the free channels in the area and determine safe transmission power

© ICST Institute for Computer Sciences, Social Informatics and Telecommunications Engineering 2018
T.F. Bissyande and O. Sie (Eds.): AFRICOMM 2016, LNICST 208, pp. 243–250, 2018.
https://doi.org/10.1007/978-3-319-66742-3_23

levels to use. There are two general approaches to meeting this requirement: the device can either (i) scan its spectral environment to determine free channels or (ii) query a geolocation spectrum database (GLSD) that responds with a list of free channels based on the device's location and parameters such as antenna height, power, etc.

Each of these approaches for protection of primary transmitters and coexistence with secondary users raises several questions. Firstly, at what height should the scanning be done? Secondly, when the GLSD provides a list of free channels, are the channels really free?

To answer these questions, which are essential for purposes of TVWS device deployment, this paper firstly looks at Received Signal Strength Indicator (RSSI) dependency on receiver height over the ultra-high frequencies (UHF). Using results of RSSI dependency on height, the prospect of influencing the transmission range by varying the receiver antenna height is considered. Next, the GLSD's view of TVWS is compared with measurements to assess the availability of channels provided by the GLSD.

The paper is organised as follows: Sect. 2 gives the related work; Sect. 3 describes the method used in data collection; Sect. 4 discusses the results; and Sect. 5 concludes the paper and outlines follow on work.

2   Related Work

Studies have been done to characterise UHF wave for point-to-multi-point propagation in outdoor and indoor environments e.g. [2,6]. Substantial work has been done in the area of propagation models used to predict path loss for purposes such as estimating transmission range, inter-system interference analysis and so forth. Propagation models use known parameters such as operating frequency, distance, transmit power, antenna and terrain characteristics, etc. to predict path loss.

Results from studies [3,4], conducted to evaluate performance of propagation models show that the accuracy of path loss variability prediction is dependent on environmental characteristics in and around the area in which the model is applied. A propagation model is considered accurate if it obtains a root mean square error (RMSE) that is below a set margin for urban and rural areas. Empirical propagation models derived from measurements in one area often have to be modified to increase the accuracy when applied in a different area.

Other studies have been done to establish dependency of propagation distance on operating frequency [5], effect of distance and transmitter antenna height on path loss [6]. Previous work [7] covering dependency of received power on receiver height reported no significant dependency for height 1–3 m however, this was study was carried out in 225–450 MHz frequency range. From the literature surveyed, the RSSI dependency on receiver antenna height for the UHF television band is a less well explored issue.

3   Methodology

The study was done experimentally. The objective of the experiment was to establish the relationship between RSSI and receiver antenna height in the UHF band. In absence of additional equipment and to avoid the need for a spectrum license, the local television broadcasting was used as a source of the reference signals. The receiving hardware setup included a R&S FSH4 spectrum analyser, a 2.1 dBi gain R&S omnidirectional antenna and short cables, all mounted on a boom lifter. The spectrum analyser was controlled over a WiFi network from within a vehicle. The setup is shown in Fig. 1.

Fig. 1. Setup used to perform measurements. Visible are the boom lifter and antenna mounted on it (covered with a low permittivity radome). The spectrum analyser is mounted under the antenna (not visible).

The measurement procedure was to lift the arms of the boom lifter (with the measurement setup), measure the actual height using a laser range finder, and perform a frequency scan (the scan was set and triggered remotely, over the wireless network.). The results of a scan would be saved into a data file. This was repeated several times for each value of height.

Each frequency scan was done from 451.25 MHz until 1,081.25 MHz with resolution bandwidth of 1 MHz and video bandwidth of 3 MHz. The choice of frequency and resolution bandwidth was dictated by two factors: (i) the need to capture the video carriers of analogue TV transmissions (which are located around 1.25 MHz from the left edge of a TV band), and by the limitations on the number of points in a single sweep which can be used by the spectrum analyser used, i.e. fixed to 631 points.

The measured values, in dBm, recorded in the data files reflect the power entering the input of the spectrum analyser. These can be translated into the power incident onto the antenna by taking into account the losses in the cables and connectors (L_c, about 1 dB) and applying the antenna gain ($G_A = 2.1$ dBi) for the selected antenna. Thus, the power incident onto the antenna, P_{inc}, may be estimated via the power entering the spectrum analyser, P_{sa}, as

$$P_{inc} = P_{sa} + L_c - G_A = P_{sa} - 1.1, (dB). \tag{1}$$

3.1   First Set of Spectrum Scan Measurements

The first round of measurements was conducted at the location with GPS coordinates: 18.423980, -34.1398. This location had one floor houses and a large number of very tall trees around the area. From the presence of tall trees, one may expect that the dependence of the signal strength on the height may be weakened as compared to more empty space. The measurements were performed at the following antenna heights: 2 m, 3.25 m, 4.57 m, 6.04 m, 7.87 m, 9.27 m, 11.57 m, over the above-mentioned frequency range. Only one frequency scan was collected at this location at each of the antenna heights.

3.2   Second Set of Spectrum Scan Measurements

This location was a residential area with one floor houses and only short trees. From this, one may expect the dependence on height to be composed of two different types of dependencies: one for the heights below the average height of houses, and another for greater heights. Measurements were conducted at antenna heights 2 m, 2.1 m, 2.66 m, 3.2 m, 3.75 m, 4.3 m, 4.9 m, 5.46 m, 6.3 m, 7 m, 7.7 m, 8.3 m, 8.8 m, 9.3 m, 10.7 m, 11.9 m. Multiple samples were collected at each height.

3.3   Data Preparation

The frequency scans were conducted from 451.25 MHz to 1081.25 MHz and the results presented focus on television channels 21 to 69 (470–862 MHz).

In order to reduce the influence of random noise, the frequency points in each frequency scan have been grouped into channels 8 MHz wide, corresponding to TV channels, i.e. a channel N starting at $470 + 8(N - 21)$[MHz] and ending at $478 + 8(N21)$[MHz]. Each channel is represented by an average of all the values which belong to this channel as well as by associated statistics. In order to reduce the effects of the noise further, the values from each channel were averaged over a number of different frequency scans at the same height. Most of the results presented in this paper are based on averages from 31 frequency scans at each level.

4   Discussion of Results

4.1   RSSI Dependency on Height

In order to provide the overview of the spectrum scan, we consider the average of samples at the main height. The results are shown in Fig. 2(a). Figure 2(b) shows the Standard deviation of the samples collected, which was computed using Eq. 2:

$$\text{Standard deviation} = \sqrt{\frac{1}{N}\sum_{i=1}^{N}(x_i - \mu)^2} \tag{2}$$

where N is the sample size, x_i are the values and μ is the mean.

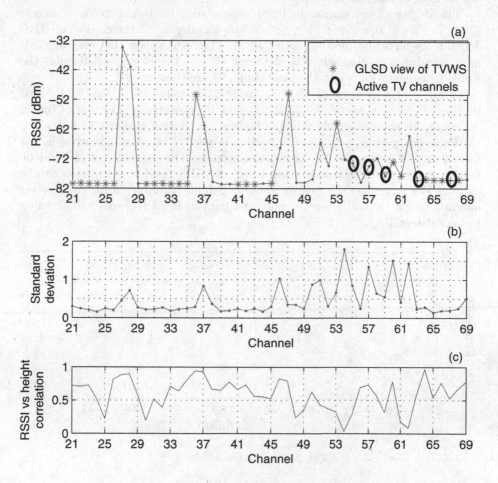

Fig. 2. Overview of the spectrum scan.

There are fluctuations in the observed standard deviation especially from channel 46 to channel 63. This could be due to changes in the spectral environment or occurrence of temporal obstructions caused by objects such as vehicles parked in the far distance thereby affecting signal propagation during the time of measurement. Spearman's Rank correlation was computed using Eq. 3 to determine statistical dependency between height and RSSI over channels 21–69.

$$\text{Rank correlation coefficient} = 1 - \frac{6\sum\limits_{i=1}^{n} d_i^2}{n^3 - n} \sum \tag{3}$$

where d_i is the difference between the ranks for $RSSI_i$, $height_i$ pairs and n is the number of pairs observed [8].

The degree of correlation in RSSI dependency on height across channels 21–69 is shown in Fig. 2(c). Figure 3 shows the degree of correlation in RSSI dependency on height plotted against RSSI. The results show that correlation is most significant on channels with strongest signal. Therefore, to determine the RSSI dependency on height the peak channels are considered.

In Fig. 2(c) correlation of 0.96907, 0.94334, 0.92862, 0.8933, 0.88153, 0.82561 is observed on channels 64, 36, 37, 28, 27 and 46 respectively. The plot of RSSSI vs. height for these channels with the highest correlation is shown in Fig. 4.

There is approximately 2.5 dBm RSSI gain per 1 m increase in receiver height from 2 m to 8.5 m across the observed channels. The dependency of RSSI on height implies that the transmission range of UHF-based wireless links can be extended by increasing the receiver antenna height. After increasing the receiver antenna height beyond 8.5 m the observed gain in RSSI plateaus and becomes less consistent.

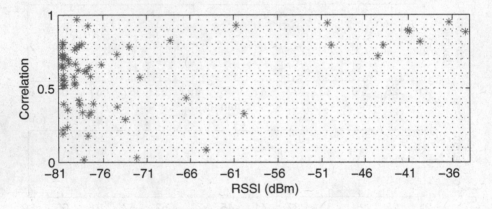

Fig. 3. Correlation vs. RSSI.

4.2   Comparing GLSD with Ground Truth

The results of the geolocation spectrum database (GLSD) query are indicated by (*) marks in Fig. 2(a). The CSIR GLSD [9] service was used to get a list of available channels or TVWS for a white space device (WSD). The GLSD's criteria for determining TVWS is based on the ITWOM+ITU-R P.1546-4(grade-B) propagation model [10] for WSD 3–10 m high and 4 W power. Details of registered television channels indicated by circular marks in Fig. 2(a) is based on information

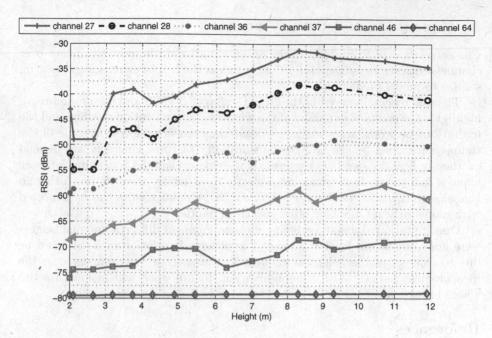

Fig. 4. RSSI dependency on receiver height at selected channels.

provided by SENTECH [11], the national licensed broadcast signal distributor in South Africa.

According to the GLSD, the following channels are free: 21, 22, 23, 24, 25, 26, 30, 31, 32, 33, 34, 35, 36, 41, 42, 43, 45, 47, 53, 60, 61, 64, 65, 66, 68. Considering the spectrum scan shown in Fig. 2(a), there is a −50.27 dBm, −49.85 dBm, −59.83 dBm, and −72.95 dBm signal present at channels 36, 47, 53 and 60 respectively, which are among the list of "free" channels provided by the GLSD.

Model-driven GLSDs use information about registered primary transmitters and compute white space at a given location based on propagation models such as ITU-R P.1546 [12]. The GLSD is required to have up-to-date information about primary transmitters but, the spectrum scan shows that some of the free channels as determined by the GLSD are in fact not free. They are tainted by unregistered sources to which a model-driven GLSD is agnostic. Furthermore, from the spectrum scan, we find (at the time) other free channels not provided by the GLSD. These findings expose the pitfalls of deploying *"sense-less"* white space devises (WSD) i.e. white space Devices with no inbuilt spectrum scanning capability. We recommend that WSDs using the GLSD for white space detection and incumbent protection supplement the query results with localised real-time spectrum scans for increased spectrum reuse and determining white space with a "finer grain".

5   Conclusion and Future Work

The correlation of RSSI dependency on antenna height is most significant over channels with strongest signal. RSSI increases as the height increases up to 8.5 m, similar to model prediction.

The differences observed in the GLSD's view of TVWS and the ground truth highlights the complex dynamics of the wireless communication medium and the limitations of propagation models. Considering the noise levels in some of the channels provided by the GLSD, the suitability of these channels will depend on the application specifics. However, it is evident that the spectrum database alone is inadequate in determining perfectly clear white space to use. Although this observation was made with TVWS GLSD, similar results can be expected with model-driven GLSD for other spectrum bands.

One limitation of this study is that measurements at different antenna heights were done one height level at a time. The observed variation in RSSI could be due to changes in the height or changes in the spectral environment over the measurement period. With this observation, future work will include a setup where measurements at different heights may be taken simultaneously.

References

1. Struzak, R., Wiecek, D.: TV White Spaces: a pragmatic approach. ICTP - The Abdus Salam International Center for Theoretical Physics (2013)
2. Porrat, D., Cox, D.C.: UHF propagation in indoor hallways. IEEE Trans. Wirel. Commun. **3**(4), 1188–1198 (2004)
3. Sridhar, B., Ali Khan, M.Z.: RMSE comparison of path loss models for UHF/VHF bands in India. In: Region 10 IEEE Symposium, pp. 330–335. IEEE, Kuala Lumpur (2014)
4. Ogbeide, O.K., Edeko, F.O.: Modification of the Hata empirical propagation model for application in VHF band in Edo State, Nigeria. Int. J. Eng. Sci. Invention **2**(8), 35–39 (2013)
5. Xiaohu, Z., Burres, T.W., Albers, K.B., Kuhn, W.B.: Propagation comparisons at VHF and UHF frequencies. In: IEEE Radio and Wireless Symposium. IEEE, San Diego, pp. 244–247 (2009)
6. Perez-Vega, C., Zamanillo, J.M.: Path-loss model for broadcasting applications and outdoor communication systems in the VHF and UHF bands. IEEE Trans. Broadcast. **48**(2), 91–96 (2002)
7. Hampton, J.R., Merheb, N.M., Lain, W.L., Paunil, D.E., Shuford, R.M., Kasch, W.T.: Urban propagation measurements for ground based communication in the military UHF band. IEEE Trans. Antennas Propag. **54**(2), 644–654 (2006)
8. Zar, J.H.: Biostatistical Analysis: Pearson New International Edition, 5th edn. Pearson Education Limited (2013)
9. http://whitespaces.meraka.csir.co.za
10. Luzango, M., Fisseha, M., Mjumo, M.: Geo-location white space spectrum databases: models and design of South Africas first dynamic spectrum access coexistence manager. KSII Trans. Internet Inf. Syst. **8**(11), 3810–3836 (2014)
11. http://www.sentech.co.za/television
12. ITU-R P.1546-5: Method for point-to-area predictions for terrestrial services in the frequency range 30 MHz to 3 000 MHz. ITU (2013)

Learning

Usage of Online Business Advisory by Micro-entrepreneurs: *Case of Cloth Tailoring Enterprises in Uganda*

Fatuma Namisango[(⊠)], Gorretti Byomire, Maria Miiro Kafuko,
and Asianzu Elizabeth

Makerere University Business School, PLOT M118 Old Port Bell Road,
Kampala, Uganda
{fnamisango,gbyomire,mmiiro,easianzu}@mubs.ac.ug

Abstract. Online platforms are becoming common and a way to enhanced interaction and wider reach. However, micro-entrepreneurs have generally not embraced online services for business development and support. Micro-entrepreneurs have largely failed during infancy owing to factors like technology use. Even with the business advisory service that is widely preached by government and non-government providers, micro entrepreneurs are still challenged. Concerns of business advisory outreach are largely raised. Using a quantitative approach the study sought to identify the advisory services needed, those accessed online and the reasons for using on not using the existing online platforms to access business advisory. The study was narrowed down to micro-entrepreneurs operating in the textile industry. The study provides insight about the state of internet-based business advisory in the micro-entrepreneurial society of Uganda. It was generally noted that micro-entrepreneurs prefer physical access to online access of business advisory although they acknowledge the benefits associated with online platforms. Limited knowledge and skills on how to use these platforms coped with the busy daily schedule limits the time available to search for advice online.

Keywords: Online usage · Business advisory · Micro-entrepreneurs

1 Introduction

Micro entrepreneurs are individuals responsible for innovations and creation of small scale income generating ventures commonly recognized as micro and small enterprises (MSEs). MSEs form the largest composition of business developments in developing countries [1] hence seen to be the largest employers and source of job creation than the large formal enterprises in these countries [2, 3]. According to [4] sustainable micro entrepreneurship is essential in driving the structural transformation from a low-income, traditional economy to a modern economy. The role micro-entrepreneurs is hampered by their inability to thrive and survive in developing economies thus greatly inhibiting their contribution to society [5]. MSEs (like those in Uganda) are known to fail in a few years or months after start [1, 6, 7].

© ICST Institute for Computer Sciences, Social Informatics and Telecommunications Engineering 2018
T.F. Bissyande and O. Sie (Eds.): AFRICOMM 2016, LNICST 208, pp. 253–262, 2018.
https://doi.org/10.1007/978-3-319-66742-3_24

Business know-how is a key success factor for small enterprises [6, 8]. [6] further indicate that micro-entrepreneurs need to access information and business training to survive in the competitive environments in which they operate. [5] also noted that new programmes and innovations for small businesses e.g. training are needed to increase firms' capabilities to offer better prospects for employment creation. [1, 10] also indicate that information flow is key but collecting and processing it is costly and may not pay off for individual micro entrepreneurs. Government and non-government organizations have thus introduced enterprise or business advisory services widely known as Business Development Services (BDS) for Micro, Small and Medium sized enterprises (MSMEs) so as to increase their survival, income generation and alleviate poverty. Business advisory services provide technical assistance, training, mentoring and access to domestic and international investment and trade information to micro entrepreneurs. Although business advisory providers in Uganda e.g. FinAfrica, Enterprise Uganda (EU), Private Sector Foundation Uganda (PSFU)'s Business Uganda Development Scheme (BUDS-scheme), Agri-business Hub have created and built basic online platforms which include interactive websites and micro-entrepreneurial communities, access and usage of business advisory services by micro entrepreneurs still remains low as these services have hardly reached out to half of the micro-entrepreneurs in small business developments in developing countries [11, 12].

Micro and Small Entreprise (MSEs) in Uganda continue to perform poorly due to internal and external factors [13]. The National Small Business Survey of Uganda (2015) indicates that the growth of MSEs in Uganda is constrained by factors such as limited finance, taxes and low technology penetration. Particularly, the survey found internet use lowest among micro entrepreneurs (at 31%). [14] advise that micro-entrepreneurs need mentorship services to enhance their entrepreneurship education and training given that many do not acquire executive and full course formal education. Unlike [14, 15] found that micro entrepreneurs in Uganda are relatively well-educated where over half have secondary education or higher. With such level of education, the skills and literacy required to use internet-based or online services are relatively available.

The outreach of business advisory services in terms of area of coverage, people and service portfolio has largely remained low overtime [11, 12]. Accessibility and the cost of procuring business advisory services are the most outstanding challenges [11]. [13] encourage that micro enterprises need affordable technical assistance. Generally, ICTs are underutilized in the delivery and access of micro and small business services [16]. Online platforms for business advisory have not been extensively used to enhance affordability and accessibility to advisory services [11, 12]. Given the high rate of mobile penetration, online platforms are cheaper to access and are ubiquitously available. However, [15] noted low internet based technological penetration among micro entrepreneurs. [17, 18] explained that studies are needed to show how small-scale pilot projects which are quite common in developing countries can be rolled out across districts as well as increasing the variety and significance of services offered over time.

2 Objective of the Study

The main aim of the study was to investigate the reasons for using or not using online platforms to access business advisory services by micro entrepreneurs. The objectives of the study were; (1) to study the social profile of micro-entrepreneurs in the cloth tailoring sector; (2) to identify the business advisory services that are needed and accessed by micro-entrepreneurs; (3) to identify the methods through which business advisory is accessed by micro-entrepreneurs; (4) to identify the business advisory services accessed online by micro entrepreneurs, (5) to identify the reasons for not using online platforms for business advisory, (6) to identify the reasons for using or not using of online platforms to access business advisory among micro-entrepreneurs.

3 Business Advisory and Micro Entrepreneurs in Developing Countries

Micro-entrepreneurship runs significantly under the Micro, Small and Medium Enterprises (MSMEs) community. MSMEs like those in Uganda are rather young enterprises with a majority of 69% aged between one and ten years [15]. MSEs are said to employ 90% of Uganda's population and engaged about ¾ of the population [19]. Micro enterprises in Uganda are indicated as those enterprises that employ less than five people [15]. There is a great entrepreneurship enthusiasm in African countries [14]. [14] continue to explain that entrepreneurship programs tend to attract more people in environments where the wage employment opportunities are limited. Entrepreneurship development in any given environment is focused on five aspects: entrepreneurship and economic growth, informality-formality relationship; entrepreneurship training and education; access to finance and targeted interventions [14]. [14] continue to enlighten that appropriate training is key for entrepreneurs but unfortunately, many entrepreneurs have limited education and cannot take academic executive courses or full-time education. The training and programs need a holistic approach to entrepreneurship development [14]. As earlier mention, micro and small enterprises face low growth rates explained by several factors including low technology adoption. Business development agencies are therefore established to nurture micro and small enterprise towards long term existence and competitiveness.

Business advisory is provided as educational and informative procedure aimed at encouraging and creating sustainable innovations and entrepreneurship amongst citizens. Business advisory services needs for entrepreneurs include; access to finance, business planning, business advice, cash flow management and book keeping, taxation and compliance, feasibility, marketing, mentorship, starting a business, techniques of production, tender advice [20]. Cheap, easy and efficient access to business advisory and support by micro-entrepreneurs encourages informed decisions on business models, financing, markets, management of enterprise and new business start-ups.

The study focused on micro-entrepreneurs in the textile industry of Uganda. The Ugandan textile industry gives little revenue to the government due to issues like illegal and unregistered ventures, collapse and failure [21]. A study of textile manufacturing was particularly on the CUT, MAKE AND TRIM (CTM) enterprises also known as cloth tailoring enterprises. These are to be largely owned by individuals and represent 90% of the sector [21]. Like other micro and small enterprises, the textile manufacturing ventures are performing poorly and hardly survive the economic turbulences in the environment [21].

4   Online Platforms, Service Delivery and Business Advisory Services

The growth of the internet has led to creation of a digital economy where services and products are increasingly accessed over online/digital platforms. [22] explain that online platforms range from small websites with a local reach to worldwide companies generating billions of revenues. Service delivery platforms (SDP) are operator solutions that provide a unified middle ground for optimized exchange of services between users, operators, and service and content providers [23]. Online service delivery platforms introduce the use of internet and mobile devices for interaction and information sharing. [24] found that broadband is an important factor in social transformation and improved service provision, particularly in rural areas, and that mobile broadband services are particularly well suited for improving the economic well-being of the poor. [23] explain the user's perspective of well-designed SDP and show that users can more easily find and make sense of available services, subscribe to and consume services across different networks and devices. Service delivery platforms enable compress administrative and technical impediments stuck between users and services [23]. An SDP comprises of end-user portal, provider portal and operator portal all of which allow and support business processes, integration and collaboration [23]. [25] adds that SDP opportunities extend to communities, personalization, on-demand computing and self-service. Furthermore, application stores on mobile devices for example can use SDP capabilities as support for application building which would support rich services and content for end-users [22, 25]. [22] identifies online platforms in five categories which are: - communication, entertainment, marketplaces, and comparison and information platforms. The provider may create one or a combination of the above delivered as one. The ultimate focus is delivery of intended processes and benefits to the users. [22] indicates that these platforms offer the following benefits to users i.e., improved convenience, greater choice, increased transparency, higher engagement and enhanced relationships at a reduced cost. [22] further indicate that clients would use online platforms for the following reasons; reduces search and transactional costs, access to a variety of services, information and knowledge from many participants, improved awareness of available products and services, social benefits i.e. easier interaction and exchange of views and experiences, actively learn and gain knowledge. Additionally, there several reasons why clients may not use an online platform as listed by [22]. These include; no time, no need, privacy and security reasons, content concerns – may not have what they need, better alternatives, too expensive, unable to use the platform. The use of online advisory could be affected by such reasons as presented above.

Online and mobile platforms have led to the emergence of information technology trends such as service ubiquity and user experience [26]. Online/internet based innovations have been undertaken in various perspectives of small and large business development spanning from product and service development and delivery, information access and sharing, operations and marketing etc. In the effort to increase business services provided to micro-entrepreneurs, it may be important to encourage engagement and use of technological platforms for greater access, information flow and collaboration. [22] notes that online platforms reduce geographical barriers, costs and allow new approaches to offering services or products. Information flow is key and has become more important especially for micro and small enterprises but quite costly [1, 10]. Consequently, [1] indicate the need for government and development agencies to focus on use of information systems or subsidize the search costs of private firms if the expected social benefits are to be derived.

There noticeable examples of firms that provide online communities for user interaction and online advisory in Uganda for example, FinAfrica Uganda – Enterprise Development Center. FinAfrica Uganda Ltd is private not-for-profit enterprise incubation, training and advisory center established in Uganda in 2009. YAMP (Young Achievers Mentoring Program) is a country-wide entrepreneurship mentoring network for Ugandan entrepreneurs provided by FinAfrica Uganda. FinAfrica Uganda build a center that supports young entrepreneurs to connect to experienced & successful entrepreneurs who may serve as personal mentors. The YAMP is aimed at encouraging the youths to raise their business mind and social capitals (ibid). The center provides e-mentoring for business sharing and U-Link for local mentoring network.

5   Methodology

A quantitative study was undertaken with the use of a questionnaire for data collection. We collected data from micro entrepreneurs operating in textile and garment tailoring in urban and peri-urban areas of Uganda. The urban and peri-urban areas comprise of the largest number of textile manufacturing in the country [19]. According to the list of operators in textiles and garments provided by Uganda Small Scale Industries Association (USSIA) a sample of 152 respondents was selected basing on [27] table for determining study samples. The data collected was descriptively analyzed and findings are presented in the subsequent sections.

6   Results

The results presented here are responses obtained from 152 respondents operating in the cloth tailoring in the textiles industry of Uganda.

6.1   Social Profile of Micro Entrepreneurs in the Cloth Tailoring Business

It is noted that most were aged 20–30 years (32.2%) and 31–40 years (31.6%). Most of them were female (53.9%). The education levels of the micro-entrepreneurs who participated was found to be basically certificate holding (45.4%) with a few who hold ordinary diplomas (21.1%) and bachelors (18.4%). Many of them are married (44.1%).

Respondents were requested to indicate the income earned from their ventures on a daily basis. It was found that most (43.4%) earn between 0 and 50,000 Uganda Shillings whereas (38.8%) earn between 50,050 and 100,000 Uganda Shillings. Very few (7.9%) are able to earn above 100,000 Uganda Shillings. The tribe orientation was mainly Baganda (46.7%), Batooro (11.8%), Banyankole (9.9%), Basoga (7.9%). Other tribe were also indicated but at very low percentages. The major language used to conduct and learn business is Luganda (73%) across all tribes. Only 4.6% indicated that they are able to use English as well to conduct and learn business.

6.2   Business Advisory Services Needed by Micro-entrepreneurs in Cloth Tailoring Business

Participating micro entrepreneurs were requested to indicate the business advisory services they need to support their ventures (Table 1). The following responses were obtained;

Table 1. Business advisory services needed by micro-entrepreneurs

Business advisory service	Yes (%)	Std. deviation
Accessing finance	73.4	.442
Marketing of products	53.3	.501
Production techniques	40.8	.493
Business planning	31.6	.466
Book keeping & cash flow management	23.7	.427
Managing business operations	30.3	.461
Compliance	10.5	.308
Feasibility analysis	9.2	.290
Starting a new business	51.3	.501
Tendering	9.2	.290
Mentorship	11.2	.316

6.3   Business Advisory Services Accessed by Micro-entrepreneurs in Cloth Tailoring Business

Participating micro entrepreneurs were further requested to indicate the business advisory services that they currently access to support their ventures. The following responses were obtained;

6.4   Access to Business Advisory Services

Using a five point Likert scale with 5 - strongly agree (SA), 4 - agree (A), 3 - neither agree nor disagree (N), 2 - disagree (D) and 1 - strongly disagree (SD), respondents were requested to indicate their level of agree about means used to access business advisory services listed Table 2 above. Here we indicated the possibility of using online (internet) platforms to access such services from business service providers or fellow entrepreneurs (Table 3).

Table 2. Business advisory services accessed by micro-entrepreneurs

Business advisory service	Physical access		Online access	
	Yes (%)	Std. deviation	Yes (%)	Std. deviation
Accessing finance	75	.434	48	.502
Marketing of products	65.1	.478	37.5	.488
Production techniques	68.4	.466	36.8	.487
Business planning	33.6	.474	-	.000
Book keeping & cash flow management	12.5	.332	-	.000
Managing business operations	11.8	.324	11.8	.328
Compliance	4.6	.210	35.5	.483
Feasibility analysis	2.6	.161	-	.000
Starting a new business	35.5	.480	48.7	.502
Tendering	-	.000	12.5	.336
Mentorship	3.3	.179	12.5	.336

Table 3. Means to access business advisory services

Means to access business advisory services	SA/A (%)	Mean	Std. deviation
Go to provider premises	34.2	2.75	1.45
Attend events, workshops or seminars	36.9	3.01	1.280
Consult fellow entrepreneurs physically	86.8	4.55	.700
Use online platforms to contact provider	39.5	2.93	1.498
Use online platforms to contact fellow entrepreneurs	44.4	3.09	1.439

6.5 Why Do Micro Entrepreneurs Go/Don't Go Online to Access Business Advisory Needed

There some reasons that were indicated by participants showing why some have chosen to use online platforms for business advisory while other have chosen not to go online for business advisory. We used a five point Likert scale with 5 - strongly agree (SA), 4 - agree (A), 3 - neither agree nor disagree (N), 2 - disagree (D) and 1 - strongly disagree (SD) to gather responses. The generated responses are indicated in Tables 4 and 5;

Table 4. Reasons for using online platforms to access business advisory among micro-entrepreneurs

Reasons for using online platforms to access business advisory among micro-entrepreneurs	SA/A (%)	Mean	Std. deviation
Reduce costs	36.9	3.12	1.478
Reduce time	47.4	3.45	1.479
Access a variety of services and information	46.7	3.47	1.244
Improve awareness of available services	39.5	3.30	1.311
Easily interact and exchange my views and experiences	42.8	3.31	1.334
Actively learn and gain knowledge	43.5	3.46	1.286

Table 5. Reasons for using online platforms to access business advisory among micro-entrepreneurs

Reasons for not using online platforms to access business advisory among micro-entrepreneurs	SA/A (%)	Mean	Std. deviation
I don't need them	27	2.65	1.450
I have not time to use them	30.9	2.69	1.418
I feel they are not private and secure	20.4	2.58	1.186
I believe they don't have what I want to know	21.1	2.41	1.397
I prefer alternative physical means of access	47.4	3.36	1.589
I don't know how to use online platforms	32.9	2.58	1.625
Using the internet is expensive	28.3	2.82	1.386

7   Discussion of Findings

From the responses generated we note that many micro-entrepreneurs have obtained the basic formal education as (National Small Business Survey of Uganda, 2015) also indicated. Mother tongue languages are the most common media of communication especially the Luganda language. Although formal education has been obtained English is not commonly used in business management at large. Micro entrepreneurs in the studied sector indicate that they seek out the following business advisory services mainly; accessing finance, marketing of products, improving production techniques and how to start up a successful enterprise. On the other hand, entrepreneurs are not much concerned about compliance issues, book keeping and cash flow management, feasibility analysis, tendering and mentorship. Among the business advisory services needed, micro-entrepreneurs indicated low access to those services as prior indicated by some scholars. Advisory on access to finance, marketing and production is the only accessible advisory service for micro-entrepreneurs in this industry. The least accessible advisory services are tendering, mentor services, feasibility analysis and compliance to regulations. Micro-entrepreneurs generally engage in physical access to business advice especially from fellow entrepreneurs operating similar ventures. For the few, micro-entrepreneurs who go online they are seeking out for advice on accessing finance as well as how to start a business enterprise. Even for the two identified as main services sought the percentages are generally low. The reason for not using online platforms was indicated to be preference of alternative physical means. Issues of cost, and benefit to be attained were not indicated as limiting factors. While online, the few micro-entrepreneurs who use online access indicate that they chose this due to enhanced interaction and learning, access to a variety of services and information, and the time saving aspect.

8   Conclusion

In addition to the prior indicated studies in the introduction, this study acknowledges to low online access to business advisory among micro-entrepreneurs in the cloth tailoring sector. According to what is found in this study, it may be necessary to investigate the reasons or circumstances that drive micro-entrepreneurs to prefer physical access to business advisory rather than through online/internet platforms despite the positive that has been noted in line with internet use or online existence.

References

1. UNIDO & gtz: Creating an enabling environment for private sector development in sub-Saharan Africa (2013)
2. Ayyagari, M., Demirgüc-Kunt, A., Maksimovic, V.: Small vs. Young Firms across the World; Contribution to Employment, Job Creation, and Growth, Policy Research Working Paper 5631. The World Bank (2011). http://elibrary.worldbank.org/doi/book/10.1596/1813-9450-5631
3. Fox, L., Sohnesen, T.P.: Household Enterprises in Sub-Saharan Africa; Why They Matter for Growth, Jobs, and Livelihoods, Policy Research Working Paper 6184. The World Bank (2012). http://www.enterprise-development.org/page/download?id=2250
4. Naudé, W.: Promoting Entrepreneurship in Developing Countries: Policy Challenges. UNU_PolicyBrief_10-04. United Nations University – World Institute for Development Economics Research (2010). http://archive.unu.edu/publications/briefs/policy-briefs/2010/UNU_PolicyBrief_10-04.pdf. ISBN 978-92-808-3083-5
5. Page, J., Söderbom, M.: Is Small Beautiful? Small Enterprise, Aid and Employment in Africa, Working Paper No. 2012/94. UNU-WIDER (2012). http://www.wider.unu.edu/publications/working-papers/2012/en_GB/wp2012-094/
6. Tushabomwe-Kazooba, T.C.: Causes of small business failure in Uganda: a case study from Bushenyi and Mbarara towns. Afr. Stud. Q. 8(4), 27–35 (2006)
7. McIntyre, R.: The Role of Small and Medium Enterprises in Transition: Growth and Entrepreneurship. UNU World Institute for Development Economics Research (UNU/WIDER) (2001). www.wider.unu.edu/...papers/.../rfa49.pdf
8. Wajahat, S., Naqvi, H.: Critical success and failure factors of entrepreneurial organizations: study of SMEs in Bahawalpur. J. Public Admin. Gov. 1(2), 17–22 (2011)
9. Shafique, M.R., Rizwan, M.R., Jahangir, M.M., Mansoor, A.M., Akram, S., Hussain, A.: Determinants of entrepreneurial success/failure from SMEs perspective. IOSR J. Bus. Manag. 83–92 (2010)
10. OECD: Small businesses, job creation and growth: facts, obstacles and best practices (n.d). http://www.oecd.org/cfe/smes/2090740.pdf. Accessed 7 Apr 2015
11. Nair, R., Chelliah, J.: Understanding key impediments to small businesses in South Pacific Island Nations: a case of Fiji. J. Glob. Bus. Manag. 8(1), 175–182 (2012)
12. Altenburg, T., Stamm, A.: Towards a More Effective Provision of Business Services, Discussion-Paper 4/2004 German Development Institute (2004)
13. Nuwagaba, A., Nzewi, H.: Major environmental constraints on growth of micro and small enterprises in Uganda: a survey of selected micro and small enterprises in Mbarara municipality. Int. J. Coop. Stud. 2(1), 26–33 (2013)
14. Schaumburg-Müller, H., Jeppesen, S., Langevang, T.: Entrepreneurship Development in Africa, Working Paper Nr. 12/2010. Centre for Business and Development Studies, Copenhagen Business School. http://openarchive.cbs.dk/bitstream/handle/10398/8208/UM_-_CBDSUM_Entrepreneurship_Workshop_final_report.pdf?sequence=1

15. National Small Business Survey of Uganda: National Small Business Survey of Uganda, NATHAN ASSOCIATES LONDON, fsdAfrica, fsdUganda and TNS (2015). http://www.fsdafrica.org/wp-content/uploads/2015/04/15-04-13-National-Small-Business-Survey-Uganda.pdf?noredirect=1

16. World Bank: World Development Report 2013: Jobs. World Bank, Washington. doi:10.1596/978-0-8213-9575-2

17. Walsham, G., Robey, D., Sahay, S.: Foreword: special issue on information systems in developing countries. MIS Q. **31**(2), 317–326 (2007)

18. Walsham, G., Sahay, S.: Research on information systems in developing countries: current landscape and future prospects. Inf. Technol. Dev. **12**(1), 7–24 (2006)

19. Uganda Bureau of Statistics – UBOS: Report on the Census of Business Establishments in Uganda 2010/2011. Uganda Bureau of Statistics, Statistics House Plot 9 Colville Street, Kampala-Uganda

20. IFC: The Role of Business Development Services (BDS). (pp.52–63) IFC GEM Brochure (2015). http://www.ifc.org/wps/wcm/connect/f75ca3004885532cade4ff6a6515bb18/IFCGEM%2BBrochure%2Bsec%2B5-6.pdf?MOD=AJPERES&CACHEID=f75ca3004885532cade4ff6a6515bb18

21. Tebyetekerwa, M., Namulinda, T.: Textile Industry of Uganda - An Overview, Textile Tribune (2015). http://www.textiletribune.com/2015/02/textile-industry-of-uganda-overview.html

22. Oxera: Benefits of online platforms, Google (2015). http://www.oxera.com/getmedia/84df70f3-8fe0-4ad1-b4ba-d235ee50cb30/The-benefits-of-online-platforms-main-findings-(October-2015).pdf.aspx?ext=.pdf

23. Johnston, A., Gabrielsson, J., Christopoulos, C., Huysmans, M., Olsson, U.: Evolution of service delivery platforms. Ericsson Rev. **1**, 19–25 (2007). http://www.ericsson.com/ericsson/corpinfo/publications/review/2007_01/files/4_sdp_web.pdf

24. Lobo, B.J., Novobilski, A., Ghosh, S.: The economic impact of broadband: estimates from a regional input-output model. J. Appl. Bus. Res. **24**(2), 103–114 (2008)

25. Carugi, M.: Telecom Service delivery platforms and application stores. In: International Workshop Innovative Research Directions in the Field of Telecommunications in the World, ITU-ZNIIS ITTC Joint Project, Moscow, Russia, 21–22 July 2011. https://www.itu.int/ITU-D/tech/events/2011/Moscow_ZNIIS_July11/Presentations/06-Carugi_IMS.pdf

26. ZTE: ICT Development Trends: Embracing the Era of Mobile-ICT. ZTE CORPORATION (2014)

27. Krejcie, R.V., Morgan, D.W.: Determining sample size for research activities. Educ. Psychol. Measur. **30**, 607–610 (1970)

28. Victoria, M., Samuel, B., Lloyd, C., Lazarus, M.: Determinants of small and medium enterprises failure in Zimbabwe: a case study of Mudavanhu, Bindu, Chigusiwa & Muchabaiwa. Int. J. Econ. Res. **2**(5), 82–89 (2011)

GIS Initiatives in Health Management in Malawi: Opportunities to Share Knowledge

Patrick Albert Chikumba[1][(✉)] and Patrick Naphini[2]

[1] University of Oslo, Oslo, Norway
pchikumba@poly.ac.mw
[2] Ministry of Health, Lilongwe, Malawi
pnaphini@gmail.com

Abstract. Knowledge is recognized as the most important resource in organisations including public organisations and its management is considered critical to organizational success. The literature suggests the development of indigenous knowledge as one of characteristics of the successful GIS implementation in developing countries. The topic of knowledge has been discussed extensively in the information system and organisation literature but much is written about *why* managing knowledge is important to organisations and little on *how* knowledge is identified, captured, shared, and used within organisations. As a contribution to '*how*', this paper discusses opportunities of sharing knowledge in the GIS implementation in health management through some initiatives in Malawi. We can confidently say that there are a number of GIS implementation activities in the health sector in Malawi which are important for knowledge sharing but they are not utilised as expected.

Keywords: Health management · GIS initiatives · Knowledge · Knowledge sharing

1 Introduction

Today, strengthening and sustaining the use of computerised health information systems (HIS) is believed to be mainly based on intangible assets such as knowledge and skills. Employee's knowledge and skills in using computer systems have become a critical factor for successful use of information technology (IT) in organisations [1]. In the case of Geographic Information System (GIS) in developing countries, there are several challenges and some of them are related to the lack of knowledge and skills. In GIS, people are the most important part who can overcome shortcomings of the other elements [2]. GIS users need certain knowledge and skills in order to use GIS properly [3]. Longley et al. [4] argue that GIS technology is of limited value without people who manage and develop plans for applying it to real world problems.

In developing countries, including Malawi, GIS is applied in various health areas such as health programs, health management, primary health care, and health research. Since 2002, there have been GIS initiatives in Malawi towards the implementation of GIS in health management with the aim of improving data integration, analysis, and visualization. The combination of GIS and health applications with decision-making processes can assist in the operational control, management control and strategic planning [5].

Knowledge is recognized as the most important resource, and its management is considered critical to organizational success [6]. Literature suggests the development of indigenous knowledge as one of the successful GIS implementation characteristics in developing countries [7]. Knowledge can be understood as information processed by individuals relevant for the performance of individuals, teams, and organisations [8]. Kim and Lee [9] have taken knowledge as a fluid mix of framed experiences, contextual information, values, and expert insight that provide a framework for evaluating and incorporating new experiences and information.

With reference to the case, this paper focuses particularly on the sharing of IT knowledge between GIS implementers and technical support teams. Proper transfer of knowledge and skills from the system implementers to target system users, particularly in developing countries, is crucial in realizing the intended benefits. López et al. [10] define IT knowledge as the extent to which the firm possesses a body of technical knowledge about elements such as computer systems (in this case, GIS). According to Taylor in 1971, cited in [10], the technical knowledge is the set of principles and techniques that are useful to bring about change toward desired ends.

The topic of knowledge has been discussed extensively in the information system and organisation literature [11], but much is written about why managing knowledge is important to organisations and little on how knowledge is identified, captured, shared, and used within organisations [6]. As a contribution to 'how' (processes of), this paper discusses opportunities of sharing knowledge in the GIS implementation in health management in Malawi through some GIS initiatives. The paper tries to answer the following two questions: Which opportunities to share knowledge exist in GIS initiatives in health management in Malawi? How can opportunities to share knowledge be utilised for knowledge sharing? These research questions have been answered through the analysis of empirical material being guided by the notion of knowledge sharing, particularly opportunities to share from Ipe [6]. The rest of the paper includes the concept of knowledge sharing, study methodology, GIS initiatives, opportunities to share knowledge and conclusion.

2 Knowledge Sharing

It has been observed that there are significant changes on how public organisations are being managed; moving from a traditional, bureaucratic approach to a more managerial one [8], in which knowledge is recognized as one of critical resources. In this context, the public organisations are treated as knowledge-based organisations, which have to contend with competition for resources [8] and there is the need for processes that facilitate the creation, sharing, and leveraging of knowledge [6]. In this paper, some processes in the GIS implementation in health management and how they can facilitate the sharing of knowledge as a critical asset have been discussed. This study takes resources as assets and capabilities that are available and useful in solving GIS-related problems or meeting GIS user needs. Generally, assets and capabilities are respectively what an organisation has and does [12]. A capability is repeatable patterns of actions in the use of assets to create, produce or offer a good or service to a particular market or user [13]. Knowledge, as an asset, needs to be acquired and accumulated [14]; this can be through sharing because knowledge multiplies when it is shared effectively [15]. When we talk of knowledge, learning can be one of the strategies for accumulating such an asset in which interactions occur between individuals, teams, or organisations and hence knowledge is shared.

Within organisations, knowledge is at multiple levels: individual, group and organisation. In this paper, the individual knowledge sharing is emphasised with the understanding that without individuals the knowledge cannot be created, and unless individual knowledge is shared, the knowledge is likely to have limited impact on organisational effectiveness [6]. Knowledge sharing refers to the provision of knowledge to help and collaborate with others to solve problems, develop new ideas, or implement policies or procedures [8]. According to Ipe [6] there are three types of individual knowledge: 'know-how' (experience-based), know-what (task-related), and dispositional knowledge (including talents, aptitude, and abilities). It is expected that knowledge held by an individual is converted into a form that can be understood, absorbed, and used by other individuals [6].

Ipe [6] suggests four major factors that influence knowledge sharing between individuals in organisations: (a) the nature of knowledge, (b) the motivation to share, (c) the opportunities to share, and (d) the culture of work environment. By its nature, knowledge exists in tacit and explicit forms whose difference is related to the ease and effectiveness of sharing [16]. Tacit knowledge is situated in the deep recesses of the human mind and non-codifiable [15] and its tacitness is natural impendiment to the successful individual knowledge sharing in organisations because it cannot be communicated or used without the knower [6]. On the other hand, explicit knowledge is recognised and expressed by formal techniques; it can be easily codified, stored and transferred across time and space independent of knower [6, 16]. Explicit knowledge can be generated through logical deduction and acquired by formal study while tacit knowledge can only be acquired through practical experience in the relevant context, which Lam [17] refers as learning-by-doing.

In order to share tacit and explicit knowledge opportunities, either formal or informal, should exist in the organisation. Acording to Ipe [6] formal opportunities are formal interactions (including training programs, structured work teams, and technology-based systems) that are designed to acquire and disseminate knowledge while as informal opprtunities include personal relationships and social networks that facilitate learning and knowledge sharing. However these opportunities alone, without personal motivation, cannot bring much influence on the knowledge sharing. Ipe [6] argues that individuals are not likely to share knowledge without strong personal motivation. Knowledge sharing is challenging because, for example, it is typically voluntary and individual's tacit knowledge is difficult to transfer [8]. Therefore, it is important to understand what motivate individuals to share knowledge; for example the perceived power attached to the knowledge, reciprocity that results from sharing, relationship with recipient, and rewards for sharing [6, 16, 18].

Generally, knowledge is actually created, shared, and used by people in organisations [6] and hence the knowledge sharing should involve dissemination of individual work-related experiences, and collaborations among individuals, subsystems and organisations [9]. Ahmad et al. [15] emphasise that the ability to share knowledge among collaborators represents possibly the greatest strategic advantage an organisation can achieve; for instance, for the public organisation the knowledge sharing represents the means for continous performance improvements.

3 Study Methodology

This case study was conducted at the national level in Malawi health sector between June 2015 and September 2016. Malawi is a landlocked country in southeast Africa and it has borders with Tanzania to the northeast, Zambia to the northwest, and Mozambique to the east, south and west. In its health system, there are five levels of management (nation, zone, district, facility, and community). The GIS application in Ministry of Health (MoH) in Malawi started as early as 2002 when a booklet of maps of the health facilities was produced and distributed in compact discs (CDs). Since then there have been several GIS initiatives and in this study the focus is on the user training, spatial data collection and mapping, and composition of technical team at the national level.

The qualitative interpretive research methods were applied in this case study. The data was collected through observations, interviews, and analysis of documents. One stakeholder meeting was organised to share experiences on the GIS related activities by various institutions in the health sector and how to work together on the GIS implementation. The first author attended that meeting as a passive observer. Participant observations were also done through out our study period in MoH. Face-to-face interviews with five participants (IT officers and M&E officers) were conducted focusing on the effort and plans on GIS implementation and activities that had been already carried out. Another issue was on the support they have been getting from other institutions and internal capacity they have on the GIS implementation. Various documents were analysed including Health Information System (HIS) policy, electronic Health Information System (eHIS) strategy, and training reports and manuals. The analysis of empirical material was guided by the notion of knowledge sharing, particularly opportunities to share from Ipe [6].

4 GIS Initiatives: From 2002 to 2016

Table 1 below summaries some GIS initiatives in MoH from 2002 to 2016. Most of these activities were carried out by MoH in collaborations with its development partners and other government agencies. The GIS initiatives are presented in three categories: user training, spatial data collection and mapping, and composition of technical teams at both district and national levels.

In Malawi the health sector governance structure has the national and district levels. To strengthen the health management information system (HMIS), MoH established Central Monitoring and Evaluation Division (CMED) in its Planning Department which involves coordination, data management, advocacy and facilitation of information use in various activities at all levels in the health sector. CMED is also

Table 1. Some GIS initiatives in health sector in Malawi

Category	Initiatives	Participation/Collaboration
User training	2008 – inter-institutional training	MoH and its partners, other government agencies; one facilitator from WHO
	2009 – intra-institutional training	Zone M&E officers, and HMIS officers from districts and central hospitals; one facilitator from Surveys Department
	2010 – intra-institutional training	Zone M&E officers, and HMIS officers from districts and central hospitals; two facilitators from Surveys Department and NAC
	2013 – intra-institutional training	HMIS officers from districts and central hospitals; two facilitators from NAC and Lands Department
Spatial data collection and mapping	2002 – mapping public and CHAM health facilities	Pioneered by a consultant from JICA with support from Surveys Department and MoH Planning Department
	2008 – mapping ART clinics (HIV/AIDS program)	NSO, MoH, NAC, CDC, University of Pennsylvania, Roads Authority, Surveys Department, WHO
	2011 – updating 2002 mapped public and CHAM health facilities	Pioneered by a consultant from JICA with support from Surveys Department and Planning Department of MoH
	2013 – coordinates for public and private health facilities	ICF International and MoH
	Since 2015 – coordinates for village and outreach clinics	UNICEF Malawi, MoH and Lands Department
Technical team	At district level	HMIS officers and IT officers
	At national level	HISP Malawi, MoH-IT unit, JHPIEGO/SSDI, Baobab Health, University of Oslo

Note: CDC – Centre for Disease Control, HMIS – Health Management Information System, M&E – Monitoring & Evaluation, NAC – National Aids Commission, WHO – World Health Organisation, CHAM – Christian Health Association of Malawi, JICA – Japanese International Corporation Agency, MoH – Ministry of Health, NSO – National Statistical Office.

responsible for implementation and management of technologies, including GIS, in HMIS. At the national level CMED has inadequate technical capacity and therefore it gets much technical support on the implementation of various technologies from its partners. In the case of GIS implementation, it has been observed that the technical expertise has been from outside the health sector in both user training and spatial data collection and mapping.

CMED has put much effort at the district level in terms of developing GIS-related knowledge to HMIS officers through training. With reference to Table 1, the first GIS training for local capacity was conducted in 2009 and participants were all HMIS officers from District Health Offices (DHOs) and central hospitals, and M&E officers from zones. The training was just for introducing GIS and was facilitated by a GIS expert from Surveys Department. A year later, second training was provided to the same officers covering the spatial data collection using GPS and facilitated by two GIS experts from Surveys Department and NAC. The same HMIS officers were also trained in 2013 by two GIS experts from Lands Department and NAC. In the past three years, CMED recruited and deployed IT officers in all DHOs and central hospitals to work with HMIS officers but they have not been given any GIS training.

Table 2 summarizes some initiatives that can facilitate knowledge sharing in GIS application the Ministry of Health (MoH).

Table 2. Some initiatives that can facilitate sharing of knowledge

Initiatives	Authors' remarks
User training	This is done to transfer knowledge from the national level to district level. In some cases it is within the same level, e.g. during the setup of DHIS2 GIS, there was a training at the national level for GIS implementation team being facilitated by some members within the team
Collaborations	The collaboration is mainly at the national level
Structured work team	It is mainly at the national level.
Learning-by-doing	This is an institutional initiative at the national level and individual initiative at the district level. Some HMIS and IT officers have learned GIS through particular tasks requested by stakeholders in their respective districts.
Codification	There is no much codification of knowledge; particularly the production of documentation. For example, in almost all user trainings presented in Table 1, there were no training manuals that would be referenced at the workplace after training. For spatial data collection there are some manuals for reference.
Workshops (or meetings)	In MoH, workshops and meetings are always available which HMIS and IT officers attended. MoH can take advantage of these activities to share experiences in GIS among officers.

5 Opportunities to Share Knowledge

In Malawi, as observed in other developing countries [19–21], there is no adequate GIS expertise and it is difficult to recruit people with all necessary GIS knowledge and skills. Alternatively, CMED has been developing such resources internally and the emphasis has been on the technical team at district level. It has been observed that CMED pays much attention on GIS user training and structured work teams which are some of formal opportunities to share knowledge [6]. In this regard, this paper discusses how these opportunities are utilised for sharing knowledge in the GIS implementation in health management in Malawi with emphasis on collaboration and learning-by-doing.

The literature of GIS implementation in developing countries emphasises the importance of collaboration [7, 20, 22]. Ramasubramanian [7] has observed that strategic alliances could promote the sharing of resources; for example, in GIS programmes of Vista University and University of Pretoria, these universities collaborated with local and international organisations and the programmes were successful. In Mozambique, despite having a number of institutions being involved in GIS activities, they face some challenges due to lack of 'strong' institutional collaboration [22]. This has also been observed in this case study; CMED collaborates with other institutions which are experienced in GIS and its use. In user training and spatial data collection, Departments of Lands and Surveys, and NAC have played great roles with their vast experiences in GIS. In terms of the knowledge acquisition and accumulation these collaborations has allowed CMED to build work teams of both experienced and non-experienced GIS users, leading to knowledge sharing. As Sirmon et al. [23] point out, if an organisation may not have the required knowledge, it might form strategic alliances with those having the desired knowledge which can be valuable to the organisation for learning new knowledge.

Training is one of the formal opportunities that help sharing knowledge. In all GIS user training, there were experienced facilitators from other government agencies, sharing knowledge with non-experienced HMIS officers. This demonstrates the collaboration aiming for HMIS officers to acquire the required knowledge. Due to the decentralization in public sector in Malawi, HMIS officers have been providing all necessary technical support at district level; such as data verification, compilation, analysis, reporting and provision of feedback to health facilities [24]. It is a good decision to invest in HMIS officers in terms of GIS knowledge because it is recommended that when building local capacity the local team should be equipped with understanding of both the application domain and the technology being implemented; this contributes towards the sustainability of the system [25]. HMIS officers have vast experience in the health information management because majority has worked with district health managers since the establishment of HMIS in 2002. Providing them with GIS knowledge and skills can equip them with both understanding of the health management (as application domain) and GIS (as technical domain) which might contribute towards the sustainability of GIS in health management.

However, it has been observed that HMIS officers are not given a conducive environment to practice what they have learnt so that they can improve their knowledge through learning-by-doing [17]. It was expected that they would be part of the spatial data collection exercises in 2013 and 2015-2016 because by then HMIS officers had been trained in GIS, but it has not been the case. In 2013 the exercise of spatial data collection was done by medical assistants and nurses during the service provision assessment at health facilities. Only two HMIS officers were involved in compiling data in this exercise at the national level. Although the spatial data collection being facilitated by UNICEF from 2015 is for mapping village and outreach clinics in their respective districts, HMIS officers are not included; instead the GIS technical support has been provided by officers from Department of Lands. In 2016, CMED has been in the process of setting up GIS on DHIS 2 for the health management and this exercise is also in the hands of GIS experts from development partners; HMIS officers are not part of the implementation team at the national level (see Table 1 – technical team at national level).

It is necessary for CMED to provide a suitable work environment for HMIS and IT officers at the district level to continuously share the individual knowledge, which in this case study has been observed as lacking. It could be better for HMIS and IT officers to be part of work teams of the spatial data collection and GIS configuration exercises so they would share knowledge and put that knowledge into practice. Another observation is that HMIS officers were trained in many occasions since 2009 but there had been no GIS applications for them to put the knowledge into practice. Now CMED is implementing GIS in the health management and it is expected that HMIS and IT officers will be providing all necessary technical support but they are also not participating in the exercise. The inclusion of these officers could create an opportunity of sharing knowledge through learning-by-doing and at the same time building social networks and relationships that may result in the continuity of individual knowledge sharing. There is a high possibility that after the GIS implementation exercise these implementers will be there and then HMIS and IT officers are to take over the responsibility of the system management and maintenance. One participant said: "*We bought GPS for HMIS officers and we trained them because they would be custodians of GIS in their respective health districts*"

Most of activities in GIS implementation have been carried out at the national level and in some cases it is difficult for HMIS and IT officers to be part of the work teams due to the culture of work environment and the nature of work [6]. There are 68 officers (34 HMIS officers and 34 IT officers) in 29 DHOs and 5 central hospitals and it is not easy to include all of them in, for example, spatial data collection or setting up of GIS. These activities require very few skilled people. In 2013 coordinates of health facilities were collected as part of the service provision assessment which involved mainly health practitioners such as medical assistants and nurses. Therefore, MoH decided not to include HMIS officers. One participant commented: "*In this exercise we felt HMIS officers would not have much work to do ... instead we trained medical assistants and nurses on collection of coordinates using GPS while they were assessing health facilities...*"

6 Conclusion

From the discussion above, we have noticed that GIS knowledge and skills are available at the national level through collaborations and there is a need to transfer such knowledge and skills to the technical team at the district level. The collaborations provide a platform for acquiring required GIS knowledge from the outside of MoH but the challenge is how to maintain it. It seems that HMIS and IT officers, who are 'prospective' custodians of GIS in the health management, are ignored in many GIS implementation activities which could help them to accumulate the relevant knowledge. Although it is fine now that the development partners are providing all necessary technical support in the GIS implementation, it reaches a point in time when majority of these GIS experts will not be available.

It has been observed that CMED takes mainly user training as a strategy for sharing the knowledge with the HMIS and IT officers and this knowledge needs to be continuously accumulated. In this context the learning-by-doing strategy [17] is essential because, for example, it provides an environment for accumulating individual tactic knowledge which contributes the large portion of individual knowledge. Apart from the user training, CMED needs to continue promoting structured work teams by including HMIS and IT officers in some GIS implementation activities in so doing the officers can have a chance to build personal relationships and social networks that may provide the environment for continuous sharing of knowledge. Some task-related (know-what) and experienced-based (know-how) knowledge [6] can be codified, for example, as documentation so it might easily be shared at any time and any place. In conclusion, we can confidently say that there are a number of GIS initiatives in the health sector in Malawi which are important for the knowledge sharing but they are not utilised as expected.

References

1. Munkvold, R.: End user support usage. In: Gordon, S. (ed.) Computing Information Technology: The Human Side, pp. 146–160. Idea Group, Hershey (2003)
2. Raju, P.L.N.: Satellite remote sensing and GIS applications in agricultural meteorology. In: DeMers, M.N. (ed.) Fundamentals of Geographical Information System, pp. 103–120. Wiley, Hoboken (2006)
3. Moffett, L.A.: Information systems in emergency management applications: evolution and integration of spatial technologies, Department of Information Systems. Baylor University, Texas (2015)
4. Longley, P.A., et al.: Geographic Information Systems and Science, 2nd edn. Wiley, West Sussex (2005)
5. Pick, J.B.: Geographic Information Systems in Business. Idea Group Publishing, Hershey (2005)
6. Ipe, M.: Knowledge sharing in organizations: a conceptual framework. Hum. Resour. Dev. Rev. 2(4), 337–359 (2003)
7. Ramasubramanian, L.: GIS implementation in developing countries: learning from organisational theory and reflective practice. Trans. GIS 3(4), 359–380 (1999)
8. Amayah, A.T.: Determinants of knowledge sharing in a public sector organization. J. Knowl. Manage. 17(3), 454–471 (2013)
9. Kim, S., Lee, H.: Employee knowledge sharing capabilities in public & private organizations: does organizational context matter? In: 38th Hawaii International Conference on System Sciences (2005)
10. López, S.P., Peón, J.M.M., Ordás, C.J.V.: Information technology as an enabler of knowledge management: an empirical analysis. In: King, W.R. (ed.) Annals of Information Systems: Knowledge Management and Organizational Learning. Springer, Boston (2009)
11. Puri, S.K.: Inregrating scientific with indigenous knowledge: constructing knowledge alliances for land management in india. MIS Q. 30(2), 355–379 (2007)
12. Galbreath, J.: Which resources matter the most to firm success? an exploratory study of resource-based theory. Technovation 25(9), 979–987 (2005)
13. Wade, M., Hulland, J.: Review: the resource-based view and information systems research: review, extension, and suggestions for future research. MIS Q. 28(1), 107–142 (2004)
14. Barney, J., Ketchen Jr., D.J., Wright, M.: The future of resource-based theory: revitalization or decline? J. Manag. 37(5), 1299–1315 (2011)

15. Ahmad, H., Sharom, N., Abdullah, C.S.: Knowledge sharing behaviour in the public sector: the business process management perspectives (2006)
16. Pardo, T.A., et al.: Knowledge sharing in cross-boundary information system development in the public sector. Inf. Technol. Manage. **7**, 293–313 (2006)
17. Lam, A.: Tacit knowledge, organizational learning and societal institutions: an integrated framework. Organ. Stud. **21**, 487–513 (2000)
18. Ahrend, N., Pittke, F., Leopold, H.: Barriers and strategies of process knowledge sharing in public sector organizations. In: Multikonferenz Wirtschaftsinformatik 2014 (2014)
19. Tanser, F.C.: Geographical information systems (GIS) innovations for primary health care in developing countries. Innov. Technol. Governance Globalization **1**(2), 106–122 (2006)
20. Chikumba, P.A.: Application of Geographic Information System (GIS) in drug Logistics Management Information System (LMIS) at district level in Malawi: opportunities and challenges, Department of Informatics, University of Oslo, Oslo, Norway (2009)
21. Fisher, R.P., Myers, B.A.: Free and simple GIS as appropriate for health mapping in a low resource setting: a case study in eastern Indonesia. Int. J. Health Geogr. **10**(1), 15 (2011)
22. Saugene, Z.B., Juvane, M., Ernesto, I.: Factors affecting geographic information systems implementation and use in healthcare sector: the case of OpenHealthMapper in developing countries. In: Rajabifad, A., Coleman, D. (eds.) Spatially Enabling Government, Industry and Citizens: Research and Development Perspectives. GSDI Association Press, Needham (2012)
23. Sirmon, D.G., Hitt, M.A., Ireland, R.D.: Managing firm resources in dynamic environments to create value: looking inside the black box. Acad. Manag. Rev. **32**(1), 273–292 (2007)
24. Chikumba, P.A., Ramussen, S.L.: Management and use of health information in Malawi and Burkina faso: the role of technology. In: Cunningham, P., Cunningham, M. (eds.) IST-Africa 2016 Conference Proceedings. IIMC International Information Management Corporation, Durban (2016)
25. Heeks, R.: Information systems and developing countries: failure, success, and local improvisations. Inf. Soc. **18**, 101–112 (2002)

Eliminate the Delay Backlog in the Conduct of Pedagogical Activities by Distance Learning

Tiguiane Yélémou[1](✉), Benjamin Sia[2],
Théodore Njingang Mbadjoin[2], and Alain Jaillet[2]

[1] School of Computer Science, Polytechnic University of Bobo-Dioulasso,
Bobo-Dioulasso, Burkina Faso
`tyelemou@gmail.com`
[2] Laboratoire EMA (Ecole, Mutations, Apprentissages), Université de
Cergy-Pontoise, Cergy-Pontoise, France
`{benjesia,mbadjoin_tic}@yahoo.fr`,
`alain.jaillet@u-cergy.fr`

Abstract. In large classes of enrolled students, Polytechnic University of Bobo Dioulasso (PUB) can not complete one academic year in 12 months. The major obstacle is the lack of infrastructure and qualified local teachers for conducting parallel coaching tutorial groups. These tutorials are carried out in group of up 50 students. The academic year can last 18 or 24 months. To address this problem, we propose a techno-pedagogical system.

Technically, this project consists in strengthen the capacities of the PUB in IT resources and optimize their use. A Learning Management System (LMS) is implemented on the local network. The campus network, accessible from all sites of the PUB and student residences, allows access to the server at a rate of at least 10Mbps. The LMS is also available on Internet. On the pedagogical and organizational level, we conducted training for content experts and tutors in design and modular structure of courses, tutoring in distance learning. A team of two techno-pedagogues are empowered to manage this training system. Theoretical courses are run-face. Group works are driven remotely with the help of remote experts. This project would enable, in two years, to reduce the duration of an academic year to 12 months.

Keywords: Elearning · Pedagogic model · Context of teacher inadequacy · Context of infrastructure inadequacy

1 Introduction

ELearning is intended as an opportunity to learn anytime, anywhere. Until the beginning of 21st century, it is a luxury for countries south of the Sahara because of poor integration of ICT in education, lack of financial resources to acquire computer equipment and low bandwidth access to remote resources. But in recent years, with the increase in computing power of electronic gadgets (smartphone, tablet, laptop) and a reduction in their cost, elearning is accessible by these low-income countries. It is a strategic challenge to up for lost time on the rest of the other continents in the field of education with modest financial resources. For five years the Polytechnic University of

© ICST Institute for Computer Sciences, Social Informatics and Telecommunications Engineering 2018
T.F. Bissyande and O. Sie (Eds.): AFRICOMM 2016, LNICST 208, pp. 273–277, 2018.
https://doi.org/10.1007/978-3-319-66742-3_26

Bobo Dioulasso (PUB) knows and accumulated delays in the conduct of academic years. In particular, promotions with large number of students can not complete two semesters in 12 months. Thus, the time it takes to pass for obtaining the bachelor's degree reached or even exceed five years. This is mainly due to lack of infrastructure and teachers to animate in parallel several tutorial groups or practical work. In this paper, we show that elearning may be a solution for this problem. After a preliminary study that allowed us to analyze the opportunity, relevance and feasibility of this training approach for this university, we propose a techno-pedagogical system as a solution to this problem. Our solution is expected to achieve the skills sought without important investment cost and reduce the academic year to 12 months in all these promotions with large numbers of students. In the remainder of this paper, we present in Sect. 2 related work. In Sect. 2, we present a diagnosis of human and material resources. In Sect. 3, we present the design of the project. Section 4 discusses the implementation of the system and tests. Finally, in Sect. 5, we present the conclusion and perspectives.

2 Related Work

For the design of this project, we studied the experience of a number of universities and training centers [Luz07] and training models of a number of experts in the elearning domain. We focus on contexts that are similar to ours marked by large number of students per class, deficiency of classrooms, deficiency of teachers.

Author in [Wil09] discusses the initiatives that Tanzania has taken to expand educational opportunities at various levels using open and distance learning (ODL) approaches. He made proposal of how to improve both access and the quality of education using emerging educational technologies.

[SL08] focuses on the progress and challenges currently facing Zambia for the implementation of the Right to Education and the role of open and distance learning in addressing those challenges.

Julien Deceuninc establishes similarities between distance teaching for great masses and shared teaching in the early nineteenth century. The shared teaching was as motivating idea: "extend the benefits of education, shorten the difficulties, reduce expenditures" [Lab18]. This form of training suitable for large numbers of learners is characterized by the standardization of educational resources and a low quality coaching which use is made of monitors [Dec07].

Jean-Marie Muhirwa in [Muh08] presents the causes of poor performance of elearning projects in South-Sahelian Africa. The author challenges poor needs analysis that failed to take seriously the impact of socio-economic and technological environment particular to developing countries and from the perennial inconsistencies of foreign aid.

Authors in [ZZC12] conducted an exploratory study on the application of e-learning standards. This standardization contributes to improving the quality of distance training offers. They focused on the description and referencing of educational resources and on the development of a standardized and interoperable learning profile adapted to the context of their university. They provide an application profile based on the Metadata for Learning Resources (MLR) allowing a standardized description and setting up a repository of interoperable educational resources.

3 The Design of the Project

To address this lack of infrastructure and permanent teachers, we propose a semi-face training for these large classes. This project concerns particularly six classes with at least 1,200 students in the domains of economics and management sciences and in the field of political and legal sciences.

Pedagogical Model

Educational resources and adequately developed learning activities are uploaded in a Learning Management System (LMS). Synchronous and asynchronous exchanges spaces are created on the virtual campus. The lectures are given in-face by the classroom teacher of the course. The tutorials are administered remotely through the LMS. These occupy more than 9/10 of the total volume of hours of supervision. This work is conducted in small groups of up to 50 learners. This last phase of training allows learners to be more in touch with the coaches and facilitates an individualized monitoring. The intervention of foreign supervisors in training animation will address the deficiency of permanants teachers. This method of training brings the benefits of classroom teaching and distance tutored teaching. Our large groups of learners training model promotes the division of labor. We distinguish content experts, mentors or instructors, technical tutors. Training modules are developed for these first two groups. A number of tutors and content experts are already formed. The LMS Moodle [moo] we offer, tolerates this proposed educational organization. It puts in scene this division for example by separating documents, activities and work performed by the students. This model is also characterized by promoting peer learning. Thus, each section or important concept is associated with a discussion forum. In order to compel in quantity and quality the participation of all learners, interventions in these exchange spaces are assessed. Group activities are systematically implemented in each module. Thus, inspired by the model of Deceuninck [Dec07], with peer learning we are contributing to reduce the coaching cost by making the learner a skill transfer agent. In this social information context where knowledge is decentralized, the only concern about the effectiveness of this model is the ease Internet access. Distance synchronous meetings are held one session for the equivalent of ten hours of lessons given in-face. The other types of activities (glossary, wiki, etc.) are implemented according to the module taught and the objectives sought. Moodle platform we offer is suitable for the implementation of socio-constructivist pedagogical approach. However, note that we disagree with the concept of assigning artifacts a learning theory in a techno-centrist drift [PARS].

IT Infrastructure

The IT infrastructure is one of the cornerstones of this project. The university already has a local network that allows accessibility of the server hosting the LMS with a minimum rate of 10 Mbps from all university sites and student residencee. This network also facilitates the use of VoIP tools for oral communication. Teachers already have laptops. Half of students have electronic devices to interact efficiently with the server. They have also at their disposal the computer rooms during periods not covered by the face training. They also have permanent access to a multimedia room of 100 machines in student residences. We have three videoconference rooms with a capacity of 100 persons that could be used for teachers who would like to make synchronous distance presentations. Internet access with a throughput of 10 Mbps is provided for this purpose.

The project has a number of strengths. Among others, we can mention a high motivation of the first university officials, the project concerns a rather theoretical training there is no practical work, a high quality techno-pedagogue team.

4 Implementation of the Project

The preliminary work of the project was a feasibility study. We conducted surveys by various means (interviews, questionnaires, data consultation, etc.) to ensure the opportunity, relevance, feasibility (technical, organizational, temporal and financial feasibility) for this project. The various actors involved in the project (university officials, teachers, students, technical support staff) were questioned. After being convinced of the relevance of the project, we proceeded to the implementation of distance learning platform. Our choice fell on Moodle for accessibility of its source code, its modularity, its adaptability to different contexts. Once installed and customized Moodle locally, we proceeded to the development of a security policy for the server room hosting the LMS and different needed services on this server. Guided by the survey results, we have prepared and hosted a number of formations. This includes design and modulary structuration of course for distance learning, mentoring and mediation in distance learning context, taking control of the Moodle platform, distance learning management. Subsequently, we proceeded to the implementation of the management team of this semi-face learning. This team is composed of two experts in e-learning domain, two computer technicians, education officer and heads of schools involved in the project. Charters have been drawn up for students and teachers. A motivating financial model was proposed to teachers. Finally, we conducted tests to ensure that teachers and the IT infrastructure are ready for the start of this e-learning the next academic year.

5 Conclusion

We are seeking short-term to reduce the delay in the conduct of pedagogic activities in Polytechnic University of Bobo Dioulasso. The Learning Management System Moodle is implemented. Teachers are trained in conception and modular structuration of courses and tutoring in distance learning. The concerned formations primarily responsible are trained in the e-learning management. A management team comprised of elearning pedagogy specialists and computer engineers respectively ensure the pedagogic and technical aspects of the proposed semi-face learning. This project will solve problems of lack of infrastructure (classrooms deficiency) and teachers for promotion with large numbers of students. It should permit, in two years, to brink back the academic year to 12 months in all promotions.

The deployment of this techno-pedagogical system is an innovation for our university. In medium term:

– It will facilitate the promotion of new educational approaches. Instead of the learner in the learning and peer learning through the forums and chat rooms associated with the learning units will be greater.
– allow the intervention (distance) of foreign experts and business professionals in our teachings.
– It will allow the development of curricula where lack of local specialists. Foreign experts be able to intervene through distance learning via this platform.
– It will reduce the very budget-Educational Missions (purchasing airfare, living expenses, insurance costs).

As another research perspective, in a mobile learning philosophy, we plan to modify the LMS Moodle by applying mobile development techniques and removing superflux services.

References

[Dec07]   Deceuninck, J.: Les campus numriques en france: ralisations, dynamiques et mergences. Technical report (2007)
[Lab18]   Laborde, A.: Plan d'ducation pour les enfants pauvres, d'aprs les deux mthodes combines du docteur bell et de m. lancaster (1818)
[Luz07]   Gutirrez Luz. Projet de formation en ligne du centre des tudes juridiques (2007)
[moo]   Moodle Open Source Software for Online Learning
[Muh08]   Muhirwa, J.-M.: Performance des projets d'enseignement distance destins au sud. le cas du Burkina Faso et du Mali. Distances et savoirs 6(1), 117–142 (2008)
[PARS]   Caron, P.-A., Becerril-Ortega, R., Rthor, S.: Modele artisanal de la formation distance: lien entre l'artefact et la pdagogie. In: Journes Communication et Apprentissage Instruments en Rseau (JOCAIR), Amiens, France (2010)
[SL08]   Siaciwena, R., Lubinda, F.: The role of open and distance learning in the implementation of the right to education in zambia. Int. Rev. Res. Open Distrib. Learn. 9(1) (2008)
[Wil09]   Komba, W.: Increasing education access through open and distance learning in tanzania: a critical review of approaches and practices. Int. J. Educ. Dev. ICT, 5(5) 2009
[ZZC12]   Zghibi, R., Zghidi, S., Chater, O.: Les normes e-learning comme garant de qualit de lenseignement distance dans le contexte ducatif tunisien: le cas de lUVT. Industries de la connaissance, ducation, formation et technologies pour le dveloppement 4, 5–23 (2012). www.frantice.net

Crypto and Services

Spatial Cryptographic and Watermarking Technique for Authentication and Security of Medical Images in a Cloud Based Health Information Systems

Quist-Aphetsi Kester[1,2,3,4(✉)]

[1] Ghana Technology University, Accra, Ghana
[2] Lab-STICC (UMR CNRS 6285), University of Brest, Brest, France
kester.quist-aphetsi@univ-brest.fr, kquist@ieee.org
[3] Satellite Communications and Navigation Systems Department,
CRITAC, Accra, Ghana
[4] Directorate of Information Assurance and Intelligence Research,
CRITAC, Accra, Ghana

Abstract. Cloud computing has provided tremendous opportunities for a lot of organizations in cutting operating cost, making data available to distributed units, provision of easy interoperability etc. Health information systems forms a critical parts of one's countries information technology infrastructure due to the sensitivity and nature of data processed over time with regards treatment history, medical records etc. And medical images form dominant part of the sensitive patient data. Hence privacy and security needs to be guaranteed for such images stored in the cloud. Most of the access security and encryption approaches are left for the cloud owners to manage and these poses a lot of insecurity if the system is compromised. In our wok, we proposed a hybrid spatial cryptographic and watermarking technique for authentication and security of medical images before storage in the cloud. Due to the sensitive nature of medical images, we were able to achieve full recoverability of the plain image after decryption and dewatermarking without pixel loss. Our results showed to be very effective and reliable for fully recoverable images.

Keywords: Cloud computing · Medical images · Health information systems · Security · Cryptography

1 Introduction

Health information systems are an integral and important part of our modern societal information technology infrastructure [1, 2]. The effective and accurate exchange of information within and between healthcare organizations helps in easy access, collection, use, and exchange of information between healthcare facilities [3]. Such information can be triggers of an outbreak, knowledge of on rare cases etc. [4]. Medical record histories of patients are very critical in understanding behavior and traits of diseases over time [5, 6]. And medical imaging has revolutionized the way healthcare

© ICST Institute for Computer Sciences, Social Informatics and Telecommunications Engineering 2018
T.F. Bissyande and O. Sie (Eds.): AFRICOMM 2016, LNICST 208, pp. 281–291, 2018.
https://doi.org/10.1007/978-3-319-66742-3_27

delivery is made across countries. Medical records are very sensitive documents in healthcare delivery and hence good care is needed to be taken to protect it [7]. Information systems adopted security approaches in securing these images. The easy of healthcare delivery and real-time and easy access to healthcare records of patience has pushed modern healthcare practices to adopt cloud storage approaches [8]. This approach then draws in a third party service provider to render services such as warehousing, interoperability, applications as a service etc. Most data stored in the cloud can leak due to malicious activities over the internet. Back door access to stored image files can compromise the privacy and confidentiality of the data stored and hence security approaches are needed in securing these medical data. Also authentication of images by mapping them using watermark approaches to patient records is also very necessary.

2 Review

The increased patient mobility in time across geographical area, combined with the fact that different health care treatments are frequently offered by different health care units, have resulted in the development of web-based electronic health care records. These have also pushed a lot of medical information systems to adopt cloud computing approaches. Although such systems facilitate access to the entire medical history of the patient, it is not straight forward to design and implement security mechanisms for ensuring the confidentiality and integrity of the data or/and the privacy of the patient, without limiting the communication of information between health care professionals and sacrificing system flexibility. In solving the above situation, Dimitris Gritzalis et al. proposed a security architecture for interconnecting health information systems and which was explained in their work [9]. The cloud architecture provides limited security control on the data for its users and a typical example of the cloud architecture is shown below which is typical of modern health information system in the cloud (Fig. 1).

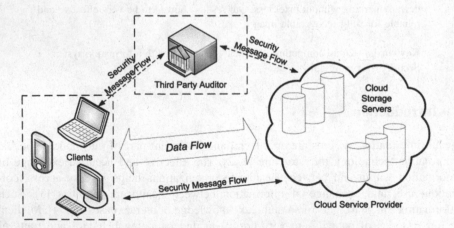

Fig. 1. Data cloud data storage architecture

The above diagram represented three different network entities that can be identified as follows: Client: an entity which uses cloud services and can either individual consumers or organizations; Cloud Storage Server (CSS): an entity, which is managed by Cloud Service Provider (CSP), has significant storage space and computation resource to maintain the clients' data; and the Third Party Auditor: an entity, which has expertise and capabilities that clients do not have, is trusted to assess and expose risk of cloud storage services on behalf of the clients upon request [10]. With the architecture above, client benefits from a lot of services advantages such as saving cost in the setup of physical information technology infrastructure setup cost, computational cost with dependency on power source for cooling centers and servers, migration of facilities during relocations and setting up other distributed access units, overhead cost for system maintenance and staff training etc. [11]. But in high hopes of these loses control or have limited oversight on user data security, system integrity, data access etc. [12]. In providing security for medical images, Abokhdair et al. in their work of Integration of chaotic map and confusion technique for color medical image encryption, proposed algorithm based on combination of scrambling and confusion processes. 2D lower triangular map used for scrambling the addresses of image pixels, and the proposed propeller algorithm was used to confuse the gray values of image pixels. Their method also was resistive to brute force attack [13]. Yicong Zhou et al. in their work, "a lossless encryption method for medical images using edge maps", showed a new lossless approach, called EdgeCrypt, to encrypt medical images using the information contained within an edge map. Their algorithm can also be applied to grayscale images or color images [14]. There have been other works such as Transmission and storage of medical images with patient information" by Acharya et al. [15], "Chaos-Based Medical Image Encryption Using Symmetric Cryptography" by M. Ashtiyaniet [16] etc. Our proposed approach to security is discussed in the following section.

3   Methodology

With our proposed approach based on the architecture in Fig. 2 by introduced a third party security service that renders a real-time session service of encryption and decryption of data between the cloud storage, streaming and other system services and the client. The third party executes the proposed a hybrid spatial cryptographic and watermarking technique for authentication and security of medical images before storage in the cloud. This means it provides services in addition to the primary security protocols between clients and the cloud as diagram below provides the detailed of the architecture behind the system. This ensures that the data stored in the cloud is secure and can only be accessed via that service as a security through a third party or via a service bus.

The pixel values of the images to be encrypted were visually encrypted using n-share of the visual cryptographic technique engaged based on pixel displacement in the RGB channels of the image. The watermarking process was based on a unique patient credential and was applied in this work to only the R-channel of the image.

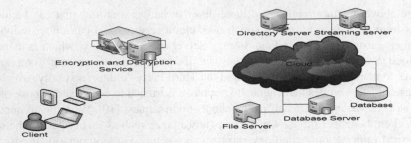

Fig. 2. Proposed process architecture

3.1   The Image Encryption Process

Step 1. Start
Step 2. Extraction of data from a plain image,
Let I = an image = f (R, G, B)
I is a color image of m × n × 3 arrays

$$
\begin{pmatrix}
R & G & B \\
r_{i1} & g_{i2} & b_{i3} \\
\vdots & \vdots & \vdots \\
\vdots & \vdots & \vdots \\
\vdots & \vdots & \vdots \\
r_{n1} & g_{n2} & b_{n3}
\end{pmatrix}
\tag{1}
$$

(R, G, B) = m x n
Where R, G, B ∈ I
(R o G) i j = (R) ij. (G) ij
Where r_11 = first value of R
   r= [ri1] (i=1, 2... m)
   x ∈ r_i1 : [a, b]= {x ∈ I: a ≤x ≥b}
   a=0 and b=255
   R= r= I (m, n, 1)
Where g_12 = first value of G
   g= [gi2] (i=1, 2... m)
   x ∈ g : [a, b]= {x ∈ I: a ≤x ≥b}
   a=0 and b=255
   G= g= I (m, n, 1)
And b_13 = first value of B
   g= [bi3] (i=1, 2... m)
   x ∈ b_i1 : [a, b]= {x ∈ I: a ≤x ≥b}
   a=0 and b=255
   B=b= I (m, n, 1
Such that   R= r= I (m, n, 1)

Step 3. Extraction of the red component as 'r'
Let size of R be m x n [row, column] = size (R) = R (m × n)

$$rij = r = I(m, n, 1) = \begin{pmatrix} R \\ r_{i1} \\ \vdots \\ \vdots \\ \vdots \\ r_{in} \end{pmatrix} \tag{2}$$

Step 4. Extraction of the green component as 'g'
Let size of G be m × n [row, column] = size (G)

$$gij = g = I(m, n, 1) = \begin{pmatrix} G \\ g_{i2} \\ \vdots \\ \vdots \\ \vdots \\ g_{n2} \end{pmatrix} \tag{3}$$

Step 5. Extraction of the blue component as 'b'
Let size of B be m × n [row, column] = size (B) = B (m × n)

$$bij = b = I(m, n, 1) = \begin{pmatrix} B \\ b_{i3} \\ \vdots \\ \vdots \\ \vdots \\ b_{n3} \end{pmatrix} \tag{4}$$

Step 6. Getting the size of r as [c, p]
Let size of R be [row, column] = size (r) = r (c × p)
Step7. Engagement of SSK which is the symmetric secret key generated. The key is then engaged to iterate the step 8 to 14.
Step 8. Let r = Transpose of rij

$$r = \begin{pmatrix} R \\ r_{i1} & \cdots & \cdots & \cdots & r_{n1} \end{pmatrix} \tag{5}$$

Step 9. Let g = Transpose of gij

$$g = \begin{pmatrix} G \\ g_{i3} & \cdots & \cdots & \cdots & g_{n3} \end{pmatrix} \tag{6}$$

Step 10. Let b = Transpose of bij

$$b = \begin{pmatrix} B \\ b_{i2} & \cdots & \cdots & \cdots & b_{n2} \end{pmatrix} \tag{7}$$

Step 11. Reshaping of r into (r, c, p)

$$r = \text{reshape } (r, c, p) = \begin{pmatrix} R \\ r_{i1} \\ \vdots \\ \vdots \\ \vdots \\ r_{in} \end{pmatrix} \tag{8}$$

Step 12. Reshaping of g into (g, c, p)

$$g = \text{reshape } (g, c, p) = \begin{pmatrix} G \\ g_{i2} \\ \vdots \\ \vdots \\ \vdots \\ g_{n2} \end{pmatrix} \tag{9}$$

Step 13. Reshaping of b into (b, c, p)

$$b = \text{reshape } (b, c, p) = \begin{pmatrix} B \\ b_{i3} \\ \vdots \\ \vdots \\ \vdots \\ b_{n3} \end{pmatrix} \tag{10}$$

Step 14. Concatenation of the arrays r, g, b into the same dimension of 'r' or 'g' or 'b' of the original image

$$= \begin{pmatrix} R & G & B \\ r_{i1} & g_{i2} & b_{i3} \\ \vdots & \vdots & \vdots \\ \vdots & \vdots & \vdots \\ \vdots & \vdots & \vdots \\ r_{n1} & g_{n2} & b_{n3} \end{pmatrix} \qquad (11)$$

Step 15. Finally the data will be converted into an image format to get the encrypted image.

3.2 The Watermarking Process

Let the host signal be defined by A as below. The following approach was used to embed the data into the image, A. For a given Image A, we have

$$A = \begin{bmatrix} x_{11} & x_{12} & x_{13} & x_{14} & \cdot & \cdot & \cdot & x_{1n} \\ x_{21} & x_{22} & \cdot & & \cdot & \cdot & \cdot & x_{2n} \\ x_{31} & \cdot & \cdot & \cdot & \cdot & \cdot & \cdot & x_{3n} \\ x_{41} & \cdot & \cdot & \cdot & \cdot & \cdot & \cdot & x_{4n} \\ \cdot & & & & & & & \\ \cdot & \cdot & \cdot & \cdot & \cdot & & & \\ \cdot & \cdot & \cdot & \cdot & \cdot & \cdot & & \\ x_{m1} & \cdot x_{m2} & x_{m3} & x_{m4} & \cdot & \cdot & \cdot & x_{mn} \end{bmatrix} \qquad (12)$$

For a given message E to be embedded in A where E < A, we have,

$$E = \begin{bmatrix} x_{11} & x_{12} & x_{13} & \cdot & \cdot & \cdot & x_{1n} \\ x_{21} & x_{22} & \cdot & & \cdot & \cdot & x_{2n} \\ x_{31} & \cdot & \cdot & \cdot & \cdot & x_{3n} \\ \cdot & \cdot & \cdot & \cdot & \cdot & \cdot & \\ \cdot & & & & & & \\ \cdot & \cdot & \cdot & \cdot & \cdot & \cdot & \\ x_{m1} & \cdot x_{m2} & x_{m3} & \cdot & \cdot & \cdot & x_{mn} \end{bmatrix} \qquad (13)$$

Where we obtain the channels of the image as R, G, B $\in$ A
(R o G) $_{ij}$ = (R) $_{ij}$. (G) $_{ij}$ and x $\in$ [i, j, m, n] and {x $\in$ I: 1 $\leq$ x $\leq$ +∞}
For x $\in$ [R, G, B]: [a, b] = {x $\in$ I: a $\leq$ x $\geq$ b} where a = 0 and b = 255

$$R = r = A (m, n, 1)$$
$$G = g = A (m, n, 1) \qquad (14)$$
$$B = b = A (m, n, 1)$$

[c, p] = s(R); is the size of R as [c, p]
Let s(R) = size of R be [row, column] = size (R) = R (c $\times$ p)

Embedding E the data into A will be

d = Eij, where d is the elements of the data to be embedded

Let the size of d be [c1, p1] = size (d)

```
for i=1:1:c1
            for j=1:1:p1
            if(c1<c)
                    R(i,j)= ((i,j)+Eij)mod256
                    G(i,j)= G(i,j)
                    B(i,j)= G(i,j)
                else
                    R(i,j)=R(i,j)
                    G(i,j)=G(i,j)
                    B(i,j)=B(i,j)
            end
            end
    end
```

4   Results and Analysis

The image below of dimension 640 × 480 pixels obtained from a UAV, vertical and horizon resolution of 72 dpi and bit depth of 24 was operated on by the proposed process and the following results were obtained from it.

The graph of the normalized cross-correlation of the matrices of the image.

The normalized cross-correlation of the matrices of is

$$\gamma(u,v) = \frac{\sum_{x,y} \left[f(x,y) - \bar{f}_{u,v} \right] \left[t(x-u, y-v) - \bar{t} \right]}{\left\{ \sum_{x,y} \left[f(x,y) - \bar{f}_{u,v} \right]^2 \sum_{x,y} \left[t(x-u, y-v) - \bar{t} \right]^2 \right\}^{0.5}} \quad (15)$$

f is the mean of the template, $\bar{t}$ is the mean of in the region under the template. $\bar{f}_{u,v}$ is the mean of $f(u, v)$ in the region under the template.

From the Table 1,

UPI = Ultrasound plain image

UEI = Ultrasound encrypted image

UWI = Ultrasound watermarked image

Table 1. Extracted features from the process.

Heading level	Entropy	Arithmetic mean
UPI	3.7603	18.5810
UEI	3.7603	18.5810
UWI	4.5355	97.8913
DWI	3.7603	18.5810
RPI	3.7603	18.5810

URI = Ultrasound recovered image
DWI = Ultrasound dewatermarked image

The results in Fig. 3 show how the ciphered image was encrypted and then watermarked. The graph of the normalized cross-correlation of the matrices of the plain, ciphered and watermarked image of the Ultrasound Image are shown in Figs. 4, 5 and 6 respectively. It can be observed from the graphs that, the distribution of pixel values are evenly distributed with arithmetic mean value of 18.5810 for the plain and ciphered image due to lossless encryption approach engaged.

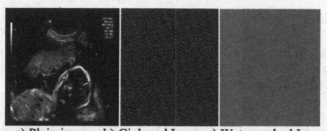

a) Plain image   b) Ciphered Image c) Watermarked Image

Fig. 3. Ultrasound Image of the womb

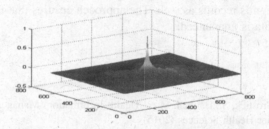

Fig. 4. The graph of the normalized cross-correlation of the matrices of the plain image of the Ultrasound Image

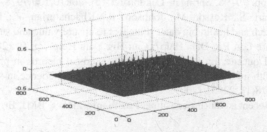

Fig. 5. The graph of the normalized cross-correlation of the matrices of the ciphered image of the Ultrasound Image

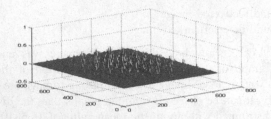

Fig. 6. The graph of the normalized cross-correlation of the matrices of the watermarked image of the Ultrasound Image

5 Conclusion

We were able to obtain a full recoverable image at the end of the process due to the fact that our proposed method can reconstruct the pixel back in the image which is very important for medical images since they contain vital information about the patient. And our proposed work was resistive against statistical and brute force attacks. The total entropy and the mean of the plain images never changed for all the ciphered images and the plain images. That is the average total pixel before encryption was the same as the average total pixel after encryption. But there was a change in pixel value during the watermarking process due to pixel expansion process. Because we engaged image features and patient identification in the ciphering process, each image is uniquely encrypted; making it safer for the images and also it is easy to authenticate the image with the patient's records as well. The approach ensures that the confidentiality of patient image data is guaranteed.

References

1. Abdelhak, M., Grostick, S., Hanken, M.A.: Health Information: Management of A Strategic Resource. Elsevier Health Sciences (2015)
2. Leventhal, J.C., Cummins, J.A., Schwartz, P.H., Martin, D.K., Tierney, W.M.: Designing a system for patients controlling providers' access to their electronic health records: organizational and technical challenges. J. Gen. Intern. Med. **30**(1), 17–24 (2015)
3. Witting, K.: Health information exchange: Integrating the Healthcare Enterprise (IHE). In: Hannah, K.J., Hussey, P., Kennedy, M.A., Ball, M.J. (eds.) Introduction to Nursing Informatics. HI, pp. 79–96. Springer, London (2015). doi:10.1007/978-1-4471-2999-8_6
4. Stuss, D.T., Amiri, S., Rossor, M., Johnson, R., Khachaturian, Z.: How we can work together on research and health big data: strategies to ensure value and success. In: Dementia Research and Care Can Big Data Help?: Can Big Data Help?, p. 61 (2015)
5. Ludwick, D.A., Doucette, J.: Adopting electronic medical records in primary care: lessons learned from health information systems implementation experience in seven countries. Int. J. Med. Inform. **78**(1), 22–31 (2009)
6. Eysenbach, G.: Recent advances: consumer health informatics. BMJ. Br. Med. J. **320**(7251), 1713 (2000)
7. Anderson, R.J.: Security in clinical information systems. Br. Med. Assoc., London (1996)

8. Mouratidis, H., Giorgini, P., Manson, G.: Integrating security and systems engineering: towards the modelling of secure information systems. In: Eder, J., Missikoff, M. (eds.) CAiSE 2003. LNCS, vol. 2681, pp. 63–78. Springer, Heidelberg (2003). doi:10.1007/3-540-45017-3_7

9. Gritzalis, D., Lambrinoudakis, C.: A security architecture for interconnecting health information systems. Int. J. Med. Inform. 73(3), 305–309 (2004)

10. Wang, Q., Wang, C., Ren, K., Lou, W., Li, J.: Enabling public auditability and data dynamics for storage security in cloud computing. IEEE Trans. Parallel Distrib. Syst. 22(5), 847–859 (2011)

11. Liu, H.: Big data drives Cloud adoption in enterprise. IEEE Internet Comput. 17(4), 68–71 (2013)

12. Tari, Z.: Security and privacy in Cloud computing. IEEE Cloud Comput. 1(1), 54–57 (2014)

13. Abokhdair, N.O., Manaf, A.B.A., Zamani, M.: Integration of chaotic map and confusion technique for color medical image encryption. In: 2010 6th International Conference on Digital Content, Multimedia Technology and its Applications (IDC), pp. 20–23, 16–18 August 2010

14. Zhou, Y., Panetta, K., Agaian, S.: A lossless encryption method for medical images using edge maps. In: Engineering in Medicine and Biology Society, 2009, EMBC 2009, Annual International Conference of the IEEE, pp. 3707–3710, 3–6 September 2009

15. Acharya, U.R., Bhat, P.S., Kumar, S., Min, L.C.: Transmission and storage of medical images with patient information. Comput. Biol. Med. 33(4), 303–310 (2003)

16. Ashtiyani, M., Birgani, P.M., Hosseini, H.M.: Chaos-based medical image encryption using symmetric cryptography. In: 3rd International Conference on Information and Communication Technologies: From Theory to Applications 2008, ICTTA 2008, pp. 1–5 (2008)

A Hybrid Lossy Compression Using 2-D Discrete Cosine Transform and Visual Cryptographic Technique for Security of Multimedia Image Data Communications in Internet of Things

Quist-Aphetsi Kester[1,2,3,4](✉)

[1] Ghana Technology University, Accra, Ghana
[2] Lab-STICC (UMR CNRS 6285), University of Brest, Brest, France
kester.quist-aphetsi@univ-brest.fr
[3] Satellite Communications and Navigation Systems Department,
CRITAC, Accra, Ghana
[4] Directorate of Information Assurance and Intelligence Research,
CRITAC, Accra, Ghana

Abstract. Security in internet of things is very critical. The computer systems that use image acquisition and processing from onboard or remote systems need to secure image data over the internet. Security of multimedia image data transmitted over secured and unsecured communications channel in today's cyberspace is of paramount consideration due to malicious activities over these channels and there has been a high demand especially for end to end security applications for mobile devices. This is to ensure safety and security as well as privacy to transmitted data and stored data in the clouds. In this paper, we proposed a hybrid approach for securing digital images for devices by engaging lossy compression using 2-D discrete cosine transform and Visual Cryptographic Technique. The DCT was used for the lossy compression process and the visual cryptography was used to encrypt the image for confidentiality. The results showed to be very effective and the implementation was done using MATLAB.

Keywords: Internet of things · Digital images · Security · Encryption · Compression · Discrete cosine transforms

1 Introduction

Communications of multimedia data over secured and unsecured channels require encryption techniques in securing its content. Over the decade, as computer processing power increase more live video transmission and streaming has also increased over the internet. These have led to tremendous efforts and many technical innovations in supporting real-time video streaming. Cost-effective large-scale video broadcast has remained an elusive goal. Internet protocol (IP) multicast represented an earlier attempt to tackle this problem but failed largely due to concerns regarding scalability, deployment, and support for higher level functionality [1]. These live data transmission over secured and unsecured communications channels have also call for concerns on

© ICST Institute for Computer Sciences, Social Informatics and Telecommunications Engineering 2018
T.F. Bissyande and O. Sie (Eds.): AFRICOMM 2016, LNICST 208, pp. 292–303, 2018.
https://doi.org/10.1007/978-3-319-66742-3_28

data security as malicious activities by hackers over the internet pose a lot of challenge to ensuring privacy and security for its users [2]. Disparate devices accessing one data source poses a lot of challenges to data compression servers since different data formats have to be made available for easy access and effective interoperability between the various disparate devices. Normally, data is compressed before encrypted for transmission but in our approach, we proposed a situation in which we provided a two security layer for the data by first engaging pixel displacement approaches to visually conceal the content of the data before compression using discrete cosine transform.

2 Review

Image compression is of key importance in transmission of images. This helps in saving bandwidth in data communications as well as reducing the rate of power usage at terminals during transmission from one point to the other. Compressed data stored on storage devices also help saves storage space cost. Security to compressed data provides confidentiality and maintains the integrity of the transmitted data until it is verified or authenticated by the receiver. In the protection of the privacy of original content of images, Qian et al. in their work of JPEG encryption for image rescaling in the encrypted domain proposed a novel protocol of encrypting the JPEG image suitable for image rescaling in the encrypted domain. In their approach, the image owner perturbs the texture and randomizes the structure of the JPEG image by enciphering the quantized Discrete Cosine Transform (DCT) coefficients. After receiving the ciphered JPEG image by a service provider, the service provider generates a rescaled JPEG image by down-sampling the encrypted DCT coefficients. They achieved this by engaging an encryption key in the process. Upon receiving the sent data via the service provider to the recipient, the recipient on the other side, the encrypted JPEG image rescaled by the service provider can then be decrypted to a plaintext image with a lower resolution with the aid of encryption keys by the receiver. Qian et al. in their work [3] of JPEG encryption for image rescaling but also provided privacy and security [3]. In securing digital videos and images, several cryptographic techniques have been developed to encrypt images and videos in recent years. Some of the encryption schemes are based on the principles of cryptography that are designed to ensure the confidentiality of multimedia data [4–7]. In most cases, such solutions may not be suitable for the effective real-time secure applications since their encryption processes require vast resources including computing complexity, time and power. Yicong Zhou et al. in their work of encryption using Discrete Parametric Cosine Transform introduced a new effective image encryption algorithm based on the Discrete Parametric Cosine Transform (DPCT). Their new algorithm transforms images into the frequency domain using the DPCT with a set of parameters, and then converts images back into the spatial domain using the inverse DPCT with a different set of parameters to obtain the encrypted images [8]. Their new algorithm transforms the original images into the frequency domain using the new 2D DPCT with the parameters P with This is shown in the Fig. 1 below. It then uses an inverse 2D DPCT with different parameters P' to convert the images back into the spatial domain to obtain the encrypted images. Its security keys are the combination of the parameters of the DPCT and inverse DPCT.

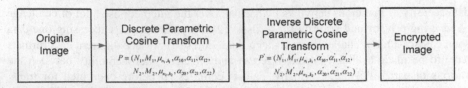

Fig. 1. Block diagram of the image encryption algorithm. In the above diagram

The experimental results of their procedure showed that the algorithm can fully or partially encrypt different types of digital images with efficiency while preserving the quality of the images. The Discrete Cosine Transform is widely used for compression of digital images and it possesses a good energy compaction property. These properties made it suitable for coding and compression, feature extraction, filtering, and image encryption. The Discrete Cosine Transform approaches for encryption schemes have been developed to protect multimedia data in the frequency domain by encrypting the DCT coefficients/ blocks [5], the quantization table [9], or Huffman table [10]. These approaches significantly lower computational cost, has the encryption speed for multimedia contents in real-time applications such as mobile computing and server-end computing [11]. The Discrete Cosine Transform based encryption methods are usually combined with the data compression process; they may not be suitable for applications requiring high quality data. In our work, we proposed a hybrid approach for securing digital images for devices by engaging lossy compression using 2-D discrete cosine transform and Visual Cryptographic Technique. The DCT was used for the lossy compression process and the visual cryptography was used to encrypt the image for confidentiality. The results showed to be very effective and the implementation was done using MATLAB.

3   Methodology

In our approach we combined lossy compression technique using 2-D Discrete Cosine Transform and visual cryptographic technique for security of multimedia image data communications. But we first encrypt the image using the visual cryptographic

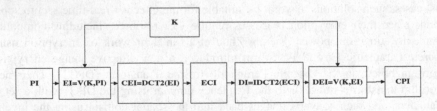

Fig. 2. Block diagram of the proposed approach: PI = Plain Image, K = Engaged key, EI = Encryption Process, V (K, PI) = the function which is the image encryption process that engages the key, and the plain image in the ciphering process. CEI = Compression of the encrypted Image process, DCT2 (EI) = the 2-D Discrete Cosine Operation on the Encrypted Image, ECI = Encrypted but Compressed Image, DI = Decompression of the compressed encrypted image, IDCT2 = Inverse of the 2-D Discrete Cosine Operation on the Encrypted Image, DEI = Decrypted decompressed ciphered Image, V (K, EI) = the function that operated on the decompressed image and the encrypted, CPI = Compressed but decrypted image

technique first, which is based on pixel shuffling and displacement, before finally applying the 2-D Discrete Cosine Transform. The Fig. 2 below illustrates the procedure.

There was no pixel loss during the encryption process due to the pixel displacement technique engaged. This means that there was pixel conservation in the process. But there was pixel loss during the compression and decompression process. The decrypted image at the end was good since critical features were still visible. Below is the explanation of the processes engaged, that is the image encryption and the 2-D discrete cosine transform process. Some image values were cut-off during the engagement of the DCT process.

3.1 The Image Encryption Process

Step 1. Start
Step 2. Extraction of data from a plain image,
Let I = an image = f (R, G, B)
I is a color image of m × n × 3 arrays

$$
\begin{pmatrix}
R & G & B \\
r_{i1} & g_{i2} & b_{i3} \\
\vdots & \vdots & \vdots \\
\vdots & \vdots & \vdots \\
\vdots & \vdots & \vdots \\
r_{n1} & g_{n2} & b_{n3}
\end{pmatrix}
\tag{1}
$$

(R, G, B) = m x n
Where R, G, B ∈ I
(R o G) i j = (R) ij. (G) ij
Where r_11 = first value of R
   r= [ri1] (i=1, 2... m)
   x ∈ r_il : [a, b]= {x ∈ I: a ≤ x ≥ b}
   a=0 and b=255
   R= r= I (m, n, 1)
Where g_12 = first value of G
   g= [gi2] (i=1, 2... m)
   x ∈ g : [a, b]= {x ∈ I: a ≤ x ≥ b}
   a=0 and b=255
   G= g= I (m, n, 1)
And   b_13 = first value of B
   g= [bi3] (i=1, 2... m)
   x ∈ b_il : [a, b]= {x ∈ I: a ≤ x ≥ b}
   a=0 and b=255
   B=b= I (m, n, 1
Such that   R= r= I (m, n, 1)

Step 3. Extraction of the red component as 'r'

Let size of R be m × n [row, column] = size (R) = R (m × n)

$$rij = r = I\,(m,\,n,\,1) = \begin{pmatrix} R \\ r_{i1} \\ \vdots \\ \vdots \\ \vdots \\ r_{in} \end{pmatrix} \tag{2}$$

Step 4. Extraction of the green component as 'g'

Let size of G be m × n [row, column] = size (G)

$$gij = g = I\,(m,\,n,\,1) = \begin{pmatrix} G \\ g_{i2} \\ \vdots \\ \vdots \\ \vdots \\ g_{n2} \end{pmatrix} \tag{3}$$

Step 5. Extraction of the blue component as 'b'

Let size of B be m × n [row, column] = size (B) = B (m × n)

$$bij = b = I\,(m,\,n,\,1) = \begin{pmatrix} B \\ b_{i3} \\ \vdots \\ \vdots \\ \vdots \\ b_{n3} \end{pmatrix} \tag{4}$$

Step 6. Getting the size of r as [c, p]

Let size of R be [row, column] = size (r) = r (c × p)

Step 7. Engagement of K which is the symmetric secret key generated. The key is then engaged to iterate the step 8 to 14.

Step 8. Let r = Transpose of rij

$$r = \begin{pmatrix} R & & & & \\ r_{i1} & \cdots & \cdots & \cdots & r_{n1} \end{pmatrix} \tag{5}$$

Step 9. Let g = Transpose of gij

$$g = \begin{pmatrix} G \\ g_{i3} & \cdots & \cdots & \cdots & g_{n3} \end{pmatrix} \tag{6}$$

Step 10. Let b = Transpose of bij

$$b = \begin{pmatrix} B \\ b_{i2} & \cdots & \cdots & \cdots & b_{n2} \end{pmatrix} \tag{7}$$

Step 11. Reshaping of r into (r, c, p)

$$r = \text{reshape } (r, c, p) = \begin{pmatrix} R \\ r_{i1} \\ \vdots \\ \vdots \\ \vdots \\ r_{in} \end{pmatrix} \tag{8}$$

Step 12. Reshaping of g into (g, c, p)

$$g = \text{reshape } (g, c, p) = \begin{pmatrix} G \\ g_{i2} \\ \vdots \\ \vdots \\ \vdots \\ g_{n2} \end{pmatrix} \tag{9}$$

Step 13. Reshaping of b into (b, c, p)

$$b = \text{reshape } (b, c, p) = \begin{pmatrix} B \\ b_{i3} \\ \vdots \\ \vdots \\ \vdots \\ b_{n3} \end{pmatrix} \tag{10}$$

Step 14. Concatenation of the arrays r, g, b into the same dimension of 'r' or 'g' or 'b' of the original image

$$= \begin{pmatrix} R & G & B \\ r_{i1} & g_{i2} & b_{i3} \\ \vdots & \vdots & \vdots \\ \vdots & \vdots & \vdots \\ \vdots & \vdots & \vdots \\ r_{n1} & g_{n2} & b_{n3} \end{pmatrix} \tag{11}$$

Step 15. Finally the data will be converted into an image format to get the encrypted image.

3.2 The 2-D Discrete Cosine Transform Process

The discrete cosine transform in general is related to the discrete Fourier transform. DCT is a separable linear transformation; which means that, the two-dimensional transform is equivalent to a one-dimensional DCT performed along a single dimension followed by a one-dimensional DCT in the other dimension. Below is the representation of the 2-D Discrete Cosine Transform engaged:

For a given 2-D spatial data sequence $\{X_{ij}; i, j = 0, 1, ..., N-1\}$, the 2-D DCT data sequence $\{Y_{mn}; m, n = 0, 1, ..., N-1\}$ is defined by

$$\tilde{Y}_{mn} = \frac{2}{N} E_m E_n \sum_{i=0}^{N-1} \sum_{j=0}^{N-1} X_{ij} \cos \frac{(2i+1)m\pi}{2N}$$
$$\times \; \cos \frac{(2j+1)n\pi}{2N} \tag{12}$$

Where,

$$E_k = \begin{cases} 1/\sqrt{2} & \text{for } k = 0 \\ 1 & \text{otherwise.} \end{cases} \tag{13}$$

Without loss of generality, the scale factor 2E, En/N will be neglected for convenience. Thus, the 2-D DCT computation becomes

$$Y_{mn} = \sum_{i=0}^{N-1} \sum_{j=0}^{N-1} X_{ij} \cos \frac{(2i+1)m\pi}{2N} \cos \frac{(2j+1)n\pi}{2N}, \tag{14}$$
$$m, n = 0, 1, 2, ..., N-1.$$

Using the row-column decomposition and denoting cos ((2k + l)rr/2N) by C &, we have

$$Y_{mn} = \sum_{j=0}^{N-1} Z_{mj} c_{nj}, \quad m, n = 0, 1, 2, \ldots, N - 1 \tag{15}$$

With

$$Z_{mj} = \sum_{i=0}^{N-1} X_{ij} c_{mi}, \quad m, j = 0, 1, 2, \ldots, N - 1 \tag{16}$$

Equations (15) and (16) are generally called "column transform" and "row transform," respectively. Performing N row transforms and N column transforms to compute an N × N-point DCT N, each row transform of Eq. (16) can be written as

$$Z_{mj} = \sum_{i=0}^{N/2-1} [X_{ij} + (-1)^m X_{(N-1-i)j}] c_{mi} \tag{17}$$

Defining

$$U_{ij}^{m'} = X_{ij} + (-1)^m X_{(N-1-i)j} \tag{18}$$

where m' = 0 when m is even and m' = 1 when m is odd, we have

$$\begin{aligned} Z_{mj} &= \sum_{i=0}^{N/2-1} U_{ij}^{m'} c_{mi} \\ &= U_{0j}^{m'} c_{m0} + U_{1j}^{m'} c_{m1} + \cdots + U_{(N/2-1)j}^{m'} c_{m(N/2-1)} \end{aligned} \tag{19}$$

Similarly, each column transform of (15) can be expressed by

$$\begin{aligned} Y_{mn} &= \sum_{j=0}^{N/2-1} V_{ml}^{n'} c_{nj} \\ &= V_{m0}^{n'} c_{n0} + V_{m1}^{n'} c_{n1} + \cdots + V_{m(N/2-1)}^{n'} c_{n(N/2-1)} \end{aligned} \tag{20}$$

Where

$$V_{mj}^{n'} = Z_{mj} + (-1)^n Z_{m(N-1-j)} \tag{21}$$

4 Results and Analysis

The plain image in Fig. 3 below with dimension of 640 × 480 pixels is having vertical and horizon resolution of 72 dpi and bit depth of 24 (Table 1). The plain image was operated on by the proposed process and the following results were obtained from it (Figs. 4, 5, 6, 7, 8, 9, 10, 11, 12, 13 and 14).

Fig. 3. The plain image

Table 1. Extracted features from the process.

Heading level	Entropy	Arithmetic mean
PI	7.8258	104.3025
EI	7.8258	104.3025
CEI	7.8366	1.5371
LI	2.3006	1.5310
DI	7.8366	104.3224
CPI	7.8366	104.3224

LI is the loss image

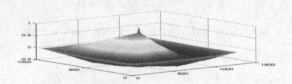

Fig. 4. The graph of the normalized cross-correlation of the matrices of the plain image

Fig. 5. The ciphered image

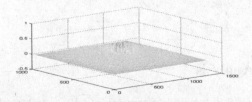

Fig. 6. The graph of the normalized cross-correlation of the matrices of the ciphered image

Fig. 7. The compressed ciphered image

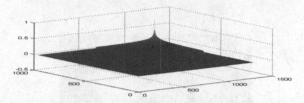

Fig. 8. The graph of the normalized cross-correlation of the matrices of the compressed ciphered image

Fig. 9. The loss image

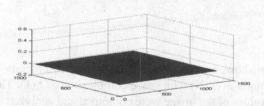

Fig. 10. The graph of the normalized cross-correlation of the matrices of the loss image

Fig. 11. The graph of decompressed image

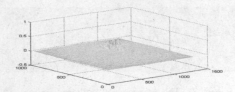

Fig. 12. The graph of the normalized cross-correlation of the matrices of the decompressed image

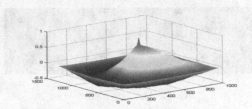

Fig. 13. The recovered image

Fig. 14. The graph of the normalized cross-correlation of the matrices of the recovered image

5 Conclusion

The implementation showed to be very successful, the complexity time of the image cryptographic technique is O (N) with space complexity of O (1). The arithmetic mean and entropy of the values of the image were computed and analyzed in the table shown. From the table, it can clearly be observed that the arithmetic mean of the ciphered and plain image is the same and that of the decompressed as well as that of the recovered image are the same. The process was successful and fast and the decompressed image was successfully recovered from the ciphered image and compressed image.

References

1. Liu, J., Rao, S.G., Li, B., Zhang, H.: Opportunities and challenges of peer-to-peer internet video broadcast. Proc. IEEE **96**(1), 11–24 (2008). doi:10.1109/JPROC.2007.909921
2. Qureshi, A., Megías, D., Rifà-Pous, H.: Framework for preserving security and privacy in peer-to-peer content distribution systems. Expert Syst. Appl. **42**(3), 1391–1408 (2015)

3. Qian, Z., Zhang, X., Ren, Y.: JPEG encryption for image rescaling in the encrypted domain. J. Vis. Commun. Image Represent. **26**, 9–13 (2015)

4. Li, T., et al.: A new scrambling method based on semi-frequency domain and chaotic system. In: International Conference on Neural Networks and Brain, ICNN&B 2005, pp. 607–610 (2005)

5. Lian, S., Sun, J., Wang, Z.: A novel image encryption scheme based-on JPEG encoding. In: Proceedings of Eighth International Conference on Information Visualization, 2004, IV 2004, pp. 217–220 (2004)

6. Chen, T.-S., Chang, C.-C., Hwang, M.-S.: A virtual image cryptosystem based upon vector quantization. IEEE Trans. Image Process. **7**, 1485–1488 (1998)

7. Kester, Q., Koumadi, K.M.: Cryptographie technique for image encryption based on the RGB pixel displacement. In: 2012 IEEE 4th International Conference on Adaptive Science & Technology (ICAST), pp. 74–77, 25–27 October 2012

8. Zhou, Y., Panetta, K., Agaian, S.: Image encryption using Discrete Parametric Cosine Transform. In: 2009 Conference Record of the Forty-Third Asilomar Conference on Signals, Systems and Computers, pp. 395–399, 1–4 November 2009

9. Sudharsanan, S.: Shared key encryption of JPEG color images. IEEE Trans. Consum. Electron. **51**, 1204–1211 (2005)

10. Zhou, J., et al.: Security analysis of multimedia encryption schemes based on multiple Huffman table. IEEE Signal Process. Lett. **14**, 201–204 (2007)

11. Wu, C.-P., Kuo, C.C.J.: Design of integrated multimedia compression and encryption systems. IEEE Trans. Multimedia **7**, 828–839 (2005)

Modelization of Recipe in African Traditional Medicine with Visual Ontology Approach, Iconic Sketch

Kouamé Appoh[1,2]([✉]), Lamy Jean Baptiste[3], Brou Konan Marcellin[1], and Lo Moussa[2]

[1] Institut National Polytechnique Félix Houphouët Boigny de Yamoussoukro, Yamoussoukro, Côte d'Ivoire
kgerappoh@gmail.com, konanmarcellin@yahoo.fr
[2] Université Gaston Berger, St. Louis, Sénégal
moussa.Lo@ugb.edu.sn
[3] Université Paris 13, Bobigny, France
jean-Baptiste.Lamy@Univ-Paris13.Fr

Abstract. The modernization of African traditional medicine (TM) using IT faces to illiteracy of most of the domain stakeholders. In order to assist traditional medicine practitioner (TMP) in theirs activities, we have propose an icon-based system to visually use plants and recipe in the drug preparation process. Therefore, traditional physicians can easily combine icons for medical prescription. For that, ontoMEDTRAD is an ontology including formal description for knowledge related to iconic representation of plants and recipes. Structurally, ontoMEDTRAD includes two modules: ontoConcept_term and ontoIcone denoting respectively the terms and the icons of concepts in this domain. Thus, avoiding any semantic issues, TMP can be free from language barriers, textual writing and reading in their work of healer. More specifically, this work aims to model plants and recipes in TM and propose compositional iconic language for plants and sketches for recipes.

Keywords: Ontology · Iconic language · African traditional medicine · Plant · sysMEDTRAD · ontoMedtrad · Icon · West Africa

1 Introduction

In West Africa (16 countries), each inhabitant of rural areas knows and uses healing virtues of the plants of traditional medicine (TM). This usage, in addition to being cultural, binds people on their land [2]. In TM, plants are used "as-is" or in simple recipes or remedies, e.g. infusions. African TM plays a growing role in primary healthcare. Some national health programs include TM in complement to modern medicine (MM), but not instead of it. In parallel to MM, 80% of West African population make calls to local MT services [19, 26]. However, TM's knowledge and experiences are disappearing because it mostly relies on oral transmission. The majority of TM practitioners (TMP) is illiterate and some of them prefer secrecy to the diffusion of their knowledge. It would be a great interest to preserve TM's knowledge,

T.F. Bissyande and O. Sie (Eds.): AFRICOMM 2016, LNICST 208, pp. 304–312, 2018.
https://doi.org/10.1007/978-3-319-66742-3_29

and this requires a dedicated setting for TMP to exchange, mutualize, share and sustain their knowledge. SysMEDTRAD [14] aims to solve this problem. It is based on a semantic wiki. Its main component is ontoMEDTRAD, itself structured in two modules: ontoCONCEPT-term, a formal ontology of TM concepts, and ontoIcone, an iconic language for the major concepts in TM. Icons have the potential for overcoming linguistic barriers and illiteracy, in a similar way than traffic signs do [6]. The wider scope of our work concerns the TM management based on a visual ontology approach. Ideally, that means to model the concepts in this field (ontoCONCEPT_term) and represent them graphically by icons (ontoIcone). We meet the major interest's requirement with three use cases (competency questions): UC1 determines disease based on symptoms, UC2 determines the recipe for producing the remedy of a given disease, UC3 specifies the administration mode for a given remedy. Here, we focus our analysis on UC2. To define a recipe, the TMP initially selects the plant(s) to be used to design this recipe. Then he determines the plant parts to be used in the recipe. Of the foregoing, it is necessary to develop a graphical approach to present visually the medicinal plants and allow them distinct recognition.

The objective of this paper contains two section strongly linked. One of the two, expresses a compositional iconic language for describing and identifying plants in TM of west Africa. The other concerns the formalization of the recipe and its iconic sketch based on plants icons and iconems of useful parts of plants. We represent each plant by an icon, created by combining several iconems (*i.e.* small icon parts). Each iconem represents a specific botanical criteria such as the color of flowers. In the following section, we describe our methods for selecting criteria, designing iconems and generating icons. Some examples will be given before discussing our approach.

2 Materials and Methods

We chosed to focus on malaria and anti-malarial plants. In the anthology of anti-malarial plants collected in TM, we targeted twenty-two (22) used in thirty (30) recipes [1, 2, 11, 12, 18, 20]. Plant plays a central role in this TM. Relatively malaria, some symptoms remain unchanged, in contrast, vary with the patient nature: child, pregnant woman, adult. So much for this collection and for the conceptual modeling, we went over several sources and results of studies in biosciences as previously mentioned. Our approach includes the benefits in terms of knowledges received from our direct collaboration with TMP (Output and field visits in Côte d'Ivoire and Senegal). We were instructed of important work references on traditional pharmacopoeia [10, 18] and seminars we attended to. We obtained documents of interest from the PNPMT (National Program for TM Promotion, Côte d'Ivoire) and from some NGOs (Non-governmental organization) as PROMETRA (Senegal).

Sometimes, a medicinal plant treats many diseases. A recipe can be limited to a single plant or can include several plants. The plant associations, mismatched, sometimes are dangerous [12] and therefore not recommended unless sufficient control side effects. In popular medicine, plant associations are enough and quite known in rural area (for enema or purge). The components of a **recipe** are plant parts such as: leaf, fruit, bark, stem, root, flower, sap or whole plant. Leaves, fruits, bark are the most often uses in recipes. Leaf and fruit are predominantly solicited at the respective rates of 60% and 15% [12]. We defined criteria to characterize and individually distinguish our twenty-two (22) plants. Started from around forty criteria mostly obtained from botanical description, we have reduced the number gradually, through an inclusive method of a learning software Weka (Ranker and Jrip) and semiotic elements. Our selection of criteria, relies on three semiological elements coming from the rules relating to the thoughts of S. Peirce (triad dimension), even if F. Saussure's ones (dyadic dimension) have just strengthened us in understanding the signs. Those elements are visual similarity, semantic association and arbitrary convention [6, 22]. The twenty-two plants are represented by icons, with seven (7) criteria ordered by their weight (in Weka's ranker algorithm) that we present in this format: **criterion: weight of criterion: order number**. Thus we have: *(i) formOfFruit: 3.1181:5; (ii) formFolioleLeave: 3.0151:2; (iii) colorOfFruit: 2.799: 19; (iv) colorOfFlower: 2.2147:21; (v) Silhouette 2.1174:1; (vi) pennation: 1.529:4; (vii) fixingOfFolioleLeave:1,352:6; botanic name* is taken for the species instances. To each value taken by a criterion for plant instance, we defined an iconem. An optimization problem appears: minimize the number of both criteria and iconems for better visual representation of all 22 plants species, while still being able to distinguish them individually. We used Python scripts and Inkscape (vectorial) drawing softwares. In part, the methodology Neon [27], was used for conceptual modeling of Plant and Recipe before their formalization under protégé. By using plural techniques and processes of information search, a prominent place was made to revival and verbatim inquries. This gives to our models a sufficient level of invariability, and thus to our ontology ontoMEDTRAD.

3   Results

A silhouette is indispensable for a plant. For the iconic need, we admitted five (5) silhouettes to represent all 22 plants, given the wide variability of botanical description. Accordingly, an iconem has been designed for each silhouette like the Table 1 shows it.

Table 1.   Five iconems silhouettes selected.

Silhouette (plant types)	tree	shrub	palm	liana	grass/herb
iconem for Silhouette					

We must recognize visually the plant through its very characteristic traits. With the seven criteria, the 22 species plants have been represented by combining iconems. We generated the icons using a Python script with Owlready-2.0 python module for ontology-oriented programming [16]. This module allowed us to make used ontoCONCEPT-term (ontoMEDTRA, owl). For example, the icon for the plant *Azadirachta indica A. Juss.(Meliaceae)*, is obtained from a silhouette tree and an elliptical shape fruit (Fig. 1).

Fig. 1. Combination of iconems for building (generating) icon of Azadirachta indica A. Juss.

NB: The leaves are green in office, and the silhouettes black. The fruits and flowers can have colors of realist appearance. The "pennation" or not, and the layout of the leaves are in black color. The flower can change color depending on the realist appearance. Another execution of python script provides the plant icon by composing more iconems as Table 2 presents that.

Table 2. Icon of Azadirachta indica A._Juss (neem) based on seven criteria

Name_botanic	Silhouette	formOfFruit	colorOfFruit	colorOfFlower	formFolioleLeave	Penantion1		fixingOfFolioleLeave
Azadirachta indica A. Juss.(Meliaceae)	tree	elliptic	green	white, yellow	entireLanceolate	imparipinnate, paripinnate		opposed
icon or pictogram								

The axiomatisation of ontoMedtrad has been enriched with Object properties and Data properties within the meaning of ontology from Gruber [21]. We give an overview via Fig. 2.

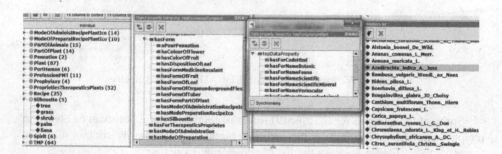

Fig. 2. ontoMEDRAD in protégé

In this work, the main concepts are Plant, Recipe, Ingredient, PartOfPlant, (FormPartOfPlant). Our selected set contains twenty two (22) anti-malaria plants in TM. FormPartOfPlant is like PartOfPlant, but with visual description. It more constant. In our context, an ingredient is an useful part of the medicinal plant. For the iconic need we determine **nine (9)** parts concerned notably *leaf, flower, fruit, stem/trunk, bark of stem/trunk, bark of root, root, sap, whole plant (grass)*. Ingredient can be formalized by a couple such *I (FormPartOfPlant, Plant)*. In application we will ensure the functional unicity of the ingredient. That means two ingredients are equal when they have the same couple's values. A set of ingredients forms the recipe on which we add preparation and administration methods. We can also add to it, the end form of preparation. Furthermore, in recipe, we must ensure that a set (singleton or not) of ingredients remains unique. An ingredient is unitary recipe. We have to avoid to get two recipes with the same set of ingredients (Table 3).

Table 3. Object properties for recipe definition.

domain	object properties	range	characteristic of object properties
Ingredient	hasFormPartOfplant	FormOfPartOfPlant	functional
Ingredient	hasBasePlant	Plant	functional
Recipe	hasForIngredient	Ingredient	no functional

In the plant icon construction, there is some difficult to integrate perceived reality related dimension. For that reason, in the recipe icon sketch, stem and trunk are been combined and denoted by the same iconem (Fig. 3).

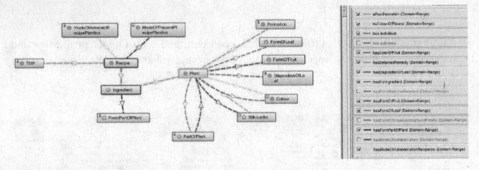

Fig. 3. Formalization of ontoMEDRAD: Plant and Recipe

Some of the iconems for the nine (9) forms of relevant useful parts can be absent in recipe icon. This is justified by the fact that plants not necessarily contain all these forms of parts. Figure 4 shows the list of those nine iconems.

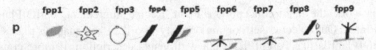

fpp = form of plant part ; P = IcoPlant; fpp1 = IcoLeaf; fpp2 = IcoFlower; fpp3 = IcoFruit; fpp4 = icoStem/trunk; fpp5 = icoBarkStem/trunk; fFpp6 = icoBarkRoot; fpp7 = icoRoot; fpp8 = icoSap; fpp9 = icoWholePlant.

Fig. 4. Nine icons: one for each form of plant's useful part

If P is in our selection of plants, then there exists at least one relevant form part of P, concerned by a recipe. The Table 4 illustrates a recipe (mTRecipe01), extracted from our ontoMEDTRAD. The mTRecipe01 is composed of two ingredients, i1 and i2.

Table 4. mTRecipe01 extracted from ontoMEDTRAD [20]

Plant (P)	Useful part (FPP)	Ingredient (I)	Recipe (R)	MP	MA
Azadirachta indica A. Juss.(Meliaceae)	Le	i1	mTRecipe01	Decoction	beverage
Senna occidentalis L. (Caesalpinaceae)	Le	i2			

Le: Leaf; MP: method of preparation; MA: method of administration

The Fig. 5 shows the iconic sketch of the recipe **mTRecipe01**.

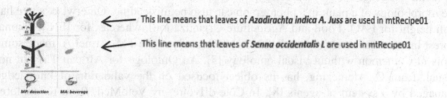

Fig. 5. Sketch icon of the recipe mTRecipe01

4 Discussion

In collecting data, we see that some renowned TMP, barely cover their determination to die with their secret [2]. Others TMP want a knowledge transmission to posterity. Between TMP, lack of trust, of mutual acceptance and knowledge sharing has been proven. Given the highly implicit and hidden character of TM, we have sensitized at least fifty (50) TMP for more openness and adherence to the project (in Côte d'Ivoire and Sénégal). In its completion, the TM discusses the moral, cultural, social and environmental dimension of the patient (overall well-being) [8]. It is sometimes used as lever for discoveries in MM, where most drugs obtained are synthetic products following a long chain of production (biology and active ingredients of medicinal plants). Thickeners, excipients, adjuvants and preservatives are products added. Between MM and TM, the procedures are different. This renders impossible the timely and automatic reuse of the existing terminological and ontological resources of MM, in our ontoMedtrad. Another specificity of the TM is that a TMP ensures inclusive two functions distinctly exerted in MM: he is both "doctor" prescriber and "pharmacist". During diagnosis for determining the disease, PMT adds metaphysical section and some socio-cultural and environmental determinants [7]. In some cases, the provision of health care by the TMP, is in the appropriate recipe form, sometimes extemporaneously. The exchange between patient and TMP is bidirectional, whereas the modern doctor [3] role, in facing the patient, is highly dominant.

After the characteristic traits of TM, degree of variability in botanic description is notorious. For the same medicinal plants, variant descriptions are given. This variability can lead to important differences and contradictions. This large degree of variability in botanic description and in TMP's point of views observed during the visits and collaboration, lead us to operate some choices in order to maintain the formal (computer uses) and visual firstness. *Lannea microcarpa,* part of our plants selection, is alternate and imparipinnate compound leaf, with 15 m high by PROTA (Plant resources of tropical Africa) [10], while the same individual plant is opposing leaf paripinnate with 10 m high according to a website [25]. The morphology of a plant species can depend on the habitat region, country. For example the tree *Adansonia digitata L* in Senegal, is physically strong and imposing, while in Côte d'Ivoire where it is more slender. This shows the limits or shortcomings to use realistic photographs as sublime means of visual recognition of medicinal plants. For this reason we proposed an iconic language rather than using photographs. The physical dimensions related to the morphology of a plant in a photograph can also be misleading. Otherwise, a tree has 5 m height for FAO (Food and Agriculture Organization), whereas, for IFN (National Forest Institute in France), it has 7 [23, 24]. Relatively to the TM, Armel A. made some tools in Cameroon without visual ontology [5]. An Ontology for African TM but not visual, from G. Atemezing, has its object focused on the validation of knowledge managed by a system of agents [8]. In Côte d'Ivoire, by VetoMed, Brou K. explores visual aspects, but does not contain an ontology [13]. In MM, the VCM from J.B. Lamy presents an iconic language for medical knowledge especially drugs, to help doctors for easy and speed reading, with visual ontology validated [16, 17].

5 Conclusion

We proposed an iconic compositional representation for the medicinal plant, the largest source in the recipes prescribed by the TMP. The botanical description is often varied to the same species. The discourse of TMP relative to the prescripted recipe from the same plants to cure the identical diseases, remains also variable. But the icons we proposed avoid this problem. The composition semi-formal, is an arduous task that must be based on a minimum of rules especially since we have a goal to integrate it into a semantic wiki for others categorizations and knowledge extraction. It's difficult, but surmountable. In perspective we must sit an iconic language in inferential goal for TMP, transcending linguistic barriers, text reading and writing. Sketch for iconic recipe is obtained in order to be achieved definitively by python program. Obviously, cover all concepts of TM, constitutes a true challenge. Another perspectives is the validation of the iconic language in two steps: the first with literate TMP group and the second with all TMP. Moreover, it seems that it would be more advantageous to indicate some realistic photos (without being reasoning objects), simply bound to icons obtained, in order to compensate the lack of education of TMP (mostly numerous), pending an acceptable level of standardization.

References

1. Lydie, A., et al.: Nephrolepis biserrata, une Ptéridophyte utilisée comme plante médicinale CI (2014)
2. Assi, L.A.: Abrégé de Médecine et pharmacopée africaines, CI, pp. 1–150 (2011)
3. Konan, A.: Place de la médecine traditionnelle dans les soins de santé primaires, (CI), pp. 54–118 (2012)
4. Amari, A., et al.: Adaptabilité des conditions d'enregistrement des médicaments génériques en CI aux médicaments traditionnels améliorés. J. sci., Lab. de galénique et législation pharmaceutique, UFR sciences pharma. et bio, Univ de Cocody, pp. 1–4 (2006)
5. Armel, A., et al.: Using METHONTOLOGY to build a deep ontology for african traditional medicine: first steps. Départ. Génie Informatique, IUT de Douala, Cameroun, pp. 1–8 (2012)
6. Nakamura, C., et al.: A taxonomy of representation strategies in iconic communication. Int. J. Hum. Comp. Stud. **70**(8), 535–551 (2012)
7. Atemezing, G., Pavón, J.: An ontology for African traditional medicine. In: Corchado, J.M., Rodríguez, S., Llinas, J., Molina, J.M. (eds.) International Symposium on Distributed Computing and Artificial Intelligence 2008 (DCAI 2008). Advances in Soft Computing, vol. 50, pp. 1–10. Springer, Heidelberg (2009)
8. Dozon, J.P.: Ce que valoriser la médecine traditionnelle veut dire, Polti. africaine, n° 28, pp. 1–12
9. Guastello, S.J., Traut, M., Korienek, G.: Verbal versus pictorial representation of objects human computer interface. Int. J. Man Mach. Stud. **31**, 99–120. Engineering, Springer, pp. 1–27 (1989)
10. Kerharo, J., et al.: pharmacopée traditionnelle sénégalaise: plantes médicinales et toxique (1974)
11. N'guessan, K., et al.: Screening phytochimique de quelques plantes médicinales ivoiriennes utilisées en pays Krobou, UFR Biosciences, Labo. Botanique., université de Cocody, pp. 5–1 5 (2009)
12. N'guessan, K., et al.: Étude ethnopharmacologique de plantes antipaludiques utilisées en médecine traditionnelle chez les Abbey et Krobou d'Agboville (Côte d'Ivoire) (2009)
13. Brou, K.M., et al.: VetoMed: un système expert à base d'icônes pour la médecine vétérinaire Traditionnelle, 8 p. (2014)
14. Appoh, K., et al.: Architecture d'un système de gestion des connaissances de la médecine traditionnelle: sysMEDTRAD, INP-HB Larima, UGB Lani, CARI, pp. 1–12 (2014)
15. Appoh, K., et al.: Modélisation conceptuelle d'une ontologie de la médecine traditionnelle (ontoMEDTRAD), INP-HB Larima, UGB Lani, CNRIA, pp. 1–5 (2014)
16. Lamy, J.B., Berthelot, H.: Ontopy: programmation orientée ontologie en Python. In: Actes du congrès d'Ingénierie des Connaissances (IC2015), Rennes, France (2015)
17. Lamy, J.B., Soualmia, L.F., Kerdelhué, G., Venot, A., Duclos, C.: Validating the semantics of a medical iconic language using ontological reasoning. J. Biomed. Inf. **4**, 615–667 (2013)
18. Arbonnier, M.: Arbres-arbustes-et-lianes-de-zones sèches de l'Afrique de l'Ouest (2002)
19. OMS/WHO: Stratégie de l'OMS pour la Médecine traditionnelle pour, 2014–2023, pp. 1–25 (2013)
20. Zerbo, P., et al.: Plantes médicinales et pratiques médicales au Burkina Faso:cas des Sanan (2011)
21. Gruber, T.: A translation approach to portable ontology specifications. Knowl. Acquis. Spec. Issue Curr. Issues Knowl. Model. **5**(2), 199–220 (1993)

22. Whiteside, J., Jones, S., Levy, P.S., Wixon, D.: User performance with command, menu, and iconic interfaces. In: Proceedings of the CHI 1985 Conference on Human Factors in Computing Systems, pp. 185–191 (1985)
23. https://fr.wikipedia.org/wiki/Arbre, (mars/16)
24. http://www.piaulealouer.com/cultbio/index.php/section-table/6-thematiques/55-arbre, (mars/16)
25. http://www.bamanan.org/index.php?option=com_content&view=article&id=81: commentaire-botanique-detaille&catid=3:linguistique&Itemid=3, (mars 2016)
26. http://www.who.int/mediacentre/factsheets/2003/fs134/en/, (mars 2016)
27. Suárez de Figueroa Baonza: M.C.: The NeOn methodology for ontology. In: Suárez-Figueroa, M.C., et al. (eds.) Ontology Engineering in a Networked World. Springer, Heidelberg (2012). doi:10.1007/978-3-642-24794-1_2

Technological Initiatives to Promote Science Growth in Mozambique

Marangaze Munhepe Mulhanga[1], Venâncio Massingue[2],
and Solange Rito Lima[1(✉)]

[1] Centro Algoritmi, Universidade do Minho, Braga, Portugal
{mmunhepe,solange}@di.uminho.pt
[2] Universidade Eduardo Mondlane, Maputo, Mozambique
venancio.massingue@uem.mz

Abstract. Deploying NREN infrastructures is considered a crucial step for fostering Science and Technology in Africa as it will allow to support advanced services for sharing science. For managing science components and players, the Current Research Information System (CRIS) has been proposed and adopted internationally. Understanding these concepts and applying them in the science ecosystem of developing countries will allow to foster science management in these countries, saving years of progress.

Facing the above, this paper discusses the challenges and strategies for the implementation of technological platforms for accessing science, taking Mozambique and its NREN as the primary goal. Answering questions such as "What is the current state of Science and Technology in Mozambique? What are the challenges and strategies to put Mozambique a step forward in science development?" is the aim of this research work. The proposals envisioned in this paper are sustained by the analysis of worldwide initiatives and recommendations regarding open access to science, CRIS inputs, the Portuguese and African context, and the Mozambican science and education ecosystem. This work also aims to provide insights for other developing countries by identifying good practices and international cooperation opportunities.

1 Introduction

Sharing knowledge in the information age is seen as a vehicle for the development of societies, being technological platforms and infrastructures for managing science used as a way of promoting the growth and dissemination of scientific production. In this context, it is important that the academic and scientific community take advantage of the benefits of advanced services provided by National Research and Education Networks (NRENs), with emphasis on Open Access (OA), since it allows to freely access academic or scientific literature using the Internet. Another aspect that should be highlighted in the knowledge management supporting service is the Current Research Information System (CRIS) concept, which should be considered to manage the scientific production of any institution. CRIS allows to provide evidence to funders and other entities, and

© ICST Institute for Computer Sciences, Social Informatics and Telecommunications Engineering 2018
T.F. Bissyande and O. Sie (Eds.): AFRICOMM 2016, LNICST 208, pp. 313–324, 2018.
https://doi.org/10.1007/978-3-319-66742-3_30

allows to measure the impact of the research carried out in the different research areas in an intelligent way.

Facing the above, it is important to look at international directives and the experience of countries which are at the forefront in terms of provision of connectivity and advanced services to the research and academic community. Portugal is recognized as a success case, due to the implementation of the national scientific OA repository (*Repositório Científico de Acesso Aberto de Portugal* - RCAAP) and the Online Knowledge Library (B-on). RCAAP and B-on are services supported by *Fundação para a Ciência ê a Tecnologia* - FCT (through *Fundação para a Computação Científica Nacional* - FCCN unit), the national entity responsible for managing the NREN, which provides high-speed connectivity and advanced services to academic and research institutions. These services have proved to be relevant to the production, sharing and dissemination of scientific production.

The challenges for deploying high-speed network infrastructures in Africa, including advanced services dedicated to the academic and scientific community, are still prominent compared to developed countries. The need for improving the quality in the higher education and research system also involves surveying the governmental strategies for science and technology, their funding and implementation. In view of the above, a careful study of the national repository of Mozambique, known as SABER, and the Mozambique Research and Education Network (MoRENet), the NREN of the country, is crucial as they will effectively support the work of the academic and scientific community of Mozambique.

The analysis of technological and scientific issues involving developing countries implies understanding science dimensions applied to each reality, the worldwide initiatives and potential cooperation synergies. Therefore, the present work discusses: (i) international initiatives for science sharing and success cases, such as the Portuguese experience on digital libraries and OA; (ii) CRIS directives and new trends; (iii) research and education network associations, with special emphasis to the UbuntuNet Alliance and AfricaConnect projects; and (iv) Mozambican strategy for science and technology. By interrelating these aspects and proposing an evolutive service model for open science in Mozambique, this work presents new perspectives to support the growth of science in this country, which can be extended to other developing countries.

The present article is structured as follows: Sect. 2 discusses the concepts related to the open access to scientific literature and research management issues, with emphasis on CRIS; Sect. 3 describes the Portuguese case study and Sect. 4 debates the African context; Sect. 5 discusses the technological guidelines for the evolution of open science in Mozambique; and conclusions are provided in Sect. 6.

2   International Initiatives for Science Sharing

The access to academic and scientific literature through digital libraries and open access repositories involves the storage of data in information systems and their access via NRENs. NRENs, providing either application and operational supporting services, represent the current trend of collaboration and sharing of scientific knowledge among various communities spread throughout the world, with emphasis on higher education institutions (HEIs), libraries, schools and, in some cases, government institutions.

2.1 Policies and Mandates

The definition of policies and mandates in the last years has been an important effort to foster OA adoption. In 2004, 34 countries members of the Organization for Economic Cooperation and Development (OECD) legitimized a Declaration on Access to Research Data From Public Funding, acknowledged the importance of OA to return the value resulting from public funding, and stressed that constraints imposed on the access to research data can influence negatively the quality of the results of science and innovation projects. With respect to the United States, the government of this country launched in 2013 a guideline through the Office of Science and Technological Policy recommending that federal agencies should organize their strategic plans of OA, i.e., that the results of research funded by public funds, including the research data, involving more than 100 million dollars should be made available in OA [1].

At European level, the European Union (EU) through the European Council (EC), continuing the 2008 FP7 Open Access Pilot project, instituted guidelines for EC funded projects regarding the improved access and re-use of data resulting from research. These guidelines stress the need for: (i) depositing research articles after peer-reviewing or manuscripts resulting from their projects in an online OA repository; (ii) effective actions to ensure free access to the same articles within 6 or 12 months (in case of publications in social and human sciences) after publication. These periods allow the scientific editors to ensure a return on investment and OA after the interdiction period has expired [2]. The Horizon 2020 Framework Program, being a recent funding program for research and innovation, highlights all the recommendations set out in previous programs concerning data and metadata in OA [3].

2.2 Research Management

Current Research Information System (CRIS) emerged as an information system of science and technology in which individual and professional information of researchers and professors, funding agencies, projects and scholarships, patents, data and products, equipment and services, are stored. CRIS is intended to assist users in registering, disseminating their work and making decisions in the course of the research [4,5]. The management of science based on CRIS can lead to multiple benefits, such as: (i) to provide administrators and science managers with tools to enable a better evaluation and report of scientific activity; (ii) to provide the academic and scientific community with means to manage their activities; (iii) to support professionals in the media, technology companies, civil society organizations and people in finding innovative ideas and interests that favor the fusion of science and society. It is within the scope of CRIS to make possible to obtain information on the results of the scientific production carried out in a given institution and its authors, and to know the ongoing activities, projects, departments, funds and portals, as a way of improving the visibility of the research outcome produced in the participant institutions. In this context, the CRIS components are depicted in Fig. 1(Left) [6].

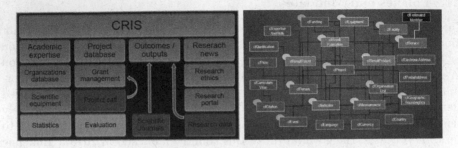

Fig. 1. CRIS ecosystem (Left) and CERIF model (Right). (Color figure online)

2.3 CRIS Evolution

The evolution of information systems for managing scientific activity has evolved, mostly in developing countries with a vast human resource capacity in ICT. Currently, the European Union (EU) has been a major engine of the debate on the development, integration and interoperability of services and platforms for managing science.

OpenAire - OpenAIRE represents an effort for the implementation of sustainable open communication technologies, assuming responsibility for the management and operation of all processes associated with the storage of research results. This involves storing and linking research results with scientific datasets and financing details in existing or future repositories, including the analysis, manipulation, monitoring and other tasks related to research results handling. In the context of Horizon 2020, OpenAIRE2020 represents a new phase in implementing and reinforcing the impact of the EC long-term OA policies, based on previous projects [7].

EuroCris, CERIF - In the European context, euroCRIS is an international non-profit organization whose aim is to promote cooperation among members for the sharing of knowledge in the areas of research and interoperability based on the use of the Common European Information Format (CERIF), the international format model for information in the context of scientific research [8]. In this perspective, CERIF encompasses several areas of interest related to knowledge management and OA, including CRIS scientific datasets and institutional OA repositories, covering the guidelines and best practices for CRIS relations between entities that are semantically defined [5,9]. In this context emerged

CERIF-XML, a language that sustains the exchange of information according to the recommendations of the EU Member States. The CERIF model, presented in Fig. 1(Right) [10], evinces the quality and robustness achieved in this model, since complex roles and relationships between the three main entities (in orange) may be defined, and other entities can be linked by role/date relationships to any or all of these three major entities. As an example, it is possible to obtain useful information, namely: "How many researchers participated in national research projects?"; "In which countries did they obtained the PhD degree?"; "How many scientific papers were published by the same researchers in year Y?".

3   NRENs and OA: The Portuguese Experience

In Portugal, FCT through FCCN unit, the managing body of the Portuguese NREN, is responsible for providing high-speed connectivity and advanced services to academic institutions and research centers. The Portuguese NREN was founded in 1987 and the evolution of its network infrastructure enabled the creation of projects supporting research and education services, especially in the last 10 years, including the access to scientific contents. With the creation of the *"Biblioteca do Conhecimento Online* (B-on)", in 2004, the digital library, supported by FCT, the national academic and scientific community can access a large number of scientific publications and electronic services. Before the creation of B-on, each Portuguese institution acquired its own scientific contents, being the contents only available to the users of the institution. Attending to this situation, the Ministry of Science and Education (then Ministry of Science of Technology) decided to centralize the budget for buying scientific publications and mandate the FCCN (currently FCT) to acquire and manage the access to information. The decision of purchasing access rights through a joint consortium proved to be advantageous as it allowed a stronger ability to negotiate with publishers. For the fulfilment of B-on mission, several entities have been working together, as represented in Fig. 2(left). B-on services are based on contents, which undergo processes of acquisition, access, support, management, evaluation and monitoring, as illustrated in Fig. 2(right).

Another service provided by FCT to NREN community is the RCAAP, the national OA repository created in 2009, available to increase the visibility, accessibility and dissemination of results from national scientific and academic activity. RCAAP is a meta-repository aggregating institutional repositories and journals, allowing free access to a vast number of scientific national publications. In 2010, to enhance the visibility of scientific contents in Portuguese idiom, a Luso-Brazilian memorandum was established, aggregating OA sources from Portugal and Brazil, and the annual CONFOA conference was created.

Currently, RCAAP has available the Institutional Repositories Hosting Service (*Serviço de Alojamento de Repositórios Institucionais* - SARI). SARI is a cloud-based repository service for institutions that do not want to assure technical aspects related to the implementation of repositories, such as servers, connectivity, maintenance, backups, upgrades and monitoring. This service is provided

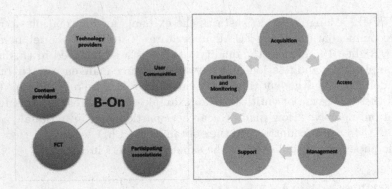

Fig. 2. B-on: (left) service entities; (right) a cycle of five processes

centrally, and institutions only have to worry with administrative aspects. From the 73 repositories participant in RCAAP, 22 are aggregated and 51 are hosted in SARI. Another service associated with SARI is the common repository, available for institutions that do not have their own repository due to their small size or low publications volume. Later on, institutions taking part of the common repository may evolve to a hosted repository, according to RCAAP policies. Apart from SARI, RCAAP supports a hosting service for scientific journals, available for institutions who want to create a journal and undergo its life-cycle, including the release of call for papers, peer reviewing and editing process.

In May 2016, FCT and Mozambique National Research Fund (NRF) signed the first protocol for cooperation between the two countries in the areas of science, technology and innovation. This protocol has resulted from the need to develop joint scientific and technological relations, which will bring mutual benefits to both institutions and their countries. This agreement recognizes the importance of science, technology and innovation in promoting the growth and competitiveness of the national economy, therefore, FCT and NRF aim to promote cooperation in these fields on the basis of equality and mutual benefit. This memorandum of understanding will operationalize the following key areas of collaboration: exchange of staff, scientists, researchers and experts; exchange of scientific and technological information, teaching and learning materials resulting from cooperation; conduct joint activities, including scientific conferences, symposia, workshops and other meetings; support joint research and technological development projects; facilitate scientific exchange among research institutions; exchange experience and expertise in information and communication technology for development; and promote the transfer of appropriate technology [11].

4   The African Context

Generically, NRENs have appeared many years ago with the aim of providing dedicated, high-speed networks to the academic and scientific community as a way to respond to the high communications costs and the lack of specific services of commercial operators. In the African context, NRENs began to be implemented just over 10 years ago, with South Africa at the forefront. However, a number of factors have pushed the African continent to the bottom regarding communication and services infrastructures, as well as on the sharing of global knowledge at both national and regional levels. The high cost of broadband access and the lack of fiber-based infrastructures at both national and international levels, have made it difficult to fulfill NRNs implementation phase, a situation that is changing due to the recent projects of international connectivity through submarines and terrestrial fiber optics cable connections. At a regional level, associations of NRENs have emerged, such as TERENA in Europe, Internet2 in the United States, and RedClara in Latin America.

In order to extend the network infrastructure to all African countries, two main regional NRENs have been created, namely the UbuntuNet Alliance in Eastern and Southern Africa, and WACREN in Western and Central Africa, which aim to provide a higher quality Internet with reduced costs, and to foster the sharing of knowledge among members, wherever they may be. The UbuntuNet Alliance currently has 15 members, and its creation in 2005 has enabled the community of member countries to share the challenges and experiences, considering their different contexts, and connect them to existing NRENs in the world. The TENET in South Africa, the KENET in Kenya and the MAREN in Malawi are success cases of NRENs operating in Africa. Regarding specific projects:

(i) the AfricaConnect project - The UbuntuNet Alliance Network was the first of its kind in Africa and was implemented between 2011 and 2015, supported by the European Commission. The AfricaConnect project expanded the existing network managed by the UbuntuNet Alliance. This network, presently, has 10 points of presence (PoPs), two of which delivering traffic in Europe (London, Amsterdam) and 8 PoPs within the regional backbone covering 7 countries members of the UbuntuNet Alliance area.

(ii) the AfricaConnect2 project - The plan defined for this project is to extend the network to all African countries and this initiative will serve to stimulate research in the global region. The social and economic differences of the involved countries is pointing out as a challenge in the execution of the project. AfricaConnect2 aims to support the development of high-capacity Internet networks for research and education across Africa. It builds on existing networks in East and Southern Africa and North Africa, and will extend connectivity to West and Central Africa. As a result, AfricaConnect2 will encompass the 3 geographical clusters and their respective regional networking organizations in coordination with Geant, UbuntuNet Alliance, WACREN and, in the North Africa, the Arab States Research and Education Network (ASREN), which operates for the League of Arab States in north. The budget for the AfricaConnect2 project will amount to e26.6m, e20m co-funded by the EC [12].

The higher education and research in Africa still needs external support for researchers and research centers to develop their projects to the level of the best that is done in the world. In this context, open access repositories and digital libraries allow researchers, even from isolated locations, as long as they have connectivity and available services, to access and share their knowledge on a global level. This is a reality that breaks down many barriers, allowing the involvement and the development of science in Africa at an equal level considering developed countries. For a long time, the access to information on the continent was scarce and, currently, the aim is to face the challenges of implementing OA platforms and associated policies so that the future looks more promising. Issues related to magazines and repositories, institutions and their departments, non-governmental organizations, national initiatives, editors, professional associations and research groups should also be considered. The production of OA Journals in Africa is still insufficient, according to the data available at the Open Access Journals (DOAJ) directory. African Journals Online (AJOL), the African directory of OA journals, created in 1998, is a non-profit organization based in South Africa, targeting health and agriculture as the most prevalent areas of research. In terms of free access to information, the Association of African Universities (AAU), the International Network for the Availability of Scientific Publications (INASP), the Research4Life and the Electronic Information for Libraries (EIFL) are organizations that have led the OA initiatives between the academic and research community. These organizations seek to create sustainable conditions to provide free or low cost scientific literature through agreements and partnerships with commercial publishers, and to establish or enhance the consortia of national libraries, the open access repositories, and the discussion and resolution of issues related to intellectual property rights.

5   Promoting Science in Mozambique

In Mozambique, ICT policies and strategies are recent, only started in 2000, focusing on solving local problems to improve the living conditions of citizens and the development of the country. In this context, the access to information and to scientific/academic production are also defined as relevant issues to frame the country in the global information society. The Science, Technology and Innovation Strategy of Mozambique(STISM) deserves a special attention in this developing scenario.

5.1   Open Access and the Repository SABER

Although it is recognized that the science academy plays a fundamental role in stimulating and disseminating the scientific production carried out in a country, the path to access the scientific literature in Mozambique is focused on the University Eduardo Mondlane (UEM). UEM was chosen to coordinate a consortium of universities (not officially created) to benefit from the support of the INASP project, managing the budget available for paying the access to scientific literature for all public and private higher education institutions in the country. Using this approach, Mozambique got the support of INASP to access 90% of publications having to pay only 10% of the real cost. From the relative analysis on the use of scientific publications, about 23,000 titles were accessed, totaling 3000 American dollars per year, which leads to a very low access rate, with downloads ranging from 5–10% per year. Thus, although having scientific information available, there are some challenges that need to be addressed, namely: (i) the investment in the training of technical staff in the libraries field; (ii) the creation of a common system that facilitates the integrated research in all databases, or where scientific literature is available; (iii) the inclusion of disciplines that encourage research culture throughout academic and scientific education; and (iv) the lack of a consortium of libraries where technicians and communities with similar interests could discuss the challenges of the access to scientific information. In particular, this last issue has led UEM to began in 2015 the creation of a consortium of HEIs and libraries but this initiative is still in its initial phase of registration of the member institutions. It should be noticed that there are particular areas of interest in which there was also the need to resort to other organizations to support the access to scientific literature in Africa, more specifically HINARI for biomedical, OARE for environment and AGORA for agriculture.

OA initiatives in Mozambique are recent and are the result of a major effort of UEM to promote access and knowledge sharing, and to make the academic and scientific production of the country's institutions visible. In this context, the first multi-institutional repository SABER was launched with the aim of collecting, preserving, aggregating and indexing the academic and scientific production carried out in higher education and research institutions in Mozambique. The SABER repository integrates six HEIs, including UEM. From the analysis carried out after 6 years of its creation, the repository contains about three thousand documents, of various types, including scientific articles, didactic materials, monographs and dissertations. From the analysis concerning the scientific contribution of each member institution, UEM is the institution with the largest number of documents deposited (98%), with the particularity that 78% documents deposited correspond to a period prior to the creation of SABER. Given these numbers and the lack of national policies on OA, it is crucial to understand and fight the existing obstacles that undermine the OA success in Mozambique.

5.2   Research Infrastructures and MoRENet

Within the scope of science and technology policies and strategies defined for Mozambique, the MoRENet project (the Mozambican NREN) was launched in 2006 in order to boost the evolution of the national science, technology and innovation system. In practice, the MoRENet project only started in 2008 after obtaining external financial support and went through several phases of implementation. At present, MoRENet deployment is as follows: (i) in terms of *network infrastructure*, MoRENet is based on fiber optic and SDH-STM technology with 5 Point of Presences (PoPs), 155 Mbps for the backbone as well as 34 Mbps for connecting institutions. It also adds 2 international links of 155 Mbps for shared Internet traffic, one for SEACOM and the other connecting the UbuntuNet Alliance network; (ii) in terms of *interconnected institutions and supported services*, at the beginning of 2016, 77 higher education institutions had been included all over the country, and the Internet was the main service provided. Presently, the efforts have been targeting the inclusion of other institutions and research centers, the analysis of the type of services to be provided, and the evaluation of the quality of service of the network.

During the different phases of MoRENet implementation, some challenges had to be overcome, namely: (i) the unavailability of operational equipment in the national market involved their external acquisition and corresponding delays; (ii) the metropolitan fiber optic infrastructure coverage was insufficient, which entailed carrying out engineering works to bring connectivity to the institutions; (iii) the cases of electric power failure in the country are frequent, as well as natural catastrophes, and it was necessary to carry out an adequate study and to implement emergency plans to improve network reliability.

5.3   Proposed Model for Science Growth in Mozambique

This section is devoted to present a model for fostering science growth in Mozambique which considers the multiple dimensions of science and takes into account specific challenges in the country that impairs science growth. In particular: (i) the lack of governmental and institutional policies covering OA and management issues, ranging from science to human resources and their qualification, is a reality in Mozambique; (ii) the need for a comprehensive metropolitan fiber optical network throughout the country is urging, as well as the creation of strategies to early respond to the acquisition of network equipment facing the country financial and technological dependence; (iii) regarding higher education and research institutions, the lack of national and institutional mandates and strategic policies for OA end up being factors that prevent the promotion of science in the country.

In this way, inspired by the OA project in Portugal RCAAP [13], an open science model and recommendations to respond to the lack of OA services and to take advantage of the existing NREN infrastructure in Mozambique are here proposed:

(i) the creation of a repository service, or the migration of SABER, into MoRENet, available to all the institutions of this NREN and being centrally managed. This brings innumerable benefits in technical and operational terms, leaving to the member institutions the tasks of documental and workflow management; (ii) for institutions with a reduced volume of publications, the creation of a common repository integrated in this repository service will be advisable; (iii) the ministry of science and technology still lacks specific guidelines regarding OA, as only recommendations for scientific knowledge dissemination were provided. Therefore, it is important that the census of rectors and the academy of sciences are involved in the actions carried out by higher education institutions, the Ministry of Science and Technology, and MoRENet; (iv) in the case of MoRENet, the QoS analysis and continuous performance monitoring is crucial to ensure that, in the future, the institutions can discard the existing connectivity services through commercial operators and that they can contribute to the economic sustainability of MoRENet. The implementation of new services, the increase of the national and international Internet access bandwidth and the reliable connectivity of the member institutions depends on a sustainable NREN; (v) the lack of technical librarians is another reality in the country and the training of specialized personal in this area to support the academic and scientific community, and content management is mandatory; (vi) a national database of researchers, similarly to Lattes in Brazil and DeGois in Portugal, should be implemented. In addition, the new trends of CRIS should be followed in the science management information system; (vii) as regards research data, in the African context, South Africa is at the frontline, with the largest number of OA repositories, being the only country with a data repository, the South African Data Archive (SADA) [14]. To consider this case study and sharing experiences is also crucial to understand and foster science in developing countries.

6   Conclusions

To efficiently manage scientific activity in developing countries and gain a global and consistent view of science participants and outcomes, the approach for NRENs, OA and CRIS needs to be rethought. In this context, this paper discussed the issues related to the evolution of science in developing countries, with emphasis on the implementation of NRENs, CRIS and OA at a global level of democratization of information access. Portugal represents a success case in terms of efforts in these areas, being here detailed and serving as a guide for this study, which had Mozambique as the main focus. For this purpose, recommendations for promoting scientific production, the sharing and disseminating of the research carried out in Mozambique were pointed out through an evolutive model for science growth in this country. This paper has also discussed the challenges and main resources for accessing information in Mozambique, to guide the proposal of recommendations for the adequate growth of science in Mozambique. These recommendations may serve as a basis for application in other developing countries, aiming at promoting their economic, scientific and social development.

Acknowledgement. This work has been supported by COMPETE: POCI-01-0145-FEDER- 007043 and Fundação para a Ciência e Tecnologia within the Project Scope: UID/CEC/00319/2013.

References

1. Stebbins, M.: Expanding public access to the results of federally funded research. Office of Science and Technology Policy (2013)
2. Directory of Open Access Journals (DOAJ). http://www.doaj.org
3. Guidelines on open access to scientific publications and research data in horizon 2020. European Commission, December 2013

4. Clements, A., McCutcheon, V.: Research data meets research information management: two case studies using (a) pure CERIF-CRIS and (b) eprints repository platform with CERIF extensions. Proc. Comput. Sci. **33**, 199–206 (2014)
5. Simons, E.: EuroCRIS and CERIF. The importance of an international standard metadata model for research information. Slovak Centre of Scientific and Technical Information (CVTI SR) (2014)
6. Moreira, J.M.: Eco-systems of research information systems: a global perspective. euroCRIS (2013)
7. Houssos, N., Jörg, B., Dvořák, J., Príncipe, P., Rodrigues, E., Manghi, P., Elbæk, M.K.: OpenAIRE guidelines for CRIS managers: supporting interoperability of open research information through established standards. Proc. Comput. Sci. **33**, 33–38 (2014)
8. Guillaumet, A.: Research information systems: what's new? euroCRIS (2015)
9. Jeffery, K., Houssos, N., Jörg, B., Asserson, A.: Research information management: the CERIF approach. Int. J. Metadata Semant. Ontol. **9**(1), 5–14 (2014)
10. EuroCRIS: The International Organisation for Research Information (2015). http://www.eurocris.org/
11. Only available in Portuguese, May 2016. https://www.fct.pt/noticias/index.phtml.en
12. UbuntuNet Alliance: What is UbuntuNet Alliance? Version 16, September 2014
13. Mulhanga, M.M., Lima, S.R., Massingue, V., Ferreira, J.N.: Expanding scientific knowledge frontiers: open repositories in developing countries supported by NRENs. In: Rocha, Á., Correia, A.M., Tan, F.B., Stroetmann, K.A. (eds.) New Perspectives in Information Systems and Technologies, Volume 1. AISC, vol. 275, pp. 127–136. Springer, Cham (2014). doi:10.1007/978-3-319-05951-8_13
14. Van Schalkwyk, F., Willmers, M.A., Czerniewicz, L.: Open data in the governance of South African higher education. Social Science Research Network (2014)

The Shortcomings of Globalised Internet Technology in Southern Africa

David L. Johnson[1] and Gertjan van Stam[2]([⊠])

[1] Meraka, Council of Scientific and Industrial Research (CSIR),
Cape Town, South Africa
djohnson@csir.co.za
[2] Scientific and Industrial Research and Development Centre (SIRDC),
Harare, Zimbabwe
gvanstam@sirdc.ac.zw

Abstract. Network protocols and applications have mostly been developed in and for a Western context and usually have an embedded set of assumptions about network performance and availability. As a result web-browsing, cloud-based services, live voice and video over IP, desktop applications and software updates often fail or perform poorly in (rural) areas of Southern Africa. This paper uncovers some of the reasons for this poor performance such as Windows TCP failing to reach capacity in high-delay networks, long DNS delays or time-outs and applications such as Office365 assuming constant connectivity to function, and describes them, set in the Southern African contexts. We address the issue of colonisation in ICT context and show the extend of such in the area of networking. These observations provide strong motivation for Africa-based engineering research to ensure that future network protocols and applications are context-sensitive, adaptive and truly global.

Keywords: Internet · Technology · Context · Africa · TCP/IP

1 A Critique of Internet Technology from an African Position

The global society relies heavily on the use of technologies to breach the imperatives of physical distances [1]. Especially Information and Communication Technologies (ICTs) are instrumental in connecting people irrespective of location, in the so-called Information Society. The assessment of the interrelationships between technologies and society depend on the academic approach and philosophical perspectives one subscribes to. In his meta-analysis of various approaches, Wolfgang Hofkichner [2] observes an academy engaged in a battle of theories, mostly bifurcated in what he calls *projectivisitic* social theories informed by social constructivism and *reductionistic* natural theories linked to technological determinism. In the mean time, society moves on. In their effort to link more users to their service platforms, corporate businesses drive target

© ICST Institute for Computer Sciences, Social Informatics and Telecommunications Engineering 2018
T.F. Bissyande and O. Sie (Eds.): AFRICOMM 2016, LNICST 208, pp. 325–338, 2018.
https://doi.org/10.1007/978-3-319-66742-3_31

settings in provisioning of access to the internet. These targets mostly address issues of connectivity, bandwidth and affordability [3,4]. Subsequently, several countries have set goals for internet access in their national laws, e.g. South Africa Connect [5].

Internet, in many narratives, is regarded crucial as an enabler of human rights like the freedom of expression and opinion, among others. The inventor of the internet, Vint Cerf [6] agrees with this notion. However, he argues, internet should be considered as a tool and not be positioned as a right itself. Tim Unwin [7] indicates that the ongoing and growing disparities in access and usability of ICTs are an important source of accelerating inequalities. He quantifies a growing gap in subscribers to mobile networks, between the so-called developed and least developed countries, till 2012. Also, he observes that technological advances in the richer countries of the world generally outstrip those in the less affluent countries. From his analysis, he derives that "the rich have been able to gain the benefits, leaving the poorest and most marginalised ever further behind" [7, p. 5].

In our African context, the utilisation of ICTs is affected by persistent poor user experiences that result from a myriad of environmental, skills and cultural factors [8–11]. There appears to be a lack of African expressions of technology [12] and a contextualised wording and local framing of the use of ICT [4]. Currently, African contributions are sub-alternalised in a dominant *lingua franca* or a single story of a globalised technology use. For technology to be truly globalised, we argue, ICTs deployed outside of their context-of-design must be subjected to a post-colonial critique. In this paper, we apply such a critique. From a reflexive stance and technical laboratory research, we discuss some of the shortcomings of internet technology in the African setting. We propose that the current and ongoing inadequacy of globalised internet technology is a sign of super-colonialism in our times. In this document, we provide insights to some of the observations focused on fundamental technical misalignments, as they are harvested from operational research in our rural environments. We endeavour to formulate integrative narratives to breach the disjunct of social and natural research approaches. Specifically, we expose the lack of contextualisation of the Transmission Control Protocol (TCP) and its effect on rural users in Southern Africa.

2   Methodology

This paper is based upon longitudinal, transdisciplinary and mixed-methods research in rural Africa, since 2003. The methods involve Participatory Action Research on internet access and wireless networks since the year 2000 and Extended Case Method analysis and technical laboratory work since 2010 [13,14]. Most of the technical findings in this paper involve retrospective analysis of data from the LinkNet network at Macha Works in Zambia, immersion in rural and urban environments in Zambia, Zimbabwe and South Africa, visits to various (rural) sites throughout Southern Africa, and literature reviews. Also, this paper draws upon laboratory simulations of the behaviour of internet systems in rural contexts. In our ethnographic work, we consider ICTs to interact with multi-level and multi-actor realities. We approach the patchwork of actors and dynamics as being entangled in techno-economic, social and political processes in order to identify issues that warrant exploration. Specific issues, like the quantitative and qualitative analysis of TCP effects, are assessed in reflexive ethnography and lab-based technical exploration.

3   Observations from an African Context

Many persons in Southern Africa lack basic ICT access, especially those at the so-called bottom-of-the-pyramid, as we witness ourselves in our in-situ research. Those in the development-scene (e.g. ICT4D) and in the corporate world (e.g. Basic Access, and Google Loon), often in an Oriental framing [15], seem to regard access provisioning as the last frontier: a market with opportunities for solutions. This battle for the so-called unreached and underserviced rages on. The discourse appears mostly framed in foreign languages with foreign interpretations of values, where renderings of aspects like freedom and democracy are at variance with the community views of the disenfranchised on morality and participation [16,17].

The perception of realities in the lived environment in rural Africa is often far removed from an epistemology that is dominant in ICT producing countries [4,12,18–20]. Andrew Feenberg [21] argues that technologies represent an embodiment of social constructs, created by people for specific purposes. Contemporary practice seems to turn this around: technologies appear to frame our social worlds (cf. [22]). The mobile phone, for instance, has been invasive, constitutive and transformative in Africa (cf. [23]). Kentaro Toyama [24] gives vivid descriptions of how ICTs force local world-views, concepts and meanings to interact with foreign concepts and expectations framed in foreign philosophies, concepts and language. Therefore, those dwelling outside the technology producing centres must cope with technology developed in an extant framing. Tim Unwin, David Nemer, and others give heed to the underlying clash of paradigms that results in widening digital divides and digital exclusion [18,25,26]. Nicola Bidwell [27] shows how the continuation of a history of colonialism and meanings embedded in ICTs is disruptive to local communication practices and results in a disconnect that reifies knowledge, disembodies voices and neglects established rhythms of life in an African village. Through ICTs, African communities interlink with a dominant, Western-centric view of the world, without—as Mark Graham [28] shows—much local content to interact with. In previous work analysing the network traffic in LinkNet's network in rural Macha, Zambia, we showed that most traffic in Macha remained within the village [29]. Also, we showed how the cultural challenges amalgamate with environmental constraints such as for electricity supply and other supply chain logistics and skills constraints in support of local ICT practitioners [20,30].

Within what Galtung [31] calls 'center-countries', especially in its centres, perceptions of internet performances seem positioned as being 'uniform'. Such uniformity implicitly assumes the availability of high quality bandwith options, relative low latencies, and an abundant electricity supply [32]. However, outside this realm, in so-called 'periphery-countries', especially in the periphery of the periphery-countries, realities are more diverse, with bandwidth options low, latencies high, and electricity in short supply.

Sabelo Ndlovu-Gatsheni [33] shows how Africa harbours multiple, competing world-views. We recognise a highly varied dialectic where multiple world-views and various positivist and interpretivist approaches compete. As a result, African practice often contends with many definitions and meanings expressed in the same continuum [18,34]. In the use of technology, these various ways of understanding come to loggerheads. Most technologies are created in a culture and context foreign to the African settings. Susan Wyche [35] shows how users long for contextual designs, and have their inputs ready. However, the culture and context of technology producing areas have particular—often oriental [36]—views on how to regard human needs [37] and others [38]. In short, orientalism combined with imperialistic practice has left its African legacy through the practice of colonialism [39]. Current coloniality in both the center and the periphery is the remnant of a history of domination, exploitation, and othering [40]. Paul Dourish and Scott Mainwaring [22] argue that the contemporary ubiquitous computing practice aligns with such a colonial intellectual tradition.

The facilities of ICT—both in their positive and negative aspects—are a most significant fact of life in the current time frame and in the global village. The technical performances of computer operating systems, network access points and internet connectivity are framed and chained as per Open Systems Interconnection Model (OSI Model), each layer and its interconnections influence the final usability by technology users. Long-term experience and observations of the introduction and growing presence of ICT in rural environments in Southern Africa sensitised us to the complexity of issues involved in this myriad of social realities and varied understandings. For instance, we recognised how technical nomenclatures and a whole range of methodologies result in a myopic understanding [9,12,18,19]. It is in the actual use of ICT within African environments that the sheer complexity and mismatch of the design and practice comes to the fore [8,19,29,41,42].

3.1 Technical Shortcomings in Rural African Internet Networks

In our daily practices in South Africa, Zimbabwe and Zambia, and during travels on the continent interacting with Africans outside of the metropolitan, we encounter an unabated stream of dissatisfied users of internet access, network services and applications. Although apportioning of guilt is not common in most African cultural expressions [43], the users we met invariably complain of a *slow internet*. Whatever the case, whether ageing or new computers or advertised high or low bandwidth network access connections, users in disenfranchised areas invariably report anecdotes of experiences that feature 'slow or no response', using devises and applications connected to the internet. These complaints remain anecdotal, as there is a general lack of elongated academic research, respectfully situated within disenfranchised areas in Africa. In our research, we have quantified the complaints in the case of the LinkNet network at Macha Works in Zambia. We concluded that, indeed, the internet can be labelled as slow, due to issues with TCP in high delay networks [8]. We observed that service interruptions are regularly experienced with video streaming, store and forward services, embedded services, banking applications, office software, among others. Also, as the applications go through frequent patches and upgrades, the user experience for the same application can change from version to version.

The persistence of the complaints over the years amazed us; this does not align with an Africa generically framed in a narrative of explosive growth, linked to the world with an ever-increasing amount of cables and higher speeds. Although we spend much collaborative effort in longitudinal research and development to facilitate contextual embedded network access for over 10 years, with community deposits of information and international academic scrutiny [13,14], the complaints remain.

We notice a continued reliance on mixed and ageing networks (GPRS, 3G, Very Small Apperture Terminal (VSAT), varieties of WiMax and multi-hop links) with poor performance aggravated by an installed base of older computer systems, relative low-grade devices, and a growing share of web-interfacing and cloud-based services [44]. An average web page size in 2012 was 68 times larger than the average size in 1995 [14, p. 86]. The inequality in the availability of bandwidth has grown three-fold in the last 10 years [7]. This is further aggravated by a growing populace accessing the internet. We conclude that there remains a defacto constant: rural networks feature congestion, high latency and poor throughput or a complete lack of availability.

3.2 Performance Deteriorations Inherent to Contemporary Transmission Control Protocol/Internet Protocols and Services

Our investigations centered on the shortcomings of the end-to-end connectivity provided by the Transmission Control Protocol/Internet Protocol (TCP/IP) and the performance of Directory Name Services (DNS). These protocols and services are among the basic building blocks of the internet. Due to the general constraints of doing research in rural areas, mostly devoid of financial or research resources, we relied on the opportunistic use of facilities, wherever and whenever available. Our first findings were presented at the Africomm conference in Cameroon, in 2012 [9].

Among the main technical hurdles remains latency [8]. Latency of at least 400 ms is introduced in case satellite connectivity. This latency is unavoidable due to the large distances between a geo-stationary satellite and the connectivity hub, due to multi-hop environments, and the frequent use of low-grade equipment with large buffering and processing-time overheads; In rural Africa, one finds all kind of equipment, including poor quality hardware platforms and devices, often with outdated and unpatched software [45].

Recently, Zaki et al. [46] confirmed our suspicion of the significance of the problems that result from the architecture of Directory Name Services (DNS). In previous work [9], we quantified the poor performance of TCP outgoing links on the Windows operating system compared to other Operating Systems (OS) such as Linux and MacOS in the LinkNet network in Zambia. Subsequent simulation in lab-environments confirmed the significant negative effects of high network delay on Windows 7 and XP machines; internet throughput in these Windows OS is unfairly disadvantaged and this effect is amplified even further when there is a mix of Windows and Linux flows present. The simulation made use of a Windows or Linux virtual machine connecting to a Linux Virtual machine over a simulated 1 Mbps link. Table 1 presents these results for a network without delays and a network with an introduced delay of 1 s. The latter is a typical delay we observed on the satellite network during peak usage periods.

Table 1. Simulation results showing TCP/IP throughputs for Linux and Windows flows in a network, single and mixed.

No delay introduced (10 ms systemic delay)	
Linux TCP flow only	892 kbps
Linux TCP flow with Windows flow added	822 kbps
Windows TCP flow only	968 kbps
Windows TCP flow with Linux flow added	151 kbps
With 1 s delay introduced	
Linux TCP flow only	860 kbps
Linux TCP flow with Windows flow added	858 kbps
Windows TCP flow only	110 kbps
Windows TCP flow with Linux flow added	57 kbps

Further investigation from 2014 until 2016—with the help of engineers at Microsoft Research Laboratory in the USA—exposed the underlying cause of the problem. Windows 7 and Windows XP use a default TCP receive-window of 16 kB while the receive-window 'auto-tuning' is disabled by default. For a 1-second link delay, the result is a maximum throughput of $16 \, kB \times 8 \, bits/1 \, s = 120 \, kbps$. This is similar to the 110 kbps seen in the simulation. Linux, on the other hand, has a default maximum TCP receive-window of 128 kB. This results in a maximum throughput of $128 \, kB * 8 \, bits/1 \, s = 1,024 \, kbps$. Furthermore, Linux has the receive-window 'auto-tuning' enabled by default.

Even upon enabling the default receive-window in Windows or enabling its auto-tuning, the TCP protocol—TCP New Reno, used by Windows 7—uses a delay-based congestion-window that adjusts throughput according to the Round Trip Time (RTT) of the last TCP packet. This makes Windows more sensitive to high delays. Linux, however, uses a different version of TCP—TCP CUBIC—that changes its congestion-window on the basis of the last occurring congestion event. As a result, Linux is less susceptible to high delays. Further investigation with Windows 8 and Windows 10 OS showed that these operating systems use the same conservative default TCP values, although they use a slightly improved TCP protocol called TCP Compound.

Modern satellite networks make use of TCP acceleration techniques, so-called TCP proxies. These proxies are implemented in the satellite modems and blur the distinction between the performance of Linux and Windows. These acceleration techniques create a virtual version of the network end-point on the client side of the satellite modem in order to cause the network to rapidly increase the TCP congestion-window and hence accelerate the throughput of the upload. However, our experiments throughout Southern Africa confirmed the issues resulting in poor performance of outgoing traffic for Windows OS persist in GPRS/Edge/3G networks as well as multi-hop wireless networks and legacy satellite modems.

The described findings affect outgoing connections only and hamper user experiences when using the internet, particularly severely when doing cloud-service uploads or using VoIP services. We observed frustrated users when they did try to upload data or used VoIP services like Skype, on Windows machines. Some users in LinkNet network became hostile to the LinkNet support staff, upon the suspicion that they were deliberately slowing down traffic for users using Windows computers compared to users utilising Apple computers or other Linux based OS, like Ubuntu. This suspicion persisted, even though the logical and technical explanation for the experiences where explained by engineers.

With Windows being the dominant OS in Africa—there are lots of legacy systems based on widely available copies of Windows-XP or Windows 7—the compromised performance of Windows' TCP/IP implementation is a significant issue. This problem is compounded by the fact that TCP/IP is continuously being developed for improved performance in high-bandwidth networks [47], potentially creating further difficulties for 'slow' networks.

In further research, we confronted the assumption of always available afford-able bandwidth for Operating Systems and Applications-updates on computers, phones, tablets and other computing devises. These updates use precious data, depleting users' data-bundles. Updates often start/stop and restart due to poor and failing data connections [8]. Users are confused because their data is used up by a process that they had no control over. We noticed that standard web proxies which could cache these updates are either not in place or are not configured correctly to be able to cache update file types. For example, the squid-proxy requires an additional entry to match .cab, .msi, .exe and .apk file types for updates. Even when the additional entries are in place, sometimes delta-updating used by some update processes will cause a cache to miss. To solve the problem of updates consuming user's data, modified and smarter caching at the internet gateway is required. Such caching stores popular updates. Possibly, public wireless access points could be placed in various places where connectivity is challenging to provide users with a local update for their device. As to make the case for more localized caching and clouds (cloudlets) to support the strong locality in the network, we developed VillageShare to allow local users to share content with each other locally without use of the internet connection beyond the gateway [44].

4   User Experience Compromised by Misaligned Internet Technologies

Technology research tends to build upon a perspective derived from research localised in center-countries [18,19,36]. Therefore, the average network performance and user experience observed in such environments pan out in the design and generic settings of software. In such relative affluent areas, in general, users are connected to low latency networks with relatively high speed connections with cloud-servers geographically relatively close-by.

Browsers like Google Chrome are set to show a web-page when all components of the web page have been received. In the Southern African environment, this means that frequently more than 10 s pass before the first information appears on the user's screen. The user calls this 'slow internet', although the actual transfer speeds might be relative high.

Web-pages embed calls for content from many different sources. Each call involves a DNS request and due to many requests, the time for the electronic signals to travel the physical distance to far-away servers, and the computing processing times, significant delays are a natural phenomena.

Cloud-services necessitate the information to travel vast distances, even if the recipient of the information is in the same community. Therefore, cloud-services add to the challenges in usability and user experiences in Southern Africa. Many internet services and products such as Google and Facebook, restrict access to a secure version of their web sites. This adds further delays to the web experience of users in Africa due to the need for requesting and processing of security certificates.

Google has set its services to time-out after a (perceived) lack of response from the client to prevent too many hanging connections. Web browsers also have default time-out values and keep-alive values. By default, these are set for typical Western networks with low latency. Due to the physical distance of Southern Africa to many network servers with the requested data, these default time-out settings can cause web pages to respond with a 'timed-out message'. In a VSAT environment, high latency is a natural given en latencies above 1 s are common. In a congested network using a satellite connection, these delays can be higher than 10 s [8,46]. Time-outs in services cause frustration and wasted internet expenses.

News applications, video applications, and software like Microsoft Office365 appear to have embedded protocols with various and non-standard time-out settings. If one of these settings times out before all interactions are finished, the user will not receive the service requested. The behaviour of the application thus cannot be relied upon. For instance, a time-out of a user licence check can disable Office365's ability to save ongoing work. In general, designers in bandwidth rich and latency low environments do not necessarily design their systems to allow local customisation and optimisation for users in bandwidth constrained and high latency environments. The fall out of these issues are real; Relationships in communities suffer, as performance differences motivate community members to accuse engineers of unfairly disadvantaging specific users.

Technological representation Mis-aligned with Language in Southern Africa

'This internet is slow' is a general statement, understood by many on the African continent. This statement, however, does not necessarily translate well into a cause and effect designation addressing the underlying issues. The technical nomenclature provided for by the (foreign designed) systems and the labelling they represent do not align with a local/African nomenclature of technology. In Southern Africa, the Bantu family of languages has a different representation of concepts. Languages tend to refer to living and movement, while European languages refer to things and allow for a deconstruction of realities [48,49]. Therefore, there appears no relationship to the (wording of) the Southern African user experience and what is needed to communicate with designers to improve the system (cf. [27,50,51]). A tool-set or an automation of context-adapted tests for adjusting application settings according to the particular link-specificities is not available. In February 2016, in Harare, a Shona speaking ICT-expert working in rural areas in southern Zimbabwe told one of us: "When I explain my mission, I find myself unable to translate English words like 'web-page' or 'application', thus I switch between Shona and English. However, my audience, with whom I wish to develop an application, does not use English much. They appear not to comprehend these English words."

The inter-cultural mix of meanings does not translate the user experience from African users into a language that the designing engineers—mostly in other environments and context—can understand. An engineering not geared for the Southern African reality and its social constructs, dis-empowers African engineers to engage with these challenges [12]. This dis-empowerment fuels an imperialist/colonialist narrative embedded in a White Saviour Syndrome, vocalising the need to 'bring technology' for the benefit of 'the other' [36,52]. As a result engineers from technology producing countries feel sanctified to fly into Africa for research, training and 'to solve issues', as technical assistants. Only when engineering companies engage meaningfully with African realities, empowering indigenous research and development in (rural) Southern Africa, can this disempowering spiral be broken [12,18].

ICT Standards Insensitive to Location and Community Contexts

As the dynamics of a networked society aids the centralisation of power, it needs a conscious effort to guard the ethical principles of neutrality, non-discrimination, equity, and reciprocity. All involved in the value chains of ICT production need the capacity to communicate over the various divides that separate people. Reflecting on an African value as Ubuntu, this can involve catering for shared identities and communal love [53]. Driven by its moral value, in general, African engineers aim to withstand the drive of self-aggrandisement and to assure a truly global and diverse community of all stakeholders and interlocutors [20]. Incorporation of previously disparate views, e.g. through listening to the subaltern, is the future source of corporate (= incorporating all) development, social responsible behaviour, and just and sustainable progress.

We see some hints of incorporating a localisation aspect in the operations of technology. For instance, Google provides for browsing on slow links in Gmail, allowing access to a less-complex web-interfacing. True localisation needs development and testing on site and in context, in an African laboratory and/or community, to see if the OS/application/hardware is truly globalised. To our knowledge, such a laboratory does not exist. Such a technical laboratory should operate in real-world, main stream (rural) African conditions, incorporating real challenges of electricity, connectivity, environment and business context in their daily operations. Many developers appear to 'have heard about Africa', but are void of an embodied experience of African contexts, meanings and effects over an extended period of time.

In an effort to alleviate the TCP/IP disadvantages in Windows and other highlighted problems, we propose that standards be developed to allow operating systems and protocols to query or check the context and assess if the system is connecting over a relatively slow/high delay link. Upon understanding the context, the technologies, such as operating systems, can evoke a contextualised TCP/IP, DNS caching, and web browsing.

Shortcomings Invisible for 'Out-of-Context' Research and Development
Many 'cause-and-effects', in reality, involve a complex chain of events. Due to the shortcomings of globalised internet in Southern Africa, the regular short-falling of realities with respect to promised user-experiences challenges the chain of engineering causes—in this case, poor TCP/IP performance, and DNS induced delays—, the performance of low grade equipment, and the underlying designs. To gain an understanding, one must be able to switch between paradigms, as they present themselves in the various parts of the world [18]. The ultimate cause of the shortcomings, we claim, is the exclusion of the voices from so-called non-technology producing countries, especially from Sub-Saharan Africa. This major omission leads to unlinked, uncontextualised and ultimately unsuitable technologies in Southern Africa. Soliciting complaints from individual users does not solve this conundrum, as such practice does not align with many cultures in Southern Africa [20,53,54]. However, the daily user experience of users in Southern Africa is consistent, albeit at variance with what users in affluent geographical areas might experience. Even the meaning of terminology like ICT or internet might be at variance, e.g. Facebook can be regarded 'the internet', with the complex aspects of coloniality playing subversive roles [33]. Thus, there are many variances and aspects influencing perceptions of understanding of causes and effects that inform the shortcomings of globalised internet in Southern Africa.

Learning from the experiences of an international health research centre situated in rural Macha, Zambia, and research at Macha Works in the same community, we experienced the benefits of research facilities to research, design and test technologies in context. Initiatives like Living Labs are promising in their efforts to circumvent the trap of localised activities being determined by a distant centre [55]. For truly globalised technologies, it is important to come to terms with, and incorporate, the diversity of contexts and experiences. We need a global understanding of a locally embedded, healthy ICT systems, in the same way that we need a locally embedded, healthy healthcare system for communities and people.

5   Conclusion

This paper gives examples of how major components in contemporary Information and Communication Technologies do not align with an African context and disenfranchise the Southern African user in ordinary circumstances. Although most users rely on such technologies to participate in a globalising world, the paper shows how the basic networks building blocks provided do not perform well in Southern Africa. Major applications, such as leading operating systems, do disenfranchise the Southern African user. More so, the paper shows how language, standards, and paradigms are major hurdles to learn from the user experience in Africa.

The impaired TCP/IP, DNS and web browser issues coming to light in Southern Africa are a general issue of the failure of global non-localised technology. Contemporary technologies fail to incorporate all experiences, perceptions and human intents, in an inclusive manner.

This paper poses the quest of changing the engineering attitude from considering technologies useful to Southern Africa to an attitude of developing technologies with Africa. Globalised technology would be sensitive to its context and is not 'one size fits all'. Apart from the obvious need to address current shortcomings in network protocols, operating systems and software applications, the paper calls for contextual Africa-based engineering research and development to ensure the development of network protocols and applications that are context-sensitive, adaptive and truly global.

References

1. Castells, M.: Information technology, globalization and social development for social development. In: UNRISD Conference on Information Technologies and Social Development, Geneva, Switzerland, 1999. United Nations Research Institute for Social Development, June 1998
2. Hofkirchner, W.: A taxonomy of theories about ICTs and society. TripleC **8**(2), 171–176 (2010)
3. Jorge, S., Goldstein, J.: The affordability report 2013. In: Alliance for Affordable Internet (A4AI) (2013)
4. van Stam, G.: Framing ICT access in rural Africa. In: 11th Prato CIRN Conference, 13–15 October 2014, Prato, Italy (2014)
5. Carrim, Y.: Electronic communciations act, 2005 (act no. 36 of 2005). South Africa Connect: Creating Opportunities, Ensuring Inclusion (2013)
6. Cerf, V.G.: Internet access is not a human right (2012)

7. Unwin, T.: Evolution and prospects for the use of mobile technologies to improve education access and learning outcomes. In: Paper Commissioned for the EFA Global Monitoring Report 2015, Education for All 2000–2015. UNESCO, Paris (2015)

8. Belding, E.M., Johnson, D.L., Pejovic, V., van Stam, G.: Traffic characterization and internet usage in rural Africa. In: Proceedings of 20th International Conference on World Wide Web, Hyderabad, India, pp. 493–502 (2011)

9. van Stam, G., Johnson, D.L., Pejovic, V., Mudenda, C., Sinzala, A., van Greunen, D.: Constraints for information and communications technologies implementation in rural Zambia. In: Jonas, K., Rai, I.A., Tchuente, M. (eds.) AFRICOMM 2012. LNICSSITE, vol. 119, pp. 221–227. Springer, Heidelberg (2013). doi:10.1007/978-3-642-41178-6_23

10. Belding, E.M., Johnson, D.L., Parks, L., Pejovic, V., van Stam, G., Zheleva, M.: The bandwidth divide: obstacles to efficient broadband adoption in rural Sub-Saharan Africa. Int. J. Commun. **6**, 2467–2491 (2012)

11. van Stam, G.: Participatory Networks: Observations from Macha works. In: Participatory Networks Workshop at PDC 2014, Windhoek, Namibia (2014)

12. Mawere, M., van Stam, G.: African engineering and the quest for sustainable development: levelling the ground for all players. In: Mawere, M., Nhemachena, A. (eds.) Theory, Knowledge, Development and Politics: What Role for the Academy in the Sustainability of Africa? Chap. 8, pp. 189–206. Langaa RPCIG, Bamenda (2016)

13. Johnson, D.L.: Re-architecting Internet Access and Wireless Networks for Rural Developing Regions. University of California, Santa Barbara (2013)

14. van Stam, G.: A Strategy to Make ICT Accessible in Rural Zambia: A Case Study of Macha. NMMU, Port Elizabeth (2013)

15. van Stam, G.: Orientalism embedded in foreign narratives of engineering for development that targets Africa. In: Mawere, M. (ed.) Underdevelopment, Development and the Future of Africa. Langaa RPCIG, Bamenda (2016)

16. Nyamnjoh, F.B.: "C'est l'homme qui fait l'Homme": Cul-de-Sac Ubuntu-ism in Cote d'Ivoire. Langaa RPCIG, Bamenda (2015)

17. Grosfoguel, R.: Decolonizing post-colonial studies and paradigms of political economy: transmodernity, decolonial thinking, and global coloniality. J. Peripheral Cult. Prod. Luso-Hispanic World **1**(1), 1–38 (2011)

18. Mawere, M., van Stam, G.: Paradigm Clash Imperial methodological epistemologies and development in Africa: observations from rural Zimbabwe and Zambia. In: Mawere, M., Mwanaka, T. (eds.) Development, Governance, and Democracy: A Search for Sustainable Democracy and Development in Africa, Chap. 6, pp. 193–211. Langaa RPCIG, Bamenda (2015)

19. van Greunen, D., van Stam, G.: Review of an African rural internet network and related academic interventions. J. Commun. Inf. **10**(2) (2014)

20. van Stam, G.: African engineers and the quest for sustainable development: levelling the ground for all players. In: IEEE PES Power Africa, 28 June–2 July 2016, Livingstone, Zambia (2016)

21. Feenberg, A.: Critical theory of technology: an overview. Tailoring Biotechnol. **1**(1), 47–64 (2005)

22. Dourish, P., Mainwaring, S.D.: Ubicomp's colonial impulse. In: Ubicomp 2012, 5–8 September 2012, Pittsburgh, PA, USA (2012)

23. de Bruijn, M., Nyamnjoh, F.B., Brinkman, I. (eds.): Mobile Phones: The New Talking Drums of Everyday Africa. Langaa RPCIG, Bamenda (2009)

24. Toyama, K.: Geek Heresy: Rescuing Social Change from the Cult of Technology. PublicAffairs, New York (2015). Kindle edition

25. Unwin, T.: Technology: the great divider? (2014)
26. Nemer, D.: Rethinking digital inequalities: the experience of the marginalized in community technology centers (2015)
27. Bidwell, N.J.: Moving the centre to design social media in rural Africa. AI Soc. J. Knowl. Cult. Commun. **31**(1), 51–77 (2016)
28. Graham, M., Geography, I.: Ethereal alternate dimensions of cyberspace or grounded augmented realities? Geogr. J. **179**(2), 177–182 (2013)
29. Belding, E.M., Johnson, D.L., van Stam, G.: Network traffic locality in a rural African village. In: Proceedings of the Fifth International Conference on Information and Communication Technologies and Development, pp. 268–277, Atlanta, GA, USA. ACM (2012)
30. Mudenda, C., Johnson, D., Parks, L., van Stam, G.: Power instability in rural Zambia, case Macha. In: Bissyandé, T.F., van Stam, G. (eds.) AFRICOMM 2013. LNICSSITE, vol. 135, pp. 260–270. Springer, Cham (2014). doi:10.1007/978-3-319-08368-1_30
31. Galtung, J.: A structural theory of imperialism. J. Peace Res. **8**(2), 81–117 (1971)
32. Krogh, B.H.: Can Africa take the lead in building a truly smart grid? In: IEEE PES Power Africa, 28 June–2 July 2016, Livingstone, Zambia (2016)
33. Ndlovu-Gatsheni, S.J.: The entrapment of Africa within the global colonial matrices of power. J. Dev. Soc. **29**(4), 331–353 (2013)
34. Harrison, S., Sengers, P., Tatar, D.: The three paradigms of HCI. In: CHI 2007, San Jose, CA. ACM (2007)
35. Wyche, S., Dillahunt, T.R., Simiyu, N., Alaka, S.: If god gives me the chance I will design my own phone: exploring mobile phone repair and postcolonial approaches to design in rural Kenya. In: UbiComp 2015, 7–11 September 2015, Osaka, Japan, pp. 463–473 (2015)
36. van Stam, G.: Orientalism embedded in foreign narratives of technology for development. In: International Conference Chinoyi University, 2–5 August 2016, Chinoyi, Zimbabwe (2016)
37. Mawere, M., Mubaya, T.R., van Reisen, M., van Stam, G.: Maslow's theory of human motivation and its deep roots in individualism: interrogating maslow's applicability in Africa. In: Mawere, M., Nhemachena, A. (eds.) Theory, Knowledge, Development and Politics: What Role for the Academy in the Sustainability of Africa? Chap. 3, pp. 55–72. Langaa RPCIG, Bamenda (2016)
38. van Zyl, I.: Technology Encounters and the Symbolic Narrative: Localising the 'Technology for Development' Experience in South African Education Settings. Universita della Svizzera italiana, Lugano (2013)
39. van Stam, G.: Experience in research and development in rural Zambia and Zimbabwe. In: RAE Workshop-4 'Enriching Engineering Education', 6–7 November 2014, Harare, Zimbabwe (2014)
40. Ndlovu-Gatsheni, S.J.: Coloniality of Power in Postcolonial Africa: Myths of Decolonization. Codesria, Dakar (2013)
41. van Stam, G.: Experience of providing wireless access to rural communities. In: Policy Dialogue by the South African Department of Science and Technology and the European Union in Partnership with the HSRC on 'Extending access and connectivity across rural communities in South Africa', 12 February 2013, Pretoria, South Africa (2013)
42. van Stam, G.: African engineering and colonialistic conditioning. In: Fifth International Conference on e-Infrastructure and e-Services for Developing Countries, Africomm 2013, 25–27 November 2013, Blantyre, Malawi (2013)

43. van Stam, G.: Ubuntu, peace, and women: without a mother, there is no home. In: van Reisen, M. (ed.) Women's Leadership in Peace-Building: Conflict, Community and Care, vol. 3, pp. 37–54. Africa World Press, Trenton (2014)
44. Belding, E.M., Johnson, D.L., Pejovic, V., van Stam, G.: VillageShare: facilitating content generation and sharing in rural networks. In: Second annual Symposium on Computing for Development (DEV 2012), Atlanta, GA, USA. ACM (2012)
45. Furnell, S., van Niekerk, J., Clarke, N.: The price of patching. Comput. Fraud Secur. Bull. **2014**(8), 8–13 (2014)
46. Zaki, Y., Chen, J., Pötsch, T., Ahmad, T.: Dissecting web latency in Ghana. In: IMC 2014, 5–7 November 2014, Vancouver, BC, Canada. ACM (2014)
47. Tan, K., Song, J., Zhang, Q., Sridharan, M.: A compound TCP approach for high-speed and long distance networks. In: 25th IEEE International Conference on Computer Communications, INFOCOM 2006, Proceedings, pp. 1–12 (2006)
48. Fuglesang, A.: About Understanding - Ideas and Observations on Cross-Cultural Communication. Decade Media Books, New York (1982)
49. Verran, H.: Science and African Logic. The University of Chicago Press, Chicago and London (2001)
50. Bidwell, N.J., Blake, E., Kapuire, G., Rehm, M.: Merging experiences and perspectives in the complexity of cross-cultural design. In: 9th International Workshop on Internationalization of Products and Systems, pp. 131–140 (2010)
51. Bidwell, N.J.: Walking together to design. Interactions **19**(6), 68–71 (2012)
52. Cole, T.: The White Savior Industrial Complex (2012)
53. Mawere, M., van Stam, G.: Ubuntu/Unhu as communal love: critical reflections on the sociology of Ubuntu and communal life in sub-Saharan Africa. In: Mawere, M., Marongwe, N. (eds.) Politics, Violence and Conflict Management in Africa: Envisioning Transformation, Peace and Unity in the Twenty-First Century, chapter 9. Langaa RPCIG, Bamenda (2016)
54. van Stam, G.: Information and knowledge transfer in the rural community of Macha, Zambia. J. Commun. Inf. **9**(1) (2013)
55. Nordling, L.: Africa's fight for equality. Nature **521**, 24–25 (2015)

Author Index

Ahmat, Daouda   88, 111
Ahouantchede, Herve   42
Aina, Alain   232
Akpona, Christian   42
Appoh, Kouamé   304

Baptiste, Lamy Jean   304
Barka, Mahamat   88, 111
Bassole, Didier   79
Belqasmi, Fatna   42
Ben Rebah, Hassen   69
Ben Sta, Hatem   69
Byishimo, Audace   145
Byomire, Gorretti   253

Chang, Wen-I   165
Chen, Chien-Hung   199
Chikumba, Patrick Albert   263
Chiu, Chien-Ching   199
Compaoré, A. Joëlle   26
Cousin, Philippe   135

Degila, Jules   42
Densmore, Melissa   186
Diop, Idy   53
Dlamini, Jabulani S.   3

Elizabeth, Asianzu   253

Garba, Aminata A.   145
Gasore, Rodrigue   145
Gaye, Ibrahima   53
Glitho, Roch   42
Gohoue, Rose   42

Hadzic, Senka   186, 243
Hoang, Pham Huy   217
Hung, Chi-Jie   199

Jaillet, Alain   273
Johnson, David L.   325
Johnson, David   186, 232, 243

Kafuko, Maria Miiro   253
Kester, Quist-Aphetsi   174, 281, 292
Koffi, Kanga   98, 122
Kogeda, Okuthe P.   3, 155, 206

Lall, Manoj   155, 206
Lamola, Magdeline   186
Liao, Shu-Han   199
Lima, Solange Rito   313
Long, Nguyen Thanh   217
Lysko, Albert   186, 243

Magoni, Damien   88, 111
Maliwatu, Richard   186, 243
Marcelin, Brou Konan   98, 122
Marcellin, Brou Konan   304
Massingue, Venâncio   313
Mbadjoin, Théodore Njingang   273
Mendy, Gervais   53
Michel, Babri   98, 122
Moussa, Lo   304
Mulhanga, Marangaze Munhepe   313

Namisango, Fatuma   253
Naphini, Patrick   263
Ndlovu, Lungisani   206

Ogutu, Achieng G.   155
Ouédraogo, Frédéric T.   33, 79
Ouya, Samuel   53

Pham, Congduc   135
Phokeer, Amreesh   232
Poda, Pasteur   26

Rahim, Abdur   135
Rouamba, Evariste   33

Safiatou, Soré   33
Saint, Martin   145
Seck, Diaraf   53
Séré, Abdoulaye   33

Sia, Benjamin 273
Sie, Oumarou 79
Somé, Borlli Michel Jonas 26

Thuy, Nguyen Duc 217
Tra, Goore Bi 98, 122

van Stam, Gertjan 14, 325

Yélémou, Tiguiane 273

Zlobinsky, Natasha 186

Printed in the United States
By Bookmasters